P9-CJF-358

D0617638

AMERICA'S
RELUCTANT
PRINCE

AMERICA'S RELUCTANT PRINCE

THE LIFE OF
JOHN F. KENNEDY JR.

STEVEN M. GILLON

DUTTON

DUTTON

An imprint of Penguin Random House LLC
penguinrandomhouse.com

Previously published as a Dutton hardcover edition in 2019
First trade paperback printing: July 2020

The Library of Congress has catalogued the hardcover edition as follows:

Names: Gillon, Steven M., author.
Title: America's reluctant prince : the life of John F. Kennedy Jr. / Steven M. Gillon.
Other titles: Life of John F. Kennedy Jr.
Description:| New York : Dutton, an imprint of Penguin Random House LLC, [2019] |
Includes bibliographical references and index. |
Identifiers: LCCN 2019014938 (print) | LCCN 2019017483 (ebook) |
ISBN 9781524742393 (ebook) | ISBN 9781524742386 (hc)
Subjects: LCSH: Kennedy, John F., Jr., 1960–1999. | Children of presidents—United States—
Biography. | Celebrities—United States—Biography.
Classification: LCC E843.K42 (ebook) | LCC E843.K42 G55 2019 (print) |
DDC 973.922092 [B]—dc23
LC record available at https://lccn.loc.gov/2019014938

Dutton trade paperback ISBN: 9781524742409

Printed in the United States of America
1   3   5   7   9   10   8   6   4   2

Book design by Nancy Resnick

To Mom and Dad, with love, as always

CONTENTS

"DON'T BE JOHN KENNEDY"

I met John F. Kennedy Jr. in the spring of 1981, when I was a twenty-four-year-old graduate student. He was a twenty-year-old sophomore history major at Brown University, and I was the teaching assistant in a class on twentieth-century American political history. Our friendship got off to an inauspicious start. Before the semester began, the professor, renowned historian James T. Patterson, told me that he wanted his assistants to deliver a lecture as preparation for a teaching career. I had applied to the PhD program in American civilization to study early American history, so I was not as familiar with the recent past. I had, however, always been fascinated with the 1960s, and the Kennedy presidency in particular. So I decided to give a critical lecture on JFK and civil rights.

I had been vaguely aware that John was on campus and had seen him several times, usually surrounded by a gaggle of giddy girls. It never occurred to me that he would take a class that would deal with his father's presidency. On the first day, I stood in the back of the room handing out syllabi to students pouring into the Manning Chapel classroom. Looking over the line of students, I spied a large mane of unruly brown hair slowly approaching me. "Please, no," I thought to myself. "Don't be John Kennedy." It was bad enough that I would be speaking in public for the first time and doing so in front of the professor I wanted as my advisor. Now I faced the prospect of criticizing a president while his son looked on. A few seconds later, John approached, reached for the syllabus, thanked me, and then sat down in the back of the room.

I would have tried switching my topic had I thought Patterson would allow it. But I would need a better excuse than "I am afraid to give a lecture about President Kennedy while John is in the class." That statement would surely have marked the end of my graduate career, and rightly so.

My talk was scheduled for March, so for the next few months, I labored to write and rehearse the lecture. It took about five weeks to write the talk, and then I spent another four weeks practicing it. Every day, I would recite the entire fifty-minute lecture before breakfast, after dinner, and again before I went to sleep. I had a lot on the line. Not only would I be giving a public lecture for the first time—and doing so in front of more than a hundred bright Brown undergraduates—but also I was auditioning for a spot as one of Patterson's PhD students. Oh, and then there was John, although I must confess, Patterson scared me more than John.

At 10:55 A.M. on the day of my lecture, I marched into the hall and took my position behind the podium, hands tucked safely in my pockets so students would not see them shaking. Professor Patterson took a seat in the middle of the room. Looking around, I took some comfort in seeing that John was absent, a not-uncommon occurrence. But just as I was about to start, the back door swung open and in he walked. Students have a natural tendency to sit as far away from the professor as possible, so the back rows were full. John kept moving forward until he plopped down in the seat directly in front of me.

John and I sat only a few feet apart that day, but we came from vastly different worlds. I grew up in a working-class family outside Philadelphia. I had been a mediocre student for most of my life but finally turned things around in college, earning good enough grades to get accepted at Brown. Education has often been the pathway to the American Dream, and that was certainly true in my case.

Getting into Brown was my big break. There was no way I was going to screw up this opportunity.

The first line of my lecture, which I can still recall almost four decades later, read: "President Kennedy was a pragmatist who did not impose moral solutions on problems." Simple enough. Yet somehow my well-rehearsed words escaped me the moment I needed them most. I stood in front of the room paralyzed by fear—fear of the one hundred students in the class, fear of my intimidating professor, and, perhaps, fear of giving a lecture about a man while his son sat a few feet away. My first public lecture thus began with a succession of "Ahs" and "Ums." My mind had gone blank. I thought, "Just look down and read the words on the page in front of you."

During times of crisis, some people are able to reach deep down inside themselves and find a vast reservoir of strength. I am not one of those people. I hyperventilate. I sweat. I grow more and more anxious. I finally looked down at my notes, but by this point everything had grown fuzzy. What in the world was I going to do? Either I said something soon, or I would be forced to run out of the room humiliated and resign myself to a short life doing manual labor.

I kept repeating to myself, *Say something. Anything.* So I did. "President Kennedy," I began, "President Kennedy. President Kennedy had no moral scruples." I have absolutely no idea where that came from, but that was what came out. As soon as the words left my lips, I realized I was in trouble. I glanced down at John, who glared up at me. Then a student in the back of the room, who was too far away to see the look of terror on my face, must have assumed that it was all a joke. She laughed and the entire class joined in. That laugh saved my career. With the ice broken, I went on to finish the lecture. I criticized JFK for being too slow to embrace the civil rights cause but noted that he eventually did, and in a famous June 11, 1963, address, he became the first president in history to refer to the civil rights movement as a "moral cause." Before he left the room, John came up, shook my hand, and said, "Great lecture."

It would be several years before John and I became friends. But once the bond formed, we remained friends for the rest of his too-short life.

Perhaps surprisingly, given that I am a professional historian, it wasn't until years after his death that I began trying to understand John through the eyes of a scholar. At the beginning of our friendship, I had decided not to read anything about him. I can remember people studying his life as if cramming for a final exam. They wanted to know what he liked and didn't, which foods he ate, which sports he enjoyed, and who his heroes were, all so they could manufacture a conversation and eventually a friendship. John was very good at weeding most of those kinds of people from his life. I wanted my connection with John to be like any other friendship. When we meet someone new, we have a chance to tell our own story. It may not be completely honest, and it certainly will contain elements of exaggeration, but it's our personal narrative. I never wanted to take that freedom away from John. Therefore, I only knew what he chose to share with me. After he died, I realized that while I had an intimate understanding of the nuances of his personality, I actually knew very little about his life before Brown.

My interest in writing this book, then, grew partly from a need to satisfy my own curiosity, along with a scholarly desire to weave together my personal recollections with the historical record to produce a fuller picture of a truly extraordinary person.

This book thus represents a mix of historical analysis and personal reflection. It combines insight gained from nearly two decades of friendship with research into all the relevant historical materials on John's life. Arthur Schlesinger Jr., who served as an advisor to JFK and who was one of the great historians of the twentieth century, serves as my model. Now, I fully recognize that I am not Schlesinger, and John was not his father. But Schlesinger's approach is instructive. In his books about both JFK (*A Thousand Days: John F. Kennedy in the White House*) and RFK (*Robert Kennedy and His Times*), Schlesinger seamlessly intertwined personal recollections with intensive research and deep historical understanding to produce a vivid portrait of his subject. If he can be faulted for anything, it was for avoiding some of the unseemly aspects of JFK's character: the womanizing and the abuse of prescription medications, among others. But I now understand more fully the challenge Schlesinger faced: as a friend, I was charged with protecting John's privacy, but as a historian, I am obligated to paint a complete portrait, warts and all. In the end, my duty as a historian supersedes my responsibilities as a friend.

As a friend, I understood the role that I played in John's life. While I knew him for eighteen years, I was not one of his closest friends. John's friends formed a wheel, with a core group who were involved in every facet of his life. They spent weekends with John on Martha's Vineyard or in Hyannis Port, went camping and kayaking with him, and spent long hours hanging out in his Manhattan apartment. The other friends resembled spokes on the wheel, each playing a specific and specialized role in his life. I was one of those spokes. I understood my place in John's life was that of the racquetball-playing "professor." When not battling each other on the racquetball court, John and I shared long conversations about politics, current events, and his father's place in history. He would occasionally share personal stories about his family and about the challenges of growing up the son of a martyred president. Sometimes he would bounce ideas off me for talks he was planning to give. Later, when he started *George* magazine, John asked me to write a few "Editor's Letter" pieces, and he gave me the title of contributing editor.

I obviously have a personal investment in telling this story. I agonized over whether I was betraying John by sharing my stories with a broader public. I always wondered why someone of John's stature took an interest in me and pursued our friendship. In large part, it was because John enjoyed spending time with people who came from backgrounds that were different from his own. But it was also because he trusted me and knew that I would never violate his privacy. He was right. But circumstances have changed, and now that he is gone, and those of us who knew him well are advancing in age, I hope to preserve his legacy by allowing the world to understand the man I knew, and the one whom I would discover in the course of conducting research for this book.

The tipping point for me came one evening when I had dinner with Rose-Marie Terenzio, who was John's close friend and gatekeeper for the last five years of his life while he was at *George*. "If John knew he was going to be dead at the age of thirty-eight," she said, "he would not want to be forgotten. He would want someone to write a book about him, and he would want you to write it." As a historian, the larger question I faced was, "Does John deserve a biography?" By any standard definition of greatness—passing legislation, building a business, demonstrating great courage, or helping the poor—the answer is a definitive no. But I believe that John's life warrants a historical biography for a number of reasons.

First, up until the 1960s and 1970s, there had been few, if any, human beings who were forced to live their lives under such intense media scrutiny. John was born in 1960, at the dawn of the television era. His father, a master of the new medium, used his young family to project a false, but highly attractive, image of himself as a wholesome family man. President Kennedy's assassination increased public pressure on John even though he was only a boy. The salute by that little boy in blue at his father's casket cemented the belief that John would be the natural heir to his father's legacy. One of John's great achievements was his ability to accept those public expectations with enormous grace while never allowing them to distort his core sense of self.

Given how the weight of celebrity has crushed others carrying far lighter burdens, including members of his own family, it is a testament to his character that he remained, in the words of another friend from Brown, "disgustingly normal."

But it wasn't easy being John. Yes, he was fabulously wealthy, strikingly handsome, and the beneficiary of his family's extensive connections. But the John I knew, and the one I discovered in researching this book, was also complex; he often struggled with the burden of expectations imposed upon him. John once told me that he was actually two people. He played the role of John Fitzgerald Kennedy Jr., the son of a charismatic president who had inspired the nation. He understood what he represented to millions of people, and he was willing to assume that burden. But he never confused that public role with his private identity. He spent his life trying to develop an authentic self, separate from that of his famous father and well-known family. He often wore a mask in public, never revealing the inner doubts that haunted him his entire life, or showing the range of emotions that he shared with only a handful of close friends. Although I was never a part of his core friendships, he occasionally opened up to me, revealing a more vulnerable side of his personality.

Second, I believe John was ahead of his time in anticipating the seamless mix of politics and culture that defines our era, but he has never received proper credit for creating *George*. For John, *George,* which he founded with business partner Michael Berman in 1995, was a natural combination of his father's fascination with politics, power, and the press, and his mother's interest in gossip and style. Unfortunately, the magazine did not survive long after John's death, but it is instructive to consider the part *George* played in forging today's popular and political cultures—as well as to imagine the role that the magazine or the man might have played if either had survived.

Finally, John is significant as a cultural symbol. What was it about America in the last decades of the twentieth century that made us need to turn John into a cultural icon? I believe that the same misplaced nostalgia that fed conspiracy theories about his father's death fueled public interest in John. Many Americans viewed the Kennedy years as a time when America stood strong in the world and prosperous at home. The troubles that followed JFK's death—a controversial war in Vietnam, student protests, angry race riots—reinforced the association between the Kennedy administration and an age of poetry and power. John served as a touchstone for many of that generation who wished to resurrect the halcyon days of the past. The public's insatiable fascination with John derived from his charm and stunning good looks, but he represented so much more. He symbolized a lost world—a world to which many Americans wished to return. Underlying this desire was a belief that John would one day lead the nation back to the promised land, to a time that existed more in people's imaginations than in reality. Ironically, Jackie Kennedy, the mother who worked so hard to protect John and his older sister, Caroline, from the intense pressures of public expectation, unwittingly helped foster them by manufacturing the Camelot myth.

I thought I knew John well, but I was surprised by many things I learned over the course of my research. I discovered that the last few months of his life were among the most difficult he had ever confronted. He was burdened with enormous personal and professional troubles: He feared losing the two people he was closest to—his wife and his best friend, Anthony Radziwill. His relationship with his sister was strained, and his magazine was failing. He had finally reached a point in his life when he was prepared to run for office, but first he needed to get his house in order. Although he felt trapped, John remained resilient, searching for ways to get his life back on track.

I also tried to resolve a question that had always bothered me: What was it about John's psychological makeup that made him so restless and willing to take risks? (Anyone who has ever been in the passenger seat of a car driven by John knows what I mean when I talk about risky behavior.) I spoke with a psychologist who offered a fascinating theory that potentially explained his restlessness and shed new light on his death. It's all very speculative, but based on my own observations, I found the comments plausible.

I was also fortunate that a number of people who had never spoken about John before were willing to share their stories with me, and even those who had already spoken offered new insights. Michael Berman, for example, who had been John's friend and business partner for more than a decade before their ugly falling-out over *George*, had refused to even mention John's name for the past two decades. But he sat down with me for more than twenty hours of interviews. President Bill Clinton, Tina Radziwill, Carole Radziwill, Elizabeth "Biz" Mitchell, Pasquale "Pat" Manocchia, Barbara Vaughn, Charlie King, Julie Baker, and many others, also participated in extensive interviews for the first time.

In addition to hundreds of hours of interviews, I gained access to Secret Service and FBI files that had been previously sealed. I went through the normal procedure for filing Freedom of Information Act (FOIA) requests, but when my requests and appeal were denied—the Secret Service claimed it had no record of anyone named John F. Kennedy Jr.—I filed a lawsuit. As part of the settlement, the Secret Service turned over more than five hundred pages of documents that offer a fascinating glimpse into the tortured relationship between John's mom and the men assigned to protect him. "She was difficult," observed Secret Service agent Clint Hill. These documents expose the frustration of agents trying to protect John while abiding by Jackie's often unreasonable demands. The presidential libraries were more cooperative and processed thousands of pages of documents in response to my FOIA requests. The William J. Clinton Presidential Library alone released more than thirteen thousand pages of new materials.

Usually biographies chronicle the lives of great people who have left a tangible record of accomplishment. Or they examine a notable person's life through the lens of their celebrity. While John was both accomplished and a celebrity, no serious examination exists of his life or considers his impact on American culture and history. Although he never had the opportunity to achieve his full potential—he had "every gift but the gift of years," his uncle Edward Kennedy said in his powerful and emotional eulogy—John, like the magazine he founded, seemed to foretell our own era, in which the line between celebrity and politics, entertainment and government, grows increasingly hazy. In the years since his death, that line has only become more distorted. This book is not just a look back at a handsome, magnetic person who died too soon. It is also a prism through which to consider the world we live in today.

Finally, many people speculate about the impact John might have had if he'd lived, raising the prospect that he might have one day returned to the White House as president. It's possible, but I believe that John should be remembered for the authentic life that he lived and not for what he might have become.

CHAPTER 1

"I WAS PROUD OF THE LITTLE GUY"

t 12:22 A.M. on November 25, 1960, John F. Kennedy Jr., who weighed six pounds and three ounces, was born in a Washington, DC, hospital to the future president and first lady of the United States. He became the first baby ever born to a president-elect.

A physician reported to the press that the delivery had been a "normal caesarean" and that both mother and baby were now resting safely. The supervising nurse also told Secret Service agent Clint Hill, stationed just outside the operating room, that the delivery was successful and that both mother and child were "doing fine"—but that the newborn had been placed in an incubator "as a precautionary measure."

However, according to Ira Seiler, a second-year pediatric resident who assisted in the delivery, the situation was actually more complicated. In a 2013 oral history, Seiler claimed that when John emerged, the anesthesiologist held him by his ankles and slapped his buttocks. After several minutes, John's face turned blue. Seiler realized that John was having trouble breathing and told the other physicians that he needed to be intubated. "He handed the baby to me, and I passed a tube into the trachea of the baby," he reflected. "I then handed the infant back to him to breathe into the baby." But the anesthesiologist appeared nervous, perhaps because he was holding the child of the future president, and accidentally knocked out the tube. Seiler grabbed John, reinserted the tube, and spent the next six minutes breathing air into his lungs. The doctor literally breathed life into the newborn. A nurse who was in the room said that John would have died had Seiler not intervened.

A few minutes later, John was transferred to the intensive care nursery.

He was diagnosed with hyaline membrane disease, now called respiratory distress syndrome, which is common in premature babies. The condition results from a deficiency of a substance called surfactant, which helps keep the air sacs in the lungs open. Without it, an infant's lungs collapse with each breath, making it harder to get enough oxygen. In some cases, the baby becomes so exhausted it gives up and stops breathing.

As the drama in the delivery room unfolded, the Secret Service tried reaching President-elect John F. Kennedy, who had left Washington earlier that evening and was flying to Palm Beach, Florida. A few minutes before landing, the pilot called him into the cockpit and informed him that his wife had been rushed to the hospital. This news was the only information available at the time. As soon as his plane landed, JFK pushed through a crowd of several hundred fans to an office, where he phoned the floor nurse of the maternity ward and learned that Mrs. Kennedy was already in surgery. He told the Secret Service that he needed to return to Washington immediately. Instead of taking his plane, he decided to jump on the much faster press plane that was already refueling.

Within fifteen minutes, the president-elect was back in the air on his way to Washington. He had no idea that John had already been born before he took off. According to published reports, JFK moved to the front section of the plane, where the pilot handed him radio earphones relaying the unexpected message, "It's a boy; both doing nicely." Campaign press secretary Pierre Salinger then announced to the press on board: "We have just been advised that Mrs. Kennedy has given birth to a boy and that both mother and baby are doing well." But Mrs. Kennedy recounted a different story. More than a decade later, when her mother-in-law, Rose Kennedy, was writing her memoir, she asked Jackie for her recollections of that evening. Jackie told her that JFK was told on the plane that his son had been born prematurely and that his health "was in doubt."

A few weeks earlier, on November 10, 1960, President-elect John F. Kennedy and his wife, Jacqueline, commonly referred to as Jackie, stood before reporters at the Hyannis Armory to greet the world's media following his razor-thin victory over the current vice president, Richard Nixon. JFK was not only the first Catholic elected to the nation's highest office; he was also the nation's first celebrity president, who, along with the first lady, looked better fitted for Hollywood than for Washington. Both were extraordinarily photogenic: Jack, forty-three, with his thick, chestnut hair, penetrating blue eyes, and high-wattage smile; and Jackie, only thirty-one years old and eight months pregnant with their second child, her square face framed by stylish brown hair that gave her "the look of a beautiful lion," observed *The New York Times.* Jackie stood proudly onstage beside her husband as he read from the congratulatory telegrams that he received from Vice President Nixon and from President Dwight Eisenhower. "My wife and I prepare for a new administration and a new baby," he concluded.

While aides from previous administrations could guide JFK as he assumed the presidency, no playbook existed for how to raise two famous children in the television age. John would be the youngest child to live in the White House since Esther Cleveland had been born there in 1893, during the second term of her father, President Grover Cleveland. John Jr. arrived prematurely, just two weeks after the Hyannis press conference, and both he and his mother suffered from poor health for weeks afterward. Despite the unusual circumstances, Mrs. Kennedy was determined to give her children as normal a life as possible while growing up in the White House. She demanded privacy even as she and her husband competed to control media access to John and Caroline. The first lady also clashed with the Secret Service, insisting that it was not the agency's responsibility to protect her children from accidents that were a natural part of growing up. She would battle the Secret Service until John was sixteen years old and lost his protective detail. Amid this conflict, having two youngsters in the White House undoubtedly added a casual informality to a typically staid setting. Caroline, born on November 27, 1957, was three years old when her father took the oath of office; John was less than two months old. Toddler John kept everyone entertained with his inquisitive personality, love of helicopters, and fascination with the military.

Both Jack Kennedy and Jackie Bouvier had faced adversity throughout their lives but dealt with it in very different ways. Jackie's father, John Bouvier, a wealthy New York stockbroker, was also a drunk and philanderer who flitted about the social scene in Manhattan and Long Island's Hamptons. His wife, Janet Lee, an accomplished equestrienne, grew tired of her husband's antics and filed for divorce in 1940, when Jackie was ten years old. Jackie had always been quiet and reserved, but the trauma of the divorce left her even more withdrawn and less trusting.

Jack, too, faced complicated family dynamics. The Kennedys were governed by the iron will of the family architect, Joseph P. Kennedy, who had made millions on Wall Street and in the film distribution business before serving as the US ambassador to Great Britain during the 1930s. By the 1950s, he had set his sights on creating a political dynasty and was willing to use his vast fortune to achieve that vision. Joseph had one overwhelming ambition—to have his oldest son elected as president. When Jack's older brother, Joe Jr., was killed while flying a dangerous mission in World War II, Jack inherited his father's burden.

"It was like being drafted," Kennedy reflected. "My father wanted his eldest son in politics. 'Wanted' isn't the right word. He demanded it." JFK, who had already gained considerable attention by swimming in shark-infested waters trying to save his crew after a Japanese destroyer rammed into his patrol boat, PT-109, returned a war hero ready to fulfill his father's ambitions. The political journey began in Boston in 1946, when Kennedy won a congressional seat. Then, six years later, he won election to the US Senate.

In addition to his domineering father, the pious and humorless family matriarch, Rose, was content to leave the task of raising her children to nannies and nurses while she traveled the world. But although Jack confronted numerous physical ailments during his life, including a crippling back condition, he dealt with hardship by reaching out to people and engaging openly with friends throughout his life.

In 1942 Jackie's mother married Hugh Auchincloss, an heir to the Standard Oil fortune with estates in Newport, Rhode Island, and McLean, Virginia. Auchincloss demonstrated coolness toward Jackie and her young sister, Lee, and both girls remained very much emotionally attached to their biological father. Jackie went on to study history, literature, art, and French for two years at Vassar College before spending her junior year abroad in Paris. In 1951 she earned her degree at George Washington University. The following year, she secured a job as the Inquiring Camera Girl for the Washington *Times-Herald* newspaper. Jackie would stop random men and women on the street to ask them a question, such as "What is your candid opinion of marriage?" She'd record their answers, snap their pictures, and weave it into a regular column. She developed a complicated personality, simultaneously appearing to be both shy and charming. Jackie possessed a breathless, childlike voice that made her appear naïve, but she was entirely capable of making ruthless calculations to advance her ambitions.

Jack and Jackie met at a dinner party in 1952 when, according to the future first lady, the congressman and soon-to-be senator "leaned across the asparagus and asked her for a date." Engaged at the time to stockbroker John Husted Jr., Jackie suddenly called off the wedding, convinced that the wealthy and well-connected Kennedy would be better suited to supporting the lifestyle she desired. Initially, JFK was reluctant to settle down, relishing his playboy role as what *The Saturday Evening Post* magazine called Washington's "Gay Young Bachelor." (*Gay* had a very different meaning in the 1950s.) He had fallen in love with Jackie, but that did not mean he was prepared for a monogamous relationship. Jack knew, however, that he needed to marry and start a family if he intended to become president one day.

Their marriage at the Auchinclosses' Newport estate, Hammersmith Farm, the next year was a social extravaganza that attracted 1,400 guests, but Jack's old habits almost brought their union to an early end. "At last I know the true meaning of rapture," Jack wrote his parents while he and Jackie honeymooned in Mexico. "Jackie is enshrined forever in my heart." But being in love with Jackie did not mean that he would be faithful. Kennedy friend Lem Billings recalled that what bothered Jackie most about being married to Jack was the "humiliation she would suffer when she found herself stranded at parties while Jack would suddenly disappear with some pretty young girl." Nevertheless, she chose to overlook his indiscretions, and they decided to start a family. Jackie lost two babies. In 1955 she suffered a miscarriage after three months of pregnancy. In August 1956, a month before the baby was due, Jackie gave birth to a stillborn infant, a girl, before successfully giving birth to Caroline in November 1957.

In January 1960 JFK announced his candidacy for the presidency of the United States. With the help of his talented group of advisors, JFK carefully cultivated the image of a youthful, robust leader, hero of PT-109, and brilliant author of the Pulitzer Prize–winning book *Profiles in Courage* (1956). Tapping into the nation's longing for youthful leadership after eight staid years of the Eisenhower presidency, JFK called for a bold effort to "get America moving again." With a crisp Boston accent, Kennedy declared, "I run for the presidency because I do not want it said that in the years when our generation held political power . . . America began to slip."

Initially, Jacqueline joined him as he traveled around the country, but when she became pregnant, her doctors instructed her to remain at home. Warned that she might have lost her daughter due to the stress associated with JFK's failed effort to secure a position as running mate to Democratic nominee Adlai Stevenson in 1956, Jackie was determined not to repeat the same mistake. But staying home did not stop her from contributing to her husband's campaign. She wrote cover stories for popular magazines and filmed a number of television commercials. She recorded the first American presidential campaign commercial in Spanish and spent the final weeks of the campaign writing a syndicated column, Campaign Wife, that appealed specifically to women voters.

Despite Kennedy's broad appeal, the election remained close till the end. Nixon skillfully capitalized on public concern over Kennedy's inexperience, especially in foreign affairs. The even bigger obstacle, however, remained JFK's Catholic faith. Anti-Catholic sentiment ran deep, especially in the Protestant South, and neither party had nominated a Catholic since New York governor Al Smith won the Democratic nomination in 1928. "If you vote for Al Smith," cried a Protestant preacher, "you're voting against Christ and you'll be damned." Smith may not have been damned, but he was trounced by Republican Herbert Hoover. Kennedy responded to the issue boldly. In September he stood before the Greater Houston Ministerial Association and declared, "I am not the Catholic candidate for president. I am the Democratic Party's candidate for president who happens also to be a Catholic."

Television played a key role in Kennedy's election. In 1960, 87 percent of American homes had televisions, representing a 25 percent increase since 1956. The turning point in the campaign came in a series of four televised debates between September 26 and October 24. Kennedy used the debates— the first ever televised between presidential contenders—to demolish the Republican charge that he was inexperienced and badly informed. He succeeded far better than his opponent in communicating his qualities of boldness, imagination, and poise. Kennedy appeared alert, aggressive, and cool. Nixon, who perspired profusely, looked nervous and uncomfortable. It is instructive that radio listeners were evenly divided over who had won the debate, while the overwhelming majority of television viewers gave Kennedy a decisive edge. The performance energized Kennedy's lagging campaign, and the debates institutionalized television's role as a major force in modern American politics. "That night," the journalist Russell Baker reflected, "image replaced the printed word as the natural language of politics."

Over the next few weeks, while the president-elect laid the groundwork for his new administration, Jackie prepared for the birth of their second child. Instead of staying in Washington, JFK interviewed potential Cabinet members at his father's six-bedroom, 8,500-square-foot, Mediterranean-style house that stretched across two acres of well-manicured lawns in Palm Beach. The campaign had left JFK both physically and mentally exhausted, and the relative seclusion of the family estate offered him the chance to regain his strength away from public view. Because she was unable to travel, Jackie stayed behind with Caroline at their Georgetown home awaiting the baby's arrival. Given her previous difficult births, doctors recommended a caesarean, which was scheduled for mid-December.

On November 23 Kennedy returned to Washington to spend Thanksgiving with Jackie and Caroline. Early the next day, Thanksgiving morning, the family drove to Virginia to scope out potential houses that could serve as a retreat from the White House. Mrs. Kennedy later recalled the bumpy roads and wondered if the jolts had impacted her pregnancy. They had Thanksgiving lunch at their home, and later that evening, JFK boarded the *Caroline*, the family's twin-engine, forty-seat Convair 240 plane, to return to Palm Beach and continue interviewing people for his administration. A separate press plane followed.

At approximately ten fifteen that evening, two hours after JFK left Washington, Mrs. Kennedy called her obstetrician, Dr. John W. Walsh, who had just finished enjoying his Thanksgiving dinner at home. She informed him that she was bleeding and enduring moderate pain. Walsh told her she needed to rush to the hospital, so he sent an ambulance to her home and jumped in his car to meet her there. The ambulance driver and his attendant found Mrs. Kennedy resting comfortably, wearing white socks, a pink nightgown, a white cardigan sweater, and a red overcoat. Walsh arrived five minutes later and, joined by two Secret Service agents, rushed to Georgetown University Hospital.

Within minutes of giving birth, Mrs. Kennedy experienced the drastic lengths to which photographers would go simply to snap a candid picture. According to Clint Hill, the Secret Service agent assigned to protect Mrs. Kennedy, a photographer from the Associated Press snuck into Jackie's hospital room in hopes of securing the first pictures of her following delivery. As she was being wheeled into the room, he jumped out of a closet and took pictures using a bright flash. Although still groggy, Jackie shouted, "Oh, no, not that!" The agents quickly seized his camera and exposed the film so that it could not be used.

Within hours, congratulatory letters came pouring in, first from President Dwight Eisenhower, followed shortly thereafter by Britain's Queen Elizabeth and Prince Philip. The birth made front-page headlines around the world. According to family friend Dave Powers, who was staying at the Kennedys' Georgetown home, the family received approximately three thousand telegrams in the first twenty-four hours, and in less than a week had broken an all-time record for floral gifts. Within a few days, the Associated Press asked campaign press secretary Pierre Salinger for pictures of the already-famous baby, pointing out that the "first pictures of John F. Kennedy Jr. will be of world interest." Salinger's reply is not recorded.

President-elect Kennedy, who arrived at the hospital at four thirty in the morning, spent a few minutes admiring his son through a thick glass window before visiting his wife. Legendary newsman Merriman Smith, who accompanied Kennedy that night, described him as "tired but unable to stop smiling as policemen and Secret Service agents softly called out their congratulations." When people asked if he had chosen a name yet, JFK responded, "Why, it's John F. Kennedy Jr. I think she decided—it has been decided. Yes, John F. Kennedy Jr."

The president-elect then went home to take Caroline for a walk around the block and to reveal that she now had a baby brother. In the weeks leading up to the birth, JFK and Jackie had promised their daughter, who had turned three in November, that her birthday gift that year would be a sister or brother. Once she learned that she had a baby brother, Caroline insisted on giving him a present: a silver brush and comb. According to Maud Shaw, the nanny, Caroline "always loved John very much. She was very dear with him." A family member, however, remembers a different story. Years later, she claimed, Mrs. Kennedy showed her drawings of animals that she kept at her

Manhattan apartment. "These are the drawings Jack did for Caroline," she recalled Mrs. Kennedy saying, "because she was so jealous of John."

After only a few hours of sleep, JFK returned to the hospital for intermittent visits: twenty minutes just before noon; again at six; then shortly after eight o'clock for about fifty minutes. In addition to seeing his wife, he also stopped by to check on Minnesota senator Eugene McCarthy, who was recovering from pneumonia, and a seven-year-old leukemia patient. A nurse had told JFK that the boy wanted to meet him, so he made a brief visit to his room and gave him an autograph.

For the first nine days of her son's life, Mrs. Kennedy had to visit him and administer his bottle in the nursery, which was across the hall from her room. On December 3 doctors finally removed John from the incubator and carried him to his mother's room for the first time.

On December 8 the fourteen-day-old was baptized in the hospital chapel. John wore the same white christening gown that his father had worn in 1917. Still weak from the delivery, Mrs. Kennedy needed a wheelchair to move from her hospital bed to the chapel. The happy occasion produced the first of many conflicts over how much access the media should have to their son. JFK saw the baptism as an ideal opportunity to show off his "all-American family" and to appeal to the working-class base that helped him win the election and that would be essential for supporting his presidential agenda. Mrs. Kennedy, on the other hand, insisted on a private event without cameras. Eventually they reached a compromise, allowing a few selected reporters to cover the event.

As soon as John was able to leave the hospital, the family traveled to Palm Beach. Upon arrival, they encountered a crowd of photographers hungry to snap photographs of the future first lady and her newborn son. "Jackie! Jackie! Look over here!" they shouted. Mrs. Kennedy turned to her husband and said firmly, "I am not talking to the press. And I don't want any photographs of the baby. I was hoping we would have more privacy down here." Although he did not say it, Clint Hill knew that "the privacy Mrs. Kennedy sought would be elusive for the rest of her life. People were fascinated by her, and there would be few places she [could] escape."

Overnight, John became the most famous infant in America. Although they were only three years apart, John's early childhood would be very different from that of his sister. When Caroline was first learning to walk, nanny Maud Shaw could take her on strolls to the local drugstore for ice cream. She could romp anonymously around local playgrounds. John would never be able to enjoy such privileges. "I think John suffered a great handicap by being brought up in the White House, surrounded by all the restrictions that have to be placed on the president's children," Shaw remarked.

The next few weeks proved difficult for both Jackie and John. The expansive Kennedy Palm Beach house lacked air-conditioning and heat, so it would get warm and humid during the day and chilly at night. Making matters worse, John remained in poor health. Jackie claimed that a Palm Beach pediatrician, C. Jennings Derrick, "saved his life, as he was going downhill." Jackie's health was also precarious: she suffered from headaches and postpartum depression. "I didn't come to meals. I couldn't hold any food down," she confessed. There was also little privacy. Jackie desperately needed rest, but aides kept coming in and out of their room offering suggestions for her husband's upcoming Inauguration Day address on January 20, 1961.

On January 18 Mrs. Kennedy returned to Washington for the inaugural activities, leaving John and Caroline behind with their nanny and nurse. JFK's address, delivered on a cold, cloudless day, captivated the nation's imagination and captured the hope and expectations of the decade. His vigor and youth stood in sharp contrast to the stodgy Eisenhower style. Calling for "a struggle against the common enemies of man: tyranny, poverty, disease, and war," he promised a "New Frontier" of opportunity and challenge. The country, he proclaimed, was ready to "pay any price, bear any burden, meet any hardship."

Over the next few weeks, while the children remained in Florida, Mrs. Kennedy worked hard to make the White House more child friendly. She turned two guestrooms into bedrooms for the children, although the new first lady did not buy new furniture for the rooms. Everything came over from the Georgetown home. Caroline's room was decorated in pink rosebuds with white woodwork, a canopied bed, and rocking horses. John's room was blue and white, with a white crib and playpen, plenty of stuffed animals, and a gas stove where Mrs. Shaw prepared his formula. Old-fashioned chintz curtains hung in both rooms. The children's rooms were filled with dozens of toys, many of them presents from strangers. At one point, the president decided they would accept gifts only from close friends and family; the rest were donated to charity.

Mrs. Kennedy also arranged to have an outdoor playground built near the president's West Wing office, including a treehouse, playhouse, swing, and slide. Over time the family added a stable for their ponies, Macaroni and Leprechaun, and doghouses for Pushinka, a gift from Soviet Union leader Nikita Khrushchev, and an Irish terrier named Charlie. The children were surrounded by a wide variety of other animals as well, including two canaries and three parakeets. White House electrician Traphes L. Bryant, who served as the unofficial Kennedy family dog wrangler, estimated that they had nine dogs at one point. Indeed, John's first memory of living in the White House was watching Pushinka slide down the metal chute of their slide. Bryant had taught the dog to climb up by smearing some peanut butter on every step.

On February 4 John and Caroline flew aboard the family plane from sunny Florida to frigid Washington, DC. The president and first lady went to the airport to greet them and bring them back to the White House in full view of photographers. Mrs. Kennedy held John close to protect him from the biting cold as they exited the plane and walked to the limousine. That evening marked their first time together as a family at the White House. But while the first lady was able to shield John from the cold, the question remained whether she could also guard him from the pressures of growing up at 1600 Pennsylvania Avenue.

While nursing both herself and John back to health, Mrs. Kennedy had to contend with her new, highly visible role as a future first lady. During her hospital stay, Jackie had read a letter from former first lady Eleanor Roosevelt, whose two youngest children with Franklin D. Roosevelt had been in college when they entered the White House in 1933. Eleanor advised her that while "most things are made easier" living in the White House, "on the whole, life is rather difficult for both the children and their parents in the 'fishbowl' that lies before you." Jackie understood the challenge. As Letitia Baldrige, the first lady's social secretary, observed years later, it was like "trying to give one's children a normal life in the middle of Disney World." In keeping with her concern for privacy, Jackie informed the press that she would not be an active first lady and that she would devote her time to raising her children. There would be no press interviews and photo opportunities. When Angier Biddle Duke, the White House chief of protocol, asked

Jackie what role she would like to play as first lady, she responded, "As little as possible. I'm a mother. I'm a wife. I'm not a public official." White House Chief Usher J. B. West remarked that if she had her way, "the White House would be surrounded by high brick walls and a moat with crocodiles."

One of her strategies for protecting her children from the press was to stay away from Washington as much as possible. Desiring a country retreat where she could escape with John and Caroline, she planned to bring them to the Kennedy family compound in Hyannis Port on Cape Cod over the summer. The family also rented the Glen Ora estate, which sat on four hundred acres in Virginia's Hunt Country and boasted a colonial home and an Olympic-sized swimming pool. But after falling out with the owner, the first family went on to purchase Wexford, a sprawling ranch-style house with stunning views of the countryside in Middleburg, Virginia. While waiting for it to finish construction, they retreated to Camp David, the presidential country home in Maryland, and were left surprised by how much they enjoyed it. "If only I'd realized how nice Camp David really is, I'd never have rented Glen Ora or built Wexford," Jackie later told West.

Though the White House could restrict access to journalists, it was much harder to prevent tourists and photographers using telescopic lenses from taking candid photos of the children. At one point, White House Press Secretary Pierre Salinger hashed out an agreement with professional photographers that they would not take pictures of the children through the fence, but he could not stop tourists from snapping revealing photos and then selling them to the wire services or newspapers. Mrs. Kennedy was so annoyed by the steady stream of photos of her children that she sent Salinger a stinging memo letting him know that he was not doing his job properly and that she wanted the pictures to stop.

Oddly enough, although denouncing the way the media violated the privacy of public figures, Jackie remained an avid reader of gossip magazines. This quality helps explain her willingness to permit her staff to release regular press updates about John's development as an infant. Given the public's fascination with the Kennedys, and John especially, these tidbits made headlines around the country. On February 3 John weighed 9 ½ pounds and had six feedings a day. On May 1 John weighed 16 ½ pounds and was 23 inches tall. He had progressed to four feedings a day: "one bottle, and three meals of either strained fruit, meat, vegetables, cereal, cottage cheese." The press reported that he slept well and "makes a lot of noise when he talks." By October 1961, he weighed 23 pounds and had grown seven teeth. "He crawls, climbs, and stands up in his crib. Has a huge appetite, makes a lot of noise, laughs all the time." By his first birthday, he weighed 25 pounds and was 29 ½ inches tall. "He is a very active boy and is into everything," the White House detailed. "He loves to turn knobs, pull handles, [and] open boxes." John had gained the ability to form sentences, his vocabulary was "rapidly expanding," and he was even learning to hold out his hand to greet guests. Weather permitting, he spent most of the day outside in a small White House playground that Mrs. Kennedy had had built on the grounds.

However, for most of the time the family lived in the White House, the press showed more interest in Caroline than in John. The Kennedys' daughter, who was three years old when they moved to 1600 Pennsylvania Avenue, had begun developing a personality, and photographers enjoyed capturing the many faces that she made. John's ability to make news was limited by the fact that he was so young. The *New York Herald Tribune* reported that Caroline "overshadows him." She was, the *Los Angeles Times* observed, "the White House's most popular attraction."

The extent of Caroline's popularity even reached into the world of children's toys. In October 1962 the chairman of the board of the Ideal Toy Company asked permission to make a commercial "Caroline" doll, which he compared with the popular Shirley Temple doll it had marketed in 1934. "Caroline is today the most loved child in the world, idolized by every little girl and an example of wholesomeness," he wrote. "This presents an opportunity for good that should be carefully considered." Baldrige called back to say that Mrs. Kennedy responded "in the negative," to protect Caroline's privacy.

Despite rejecting such requests and prohibiting photographers from taking pictures of her children, Jackie was shrewd enough to know that one of the best ways to keep the members of the press satisfied was to feed them carefully scripted images. According to Clint Hill, "she would think up little stories, or agree to certain photographs, and filter them through the press. As long as she was the director, it was all right." Indeed, Jackie was not opposed to pictures of John as long as she controlled what images the public would see. Her main concern was that the children not be captured at awkward moments or presented in a negative light. She feared they would be used as political props, tossed before a ravenous press to further a partisan agenda.

Instead, the first lady preferred photos that highlighted their "happy" family life. She turned to *Life* magazine's Mark Shaw to snap many of those photos, occasionally inviting him to the White House to take candid shots of the children. Shaw had covered her during the campaign, and she came to trust him because he gave her final approval of all pictures. In addition to feeling comfortable with Shaw, Jackie also preferred *Life* over the other major photojournalism magazine in America, *Look*, because *Life* appealed to a more sophisticated and better-educated reader.

Meanwhile, the president and his media-conscious staff understood how photos of John and Caroline could influence the public's perception of the administration. In their minds, the more pictures of the children, the better. "When the average person needed to be cheered up," wrote Mrs. Kennedy's secretary Letitia Baldrige, "it helped for him or her to hear the latest on those two children at 1600 Pennsylvania Avenue." Whenever JFK needed a media boost, she observed, "the powers that be in the West Wing would decide it was time to stage a photo-op with the children, with probable touchy-feely results." Since they knew that Mrs. Kennedy would object, they waited until she was out of town, or even riding horses in Virginia, before inviting John and Caroline into the Oval Office for photos. "The photo results were inevitably adorable and made the front page of every newspaper in the world," Baldrige recalled, adding that the president "always heard back from the first lady when this happened, in no uncertain terms."

In order to ensure that the public received a steady stream of flattering pictures from the White House, JFK hired Cecil Stoughton as the first White House photographer in history. Kennedy liked the photos that Stoughton, a retired officer with the US Army Signal Corps, took of Inauguration Day and hired him to work full-time in the administration, documenting both official events and behind-the-scenes family life. The president had a buzzer installed in Stoughton's West Wing office and a special phone mounted at the photographer's Virginia home so he could call on him at any time. "Prior to JFK," Stoughton reflected, "we had Eisenhower, and there was no need for a photographer. He was about sixty-three years old, and he didn't have the charm and charisma of President Kennedy, and he didn't have a family that engaged the American public."

The timing could not have been more perfect, as the beginning of the 1960s witnessed the merger between "humanitarian" photography and human interest. Magazines including *Life*, *Look*, *Time*, *Paris Match*, and a host of women's glossies started combining serious news stories with the "human face" of public figures. Over the next four years, Stoughton captured more than eight thousand pictures. His photos helped create the public image of a vibrant young family and forge an enduring emotional bond between the president and the public. John, who was never camera shy, used to plead, "Take my picture, Taptain Toughton." Stoughton's favorite set of images, taken in October 1962, depicted John and Caroline dancing around the Oval Office while their father clapped and sang. After reviewing one of the photos, JFK asked Stoughton, "Why can't we give this one to the press for the birthday picture which they are always demanding?" These photos communicated so powerfully that Barbara Baker Burrows—who later became the photography editor at *Life* in 1966—reflected that they "helped create the aura that later came to be called Camelot."

Although both the first lady and the president proved adept at exploiting the new power of television, they disagreed about how much exposure the children should have to the camera. JFK was convinced that he "couldn't survive without TV" and saw his children as central to the image he wished to project to the nation. "Memories of the Kennedy days are memories of television," recalled a prominent television producer. Kennedy was the first president to allow live broadcasts of his press conferences. By May 1961, nearly 75 percent of the public had seen one, and the vast majority—more than 91 percent—gave him high marks for his performances. The first lady received similar praise when, on Valentine's Day in 1962, she gave a CBS News correspondent the first-ever televised tour of the White House. The broadcast, carried live by all three networks, reached more than eighty million people. But while Jackie was willing to use the cameras to highlight her restoration of the White House, she did not want the children appearing too often on television screens in the homes of millions of Americans.

Given this ongoing conflict between the president and first lady, the rules governing how the press could cover the children changed every day. "It depended on who was making the ground rules, whether it was going to be the president or Mrs. Kennedy," recalled Assistant Press Secretary Christine Camp. When Mrs. Kennedy was in the White House, "there was an absolute rule of divine right that no photographer ever would photograph the children."

The struggle affected issues as small as landscaping. In March 1961 Mrs. Kennedy tried to block tourists and the press from seeing the children's playground by planting thirty-six-foot-tall rhododendrons around the southwest gate. These plants would cut off the view of the White House grounds from the South Lawn, a favorite spot for tourists. The president, who had not been informed of the decision, looked out from his office one morning and saw National Park Service gardeners installing the large bushes. "What's that army doing out there?" he asked J. B. West. "Shielding your children," the chief usher answered. The president shook his head. "I hope it doesn't obstruct the tourists' view of the house," he responded. The bushes stayed.

The scuffle over image also led to clashes over matters as simple as John's hairstyle. The president and first lady gave John's nanny, Maud Shaw, different instructions. Mrs. Kennedy wanted to grow it long, while the president preferred a shorter cut. One Easter at Palm Beach, Mrs. Shaw groomed John's hair in the style that Jackie liked. When they posed for a family picture, the wind blew John's hair and left it unruly. The president proceeded to request that Shaw cut John's hair. Reluctant to tell him that Mrs. Kennedy preferred it long, she promised to fix it the next day, but she ended up not cutting it as short as the president wanted. When JFK entered the nursery and saw that John's hair was still too long by his standards, he asked, "Mrs. Shaw, when are you going to cut John's hair?" Frustrated, the nanny blurted out that she *had* cut it, "but Mrs. Kennedy—" She caught herself before finishing, but JFK got the message and told her to cut it shorter. "If anyone asks you," he said, tell them "it was an order from the president."

Like his wife, JFK had a favorite photographer, Stanley Tretick, who covered the Democratic nominee as the United Press International (UPI) pool photographer. According to photojournalist Dirck Halstead, Stanley and the candidate shared a unique bond. They had a system arranged so that if Kennedy spotted a "jumper"—an attractive woman who jumped up and down with excitement at seeing him—he would subtly signal Stanley, who would then invite her back to Kennedy's hotel room for drinks.

That bond of trust did not go unrewarded. After the election, Tretick asked UPI to make him its full-time White House photographer, but his editor insisted that he share the assignment on a rotating basis with other photographers. When he informed the president, JFK told Tretick to search for another publication and to tell them that the president would guarantee him regular and exclusive access to the White House. *Look* magazine took the president up on his offer and gave Stanley the plum Washington assignment.

From that moment on, Tretick practically served as an official White House photographer, creating an ideal relationship between the two men. He promised the president "complete control" over which pictures would be used, assuring him that any negatives JFK rejected would be turned over to the White House to be destroyed. He even told the president that he would not report anything negative that could potentially harm his image. At the same time, Tretick was a respected photographer who was theoretically independent of the White House, which gave his pictures more credibility than those of an official photographer.

JFK worked with Tretick behind the scenes to capture some of the most iconic pictures of the Kennedy children. But the photographer soon clashed with Mrs. Kennedy when he took a photo spread of Caroline arguing with her cousins over the July 4, 1961, weekend in Hyannis. Jackie insisted that the photos not be published. Tretick, however, took his orders from JFK, not her. Initially, he agreed, but after Jackie allowed her favorite photographer, Mark Shaw, to publish *his* photos of Caroline in *Life*, Tretick's editors overruled him and included the photos as part of an August 1962 cover story, "Caroline's Wonderful Summer." The president feigned anger, most likely to placate his wife, but White House aide Kenneth O'Donnell told the photographer that JFK liked the pictures. "Oh, come on, the president's not upset," he confided. "The president loves those pictures."

The timing of this conflict over Caroline's photos could not have been worse. In late 1962 Tretick was angling to be the first to publish exclusive pictures of John, ideally for his second birthday in November. But the photo spread of Caroline had angered the first lady and complicated his plans. JFK now kept putting Tretick off, not wanting to risk a confrontation with his wife. Mrs. Kennedy did not oppose having John's photo taken, but she insisted that only her photographer, Mark Shaw, do so. On August 6, 1963, she sent a memo to Pierre Salinger asking if her husband would pursue the possibility of getting Shaw to do the photo shoot of John. "The excuse you could give to *Look*," she told him, "is that Mrs. Kennedy prefers to have only one photographer shoot her children so that they are not made self-conscious by being photographed often, and that they know Mark Shaw now and pay no attention to him when he is around." She said she had nothing against Tretick but saw "no reason why he should ever come near my children again."

The president clearly wanted Tretick to take the pictures, but he needed to find a time when Jackie was away from the White House. "Why don't you ask me the next time Mrs. Kennedy goes out of town?" he told him. A few weeks before she was scheduled to visit Greece in October 1963, Tretick called the president's secretary, Evelyn Lincoln, to set up an appointment. "You better call me a little later," she told him. "You mean, like, Friday after eleven o'clock or something?" he asked, referring to the time Jackie would leave the White House. "Well," she responded, "I didn't say that, but it might be a good idea."

On October 9, after Jackie had departed the White House, Stanley sat in a chair outside Mrs. Lincoln's office waiting for John to show up. Even though the first lady would be away for weeks, JFK was nervous. "Now, you know we better get this out of the way pretty quick," the president told him. "Things get kind of sticky when Jackie's around."

John showed up that evening at 7:10 wearing his pajamas and robe. "I'm going to my secret house!" he yelled as he ran toward the president's desk. He crawled under the carved oak and timbers of the British ship HMS *Resolute*. (The ship had been trapped in the Arctic in 1854 and was later recovered by the United States and returned to Queen Victoria, who had a desk constructed from its timbers.) Seconds later, the front panel suddenly flew open and John looked up as Stanley snapped pictures. John jumped out, scampered around the president's feet, skipped about the Oval Office, and then dove under the desk again, giving Stanley a series of juicy photo opportunities. "I almost fainted," Tretick recalled about the scene. "You know instinctively that that's a hell of a picture. When JFK saw the pictures of John under the desk he said, 'You can't miss with these, can you, Stan?'"

The photos captured the genuine loving and playful relationship that JFK shared with his son. Whenever the president opened his office door and saw John and Caroline outside, he would act surprised, which inevitably produced giggles. "Hello there, Sam, how are you?" he would say to John. "I am not Sam," came the response, "I'm John. Daddy, I'm John." *Washington Post* editor and Kennedy family friend Ben Bradlee recalled how John would walk up to his father and whisper gibberish into his ear. When the president threw his head back in mock surprise and asked, "Is that so?" John would laugh until he drooled. JFK would ask Ben to pick up John and toss him in the air because John loved it so much and the president could not do it because of his bad back. "He doesn't know it yet," JFK said, "but he's going to carry me before I carry him." According to Bradlee, JFK could get down on his knees and shout, "I'm going to get you!" while tickling John until "he wets his pants with uncontrolled delight."

Tretick was not the first to witness John playing under his father's desk, but he was the first to record the moment. (Stoughton was in the room later and took pictures as well, but it was Tretick's photos that graced the cover of Look.) Journalist and socialite Katherine Murphy Halle remembered being in the office with her close friend Randolph Churchill, the only son of Sir Winston Churchill, when they "saw a strange movement under the president's desk, and then the door opened and out popped John's head." White House military aide Chester Clifton Jr. recalled how John would hide inside the desk. Sometimes staff meetings would continue despite the obvious sound of a child playing under the furniture.

Along with the photo of John saluting his father's casket following his assassination, the picture of him playing in the Oval Office became part of America's photo album. John did not speak often about his memories of living in the White House. Later in life, when he was promoting George magazine, he sat down for a series of interviews in which he gave away snippets of his past. He shared some with me as well. The one I remember most vividly was his explanation of why he liked to play under the desk. He told me that he hid there because his mom would not allow him to chew gum anywhere in the White House. Often when he came into that room, his dad would hand him a stick of gum, which he would then chew under the desk so that he would not get caught.

Mrs. Kennedy was furious when she returned home and found that Jack had ignored her wishes and allowed Tretick to take the photos. "All hell broke loose," recalled Camp. "You tell Look magazine to never publish a picture!" she demanded. "Stan and Jack were like two sneaky little boys," she told a Look editor. "The minute I left town, they would let you in to do these things that I didn't particularly want done." Despite Mrs. Kennedy's objections, *Look* scheduled the photos for its December 3 issue. It hit the newsstands a few days after the president and first lady traveled to Dallas.

Whether *Life* or *Look* published a photo, the result was the same: the images contributed to crafting a mythical portrait of the Kennedy family. A new generation of baby boomers, the seventy-six million people born between 1945 and 1964, had been raised to embrace the idealized image of the American family portrayed on television sitcoms such as *Leave It to Beaver* and *Father Knows Best*. The steady stream of sanitized images flowing from the White House depicted the Kennedys as the embodiment of that very ideal. Just like the families portrayed on television, the Kennedys—the dedicated and handsome president, the stunning first lady, and their two adorable children—were wholesome and caring, healthy and happy, their relationships devoid of conflict.

We now know that much of that image belonged to a myth manufactured by the While House, disguising the ugly reality that JFK was sickly and unfaithful. Although information about JFK's private life started leaking in the 1970s, it was not until Robert Dallek's masterful 2003 biography, *An Unfinished Life: John F. Kennedy, 1917–1963*, that the public learned the full story. While JFK sought to project youthful energy, he suffered from a variety of debilitating ailments, from Addison's disease—an adrenal gland deficiency that required regular injections of corticosteroids—to colitis, to degenerative back problems. For relief from pain, he often turned to Dr. Max Jacobson, the infamous "Dr. Feelgood," who regularly administered amphetamines and painkillers. When questioned about the injections, JFK snapped, "I don't care if it's horse piss. It works."

Kennedy was also a serial womanizer who would sometimes leave Jackie at events while he slipped away to have sex with a young woman. He even seduced a nineteen-year-old Wheaton College student named Mimi Beardsley, luring her into his bedroom and also encouraging her to engage in oral sex during nude swims in the White House pool. Jackie tolerated his antics. Once, while giving a *Paris Match* reporter a tour of the White House, she passed the desk of a staffer with whom the president was having an affair. "This is the girl who supposedly is sleeping with my husband," she said to the stunned journalist.

The public saw a distorted picture of the Kennedy family, and these images helped forge the expectations that would shape the way the nation viewed John. Pictures of John and Caroline romping around the Oval Office, along with another showing them horse riding with their mother in Glen Ora, appeared on the front page of newspapers around the country on November 25, 1962. These photos would become part of the nation's scrapbook, allowing the public to feel it shared a personal connection with John. Ironically, John had no specific recollection of any of them. After all, he was only three years old when he left the White House. Years later, John confessed that he had seen the images so many times that they blended in with his real memories, the two becoming indistinguishable.

Over time the public would see John as an innocent embodiment of a mythical past. JFK Jr. triggered a nostalgic response in people he encountered, especially those who had been old enough to remember the family's years in the White House. Strangers who approached him on the street always felt compelled to tell him how much they loved his mother and father and still recalled the pictures of him as a child. Those photos reminded them of an allegedly simpler time, not only in their own lives but also in the life of the nation. The public struggled to separate the idealized image of the past that John represented from the flesh-and-blood man that he became.

Clearly, privacy remained Mrs. Kennedy's paramount worry, but not just from the prying eyes of reporters. Of more immediate concern was the Secret Service detail assigned to her and her children. While John was an infant, two agents served as part of the "kiddie detail": Bob Foster and Lynn Meredith. Once John could walk and he and Caroline began engaging in separate activities, the Secret Service added a third agent, Paul Landis. The agents developed code names for the first family, all beginning with the letter L. JFK was Lancer, Mrs. Kennedy was Lace, Caroline was Lyric, and John was Lark. Maud Shaw said the agents were so close to the children that they became "a trio of uncles."

While recuperating at Palm Beach after John's birth, Mrs. Kennedy spoke to Clint Hill about her privacy and the role that the Secret Service would play in their lives. At one point, she asked him to join her by the pool. "I'm worried, Mr. Hill," she said, "about losing all semblance of privacy." As she looked at the agents surrounding the property, she asked, "Are these Secret Servicemen and other agents going to be around us constantly? Even in the White House?" Hill reassured her that there would be no agents in the private residence of the White House, but she remained unconvinced. "Well, that is good to know," she said. "I'm just so worried about Caroline and John growing up in such a restricted environment. I want them to have as normal a childhood as possible." Hill knew that her children would never enjoy such a luxury, but he kept his thoughts to himself.

Congress originally created the Secret Service in 1865 to investigate counterfeiting, but expanded its mandate to provide protection to the president following the assassination of President William McKinley in 1901. At the time, there were only two men assigned to the White House detail. Over the next few decades, the service saw its budget grow and its responsibilities expand. In 1950, after a failed assassination attempt against President Harry Truman, Congress enacted legislation that permanently authorized Secret Service protection for the president, his immediate family, and the president-elect. But the Kennedys provided the agency with a new challenge because it had never before protected two young children.

The agents saw their role as straightforward: to shield the children from all potential threats. They soon discovered, however, that Mrs. Kennedy held a very different view of their job. She raised a basic question, and one that the service had not dealt with in modern times: At what point did the Secret Service's responsibility to protect the family interfere with a parent's right to decide how her children would be raised? Over the next sixteen years, Mrs. Kennedy and the Secret Service would debate this issue back and forth. Jackie believed that her parental rights superseded the service's legal obligation to safeguard the family. In many ways, she would come to see the Secret Service as more intrusive than reporters and photographers.

After just one month in the White House, Mrs. Kennedy established specific ground rules for how she wanted the Secret Service to deal with her. When traveling by car to a publicly announced event in Washington, DC, or whenever she was in the car with her children, she wanted the agent to sit in the front right seat with the window divider raised for privacy. When shopping unannounced in Georgetown, she insisted on being accompanied only by the driver—and on those occasions, she would sit in the front right seat. If the agent could not find a parking spot near the entrance, he could drop her off, and she would walk. Once the agent parked the car, he would have to find her. "The agent," she insisted, "will not enter small shops but will remain at a distance to observe." If she decided to drive the children, she asked that two agents follow her in a separate car. Once they arrived at their destination, usually a playground, one agent would stay with the car and the other would "follow on foot at a very discreet distance, whereby he will not be noticed by the children or Mrs. Kennedy."

The following year, she devised even clearer guidelines for how the Secret Service was to protect John and Caroline. The head of the service spelled out Jackie's demands in a memo distributed to the agents in charge of their protection. She insisted that whenever she was driving the children, the follow-up car needed to remain far enough behind that the children would not see it if they happened to turn around. Furthermore, she was "horrified" to see agents doing chores for the children and nanny Maud Shaw. "Mrs. Kennedy is adamant in her contention that agents must not perform special favors for Miss Shaw and Caroline or wait upon them as servants," the memo read. She believed that the agents were acting like caregivers, and "it is bad for the children to see grown men constantly doing things for Miss Shaw or waiting upon the children." It was "imperative" that the agents "drift into the background quickly when arriving at a specific location, and remain aloof and invisible until moment of departure."

She also established precise instructions for the way agents should behave at the White House, Hyannis Port, and Palm Beach. She did not want an agent with her when she took the children out for boat rides in Hyannis, nor did she want to see them in a follow-up boat when they were waterskiing. She made clear that "drowning is my responsibility." That rule applied to all the activities that the children participated in. "She insists," the memo read, "that the Secret Service is not responsible for any accident sustained by the children in the usual and normal play sessions; accidents and injuries while at play are the sole responsibility of Mrs. Kennedy, herself, or the attending nurse." She did not believe the service was responsible for sheltering her children from the usual challenges of childhood, but rather for "preventing kidnapping, abduction, molestation, rape, all crimes of violence, and undue infringement of her children's privacy by the general public."

"She was difficult," Hill reflected. "She wanted us to be almost invisible." He recalled that her top priority was that "the children not be spoiled or treated any differently than any other child." But that demand proved unrealistic: they were not like other children. Their father was the president, they lived in the White House, the public was fascinated by them, and the constant threat existed that someone might harm them. "But," he pointed out, "the guys really made an effort to follow her wishes and allow John to grow up as normal as possible, have friends, and go through the bumps and trials and tribulations of childhood like every other kid."

Mrs. Kennedy's orders—specifically the contention that "drowning was my responsibility"—were put to the test shortly after she announced them. On June 28, 1961, John and Caroline attended a picnic at the home of a friend in Bethesda, Maryland. According to the Secret Service report, at eleven thirty Caroline "entered the swimming pool and pushed away from the edge" in an inflated tube. When she reached the center of the pool, she "apparently lost her grip on the tube and dropped through the tube, with her head submerging under the water." One of the mothers jumped into the pool and pulled Caroline to safety. The agent in charge assured his superiors that there "was no need for artificial respiration," but it was also clear that Caroline could have drowned had it not been for the immediate intervention of an adult. The agents did not see Caroline struggling because they were following Mrs. Kennedy's instructions to remain out of sight "and approximately 50 to 75 feet from poolside." From their vantage point, they could not see the surface of the swimming pool. "On any future occasion, this agent will try to forestall the necessity of a fully dressed, pregnant mother jumping into the swimming pool to rescue Caroline. But under existing instructions from Mrs. Kennedy, it won't be easy to do, and the only proper way to handle the situation is to have a special agent, of the service, in a bathing suit close enough to the pool to observe all activity in and around it."

Following the incident, the agents asked the first lady to relax some of the limitations that she had placed on them. She refused. "Mrs. Kennedy feels that the Secret Service was in no way negligent in the performance of their duties and that their actions on this occasion were in conformity with existing policy," Agent James Jeffries wrote. "Mrs. Kennedy is not in favor of revising security measures. She insists that the Secret Service is not responsible for accidents which the children might be involved in, and that our only interest should be to protect her children from kidnapping."

Although she left very specific guidelines about the agents maintaining their distance, Mrs. Kennedy could become irritated when they failed to control crowds. While in Hyannis that same summer, Jackie took John and Caroline to a news shop. The agents reported a few curious onlookers, but no one appeared to be a security risk, so they adhered to her demands and did not enter the store or keep her path open. The agents reported that "several elderly ladies with cameras" tried to take Jackie's picture as she made her way back to her parked car. According to Agent Lynn Meredith, "The first lady turned a cold shoulder and refused to permit any photographs." Afterward, she complained that the agents did not clear a path for her or prevent onlookers from trying to talk with her or take her picture.

The most dramatic test of the conflict between Mrs. Kennedy's rules and the Secret Service's legal obligations came during the Cuban Missile Crisis. In October 1962 an American U-2 spy plane discovered Russian offensive nuclear missile sites in Cuba, just ninety miles from Florida. JFK delivered a nationwide television address to the American people. Declaring the Russian tactic in Cuba "deliberately provocative and unjustified," he insisted the United States must respond "if our courage and our commitments are ever again to be trusted by either friend or foe." Kennedy then established a quarantine of the island that was enforced by a naval blockade. For days, the nation and the world teetered on the edge of nuclear war.

Amid the crisis, as Soviet ships inched closer to Cuba and no one knew whether nuclear war with the Soviets loomed, Hill counseled Jackie that in the event of a Soviet attack, she and her children would be escorted to a secure bunker beneath the White House. She interrupted him before he could finish. "Mr. Hill," she said, "if the situation develops that requires the children and me to go to the shelter, let me tell you what you can expect." According to Hill, she then lowered her voice into a deep whisper, "If the situation develops, I will take Caroline and John, and we will walk hand in hand out onto the south grounds. We will stand there like brave soldiers and face the fate of every other American." Hill responded politely, "Let's pray to God that we will never be in that situation." But he also told himself that his job was to protect the first lady and the children. If necessary, he reflected later, he would have "picked her up, kicking and screaming, and dragged her into the shelter." Fortunately, rational heads prevailed, and after a nerve-racking thirteen days, Russia backed down, and the crisis was averted.

For Mrs. Kennedy, raising John and Caroline was her highest priority. "A mother's responsibilities to her children are enormous, especially where they see less of the father," Jackie told a reporter in 1963. "The insecurity of much coming and going, the irregularity of schedules, and the strange people all affect the children." She went on to say that it was not fair "to children in the limelight to leave them to the care of others and then to expect that they will turn out all right." Children, she continued, needed "their mother's affection and guidance and long periods of time alone with her. That is what gives them security in an often confusing world."

As much as Mrs. Kennedy spoke about "a mother's responsibilities," her idea of what constituted "raising" children reflected her own wealthy upbringing, in which daily needs were handled by nannies, maids, and nurses. In fact, Jackie traveled often—either with the president or on solo trips—and when she went abroad, she could be absent for weeks at a time. Before leaving, Mrs. Kennedy would fill out postcards to be given to Caroline and John every day that she was away. Furthermore, even when she was home at the White House, Mrs. Kennedy kept irregular hours. Whenever she woke up, whether as early as eight or as late as noon, she always requested breakfast served in bed. The only consistent time that Jackie spent with the children was in the evening, the "children's hour," when she would read to them and watch as they ate dinner.

Although not a constant presence in their lives, Mrs. Kennedy stayed very clear about the way she wished them to be raised. According to Letitia Baldrige, the first lady did not want them showered with praise due purely to the accidents of their birth. While she believed they should be proud of their father's success, she insisted that they earn respect through their own accomplishments. Though they were surrounded by the trappings of wealth and power, she raised her son and daughter to be humble and unfailingly polite. "When people spoke, they listened," Baldrige wrote. "When people gave them presents, they said thank you with grace and a minimum of prompting." It was during his years in the White House that John developed his lifelong habit of bowing as he shook the hand of someone he deemed important—which was just about everyone he met as a child.

In actuality, the person who bore most of the burden of raising John and Caroline was Maud Shaw. The nanny changed diapers, dressed and fed them, readied them for naps, and took them to the playground. Whenever John had a restless night, it was she who would rock him back to sleep. Shaw, then in her midfifties, had started working for the Kennedys when Caroline was only eight days old. Shaw had a distinct British accent and always wore a crisply ironed white uniform. She lived simply, in a dressing room closet connected to Caroline's room on one side and John's on the other. "She won't need much," Mrs. Kennedy told J. B. West. "Just find a wicker waste-basket for her banana peels and a little table for her false teeth at night." The rooms sat atop the portico, looking down on the lawn and gardens at the front of the house. Shaw was up at six every morning to feed John, and then an hour later, she would give Caroline her breakfast. When they finished eating, she took them to visit the president, who was served breakfast in his suite at eight fifteen.

The president was woken up every morning at seven forty-five by George Thomas, his African American valet. JFK would go into his separate bed-room and eat breakfast, allowing Jackie to sleep later. He would be sitting in a chair with his breakfast on a tray, reading briefing books, when John and Caroline came rushing into the room. They would turn on the television with the sound blasting. Sometimes they watched cartoons, but they also enjoyed exercising along with fitness guru Jack LaLanne, the host of a long-running, popular home TV exercise show. JFK sometimes would "touch his toes with John a bit," Jackie told the historian Arthur Schlesinger in 1964. "He loved those children tumbling around him."

Beginning in 1962, Caroline spent from nine until noon at a special school with about ten classmates, mainly the children of family friends, on the third floor of the White House. It served double duty as both a school-room and an indoor playground, complete with a sandbox, plants, an aquar-ium for goldfish, and cages for rabbits and guinea pigs.

Once old enough to walk, John would often accompany his father to the West Wing. As the president got up to leave his bedroom and head to the Oval Office, John would shout, "Don't leave me! We've got to go to work!" Still in his pajamas, he would then follow along closely behind his father. John used to bombard Shaw with "his machine-gun burst of questions about everything and anything." He had a hard time pronouncing "Caroline," so he referred to his sister as "Canon." For her part, she never grew tired of re-sponding to his cries of "Canon! Canon!"

When Caroline's class was having morning recess, the president would walk out and clap his hands to get their attention. Within seconds, he would be surrounded by children. He would often shout John's name, saying it in rapid succession so that it sounded like "John-John." The moniker caught on, and soon everyone in the White House, including the press corps, called him by that name. John would spend most of his adult life trying to convince passersby that, as he often repeated, "One John will suffice."

One morning the president called John's name, but he did not appear. The president turned to Agent Tom Wells and asked, "Where's John?" Wells told JFK that a few minutes before, John had accidentally knocked out his front tooth and that Agent Bob Foster had escorted him to the doctor's office. JFK hesitated a minute before asking, "It's a baby tooth, isn't it?" Wells responded, "Yes sir, as far as I know." JFK seemed unconcerned. "He will be all right," he stated. "He will grow another one."

By 1962, Caroline had a daily schedule because of morning school, but John's time was still unstructured. In the afternoon, following lunch, Caroline would nap for about two hours. Then, weather permitting, she would go outdoors and play, often with John. Sometimes she would return to the Oval Office to see her father in the afternoon. She would be back in her room in time for children's hour and then eat dinner around six thirty or seven. Meanwhile, John followed no set pattern. "He eats, sleeps, and plays, all with gusto," the White House reported.

After dinner, Shaw would bring the children down to their father's office. They would stop by to see secretary Evelyn Lincoln, crawl around her office, and play with her typewriter while they waited for their father to finish his meetings. On some days, the president would take the children down to the indoor swimming pool for an evening dip. Afterward, John and Caroline would return to the second floor, where they played for a short while before going to bed. The president and Mrs. Kennedy would come up in the evening and give them their good-night kisses. During his time in the White House, whenever he was at home, the president never failed to see his children tucked into bed.

In Hyannis, where John and Caroline spent most of the summer, they followed an entirely different schedule. Here they would be surrounded by more than a dozen cousins, along with aunts and uncles. In addition to Jack's younger brothers—Robert F. Kennedy, the US attorney general, and Edward "Ted" Kennedy, who in 1962 was elected to JFK's vacant seat in the US Senate—were his younger sisters Eunice Shriver, Jean Kennedy Smith, and Pat Lawford. Jackie's sister, Lee, used to visit occasionally. Because there were so many kids around, the adults made sure their days were structured and full of activities. The mornings would begin with Caroline going horse riding with friends. While she was off riding, John, Maud Shaw, and a Secret Service agent would head to the beach, swimming and playing until lunchtime. They usually picnicked for lunch, consuming large quantities of ice cream, fruit, and soda. Normally the children were not permitted to have sweets, but in Hyannis and on holidays, they could eat whatever they wanted. The biggest bonus was that they were allowed unlimited Coke.

One afternoon, Shaw and the two children visited a neighbor's house to play on the beach. Shaw spotted a strange woman walking toward the group of children. The Secret Service watched from a careful distance but did not deem the woman a threat. "Say, I hear the Kennedy children are coming down here today," she told Shaw. "Do you know when they are arriving?" The first family's nanny played dumb and told her she knew nothing. "Gee, I'd sure like to see them," the stranger said. "I guess they must be real nice kids." As she talked, she patted young John on the head, oblivious to who he was. On most occasions, however, whenever a stranger approached, John would blow his cover by declaring proudly, "I'm John F. Kennedy Jr."

The presence of children running around added a casual informality to the White House. Once, when a reporter asked three-year-old Caroline where her father was, she responded, "He's upstairs with his shoes and socks off, doing nothing." Baldrige remembered the White House as "full of children morning, noon, and night." Male houseguests would use the same bathroom where JFK took his hot baths and would find rubber ducks lined up along the side of the tub. Mrs. Kennedy bought the ducks to keep John Jr. occupied when he lounged in the tub with his father, who often used the time to read newspapers and memos from his staff.

Although he lived amid the formal grandeur of the White House, there was little doubt that John was a child and often acted like one. On one occasion, the president wanted Grand Duchess Charlotte of Luxembourg to meet John and Caroline, so Shaw made them practice for the formal reception. She taught Caroline how to curtsy and John to bow. Caroline had the curtsy down, but John struggled with his gesture. Although worried about whether John would perform adequately, Mrs. Shaw sent them to the reception. Within a few minutes, she was called in to have John removed. Not only had he failed to bow, he'd also thrown himself on the floor in a temper tantrum.

"What on earth did you do that for?" Shaw scolded as she escorted him out of the room. John informed her that they did not give him his cookie. He would perform at these events only after having a cookie and ginger ale, but when neither arrived, John decided to let his displeasure be known.

While the first lady tried her best to insulate the children from outside pressure, she could not shield them from a tragedy closer to home. In the summer of 1963, the whole family learned excitedly that Mrs. Kennedy was pregnant again. They agreed that if it were a boy, he would be named Patrick, and if it were a girl, Caroline insisted, her name would be Susan. On August 7 Jackie went into labor while at their home in Hyannis Port. She was rushed by helicopter to Otis Air Force Base Hospital in Falmouth, where she gave birth to Patrick Bouvier Kennedy. He was born at thirty-seven weeks and weighed only 4 pounds, 10 ½ ounces. The infant was quickly diagnosed with hyaline membrane disease, the same lung ailment as John. As his condition worsened, Patrick was transferred to Children's Hospital in Boston but died after only thirty-six hours. The president broke the news to Caroline, who was visibly upset. He simply told John the baby wasn't coming home, but John was not old enough to understand the meaning of death.

Nevertheless, Patrick's memory stayed alive, either by Jackie's choice or John's own. Even when I knew him, John would often refer to his "brother Patrick." I remember being stumped at first because he seemed to speak about him in the present tense. I knew my Kennedy family history was rusty, but I probably would have known if John had a brother walking around. Only after asking a friend did I learn the sad truth. Often John would bring up Patrick out of the blue. Once, when a friend told him that his birthday was in August, John did not miss a beat. "Oh," he responded, "that's my brother Patrick's birthday."

Patrick's death appeared to signal a turning point in the president's relationship not only with his wife but also with his children. Clint Hill noticed that after the death JFK grew more affectionate with Jackie and spent more time with both John and Caroline. When he returned to the Cape, JFK went swimming with his brother Teddy and John, and Teddy noticed a change in his attitude. "Jack was absorbed in everything that his small son was doing,"

Teddy wrote in his memoir. "In the few months left to him, my brother showed an even greater preoccupation with the activities of his son and daughter than I had seen before."

Walter Heller, who served as chairman of the Council of Economic Advisers, offered a rare insight into how John added to the informality of a typically formal White House. A detailed notetaker, the economist recorded two encounters with John in the final months of the Kennedy presidency. In October 1963 the president walked into a breakfast meeting with John in tow. The meeting started with John circling the table to shake hands with all those in the room, bowing as he did so. John then climbed into an empty seat. When his father asked him to leave, John answered loudly, "No, Daddy, I want to stay here." The president proceeded with his usual opening statement: "What have we got today?" Before anyone could respond, John declared, "I've got a glass of ice water." When Mrs. Shaw came in to retrieve him, John protested, "I want to stay with Daddy." She eventually managed to hustle him out of the meeting by promising that he could play with Caroline and return to the office later in the day. The president, Heller pointed out, "suggested that we all take note of the nurse's technique," adding that "if she or I had ordered him out, he would've cried and said 'no.'"

Two days before JFK and the first lady left for their fateful trip to Texas, Heller went to see the president in the evening to discuss "the status of his thinking on the assault on poverty." When he arrived in Evelyn Lincoln's office, "[T]here were Caroline, drawing pictures at one side of the office, and John-John, with a mighty bruise and scratched nose, playing with the children's tea set at the other end of the room." Caroline was showing Heller some of her drawings when John came over with a little aluminum plate, saying he was serving "terry-manilla pie," which Heller quickly realized was childspeak for cherry vanilla. John then handed him a spoon, and Heller ate a piece. As he finished, National Security Advisor McGeorge Bundy exited the president's office, and he, too, tasted John's concoction before leaving.

By all accounts, John was a normal, highly energetic child. Clint Hill described him as "a typical little boy; he loved to climb and jump, and as soon as he learned to walk, he rarely walked—he ran." In her oral history for the John F. Kennedy Presidential Library, Shaw reflected that "John is one hundred percent boy. He was a boy that every man would be proud of. There was no silly nonsense that you have with a child. No matter where he went, he showed off his best. He has very good manners, and his father was always very proud of him."

John was fascinated by helicopters, and he enjoyed watching military rituals. "Helicopters and his dad were like two lollipops in his life," observed Agent Thomas Wells. John loved traveling by helicopter with his father to Andrews Air Force Base outside Washington, DC. "Any time the president was leaving and John was aware of it, he wanted to ride the helicopter out to Andrews," Wells recalled. "If he didn't make that trip, he was put out." Famous footage shows John rushing toward the president after his helicopter landed at the White House. Most people interpreted it as John rushing to embrace his father. But John once confessed to me that he was actually running to get on the helicopter. It just so happened that his father was in the way.

Shaw remembered when John accompanied his father for a helicopter ride from the White House to Andrews, the home base of Air Force One. Everyone on the specially equipped presidential jet was ready to take off, but the president spent extra time with John. "Everybody was very impatient, tearing their hair out," Shaw reflected in an oral history, but the "president was taking his time," allowing John to walk up the ramp to the plane even though he was not going on the trip. He let John get seated and strapped in before telling him that he needed to return home to the White House. Not surprisingly, John let loose a torrent of tears as he was led off the plane."

John also preferred to fly by helicopter to Camp David. Clint Hill recalled the boy's excitement as he stood waiting for Marine One to land in the back to transport them to their official getaway. "He was bouncing around the room, so excited he could hardly contain himself." Once on board, John sat on his mother's lap with his nose pressed against the window as the helicopter maneuvered past the Washington Monument. Hill noted that John "could barely sit still."

At Camp David, if John arrived before his father, he would stand by the landing pad, waiting patiently to hear the whirling sound of the helicopter's blades. On one occasion, John traveled to the retreat on Friday afternoon, and the president wasn't scheduled to arrive until the next day. John spent most of Friday hanging out by the landing patch, gazing up at the sky. When he finally heard the copter approaching, he started dancing with excitement.

"The chopper's coming, Mrs. Shaw! The chopper's coming!" Sometimes he referred to Marine One as "Daddy's hebrecop."

But landing the helicopter was just the beginning. John would drag his father into the hangar just so they could sit at the controls. Whenever John went missing, Mrs. Shaw knew where to find him. John would put on a helmet and bark orders to his father, telling him which buttons to push and which lever to pull. The commander in chief followed instructions dutifully, and John would start mimicking the sound of the helicopter lifting from the ground.

John's fascination with flying also extended beyond helicopters. The president kept copies of aviation magazines in his office, and John would flip through the pages and admire the pictures. Noticing John's excitement after a flight on the Goodyear blimp, Mrs. Kennedy made a prediction about his future. "You know how much John loves airplanes and flying," she said. "I think someday he is going to be a pilot."

John's love of flying was matched only by his fascination with the military. Whenever a formal ceremony occurred for a head of state, Mrs. Kennedy would take John to the South Lawn to watch the marching bands and the soldiers in uniform with shiny medals covering their chests. In October 1962 Prime Minister Ahmed Ben Bella of Algeria visited the White House and was given an official ceremony, including a military review. Mrs. Kennedy and Maud Shaw brought John down to the Rose Garden to observe the ceremony. "Come, John," Jackie said as she lifted him into her arms. "Let's go watch the ceremony. You can see all the military men in their uniforms." They positioned themselves out of sight behind a hedge, where she held him up high enough so that he could have a clear view. He peppered her with questions. "What's that?" he asked eagerly. "Why are they doing that? What are all those flags?"

Like many young boys, John enjoyed playing with imaginary guns and rifles and pretended to be in the army. At both Camp David and Wexford, while Jackie and Caroline rode horses, John explored the woods wearing cowboy boots and an army helmet. At Camp David, the Secret Service set up a tent in the woods for John, and he spent hours marching around with his toy guns, giving orders to the agents and other imaginary friends.

Yet as much as he loved the pomp of military ceremonies and tried to imitate the way the soldiers marched, John struggled with one important gesture: the salute. When "General John" issued orders, the Secret Service agents would salute. He would always salute back with his left hand. "No matter how many times we told him to use his right hand," Hill recalled, "his instinct always seemed to be to use his left hand."

Family friend Dave Powers, who spent part of his day entertaining John, took it upon himself to teach John the proper way to salute. After considerable practice, the two-year-old seemed to have mastered the gesture. On October 25, 1963, Powers had John show off his salute to a friend, William F. Connors, the New England regional manager of the Veterans Administration, as they waited outside the president's office. "What do you do when you see the soldiers?" Powers asked John. According to Connors, John "whipped up his arm in a right-hand salute."

A few weeks later, Mrs. Kennedy tried to prepare John for the Veterans Day ceremony held at Arlington National Ceremony. She told him that since his father was the commander in chief, all of the soldiers were going to salute him. "Now, John," she said, "when you see the other soldiers salute Daddy, you can salute him, too." On November 8, 1963, as his father placed a wreath on the Tomb of the Unknown Soldier, the uniformed color guard saluted. On cue, John raised his right hand and saluted his father. "I was proud of the little guy," Agent Bob Foster said.

CHAPTER 2

"PLEASE, MAY I HAVE ONE FOR DADDY?"

The Kennedy family considered November to be a month of celebration. In addition to gathering at Thanksgiving, the family held birthday parties for John and Caroline, and they observed the anniversary of JFK's election to the presidency. November 1963 appeared no different from the past two in the White House. John's mother and father were already preparing for John's third birthday on November 25, but first they needed to make a trip to Texas to shore up support for the upcoming 1964 presidential election.

Thursday, November 21, began like most other days at the White House. John, dressed in plaid short pants, and Caroline, wearing a blue velvet dress, joined their father while he was eating breakfast. Maud Shaw had told them that their parents would be leaving soon for Dallas. What mattered most to John, however, was that his father had invited him to fly on the helicopter to Andrews Air Force Base. (In bad weather, they traveled by motorcade.) While the children played and Mrs. Kennedy combed her hair in the other room, JFK waded through newspapers and made phone calls. At nine fifteen Caroline hugged her father and whispered, "Bye, Daddy," before making her way up to the third-floor school. John accompanied his father to the West Wing and kept himself occupied with toy planes while the president prepared for his trip.

The visit to Texas carried special importance for JFK. As he geared up for his 1964 reelection campaign, Kennedy wanted to keep the state's twenty-five electoral votes in the Democratic column. That feat would be difficult: the state Democratic Party had split into rival liberal and conservative factions, and the president's recent support for a civil rights bill banning segregation in public facilities made him wildly unpopular in the South.

To help soften his image, he asked Jackie to join him. It was her first political event since losing Patrick in August, just three months earlier. The public had missed Jackie, who had become only more popular over the past three years. JFK had always worried that her sophisticated style, along with her elegant and expensive taste in fashion, would be a political liability. But the opposite happened. She added to the luster of the Kennedy White House, underscoring that the dowdy Eisenhower days had come to an end and been replaced by a new sense of panache and elegance. Her regal style, both pre- and post-motherhood, and refined taste had transformed her into a cultural icon, making her the most admired woman in America.

John brimmed with excitement as he walked with his parents to the South Lawn to board Marine One. When they landed at Andrews Air Force Base a few minutes later, his mother and father hugged him and said goodbye inside the helicopter. "It's just a few days, darling," Jackie said to console him. "And when we come back, it will be your birthday." A few photographers had already assembled nearby, so JFK decided not to give them shots of John having a meltdown on the tarmac. "I want to come!" John protested. "You can't," the president said gently. JFK kissed his sobbing son and then turned to Secret Service agent Bob Foster. "You take care of John, Mr. Foster," he said. John sat on Foster's lap as his parents boarded the plane, letting out a sigh as the majestic Air Force One lifted into the clouds.

Mrs. Shaw and the members of the kiddie detail managed to keep John and Caroline occupied for the remainder of the day. Caroline spent the afternoon at a birthday party while Shaw struggled to persuade John to take a nap. She felt relieved when Foster offered to escort him to a toy store on Wisconsin Avenue. "Mommy and Daddy will be back soon," the agent assured John as they walked through the aisles. "Just in time for your birthday."

After dinner, the children played games with the agents. Shaw then bathed them and readied them for bed by reading stories. John slept that night surrounded by toy trucks and helicopters; Caroline preferred stuffed animals. Before Shaw turned off the light, Caroline reminded her brother that tonight was the first time they would be sleeping without relatives in the house, so they needed to be on their best behavior. They had spent nights without their parents, but always with a relative in the house, usually Jackie's mother.

The next morning, November 22, John and Caroline strolled into Maud Shaw's tiny room at seven o'clock and chorused politely, "Good morning, Miss Shaw. May we get up now?" Usually, after getting washed and dressed, they would rush to their father's bedroom. Instead, Shaw escorted them into the family dining room for breakfast. Afterward, Caroline headed to school while Shaw took John outside for a short walk. At noon, after Caroline's class ended, they shared lunch together with Ted Kennedy's children, Edward Jr., two, and three-year-old Kara. Much of their conversation that day revolved around birthdays. John was about to turn three on Monday, and Caroline, six, on Wednesday.

Meanwhile, after successful events in San Antonio and Houston on Thursday, the president and first lady started the morning in Fort Worth. There President Kennedy; Vice President Lyndon Johnson, a native Texan; and a handful of Texas politicians stood in misty rain in a parking lot across from their hotel to speak to a large crowd of well-wishers. Although the two most powerful political figures in the country had come to the Lone Star State, it was the first lady who seemed to attract the most interest. When the president appeared at the rally without Jackie, the crowd conveyed disappointment. "Mrs. Kennedy is organizing herself," JFK joked. "It takes longer, but, of course, she looks better than we do when she does it."

Afterward, they moved inside for the main event: a breakfast meeting at the Hotel Texas for 2,500 guests sponsored by the chamber of commerce. Mrs. Kennedy entered the room late. "Two years ago, I introduced myself in Paris by saying that I was the man who had accompanied Mrs. Kennedy to Paris. I am getting somewhat that same sensation as I travel around Texas," JFK observed. "Nobody wonders what Lyndon and I wear."

At 10:35 A.M. the presidential party left the hotel for the short trip to Carswell Air Force Base and the eight-minute flight to Dallas's Love Field. The president's political advisors decided to fly the thirty miles to Dallas so they could arrive in time for a midday motorcade through downtown to attract the largest possible crowds. According to presidential aide Dave Powers, when the president and first lady stepped off the plane "a great roar went up from thousands of throats." They "looked like Mr. and Mrs. America," he said. Jackie wore her now-iconic outfit: a pink wool suit with a matching pillbox hat.

At 11:55 A.M. JFK took his seat in the back of a specially designed 1961 Lincoln convertible. Jackie positioned herself on his left. Texas governor John Connally and his wife, Nellie, sat on the jump seats directly in front of the first couple. To guarantee maximum exposure, Kennedy aides chose a circuitous path through the most populated parts of the city en route to the Dallas Trade Mart, where he was scheduled to speak at a luncheon for local businessmen. It took the motorcade eight minutes to travel down Main Street. At 12:29 the car passed the Old Court House and turned right onto Houston Street. As they approached Dealey Plaza, the presidential limousine made a sharp left turn onto Elm Street and proceeded down a slope, leading to an underpass and a highway ramp that would take them to the Trade Mart. Jackie had been uncomfortable all morning sitting under the bright sunlight, but her husband insisted that she not put on her sunglasses. Now she hoped the shade from the underpass would provide a brief reprieve from the sun. "I thought it would be cool in the tunnel," she recalled.

Before they reached the shade, Lee Harvey Oswald, a disgruntled former US Marine who'd defected to the Soviet Union in 1959, only to return to the States two years later with a Russian bride, fired three shots at the motorcade from the sixth floor of the Texas School Book Depository building. The first bullet missed its mark. The second tore through Kennedy's throat and struck John Connally in the back. "My God!" the governor shouted. "They're going to kill us all!" Nellie Connally pulled her husband into her lap and covered his body when a third shot rang out, exploding Kennedy's head and showering Jackie with blood, bone, and brains. "They've killed my husband! I have his brains in my hand!" she cried.

No doubt existed among those who witnessed the fatal third shot that Kennedy was dead. Agent Paul Landis, riding in the backup car, described the sound of the bullet hitting Kennedy's head as "the sound you would get by shooting a high-powered bullet into a five-gallon can of water or shooting into a melon." Devastating results followed. "I saw pieces of flesh and blood flying through the air, and the president slumped out of sight toward Mrs. Kennedy. . . . My immediate thought was that the president could not possibly be alive after being hit like he was," Landis testified. Another agent, Clint Hill, ran toward the car and leaped onto the back of the limousine. He quickly examined the president's wound and signaled thumbs-down with his hand.

Around one thirty in Washington, DC, just as the first shot rang out in Dallas, Caroline hopped into the backseat of a Country Squire station wagon driven by the mother of her best friend, Agatha Pozen. Mrs. Kennedy had given Caroline permission to sleep over at the Pozen household. It would be her first sleepover without her parents or relatives present. In keeping with Mrs. Kennedy's orders, Agent Tom Wells maintained a respectable distance in the follow-up car. About halfway between the White House and the Pozen residence on Connecticut Avenue, Wells heard over the radio that shots had been fired at the presidential motorcade. He flashed his lights, pulled over the wagon, and asked a reluctant Caroline to return with him to the White House. "I don't want to go," she protested. She complained all the way back. "But why?" she asked confusedly. "Why do we have to go home?" Wells did not want to divulge the real reason. "Mummy is coming back early," he said. "She's changed her plans, and she wanted you and John to be home."

While Caroline was being driven back to the White House, the car containing her parents scrambled madly to nearby Parkland Hospital, where doctors engaged in a Herculean but futile effort to save the president's life. JFK was declared dead at one o'clock. Shocked and numb, the presidential party rushed to Air Force One for the lengthy flight home. But Lyndon Johnson insisted on taking the presidential oath before the plane took off, and he asked Mrs. Kennedy to stand beside him as a sign of continuity to both the nation and the world. Visibly shaken, the now former first lady insisted on wearing her bloodstained dress so the world could see "what they did to my husband." As soon as the brief ceremony concluded, the plane carrying Mrs. Kennedy and the body of her slain husband departed for the long, solemn trip back to Washington.

Meanwhile, Mrs. Shaw remained unaware of the tragic events unfolding in Dallas. She was waiting for Ted Kennedy's children to leave so that she could ready John for his afternoon nap. But he resisted. Apparently no one wanted to break the news to the nanny or explain why Caroline had been sent back home. She recalled Caroline and John sitting in the living room when she received a phone call from Nancy Tuckerman, the first lady's secretary.

"Mrs. Shaw," Tuckerman said gravely, "I have some bad news for you. I'm afraid the president has been shot." She had no details. "This is all we know right now," she stated. "I'll call you back as soon as I hear how it is."

Shaw was not sure what to do but decided to let the children take their usual naps. "Come along, children," she said, hiding her fears. "It's time for you to rest now." Surprisingly, John, who would often play under the covers for twenty minutes before charging out without ever having closed his eyes, gripping a toy plane or helicopter, fell asleep immediately, and Caroline read from her book before dozing off.

While they napped, a "pale-faced and ill" Secret Service agent informed Shaw that the president had died. The agents had drawn lots to determine who would break the news to her. The Kennedys' longtime nanny broke down in tears, not only over the death of the president but also over how his death would shatter the lives of the two children now sleeping peacefully in their rooms. "I loved them both," she reflected, "and it broke my heart to think of the pain and shock that now lay in store for them."

Around the same time, the nation was also learning the somber news. At 2:35 P.M. EST the United Press International teletype machines reported around the world: "Flash: President Kennedy Dead." CBS anchorman Walter Cronkite, dubbed "the most trusted man in America," made the official announcement at 2:37 P.M. "From Dallas, Texas, the flash, apparently official. President Kennedy died at 1:00 P.M. central standard time, two o'clock eastern standard time." The normally stoic newscaster paused for a moment and looked at the studio clock, stunned. "Some thirty-eight minutes ago." Fighting back tears, Cronkite removed his eyeglasses and cleared his throat.

Television came of age that ominous day. Never before had a news story traveled so far, so fast. Thirty minutes after the shots rang out at Dealey Plaza, two out of three Americans had heard about the assassination. Most people learned of the shooting itself from friends or colleagues, but they were sitting in front of televisions or radios when word arrived of Kennedy's death. Within two hours of the shooting, 92 percent had received the news that the president had been shot. By six o'clock EST, nearly every adult in America—99.8 percent—knew that Kennedy had been assassinated. The three major networks canceled all commercial broadcasting for the weekend. More than 90 percent of homes followed the assassination coverage during those three days, and they watched for an average of 31.6 hours—more than ten hours a day.

Americans growing up in the 1940s and 1950s had experienced a variety of big news stories, but none possessed the shock value of the Kennedy assassination. JFK's death paralyzed the country. The nationwide telephone system crashed from the demand of calls. On street corners and in department stores, crowds gathered around radios and televisions to follow every detail of the news. In New York City, traffic came to a halt as drivers stopped cars and hunched over dashboards, glued to their radios. The garish brilliance of Times Square was replaced by darkness as the massive advertising displays were turned off. Broadway performances were canceled. Nightclubs closed. "In many respects, the biggest city in the nation turned into something of a ghost town," reported *The New York Times*.

The same television cameras that had helped forge such a strong emotional bond between the young, charismatic president and the nation he led now transformed his death into a uniquely personal event for millions of Americans. The nonstop TV coverage, which began within minutes of the shooting and continued until after the funeral on November 25, enabled all of America to experience the tragedy firsthand.

On November 22 I was in the first grade at St. Clements Catholic school in southeastern Philadelphia. After lunch, the sisters started scurrying around in the hallway, and when my nun returned a few minutes later, she was crying. She kept pulling tissues, one after the other, from the arm of her habit, which left me wondering what else she had stored up there. Within several minutes, the mother superior announced over the intercom that the president had been shot and instructed us to pray for him. The sister took out her rosary, but before we could start our prayers, the mother superior's voice came back on the intercom and declared that the president was dead. At that point, she put the microphone up against the radio, and we sat, hands folded in front of us, listening to the live broadcast for the rest of the afternoon.

I'm ashamed to admit it now, but the seriousness of what had occurred did not register on me that day. I was just shy of my seventh birthday, old enough to be aware of world events. Reflecting on that time, however, I was a rather dull kid who was largely oblivious of the outside universe. Growing up in an Irish Catholic family, I knew that JFK was a Catholic, and my elders told me that his Catholicism was a good thing. In fact, my dad used to call himself a "Kennedy Democrat," but it was not until years later that I understood what the phrase meant. I knew that something momentous had happened because everyone around me seemed to be either crying or on the verge of tears. When I arrived home, my mom was watching television keenly, but I just went outside and played. What I remember most was being glad that Monday was going to be a holiday.

Inside the family quarters of the White House, a new challenge emerged: to insulate John and Caroline from the tragic news and to keep them occupied until their mother returned later that evening. Nancy Tuckerman invited *Washington Post* editor Ben Bradlee and his wife, Tony, to spend time with the children. They were both close friends of the family, and Ben had developed a fun, playful relationship with John. The two of them entertained the children in the Oval Room, which was the family's living room. John asked Bradlee if he would tell a story, so as they lay on the floor, Bradlee began spinning adventures about a three-year-old boy named John. The real John listened intently before showing Ben the military salute that he had been practicing. He then ordered Bradlee to "chase me around the house," and the editor obliged.

As they played, helicopters began landing on the mansion's South Lawn. Every time John and Caroline heard the whir of a helicopter rotor approaching, they raced to the windows, shouting, "That's Mommy and Daddy! Mommy and Daddy are coming home!" Unsure what to say, Bradlee simply responded, "Daddy will be back later." Ben would never forget "those bloody great choppers, one after another, drowning everything out." Tuckerman believed that Caroline sensed something was wrong, but John seemed oblivious. With the sound of every helicopter blade, he jumped with excitement. "Here they come! Here they come!"

Around five o'clock, as it grew dark outside, Agent Foster called and told Shaw that he had received a coded message from Clint Hill aboard Air Force One. Apparently, Mrs. Kennedy wanted the children taken to the Georgetown home of her mother, Janet Auchincloss. While they were speeding back to Washington on Air Force One, Hill had decided that the first lady would not want John at the White House, where he would hear Marine One land on the South Lawn but not see his father emerge. He concluded it would be best if John and Caroline stayed with their grandparents.

The decision surprised Mrs. Auchincloss, who believed her grandchildren should remain at the White House, but she agreed that if they had to be moved, the best option would be for them to remain with her. Foster informed Shaw that the children needed to be out of the White House by six o'clock, when their mother was expected to land. Shaw wasn't sure how long the children would be away, so she went into their rooms and started stuffing their suitcases with clothes. John and Caroline then hopped into the family station wagon and arrived at their grandmother's house a few minutes later. If they knew something was wrong, neither of them let on. They both ate hearty dinners while chatting contentedly with each other. "I was shattered by the thought that such carefree happiness would have to be shattered so soon," Shaw reflected.

The plane carrying Mrs. Kennedy and JFK's body arrived at Andrews as scheduled at six. The new president, Lyndon Johnson, delivered a short speech before taking a helicopter back to the White House. Jackie decided to go to Bethesda Naval Hospital, where doctors planned to conduct an autopsy. By seven, family members had joined Mrs. Kennedy on the hospital's seventeenth floor while doctors examined the wounds on JFK's body in order to determine the trajectory of the shots that had killed him. Jackie described in graphic detail every aspect of the shooting and the horrific minutes that followed. "I was so startled and shocked she could repeat in such detail how it happened," recalled Robert Kennedy's wife, Ethel. Her personal physician, Dr. John W. Walsh, thought it would be good for her to talk about the day. "It's the best way," he said. "Let her get rid of it if she can." A few hours later, fearing that she would collapse from exhaustion, Dr. Walsh injected her with a powerful sedative. It had absolutely no impact.

In an instant, Jackie's world had been upturned. She worried what it would be like to raise her children without their father. "Bobby is going to teach John," she said. "He's a little boy without a father, he's a boyish boy, he'll need a man." She knew that she would have to vacate the White House now that her husband was gone. Her plan was to move back into the Georgetown house they had occupied while Jack was in the Senate. "That was the first thing I thought that night: 'Where will I go?'" she recalled. "I wanted my old house back." She would soon learn, however, that the house was no longer on the market.

Janet Auchincloss, who had rushed to the hospital, tried comforting her daughter by assuring her that the children were safe at her house.

"You know they are at O Street now."

"What are they doing there?"

"I had a message that you had sent from the plane that you wanted them to come and sleep there."

"I never sent such a message."

"You don't want them to be there, then?"

"No, I think the best thing for them to do would be to stay in their own rooms with their own things so their lives can be as normal as possible. Tell Mrs. Shaw to bring them back and put them to bed."

However, before Janet Auchincloss could make the call, Clint Hill, who had overheard the conversation, called Agent Wells and told him the first lady's wishes. Wells then relayed the message to Foster. "Mrs. Kennedy is coming back tonight and wants the children in the house with her," Foster informed Shaw, who then packed up the children for a second time. The nanny recalled that Mrs. Kennedy instructed that she did not want the children "disturbed" and that it was important for them to keep their normal routine until she figured out how to reveal the awful news. "Come on, John-John," Caroline urged. "Put your coat on, we're going home again."

By the time they returned to the White House at eight o'clock, more than a thousand people had gathered outside in a silent vigil. "What are all those people there for?" Caroline asked as she clambered out of the car. "To see you," Shaw responded as they scurried back into the White House and up to their second-floor bedrooms.

Mrs. Kennedy had numerous issues to consider, including planning a state funeral, but one central question lingered: How would she tell John and Caroline that their father was not coming home? Did they even understand the concept of death? Her mother pressed her on that question at the hospital. "Jackie, are you going to tell the children, or do you want me to, or do you want Mrs. Shaw?" Jackie wasn't sure and asked for advice. "Well," Janet contemplated, "John can wait. But Caroline should be told before she learns from her friends." Jackie agreed and suggested that Shaw should use her own discretion. Janet, however, delivered a different message, saying that Mrs. Kennedy wanted Shaw to tell the children, leaving out the part about using her own discretion. Shaw objected. "I can't take a child's last happiness from her. I don't have the heart. I can't destroy her little happy day." Janet, however, insisted. "I know, but you have to." Shaw agreed eventually and said it would be best to tell Caroline before she went to sleep. "You know," she told Janet, "when children are Caroline's age, they do sleep at night, and it's better for them to get a sadness and a shock before they go to sleep at night so that it won't hit them very hard when they wake up in the morning."

Shaw tucked in John and recited prayers with him before going into Caroline's room and sitting on the edge of her bed. She read to the five-year-old from one of her favorite books, knowing the whole time that she was about to break the little girl's heart. As Shaw held Caroline in her arms, Caroline could sense that she was upset. "I can't help crying, Caroline, because I have some very sad news to tell you." She told Caroline that her father had been shot. "They took him to a hospital, but the doctors could not make him better." She continued, "So your father has gone to look after Patrick. Patrick was so lonely in heaven. He didn't know anybody there. Now he has the best friend anyone could have." Caroline buried her face in the pillow and cried herself to sleep.

Shaw claimed that it was decided that the president's brother Robert should be the one to tell John. But there is no evidence that such a conversation ever took place, and John probably learned about his father's death the next morning.

The children also weighed on the mind of Lyndon Johnson. Before leaving his office for the night, the new president of the United States wrote notes to them. "Your father's death has been a great tragedy for the nation, as well as for you, and I wanted you to know how much my thoughts are with you at this time," he wrote in longhand. He placed the notes in envelopes and sealed them, planning to deliver them in person.

While she awaited the autopsy and embalming at Bethesda Naval Hospital, Mrs. Kennedy phoned a family friend, artist William Walton, and asked him to consult a book of sketches showing Abraham Lincoln lying in state at the White House in 1865. She wanted her husband's viewing and funeral modeled after that of Lincoln, the first American president to be assassinated. Historian and Kennedy aide Arthur Schlesinger Jr. and speechwriter Richard Goodwin rushed to the Library of Congress and spent the night researching details of the Lincoln rites.

The family arrived back at the White House with the body of President Kennedy at 4:35 that morning. Workers spent most of the night and early morning preparing the East Room for the viewing. Schlesinger described the scene as Kennedy returned to the White House for the final time. "The casket was carried into the East Room and deposited on a stand. It was wrapped in a flag. Jackie followed, accompanied by Bobby. . . . A priest said a few words. Then Bobby whispered to Jackie. Then she walked away. The rest of us followed."

Jackie retired to her room, but Bobby returned and asked Schlesinger to view the body and make a recommendation about whether to have an open casket. Schlesinger recorded his thoughts in his journal later that day: "And so I went in, with the candles fitfully burning, three priests on their knees praying in the background, and took a last look at my beloved president, my beloved friend. For a moment, I was shattered. But it was not a good job; probably it could not have been with half his head blasted away. It was too waxen, too made up. It did not really look like him." Schlesinger reported back to Bobby, who made the decision to have a closed-coffin ceremony.

Mrs. Kennedy went to sleep that night without seeing her children. She slept for a few hours with the help of another powerful tranquilizer. The next morning, she had to handle the dizzying preparations for the funeral, but, more important, she needed to help her children face the reality that their father was dead.

I had little interest in the assassination until my senior year at Widener College in Chester, Pennsylvania, which was a few miles from my home. I was walking home from the library one evening when I saw a poster announcing a presentation about the "conspiracy" to kill Kennedy. I was curious enough to stop by, thinking I would stay for only thirty minutes. But the show—and it was more of a show than a dry, academic presentation—turned out to be wildly entertaining and quite disturbing. Leading the performance were roughly six young, bearded men, all of whom looked as though they had just graduated college. They presented the Zapruder film, the famous 8mm silent color home movie footage of the assassination taken by Abraham Zapruder, to make the point that the fatal head shot must have come from the front, in the area by the grassy knoll, a gently rising slope to the front of the limousine. I learned for the first time about the mysterious "umbrella man," who had been wearing a trench coat and carrying an umbrella on a sunny, warm day. Without a doubt, they argued, the umbrella shot a poison pellet directly into the president's throat. They challenged all the major conclusions of the Warren Commission, established by Lyndon Johnson and chaired by the chief justice of the Supreme Court, Earl Warren, by charting the path of the "magic bullet" as it meandered through Kennedy's body and then Governor Connally's. Clearly, they claimed, there must have been at least two shooters, maybe even more. It seemed by the end of their presentation that everyone in Dealey Plaza that day, with the possible exception of Mrs. Kennedy, had a motive to kill Kennedy. The military, the Secret Service, the CIA, the FBI, and the Mob apparently conspired with various outside forces—the Soviets and the Cubans—to murder JFK and then orchestrate a cover-up. Oh, wait, I forgot Lyndon Johnson. He was in on it, too.

When I met John in 1982, I stood firmly in the conspiracy camp. By the 1990s, I had not only abandoned conspiracy theories entirely but also had lost interest in the whole debate over the assassination. It was settled history, and I never raised the topic with him. It came up only once, around the time when director Oliver Stone's conspiratorial megahit movie JFK hit theaters in 1991. I don't recall the context of the conversation, but John stated cryptically, "Bobby knew everything." Years earlier, I would have seen that statement as an acknowledgment of conspiracy. By then, however, I was not even curious enough to pursue the subject further.

Early on the morning of November 23, Caroline entered Maud Shaw's room looking "pale, and her big eyes were sad and puzzled." John appeared a few minutes later. Their nanny told them gently that their grandparents were sleeping in the president's bedroom and that they should go see them. It is likely that she also broke the news to John about his father's death. Janet and Hugh Auchincloss, who had accompanied Jackie and the president's body back to the White House, slept for only an hour before John and Caroline wandered into the room at seven o'clock. Caroline was carrying a stuffed giraffe that her father had given her, and John was pulling a toy behind him. The first daughter headed to the bed and pointed to a picture of her father emblazoned on the front page of that morning's newspaper.

"Who is that?" she asked.

"Oh, Caroline," Janet responded. "You know that's your daddy."

Caroline looked at her and responded, "He's dead, isn't he? A man shot him, didn't he?"

Jackie managed only a few hours of sleep. When Robert Kennedy, who'd slept in the Lincoln Bedroom, walked down the hall, he found his sister-in-law sitting on her bed talking to John and Caroline. By this point, John clearly knew about the loss because when his uncle entered, John told him that "a bad man" had shot his father. Caroline added that her father was too big for his coffin.

Although still traumatized, Jackie needed to prepare for a Mass that would be held in the East Room for seventy-five family members and close friends. As she had requested, White House workers labored through the night to make the room look exactly the way it had in 1865. It was decorated entirely in black. The bulbs in the great chandeliers were dimmed. The president rested in a closed flag-draped casket supported by a platform called a catafalque. Flickering candles adorned each corner.

Shortly before ten o'clock, Mrs. Kennedy gathered the children so they could say good-bye to their father. Jackie wanted to place mementos in the coffin, so she helped John and Caroline write scribbles. "I would like you to write a letter to your father, telling him how much you loved him," she told them. John drew an X on a piece of paper. Caroline wrote, "We're all going to miss you, Daddy. I love you very much." Jackie composed her own long letter that began with "My darling Jack." She took the children by the hand and led them downstairs, where they knelt in front of the casket and prayed.

She also collected several of President Kennedy's most cherished items, including gold cuff links she had given him on their first anniversary and a PT boat tiepin. She and Bobby carried the items down to the East Room to place them in the coffin. RFK ordered that the casket be opened and that the guards turn their backs to give them privacy. Jackie kissed her husband, cut off two locks of his hair, and put them in a small ceramic frame. She kept one and gave the other to Bobby. "I had never seen her looking so wan and desolate," observed her secretary Mary Gallagher. "She seemed on the verge of fainting."

John and his sister did not attend the Mass but watched it through the open doors of the Green Room. Once the Mass ended, Kennedy's body remained in the East Room for the next twenty-four hours as the Cabinet, congressional leaders, governors, diplomats, the Supreme Court, and the White House staff walked solemnly past the casket. The public would get its chance on Sunday, when the body would be moved to the great Rotunda in the Capitol until the burial on Monday.

Mrs. Kennedy wanted to keep the children busy, so she asked the Secret Service to take John and Caroline to Andrews Air Force Base to watch the planes take off and land. While Caroline was old enough to realize that her father would not be coming back, John did not fully grasp the finality of death. One minute he would tell the agents, "A bad man shot my daddy." A few minutes later, he would ask them to take him to the office to see his dad. John still associated Andrews Air Force Base with JFK, since just two days earlier he had watched from the tarmac as his father left for Dallas. At one point, he cried, "Whoosh! Here comes my daddy, and he's landing!" Mrs. Shaw explained to him that his father had gone to heaven. "Did he take his big plane?" John asked. "Yes, John, he probably did," Shaw responded. Shortly afterward, John wondered out loud, "When is he coming back?"

Later that afternoon, Janet Auchincloss and Jackie's half brother, Jamie, took John and Caroline to the battlefield at Manassas, the site of two momentous clashes between the Union and Confederate armies in the early years of the Civil War. They also brought with them two family dogs: a German shepherd and a French poodle. At first, they walked the dogs on a leash but then decided to let them run. The animals raced off and ended up in the visitor center, where they were greeted by an angry National Park Service ranger shouting, "No dogs allowed!" But as soon as he uttered those words, he saw John and Caroline rushing to retrieve the dogs. "At that moment," recalled Jamie, "he realized that he was talking to the children of the slain president. His jaw flew open, and he had a hard time controlling his emotions."

When they returned home, Jackie and Janet went to the nursery to see them. Jackie, who had been so controlled all morning, could no longer contain her emotions. Tears streamed down her face as she embraced John and Caroline. She pleaded with Mrs. Shaw to entertain the children. "That is all you can do for me. As long as I know they are happy, it will be a great help."

While everyone did his or her best to keep John occupied, he clearly felt his father's absence. Later that day, he wandered around the White House, complaining, "I don't have anyone to play with."

On Sunday John joined his mother and sister for the ride to the Capitol, where President Kennedy's body would lie in state until the funeral on Monday. As the family gathered in the East Room, the major networks, which were providing live coverage of the procession to the Capitol, cut away with a news flash that the president's alleged assassin, Lee Harvey Oswald, had been shot down in the basement of the Dallas city jail as he was being transferred to the county jail. The assailant, Jack Ruby, was a local nightclub owner with close ties to the police.

The news did not faze the Kennedys, who no longer wanted to hear about anything happening in Dallas. They stood together on the steps of the North Portico as the caisson moved slowly down the drive. Mrs. Kennedy wore a black wool dress. John and Caroline wore similar pale blue coats and red shoes. Behind the caisson, following military tradition, came a riderless bay gelding, with the military boots reversed in the silver stirrups. When John pointed at the animal, his mother leaned down and told him that the horse was a symbol representing the nation that had lost its leader. Jackie, along with John and Caroline, joined by President and Mrs. Johnson and Robert Kennedy, all piled into the first of the ten-car procession to the Capitol.

An estimated crowd of three hundred thousand lined Pennsylvania and Constitution Avenues to witness the caisson carrying the slain president travel from the White House to the Capitol. While riding in the car, RFK noticed that John was wearing gloves and instructed him to remove them. A few minutes later, Jackie noticed that John was not wearing the gloves. "Where are John's gloves?" she asked. "Boys don't wear gloves," Robert responded. The gloves stayed off. When they reached the Capitol, Mrs. Kennedy and her children walked up the marble steps, trailed the flag-draped coffin into the Capitol Rotunda, and took their places in a small section that had been roped off for them.

The entire ceremony proved overwhelming for John. A reporter described him that morning as "wild eyed and bewildered." As he grew more restless and rambunctious, Shaw whispered to Agent Foster, "This is no place for a little boy." Foster picked him up and carried him to the Speaker of the House's offices. Agent Wells followed and stood outside the door, where he heard John ask, "Mr. Foster, what happened to my daddy?" Foster never figured out an answer, but John became distracted by a wooden stand containing miniature flags from all the nations. A guide asked John if he would like one of the flags. "Yes, please," he said. "And one for my sister, please." The guide handed him two flags. "Please, may I have one for Daddy?"

At the end of the ceremony, Mrs. Kennedy and Caroline stepped a few feet forward and touched the flag and the coffin beneath. Mrs. Kennedy knelt and kissed the coffin, then led Caroline away to the top of the Capitol steps, where they were rejoined by John. Clasping John's and Caroline's hands, she slowly descended the long flight of steps before entering a limousine for the trip back to the White House.

As they made their way home to 1600 Pennsylvania Avenue, the news flash announced that Oswald had died from the single gunshot to his abdomen.

On Monday morning, November 25, Shaw organized an intimate breakfast celebration for John's birthday. The three-year-old sat in the dining room while Shaw and Caroline sang "Happy Birthday" and gave him two presents: Caroline, a helicopter, and Shaw, a book.

The formal remembrances concluded that afternoon with a Mass at St. Matthew's Cathedral and burial at Arlington National Cemetery. Mrs. Kennedy, along with Robert and Ted Kennedy and hundreds of visiting heads of state and dignitaries, walked the seven blocks from the White House to St. Matthew's. John and Caroline traveled by car and met their mother at the base of the church. Bewildered, John looked around and started crying. His mom whispered something to him, managing to calm him down. They then ascended the steps of the cathedral, and there waiting was Richard Cardinal Cushing of Boston, who had married the Kennedys in 1953 and had baptized both children. Mrs. Kennedy, holding her son's and daughter's hands, went inside and proceeded down the aisle to their seats. The church was already packed with 1,200 mourners who had been admitted by special invitation. The president's casket rested in front of the altar just underneath the soaring dome.

Once again John grew restless. Someone gave him a copy of a booklet—*The Church Today: Growth or Decline*—from the literature rack in hopes of distracting him. The gesture did not work. "Where's my daddy?" he was heard saying. "My poor mummy's crying," John said, "and she's crying because my daddy's gone." He then lifted his arms in the air. "Somebody pick me up." Agent Foster swooped in, picked up John, and carried him into an anteroom. In an effort to keep him occupied, Foster asked John to practice his salute. Old habits proved hard to break. On Veterans Day, just two weeks earlier, John had pulled off a perfect right-hand salute, but now he had reverted to using his left hand.

A marine colonel was watching John and offered to help. "Why don't you give the colonel a salute?" Foster urged. When John once again used his left hand, the colonel corrected him gently. "John, you are doing it all wrong. This is the way you salute." In one demonstrative move, the marine stood upright and offered a crisp salute. It clearly had an impact on John because he immediately started using his right hand again. By this time, the Mass had ended, so Foster brought John, still grasping his church booklet, out to join his mother and sister as they exited the church.

Mrs. Kennedy, with Caroline and John on each side, led the mourners from the cathedral and then stood on the outside steps while the casket was removed and placed on the caisson, which was positioned directly in front of the Kennedy family. Once the casket was secured, the military rendered a salute to its fallen commander in chief. At that point, Mrs. Kennedy leaned down and whispered, "John, you can salute Daddy now and say good-bye to him." John handed her his church booklet, took a small step forward, stood tall, and then lifted his right hand to his brow. With the entire world watching, three-year-old John saluted his slain father. "It was almost more than I could bear," recalled Clint Hill. "I looked around and saw colonels and generals and colleagues—some of the toughest men I knew—and they too were fighting to hold back tears."

The original plan had been for John and Caroline to accompany their mother to Arlington for the burial, but at the last minute, she decided to send them back to the White House. After the funeral services, Mrs. Kennedy invited 220 foreign dignitaries and diplomats to the White House for a reception. As the guests started to leave, Dave Powers kept John busy by playing the role of drill instructor. "One, two, three, four—cadence count!" he proclaimed as he led John to the end of the south hall and back into the dining room.

Mrs. Kennedy decided to proceed with a planned birthday party for John that evening. She wanted to disrupt his life as little as possible. The party was a tradition that she would continue for the rest of her life. It served as much as a distraction from the ritual media focus on the assassination as it did a celebration of John's life. At seven o'clock she left the reception and went upstairs to the celebration. "I couldn't disappoint little John," Jackie told family friend Countess Vivian Crespi. The entire Kennedy family, including distant relatives in town for the funeral, attended the event. When cousin John Davis walked into the dining room, he saw John with a paper hat on his head and a toy rifle over his right shoulder. "He had been seen marching all day and could not get it out of the system," he recalled. By contrast, Caroline sat somberly, not saying a word. Eventually John put away his rifle long enough to start opening his presents. The guests applauded every time John ripped the wrapping paper off the gift. Mrs. Kennedy laughed when John took a deep breath and blew out his three candles. "I'm glad they are happy," she said quietly.

"Of all Monday's images, nothing approaches the force of John's salute," wrote William Manchester in *The Death of a President*, a masterful account of the day's overwhelming events. Millions of Americans had watched the funeral live. But I was not one of them. I spent most of the day outside exploring the woods near our home in Darby, Pennsylvania. My best friend could not join me because his mother made him stay home and watch the ceremony. Even then, it was impossible to escape the image. The television in our house stayed on all weekend. That evening, I saw the shot of John for the first time in a news summary, and it was plastered on the front page of the local newspaper the next day. But somehow it did not resonate with me. I suspect that until I saw the picture, I was not aware that the president even had a son.

Over time that image has branded itself on our public consciousness. Before that moment, John had been a cute little boy who romped around the White House, hid under his father's desk, and danced to his father's claps. But with that single gesture, he became identified with so much more. As the heir apparent, all the unfulfilled hopes and expectations of his father's presidency transferred to him. In the short run, while John was still a child and young adult, his uncles Robert and Teddy would seek to fulfill their slain brother's legacy, but John was always the prince in waiting.

JFK's hold on the public imagination actually exceeded his modest accomplishments in office. In death, Kennedy was transformed into a martyr for causes he championed reluctantly as president. Only after intense pressure from civil rights activists did JFK agree to submit a watered-down civil rights bill to Congress. Many of his campaign promises to stimulate the economy remained bottled up in Congress. He skillfully guided the nation through the Cuban Missile Crisis, but his administration's obsession with ousting Fidel Castro, often by extralegal means, helped set the stage for the confrontation in the first place. Furthermore, JFK expanded America's involvement in Vietnam and showed little inclination to avoid a wider war.

Indeed, his legacy has largely been defined by his sudden death. By the mid-1970s, the tragic series of events that followed the assassination—a lost war in Vietnam, racial violence, student protests, and the Watergate scandal that brought down JFK's onetime political foe Richard Nixon, who'd ascended to the White House after all—made America nostalgic for the bright idealism of the Kennedy years. Citizens overlooked his limited achievements and turned him into a symbol of a time when the United States apparently stood strong in the world and felt united; when life seemed simpler. As the American Dream slipped further from the grasp of most people and as faith in government diminished, Americans clung ever more tenaciously to a mythic view of Kennedy.

Mrs. Kennedy played a vital role in manufacturing that myth. Similar to how she sought to control media access to her children, she grew determined to shape the public's perception of her husband's presidency. A few days after the assassination, she sat down with the journalist Theodore White to detail her view of JFK's administration as resembling the fictitious kingdom of Camelot. "Don't let it be forgot, that once there was a spot, for one brief shining moment, that was known as Camelot," she told White, quoting the lyrics to the song "Camelot," from one of JFK's favorite Broadway musicals.

Ultimately, John would spend his life burdened by the expectations of that myth. It did not seem to matter that John had no memory of that weekend, let alone his salute. The millions of people who *did* remember no longer saw him as John-John (though many continued to call him by that name) but as John Fitzgerald Kennedy Jr., a living embodiment of his illustrious father. Years later, John was having lunch with his friend and future business partner Michael Berman. "It must be interesting being you," Berman noted. "We are sitting in a restaurant, I don't know a soul here, and no one knows me. You don't know a soul here, but they all know who you are."

John paused for a moment before responding.

"That's not the odd part," he said. "The weird part is that they remember, and I don't. They look at me, and they know me because of what they remember. And they remember more than I do. It's uncomfortable for me."

John's observation captured the central dilemma of his life. The public viewed him as a symbol of a different time in the nation's history and, perhaps, in their own lives. John learned to gracefully acknowledge and respect those deep feelings. But in order to live a fulfilling life, he needed to define himself separately from his father and beyond the expectations that he had inherited. After November 22, 1963, he confronted that challenge every day of his life.

"Honey, you stay as long as you want," a gracious LBJ assured Mrs. Kennedy, but Jackie was eager to leave the White House. Staying a few extra weeks, however, allowed John to maintain his routine in the only home he knew. On December 2 he wandered into Mary Gallagher's office. "Do you have some gum for me?" he asked. He was disappointed when she said no. "But I'll bet I have something else that you'll like even more!" John approached her desk to see what she planned to give him. "Oh, not here," she told him. "It's something that doesn't even fit into my desk drawers." John went gleefully around the room, looking under furniture to find his mystery gift. Finally, he confronted a closet door, slowly turned the knob, and let out a shriek when he discovered that his gift was a toy airplane. "Look, Miss Shaw!" he shouted with excitement. "I have a new airplane!"

On December 7 Jackie accepted an offer from diplomat and family friend Averell Harriman and his wife to move into their eleven-room, three-story home on N Street, which was just a few blocks from where Jack and Jackie had lived before taking up residence in the White House. It would be a temporary move until she could purchase her own house. Jackie's room was located on the second floor, and the children and Miss Shaw occupied the third floor. The first floor brimmed with activity. A navy cook made meals, the Secret Service monitored phone calls and searched unknown packages, and Mary Gallagher frantically tried to keep up with correspondence.

The children made the best of their new home. They brought with them their favorite toys: for Caroline, a doll named Mary and her Raggedy Ann; for John, an armory of military equipment—guns, rifles, toy soldiers, and swords for hand-to-hand combat. He had also received a military uniform for his birthday and wore it all the time around the house. Unfortunately, the Harriman house lacked some of the comforts that John had enjoyed while living in the White House. He was not happy that the house had no elevator, which meant that he had to climb three flights of stairs to get to his room.

By all accounts, Mrs. Kennedy was suffering from severe depression and was emotionally unavailable to her children. She rarely left her bedroom on the second floor. "After the busy days moving from the White House, her depression set in," observed Gallagher. She confided in friends that she was drowning in grief. "Sometimes I become so bitter—only alone—I don't tell anyone," she wrote former British Prime Minister Harold Macmillan in January 1964. Robert Kennedy, concerned about her mental state, began brokering meetings between her and a Jesuit priest, Rev. Richard T. McSorley. That spring, she told McSorley that she was contemplating suicide. The priest recorded some of their conversations in his diary.

"Do you think that God would separate me from my husband if I killed myself?" she asked on April 28, 1964. "I feel as though I am going out of my mind at times. Wouldn't God understand that I just want to be with him?" In a letter that summer, she thanked McSorley for his assistance. "If you want to know what my religious convictions are," she wrote on July 15, "they are to keep busy and to keep healthy—so that you can do all you should for your children. And to get to bed very early at night so that you don't have time to think."

As part of her intent to "keep busy," Mrs. Kennedy made sure that the children remembered their father and Irish heritage and that John had plenty of male role models. In addition to his responsibilities as attorney general, RFK consoled Jackie and spent time playing with John. Like clockwork, Dave Powers came every day at noon to entertain John and regale him with stories, often about his father. John would sit for long periods listening raptly as Powers told him about everything from his father's bravery during World War II to his victory over Khrushchev during the Cuban Missile Crisis.

I got a taste of Powers's storytelling prowess in the 1980s. For my dissertation, I needed to spend countless hours at the newly opened JFK Presidential Library in Boston. Since no cafeteria existed at the time, researchers had to buy sandwiches from a food truck outside and bring them back to a small, spartan room, with only a handful of tables, off the main reading area. I must have made a dozen trips to the library, and every day at noon, there was Dave Powers, who held the title of museum curator, sitting in the lunchroom and captivating us with stories about JFK and his time in the White House. What was most impressive was that he repeated the stories exactly the same way each time—the same pauses, inflections, and tone. By then, he was so well rehearsed that he appeared to be on autopilot. He had started practicing his stories back in 1963 with two young children as his audience. And like John, I never grew tired of listening to those tales.

Despite their new surroundings, the children maintained much of their same routine. LBJ allowed Caroline to finish the school year at the same White House school that she'd attended before the assassination, riding back and forth with a Secret Service escort. John played with Maud Shaw as usual, though the British nanny did discern something different about him. "I could not help noticing his bright little face clouding over sometimes as he struggled to understand what had happened to him," she reflected. John had trouble comprehending why they no longer lived in the "big White House" in Washington. Whenever he saw a picture of the White House, he would turn to Shaw and query, "That's where we live, isn't it, Miss Shaw?" Shaw would then remind him again that they didn't live there anymore. Eventually she overheard him comment to his sister as they looked at a picture of the White House, "That's where we used to live, Caroline."

John still struggled with the whole idea of death as well. In the White House, he had begun most mornings in Evelyn Lincoln's office, crawling on the floor and playing with the typewriter. Naturally he missed her. One day John asked Mary Gallagher, "Where's Mrs. Lincoln?" He continued to interrogate her about Lincoln's whereabouts until Shaw intervened, deciding it would be best if John spoke with Lincoln on the phone. That conversation started a daily habit of phone calls. One day John stated that he planned to visit her.

"That would be lovely, John. I'm looking forward to seeing you."

"Me too. Mrs. Lincoln?"

"Yes, John."

"Is Daddy there?"

Lincoln was too overcome with emotion to respond.

As they had done for the past few years, Jackie took the children to Palm Beach to celebrate Christmas with their grandparents Joe and Rose

Kennedy and the extended Kennedy clan. Joe, who suffered a massive stroke in December 1961, was now confined to a wheelchair and unable to speak. Caroline hung lights on the Christmas tree while John tossed tinsel "over everything and everyone." Afterward, John, Caroline, and a few cousins performed a Nativity play for the adults. The occasion brought back memories of past Christmases they had celebrated with their father. "Will Patrick be looking after him in heaven?" Caroline asked. Before anyone could answer, John piped up, "Do they have fish chowder in heaven?" Everyone knew that fish chowder was the president's favorite dish.

The Secret Service took elaborate precautions to protect the family during their stay, which lasted until January 5. Agents were no doubt still on edge about losing the president the previous month, and it did not help matters that two days after the family arrived, the West Palm Beach Police Department received an anonymous call from a man saying that he "planned to kill the rest of the Kennedy family that night." Jackie and the kids were spending the vacation at the home of Colonel Michael Paul, who lived just up the street from the Kennedy compound. In order to make the Paul residence more secure, the Secret Service established a security room in the main garage, installed a new telephone system that connected to each of the security checkpoints, and created four security posts outside and two inside the property.

The added layers of security did little to dampen spirits on Christmas morning at the compound. The children seemed to have forgotten about recent events as they ripped open their gifts, cluttering the living room with wrapping paper and boxes. "There were hugs and kisses and thank-yous and a great deal of shouting and laughter," Shaw recalled, "which became so infectious that the grown-ups temporarily forgot the grief of a month before and joined in."

But reality soon greeted them again. On January 6 the family returned to the Harriman house only to find more than four hundred spectators camped outside hoping to get a glimpse of the grieving widow and her children. They planned to stay there only a few days, since Mrs. Kennedy had purchased a new house just down the street: a three-story, fourteen-room brick Colonial with two large magnolias in front. The first few weeks were difficult for Mrs. Kennedy as she waded through boxes of pictures and other mementos reminding her of her husband. At one point, she walked into Gallagher's office with an envelope full of material related to JFK. She insisted that the secretary remain in the room while she sorted through the contents. "It's so much easier doing it while you're here than at night when I'm alone," she confided. "I just drown my sorrows in vodka."

Despite the presence of two lively children, Gallagher found the house eerily quiet. "During the hours that I was there, I saw few people," she recalled. John was relieved that this house had an elevator to take him up to his room, and he continued receiving noontime visits from Dave Powers. "They would lunch together," recalled Gallagher, "tell stories, march through the rooms, or do just anything to occupy the time happily." There was also a paved backyard so that John could ride his tricycle. "President Kennedy's son is described these days as all boy," wrote *The Washington Post* in May 1964. "A tricycle terror in his own backyard, he sometimes corners on two wheels around the flagstone-paved area. He has a delightful time tumbling with Shannon, the family's cocker spaniel. He tangles with the living room draperies. And he scrambles with his uncle, Attorney General [Robert] Kennedy, who dropped by almost every day to see him."

RFK and Jackie had bonded in their grief. They made almost daily trips to Arlington, where they prayed at President Kennedy's grave. Along with Dave Powers, Bobby became the other central male figure in John's life in the year following the assassination. He observed a clear difference in the way John and Caroline dealt with their anguish. John, always an energetic child, seemed to grow even more rambunctious. After one hectic morning, an exacerbated Mrs. Shaw complained, "You know, he's a boy and a half!" But while RFK described John as mischievous, he noted that his sister became more withdrawn, saying, "Caroline doesn't let people get close to her."

Robert did his best to fill the void in John's life left by his father's death. He roughhoused with him, just like his dad had done. They played games, especially John's favorite, hide-and-seek. "Where's John?" he'd ask as he searched for his nephew, who was usually hiding in plain sight. By the spring of 1964, Robert would pick up John most mornings and let him spend several hours with him at the US Justice Department, where he was usually joined by two of RFK's children, his cousins Kerry and Michael.

Just when people thought that John did not understand that his father was dead, he would say something surprising. One morning, an Associated Press photographer was hanging around John as he played at a Georgetown playground under the watchful eye of the Secret Service. "We knew him," recalled Tom Wells, "and did not consider him a security risk, but Bob Foster warned him to keep his distance." Nevertheless, the photographer kept pursuing John. At one point, as Agent Foster picked up John so he could drink from a water fountain, the photographer kept moving toward him. John, seeing what was happening, turned toward the man and demanded, "Why do you want to take my picture? My daddy is dead." Hill reflected that John's outburst represented the "first real recognition the agents who worked with him had that he was fully aware of his father's death and that it was affecting him."

The crowds of tourists became too much for Mrs. Kennedy, and Washington contained too many bad memories, so she decided to relocate her family permanently to New York. Situated right on the street, their Georgetown house practically welcomed tourists to approach and peek into the windows. Jackie felt like a prisoner. Packed tourist buses pulled up and unloaded their passengers directly in front of the residence. "I do wish they would go away," Mrs. Kennedy lamented. "I know they mean well, but I can't stand being stared at like that every time I go out on the street." The scrutiny also annoyed John. "What are the silly people taking my picture for?" he would complain. Jackie started spending more time away from Washington. She took the kids skiing in Stowe, Vermont, and made frequent trips to New York City, where they stayed at the Carlyle hotel while she considered their future in the city.

You could fill a small library with the many books and articles that have been written about the way the assassination impacted the adults who surrounded the president, especially Jackie and Robert. But nothing has been written about how John processed the trauma of not only suddenly losing his father but also of moving three times in less than a year. John F. Kennedy's only son would grow into a remarkably well-adjusted adult, which no doubt owes a great deal to his attending therapy continuously his entire life. But John also possessed two qualities that separated him from others: his profound restlessness and his willingness to take risks.

One question has crossed my mind more than a few times: How much of John's personality was shaped by the trauma of his father's death?

For answers to that question, I turned to Dr. Susan Coates, clinical professor of medical psychiatry at Columbia University and a leading expert in childhood trauma. Coates was careful to make clear that it is impossible to know for sure how any individual deals with trauma, but she pointed out that a large body of literature has identified general characteristics exhibited by children who experience trauma.

As I listened to Coates describe some of the typical ways that children process trauma, much of the information sounded all too familiar. She explained that three-year-olds do not understand the finality of death, but they "take their cues in understanding a traumatic loss from their primary attachment figure, who is most often their mother. In John's case, he would have known that something very terrible had happened from observing his mother's reaction." For John, his father's violent death marked the first in a series of traumatic events that would shape his personality. "In one fell swoop, he loses his father. He loses his mother in the sense that he has likely lost her emotional accessibility because she is in mourning. He also loses his home, the White House. It is an overwhelming trauma for the child."

For John, the trauma was not limited to a single event. Even the ongoing presence of Secret Servicemen could have reinforced and worsened his distress by serving as a daily reminder of his father's death. Psychiatrists refer to this repetition as "strain trauma." As Coates explained, "Although single traumatic events can have a big impact on a person, what most often shapes character are experiences, particularly interpersonal experiences, that happen over and over again."

Were John's risk taking and restlessness as an adult possibly outgrowths of the trauma he suffered as a child?

Quite possibly, according to Coates. The way that children deal with trauma can vary widely based on their emotional makeup. What's more, given his family history, John was likely genetically predisposed to take risks. But the events of his childhood probably fostered even further a sense of rebellion and thrill-seeking behavior. "Some children react to traumatic loss by becoming withdrawn. Others become more outwardly dysregulated and act out in impulsive and aggressive ways," she noted. Many children, especially boys, develop a "counterphobic defense" against the anxiety produced by traumatic events. Society teaches them that feeling anxious is unacceptable, so rather than acknowledging their anxiety, they deny it and move in the opposite direction by exposing themselves to risk.

Children undergoing trauma must also confront the realization that life is both fragile and precious. "When a catastrophic loss occurs, you lose the sense of living with a mantle of safety around you," Coates continued. "You now know that something catastrophic can happen out of the blue." Since life can be stolen at any moment, it is important to live it to the fullest—but traumatized children may come to interpret *fullest* in extreme, potentially dangerous ways.

While all of this discussion remains highly speculative, it does raise a tantalizing question: Did the trauma surrounding his father's death produce personality traits that led John to accept unusual, even foolhardy risks? If so, this theory may help explain why on a hazy night in July 1999, he would choose to fly a plane without proper instrument training.

CHAPTER 3

"JOHN, WHAT DO YOU WANT
TO BE WHEN YOU GROW UP?"

I n September 1964, after spending a few weeks at the Carlyle hotel waiting for renovations to be completed, Mrs. Kennedy took possession of
her fifteen-room apartment at 1040 Fifth Avenue. It would be John's
fourth home in less than a year. While not as spacious as the White House,
the new apartment occupied the entire fifteenth floor of a sixteen-story
building and sat across the street from Central Park. Ironically, there were
already two other John F. Kennedys in the building. One of the men who
operated the elevator was also named John, and his son, John F. Kennedy Jr.,
was a doorman. The only difference was that they shared the middle name
Francis, not Fitzgerald.

According to Maud Shaw, who accompanied the family to New York, the
move lifted everyone's spirits. It was an improvement over living in Washington, where they were hunted by intrusive tourists hoping to catch a
glimpse of the grieving widow and her now-famous son. While reporters still
followed Mrs. Kennedy, New York provided her and the children with a degree of anonymity. "In New York," Shaw noted, "people seem to accept the
presence of the Kennedy children without staring at them or doing anything
so ridiculous as asking for their autographs."

Understandably, Jackie remained haunted by her husband's tragic death
and held herself responsible for not reacting quickly enough to prevent the
third, fatal bullet from lodging in his head. She now decided to channel her
grief into shaping how the public viewed JFK and his presidency. After sitting for long interviews with journalist Theodore White and historian Arthur Schlesinger, she sought to counter the official explanation that his death

was the result of a random and senseless act of violence. In hopes of breathing some meaning into JFK's death, she initially approached two established authors—White and Walter Lord—to write an authorized account of November 22. Both declined, however, mostly because she demanded final review rights of the book. William Manchester, a former correspondent for the *Baltimore Sun* and editor at Wesleyan University Press, was her third choice.

Once she had settled on Manchester, Jackie rebuffed other efforts to detail the story of that tragic day. Just four days after Kennedy's burial, veteran reporter Jim Bishop wrote White House Press Secretary Pierre Salinger to inform him that he was writing a book called *The Day Kennedy Was Shot*. He had already published similar books about the deaths of Jesus Christ and Abraham Lincoln, and now he planned to adapt the formula to Kennedy. "I am sure that this will be attempted by several writers," he said, but he was hoping that Mrs. Kennedy would designate him as the authorized writer. She rejected the request, but the undeterred Bishop later announced plans to write his own book. Mrs. Kennedy again begged him "to please not go ahead with your intended book." The family, she wrote, had hired Manchester "to protect President Kennedy and the truth." She told him bluntly that "none of the people connected with November 22 will speak to anyone but Mr. Manchester—that is my wish, and it is theirs also."

Her relationship with Manchester quickly soured, however. The Kennedy family gave Manchester unfettered access, and Jackie sat down for long interviews with him. But as the book neared publication, Mrs. Kennedy expressed reservations about the project. She complained that Manchester had violated her privacy by exposing too many private details about her actions and thoughts in the hours following the assassination. She insisted that he make significant changes to the manuscript. When he produced only minor revisions, she filed suit to block publication. Eventually the two sides reached a settlement that required Manchester to remove all references to his interviews with Mrs. Kennedy. Despite the back-and-forth, the book became an instant bestseller once it was published in early 1967.

In addition to controlling the narrative of events, Mrs. Kennedy lobbied to have monuments named after her slain husband. She urged President Johnson to modify the name of Cape Canaveral, the launch site of the US Space Program, to Cape Kennedy. A month after the assassination, New York City mayor Robert F. Wagner Jr. changed Idlewild Airport in Queens to John F. Kennedy International Airport. Mrs. Kennedy also took an active role in the building of a new presidential library, and she spearheaded the drive to name a national center for the performing arts after her husband.

Yet in her efforts to preserve and define JFK's legacy, Mrs. Kennedy inadvertently increased the burden on John to live up to an impossible ideal. By perpetuating the myth of Camelot, she fed the perception that her husband's death marked a critical turning point in our history, that if only he had lived, the future would have been brighter. Many Americans responded to the shock by transferring their unrealistic hopes to the president's namesake. Mrs. Kennedy saw the public pressure building on John even as her actions encouraged it. At one point, she confessed to friends that she regretted having named John after his father.

Despite these looming pressures, however, John appeared to adjust well to his new environment. While he missed the helicopter trips to Andrews Air Force Base, he enjoyed living across from Central Park, where he spent hours playing on the swings and going for boat rides on the lake. Maud Shaw would take him and Caroline to the zoo cafeteria for lunch. John, always the animal lover, enjoyed seeing the creatures behind fences, though he preferred the Bronx Zoo because there they could go for camel rides and watch the lions being fed. While Caroline was in school, John's nanny would guide him through museums and exhibitions, always ready to respond to his rapid-fire questions.

John's playtime was also occupied because so many of his cousins lived nearby. Pat Kennedy, her husband, British actor Peter Lawford, and their four children (Christopher, born in 1955; Sydney, 1956; Victoria, 1958; and Robin, 1961) lived only a few blocks away, as did Jean Kennedy Smith, her husband, Stephen, and their two kids, Stephen Jr. (1957) and William (1960). (They would later adopt two more children, Amanda in 1967 and Kym in 1972.) Caroline spent most of her free time playing with Sydney Lawford, who was about fifteen months older. According to Shaw, the two felt "like sisters." Before he started school, John played the role of a typically annoying little brother. He occasionally tried to play checkers with Caroline and Sydney, but most of the time, he would end the game by tossing the pieces on the floor.

In February 1965 John started classes at St. David's School, an independent Catholic boys' school founded in 1951. John's class had twenty-one boys, and the tuition cost $825 a year (today's equivalent of $6,518). Jackie walked her son to school, accompanied by a small group of reporters and the ever-present Secret Service. His cousin William Kennedy Smith attended the same school, and the two spent plenty of time together, forming a strong friendship. More important, John finally left his sister alone. The day began with morning prayers in the school chapel, followed by classes. When school ended, John and his new friends rushed to Central Park to play sports.

Members of his Secret Service detail taught John how to box, and he put those skills to use within the first few weeks of school. "The new boy punched me in the nose," a classmate told his mother. "Oh," she said, "I didn't know there was a new boy. Who is he?" The youngster replied that he did not know him but that "he says his name is John Kennedy." Jackie, already concerned about John's rowdy behavior, spoke with RFK about the incident, but he seemed unconcerned. The only question that Robert Kennedy asked was whether John had won the fight.

Shortly after her move to New York, Mrs. Kennedy hired Kathy McKeon, a nineteen-year-old Irish transplant, to assume the role of her personal assistant. John inadvertently helped her land the job. While she was sitting in the living room, John came bounding in with a black-and-white cocker spaniel. "Hello," he greeted her. "I'm John. Do you want to see my dog do a trick?" Kathy smiled back and nodded.

"Shannon! Roll over!"

On cue, the dog flopped down on his side and rolled over. "Roll over again!" John declared, and once again Shannon did as told. "Shanny, get the bone!" The dog went searching between the cushions and found the bone. What Kathy did not know was that Mrs. Kennedy was watching the whole episode and liked the way the young woman interacted with John so much that she offered her the job on the spot. Thereafter, Kathy lived in the residence, was paid $75 a week, and was required to refer to Mrs. Kennedy as "Madam."

Over time Kathy also assumed many of Maud Shaw's responsibilities of caring for the children. Mrs. Kennedy felt that Shaw, who was now in her sixties, lacked the energy to watch over John. She'd been an ideal nanny for John and Caroline as infants, but now Caroline could sit for hours occupying herself, while John was in perpetual motion. In the White House, John would eventually give in to Shaw's insistence that he take an afternoon nap; now he would stay in his room until Shaw disappeared into her room and then roam around the apartment in search of a playmate. One day he exploded an old firecracker that he had found in a drawer. The blast aroused the Secret Service agents on duty, and they came running into the room with their guns drawn. John was shaken but unhurt. The problem was that Shaw's patience was beginning to wear thin. She devised a way to keep John in his room by having maintenance install a chain lock on the *outside* of his bedroom door to prevent him from leaving. Mrs. Kennedy was not pleased when she learned what Shaw had done, and it likely expedited the nanny's departure the following year.

While John had always been an active child, it appears that his behavior grew unrulier following the assassination, a change that no doubt resulted from the trauma he experienced compounded by moving so frequently. McKeon described John as "hyperactive" and noted that a doctor had prescribed medication to treat the condition. The staff was also careful to limit his sugar intake; otherwise, she noted, "he'd really start bouncing off the walls." Though John was not "destructive or bratty," McKeon stated, "both his energy and curiosity were endless." John was always the first one to rise in the morning, so he would "proceed to make a racket, rolling his favorite wooden truck up and down the hallway until someone—me, generally—came out to shush him."

When John was home, there was never a dull moment. If cousin William was there, they would be running around playing cops and robbers. John also loved animals, but he was often too forgetful to care for them properly. One of his favorite toys was a semitruck with a back door and an empty compartment in the rear. Occasionally he would put his guinea pig inside the truck to give it a ride. But one morning, when he went looking for the guinea pig in its cage, he could not find it. They eventually discovered the animal still sitting in the back of the truck. John also had a two-foot pet snake that lived in a terrarium in his room. Often he would walk around the apartment with the snake draped around his neck. But one day the snake escaped, most likely because John had forgotten to properly seal the top of the terrarium. A few days later, the building super called to let them know that a snake had appeared in the toilet of a downstairs neighbor. The Secret Service retrieved the snake, and Mrs. Kennedy wrote a letter of apology.

John was a clown and a natural mimic, skills that he would fine-tune over the years. In 1964 the Beatles captured the hearts of countless teenage

Americans after TV appearances on the popular *Ed Sullivan Show*. In the first of three consecutive Sunday-night appearances, the Beatles attracted an audience of seventy million viewers—the largest for any television show up to that point. The following year, John was one of fifty-five thousand fans at New York's Shea Stadium when the Beatles toured the United States. Afterward, he entertained Jackie with his imitation of the Beatles. He would stand, hips swaying, pretending to play guitar and singing, "She loves you, yeah, yeah, yeah!"

While living in the White House, John's parents often clashed over how he should wear his hair, with Mrs. Kennedy willing to let it grow long and JFK insisting on keeping it short. Now in New York, Jackie allowed John's hair length to reflect the trend toward longer hair inspired by the Beatles. John quickly became a trendsetter in young boys' fashion, usurping the spot formerly held by Prince Charles, heir to the British throne. Mothers across the country took their young boys to barbers and insisted on the "John-John." (While the public continued to call him by that name, John made his displeasure known, and the family reverted to calling him simply John.) The instructions were clear: lengthen the sides, shorten the bangs over the eyebrows so the width of an adult finger is visible, and let the hair touch the collar in the back.

John's influence extended beyond just haircuts and into the world of fashion. My friend Sam Stoia, who grew up during the 1960s in an Italian Catholic family in Newark, New Jersey, recalls his mother instructing his barber to give him a "John-John." She would also buy outfits for Sam and his brother, who was ten months older, that imitated what she saw John wearing as a child. Although too young to understand the significance of his trendsetting power, John clearly "set the bar for American families and particularly young boys" in the years immediately after the assassination.

The move to New York did nothing to diminish John's fascination with the military. He remained largely oblivious to the debates raging over the wisdom of America's involvement in Vietnam—a conflict that his father had escalated and President Johnson expanded with the introduction of ground troops in 1965. At least for the first few years, the war remained popular, primarily because the administration assured the public that America was winning. As a six-year-old, John's favorite song was the patriotic song "The Ballad of the Green Berets," the number one hit in the country throughout

March and part of April 1966. He'd likely seen it performed on *The Ed Sullivan Show* by Sergeant Barry Sadler, himself a Green Beret who'd seen action in Vietnam. John still loved to salute, as well as to teach others how to imitate him. McKeon recalled John ordering her to march around in circles and also instructing her on proper saluting. Like John before November 22, 1963, McKeon mistakenly used her left hand until John corrected her. "No, Kat, like this!" he would say before demonstrating the correct right-handed salute.

Most people remember John as he was later in life: a strapping young man who loved to play touch football in the park and was allergic to wearing a shirt. However, as a young child, John was small and sickly, suffering from asthma and other respiratory problems. Although he enjoyed casually tossing a Frisbee or playing touch football with his friends in Central Park, he avoided the rough-and-tumble of Kennedy-style family sports. He found his cousins to be too aggressive and too competitive. According to McKeon, during their fiercely played touch football games in Hyannis, the other Kennedy boys "homed in on John as the runt of the litter and liked to pick on him the way big brothers do, seeing if they could make him cry." John would make up excuses for not participating, but no one believed him. "The only part of dear, sweet John that was Irish," she joked, "was his pitiful lack of imagination and commitment when it came to lying."

Perhaps because he was so sickly and unwilling to play competitive sports, Mrs. Kennedy felt even more strongly that John needed dependable male figures in his life. Although no longer seeking counseling from Father Richard T. McSorley, she invited him to New York to spend time with John. In the fall of 1964, John greeted Father McSorley at the door, begging the priest to take him to the World's Fair. Jackie handed him a list of places that she thought would interest John. Later that day, McSorley also took John to the Central Park Zoo to observe the animals. When they returned after their long outing, Jackie asked the priest to say a few prayers with her son. They knelt together beside the bed, and the priest watched as John blessed himself and uttered prayers for his father, mother, and other family members.

When they finished, Jackie came in and tucked John into bed. "Maybe Father will sing you a song," she said. "His daddy used to sing him 'Danny Boy.' Could you sing that, Father?" Although he did not know all the words, the priest did his best. "As I sang through it, John listened with complete attention and Mrs. Kennedy's eyes filled with tears," McSorley noted in his diary. Jackie kissed John on the forehead and wished him good night, but John asked his mother to sing one more song: "America the Beautiful."

When the priest returned after the Christmas holiday in January 1965, Jackie asked him a very difficult question. "Maybe, sometime, you will get the chance to answer the question that comes to John: 'Why did they kill him?'" Jackie stated. She explained that John was learning about his father's death by watching television or hearing from friends. "I don't know what to say. I don't know what's a good answer, and I feel inadequate about saying anything."

Sure enough, the topic came up when the priest and John went driving through Manhattan and passed Grant's Tomb.

"Who lives there?" John asked.

"Grant."

"Can we visit him?"

"No, because only his body is there. His spirit went to meet God."

"Does everybody here go to meet God when they died?"

"No, only those who are good meet God."

"Did General Grant see Daddy? If we visit Daddy's grave, can we see him?"

The priest explained to John that the grave contained only his father's body, which would turn to dust. But the idea of a separate soul and body confused John. "How can you go to the bathroom if you don't have a body?" he asked innocently.

Mrs. Kennedy traveled a great deal on her own, leaving John and Caroline in the care of staff members. John told me once that in the years after his father died, his mom became a different person. She drank a lot and was absent for long periods. When she was at home, she appeared emotionally distant, clearly consumed by her own grief. He said cryptically that it was "a difficult time" for him, although he did not elaborate further, and I did not probe.

Jackie did, however, organize extended family trips during the summer. In 1965 she took John and Caroline out of school early so they could travel to England. When the teacher called attendance at St. David's on May 12, one of John's friends stood up and announced, "John's not here. He's gone to London to see the Queen."

John and Caroline journeyed to England accompanied by their uncles and cousins. There Queen Elizabeth granted three acres of land for a JFK monument in Runnymede, the site where, in 1215, British barons forced King John to sign the Magna Carta—"the Great Charter of the Liberties"—which established limits on kingly power and remains one the most sacred documents in the birthplace of Western freedom.

In the weeks leading up to the May 14 ceremony, Shaw rehearsed John and Caroline for their meeting with the Queen. Playing the role of Elizabeth, Shaw watched as Caroline curtsied and said politely, "Good afternoon, Your Majesty." "Perfect," the British governess thought. But John, a few years younger and with a short attention span, struggled to get it right, marching up to Shaw and barking, "Good afternoon, My Majesty." Shaw corrected him. "No, John, that's not quite right. We have to call the Queen 'Your Majesty.'" John walked to the back of the room, collected his thoughts, and gave it another try: "Good afternoon, My Majesty." The four-year-old grew increasingly frustrated as Caroline laughed hysterically at her brother's ineptitude. After a few more tries, he finally got it right, but no one knew what would happen at the actual event.

Since Secretary of State Dean Rusk was leading the delegation on behalf of the United States, President Johnson offered to fly the family on Air Force One, but Mrs. Kennedy asked for a different plane to avoid the painful memories of her trip back from Dallas in November 1963. Still, the plane LBJ sent was one the family had used many times on excursions to Palm Beach and Hyannis. John immediately recognized it. "Look!" he shouted. "Daddy's airplane!" Shaw recalled that "the atmosphere onboard the plane was that of a holiday trip." Mrs. Kennedy remarked, "This brings back some wonderful memories, doesn't it?" Then she added, "There's only one person missing."

They arrived in London early on Friday morning, May 14, and headed directly to the ceremony. The extended Kennedy family walked through the trees and grassy slopes to the memorial. John knew that he was meeting the Queen, but it was not clear whether his cousins Anthony and Tina Radziwill, the young son and daughter of Jackie's sister, Lee, and her second husband, Prince Stanislas "Stash" Radziwill of Poland, would have the same honor. "We knew the Queen was going to be there, but I wasn't sure if I was going to get to meet her," Tina recalled. "Don't worry," John reassured her, "maybe she will give you a crown." Only John and Caroline were introduced to the Queen, and all of their practice paid off. Even John did not flub his lines.

The Kennedy Memorial, made of Portland stone—a limestone that dated back to the Jurassic period and is found on the Isle of Portland, Dorset—bore the words from JFK's inaugural address: "Let every nation know, whether it wishes us well or ill, that we shall pay any price, bear any burden, meet any hardship, support any friend or oppose any foe, in order to assure the survival and success of liberty." As the ceremony began, John sat in a silver chair, holding hands with both his mother and Prince Philip. "With all their hearts, my people shared his triumphs, grieved at his reverses, and wept at his death," declared the Queen. Dean Rusk rose to accept the memorial on behalf of the United States.

Once the ceremony ended, the family joined the ranks of thousands of other American tourists in London. They turned down an invitation to stay at the US embassy and instead lived with Lee, now a princess, and the prince. Since they planned to spend six weeks there, Mrs. Kennedy enrolled John in school with his cousin Tina. "I was only a year older than John, but he was quite a bit smaller," reflected Tina, who, like her mother, was also a princess. "I felt very protective of my little cousin who had come all the way from New York. So I kept my arm around him until a nice, very British teacher said, 'You don't have to put your arm around your cousin. He's absolutely safe as he is.'"

After school, Jackie took John and Caroline, along with Tina and Anthony, to sightsee. She tried slipping out the back door of the Radziwill residence, but the British press caught on to this maneuver and followed the family everywhere they went. For John, the highlight of the trip was visiting the Tower of London, where he kept interrupting the guide with detailed questions about executions. Somehow he managed to touch the suits of armor and play with the swords. He even stuck his head inside one of the cannons and crawled in as far as he could until only his feet were dangling outside. John was also mesmerized by the changing of the guards and made sure to show off his well-rehearsed right-hand salute.

John's fascination with the swords and gory side of the Tower of London only reaffirmed Shaw's belief that he was "bloodthirsty," a description that McKeon echoed after watching John feed a mouse to his snake. One time, Shaw took John to a movie that included a character who threatened to chop off people's heads with an axe but who always found an excuse not to actually use his weapon. John grew impatient, nudging Shaw throughout the movie and asking, "Why doesn't he chop someone's head off?" When the film ended, John was disappointed that all the characters still had their heads.

By the fourth day in London, Mrs. Kennedy had grown tired of the flock of reporters trailing her children and issued a plea for privacy. "In view of the full coverage given to the children already," she said, "it is very much hoped that the remainder of the visit here can be kept private." But the storyline— American royalty meets real British royalty—was simply too good to pass up, and the reporters continued to stalk them for the rest of the trip.

Near the end of the trip, Maud Shaw brought John and Caroline with her to see the modest house in which she grew up. Upon entering, John announced, "I like this dumpy little house." He was especially pleased that it had only two stories. At the Radziwill home, John, still a fan of elevators, had to walk up four flights of steps to get to his bedroom. "I'm tired of stairs," he declared. But some luxuries he clearly missed. As he looked around, he asked, "Where's the cook and butler?"

As the family packed for their return to the United States, they left their beloved nanny behind. Mrs. Kennedy was well aware of how attached the children were to Shaw, who had been with the Kennedys since Caroline was eleven days old. To ease the transition, Mrs. Kennedy told John and Caroline that Miss Shaw was taking a short sabbatical but would be back in New York in a few months. Shaw never returned, but she kept in touch with the children for years afterward.

After returning to New York, Mrs. Kennedy continued her correspondence with Harold Macmillan, which had started after the assassination. While in London, Jackie managed to spend time with the former prime minister, who had delivered eloquent words of praise for President Kennedy at Runnymede. The two were kindred spirits, bound not only by their mutual affection for JFK but also by their own suffering. Macmillan had been seriously wounded during the First World War and, just shy of his seventieth birthday, grieved for all the friends he had lost. He asked many of the same questions that Jackie now pondered: "How can we accept it? Why did God allow it?" She confided to him that she had decided to move past the tragedy by focusing on raising John and Caroline. "I have consciously tried to put him out of my mind—since I moved to New York—because of his two children. . . . I can make his children what he would have wanted them to be. They are such little things who bear so much upon their shoulders—never to disgrace him is a burden when you are four and seven." What she did not (and could not) appreciate was that JFK's legacy would remain a burden for the rest of their lives.

Mrs. Kennedy penned Macmillan another letter on her distinctive blue stationery on September 14, 1965, the last day of their visit to Janet and Hugh Auchincloss's Victorian mansion and three-hundred-acre estate in Newport, Rhode Island, where Jackie had grown up. Hammersmith Farm was also the site of her and Jack's wedding reception in 1953. She and the children would be returning to Manhattan for the start of school. It was, she wrote, a "wonderful" summer, as they kept themselves occupied by playing in the sun, gathering shells, and eating lobster and blueberries. It was like past summers, except that her husband did not fly out to meet them on weekends. Jackie was proud that she had pulled herself "together enough to be helpful to my children." She referred to John as "the boy with the quicksilver curiosity and intelligence of Jack covered by a warm four-year-old body but waiting to burst out." Finally, she reflected that if John and Caroline "grow up to be all right—that will be my vengeance on the world."

Back at St. David's, John provoked varying emotions among his peers, as he would throughout his life. There would always be groupies who used their access to him as a status symbol. A friend told the author Wendy Leigh that when John invited classmates to his mom's apartment, some used to steal family photos on display. Then there were others who were intimidated by him and kept their distance, refusing to invite either John or Caroline to parties they threw for other classmates. Jackie gently intervened, writing notes to all the parents, reminding them that her children were no different from their own.

The anniversary of the assassination was always challenging. "You have no idea how difficult November 22 is in my house," John told me once. On the second anniversary, while Jackie was walking him home from school, a group of boys, including one from St. David's, followed them, taunting cruelly, "Your father's dead, your father's dead!" John, though only four years old, never lost his composure. Instead, Jackie said, "He just came closer to me, took my hand, and squeezed it as if he were trying to reassure me that things were all right."

As soon as the school year ended, the family traveled to Hyannis. On May 29, 1966, on what would have been his father's forty-ninth birthday,

John received a classic Piper Cub observation plane, minus the engine and propeller, that sat on the grass of the Hyannis estate. In doing so, Jackie was fulfilling a promise made to him by his late father. As she explained to JFK's longtime friend Chuck Spalding, "Jack always said he was going to give John a real plane when he grew up. Well, it's a little early, but now he has it: a real airplane." According to McKeon, John "loved to sit in the pilot seat and fiddle with all the levers, making engine noises as he pretended to take off. The rest of the Kennedys may have felt the pull of the sea, but John always belonged to the sky."

Jackie also organized a game for John, Caroline, and all the other Kennedy cousins at her mother's estate at Hammersmith Farm. She hid a wooden treasure chest, and once they discovered it, a boat showed up with parents, including Secret Service agent Jack Walsh, pretending to be pirates and demanding back their loot. As the ship approached, the cousins scurried to the house, but John remained unfazed. "John was so not afraid," writer George Plimpton, a family friend, told the journalist Christopher Andersen. Instead, he grabbed a rubber sword and started waving it above his head. Revealingly, the only time John became upset was when the cousins decided that the pirates needed to walk the plank. Realizing that Walsh was one of the buccaneers, he burst into tears. "You can't die!" John sobbed. "You can't die!"

Later that summer, the family packed its bags for a seven-week vacation to Hawaii. The trip got off to an inauspicious start. On June 9, 1966, just four days after their arrival, Caroline cut her foot on jagged coral and required stitches. She spent the next few days hobbling around on crutches. Then, on July 1, John had a serious accident that made national news. According to the Secret Service agent on duty, John was on an overnight camping expedition with his mother and sister. Upon waking up at seven in the morning, he started pulling his sleeping bag across the ground "when he lost his grasp on the sleeping bag and fell backwards into a lighted campfire." At the time, the five-year-old was wearing only a bathing suit.

The agents rushed John to a local clinic, where he was treated for burns on his right arm, hand, and buttocks. Dr. K. E. Nesting, who treated John in the emergency room, characterized the injury as "significant enough to be concerned" but stopped short of calling it serious. "It is not life threatening," he told reporters. Shortly after noon, Mrs. Kennedy flew with John to

Honolulu, where burn specialists told her he had suffered second-degree burns. While he would not require skin grafts or special surgery, some of the burned skin had to be cut away.

Four days after returning from Hawaii, John attended the wedding of Jackie's half sister, Janet Jennings Auchincloss, at St. Mary's Roman Catholic Church in Newport, Rhode Island, where his rough behavior was again on display. Perhaps it was the thousands of spectators, some of whom had climbed poles and roofs to get a glimpse of his famous family. It also did not help that as a page boy with many of his other cousins, John was required to wear a ruffled shirt, a blue cummerbund, and white shorts. As Secret Service agents formed a phalanx around the family and forced their way through the crowd, a spectator called John a sissy. Later during the wedding reception, John got into a fight with another page, and the two ended up rolling around in mud, ruining their clothes. A relative disapproved of his conduct, grumbling, "That boy travels ninety miles an hour, at right angles to everyone else." John even chased ponies into the reception tent and, the next day, threw sand on bathers at the exclusive Bailey's Beach.

During the summer of 1967, the Kennedys traveled to Ireland for a month. In preparation for the trip, John brushed up on his Irish geography by holding mock debates with the Irish members of his mother's staff. "Which is better: Monaghan or Sligo?" he would ask Kathy and May, an Irish maid, while he sat at the kitchen table with his cookies and milk after school. "Monaghan's farmland is more fertile," Kathy responded. "Sligo was the home of William Butler Yeats!" May answered. "Point to Kathy!" John shouted. But May refused to concede the point. "Sligo was much prettier," she insisted, but Kathy pointed out that they were "still working the fields with donkeys in Sligo." "Two points Kathy!" John shouted as he slapped his hand on the table for emphasis.

According to McKeon, with the exception of the family's public tours, the Irish press was much more respectful than the British reporters had been two years earlier. In fact, she claimed they had more privacy than they had at home in New York. One of the few American headlines to emerge from the trip came when John went into a small candy store. "What do you want, dear?" the shopkeeper asked. "I want everything," John declared. "Now, John," his nanny chided gently, "you know you can't have everything."

"I can too!" he replied.

Mrs. Kennedy was resolute in her efforts to ensure that the children remembered their father, filling John's bedroom with mementos of JFK. On one occasion, Jackie told Robert McNamara, the secretary of defense under both her husband and now President Johnson, that she believed the ratification of the 1963 Nuclear Test Ban Treaty between the United States, the Soviet Union, and the United Kingdom (and eventually more than 120 other countries) marked her husband's greatest accomplishment. McNamara proceeded to give her one of the pens that JFK had used to sign the landmark treaty, which banned all atmospheric testing of nuclear weapons. She had the pen framed and, along with a photo of JFK signing the document, hung it proudly in John's room.

During summers in Hyannis Port, John spent considerable time with his uncle Teddy, who'd handily won reelection to the US Senate in 1964. At the time of his easy victory, the youngest Kennedy brother was still convalescing in a Boston hospital from injuries sustained in a near-fatal plane crash in June. The pilot and one of Ted's aides were killed in the crash of the small plane while on the way from Washington to Massachusetts. He suffered a collapsed lung, two broken ribs, and three fractured vertebrae. He spent five months in the hospital.

Teddy took John out to Nantucket Sound aboard Jack's sailboat. A master storyteller, Teddy regaled John with tales, most of them true, about his father. Over time Teddy would become the one constant father figure in John's life, and they would be bound by deep bonds of affection and respect. Teddy outlived all the others, including, tragically, John himself.

In the immediate aftermath, however, Robert F. Kennedy filled the gap left by JFK's death. With Joseph P. Kennedy crippled from the stroke and Jack dead, Bobby stepped comfortably into the role of family patriarch. On August 22, 1964, RFK resigned as US attorney general and the following month announced his candidacy for the US Senate seat from New York. His victory in November allowed him to spend more time in the city with Jackie and the kids. He tried to have dinner with them at least once a week. Whenever he showed up at the front door, John and Caroline would race to embrace him. "Bobby would toss John into the air and catch him, then get down on the floor to play," McKeon observed. They both worshiped him. If they ever did something wrong, Mrs. Kennedy would threaten to tell Bobby, which, McKeon noted, was "like telling the kids Santa Claus was going to find out."

His brother's assassination radically altered the trajectory of RFK's life. He suffered for years and seemed, according to an aide, to be in constant emotional pain, "almost as if he was on the rack, or as if he had a toothache or . . . a heart attack." Coming to terms with his own pain, however, made him more sympathetic to the suffering of others. Bobby developed a visceral connection to the poor, whether it be Chicano farm workers in California, Native Americans on reservations in Oklahoma, or urban blacks in Harlem, New York. The journalist Murray Kempton claimed boldly that RFK became "our first politician for the pariahs, our great national outsider, our lonely reproach, the natural standard held out to all rebels."

Like many Americans, he agonized over the ongoing Vietnam War. JFK had sent military advisors to support the corrupt and failing South Vietnamese government. In 1965 LBJ expanded the conflict by committing ground troops to prevent a Communist takeover. As the war dragged on and the death toll rose, Americans grew weary of the conflict. But Johnson continued to expand US involvement, sending more and more troops even as he spoke about peace. By the summer of 1967, wrote *Time*, "a profound malaise overcame the American public." In August Johnson sent forty-five thousand more troops to Vietnam, bringing the number of troops up to five hundred thousand, and asked for higher taxes to finance the war. The horrors of this overseas debacle flashed into the homes of most Americans on evening newscasts, accompanied by disturbing images of racial violence in thirty of the nation's cities. In one week alone in August, forty-five people were killed, thousands were injured, and property damage from fires and riots ran into billions of dollars. Then, in October, the antiwar movement staged a march on the Pentagon. One hundred thousand angry students converged on the Pentagon, aiming to shut down "the American military machine" in one act of civil disobedience. By October 1967, only 31 percent of the country approved of Johnson's handling of the war.

The war represented a complicated issue for RFK, as his brother's administration had publicly supported the South Vietnamese and had sent advisors and military aides to prop up their government. By 1967, Senator Kennedy had become a fierce critic of the war, yet he offered no realistic plan for ending US involvement. Antiwar liberals pushed him to challenge LBJ for the Democratic nomination, but Kennedy resisted, believing he had a better chance of winning in 1972. RFK's real passion lay in giving voice to those who had been left behind by American prosperity, and he feared that the millions of dollars spent on tanks and bombs could be spent more wisely at home providing poor children with better schools.

Robert discussed these issues with John and Caroline, explaining to them the need to get involved in public life. He did not want them to grow up in a privileged bubble. As he tucked them into bed, he would share stories about the plight of poor people in America, reminding them that children their age were living in horrid conditions only a few miles away in the ghettos of New York.

John once told me a story that revealed both RFK's intensity and how he planned to instill in John an unwavering sense of public service. One Christmas John received an Easy-Bake Oven. Introduced in 1963, these toy ovens used the heat from two ordinary lightbulbs to bake actual mini desserts. One evening Robert came into his room and saw John playing with it. RFK sat down next to his nephew and asked, "John, what do you want to be when you grow up?"

"A chef." Apparently that was the wrong answer. John remembered his uncle grabbing him gently by the shoulders and lecturing him about his responsibilities to serve those who were less fortunate. "You're a Kennedy," Robert insisted sternly. "You can't just be a chef. You have been given special privileges, and you have a responsibility to help other people."

As RFK became more outspoken in his criticism of Vietnam, his already fraught relationship with LBJ turned decidedly worse. The two men were a study in contrasts. The president, seventeen years older and six inches taller, seemed to be a natural politician: an expansive, back-slapping, practical deal maker, always willing to bend facts to serve a larger purpose. Meanwhile, RFK was an introvert who loved politics but disliked politicians. Johnson, he told friends, "lies all the time." Kennedy viewed the Texan as embodying all the qualities of the old-school politics that his brother had come to Washington to abolish. Johnson, who resented RFK's sense of privilege, dismissed him as a "snot-nosed little son of a bitch."

Jackie found herself caught between them. Although she distrusted Johnson and had become a bitter critic of the Vietnam War, she appreciated his kind gestures toward John and Caroline. LBJ never forgot their birthdays, and he and his wife, Lady Bird Johnson, sent cards every year. "Being four years old is a mighty important event in a young man's life," LBJ wrote in 1964. "All the Johnsons send you their love and their friendship." Mrs. Kennedy always wrote back to thank the president for his consistent messages. "You are a marvelous child psychologist," she responded in 1966, "saying just the right thing to a boy and a girl." She told him that John could "quote his letter by heart."

Letters to John and Caroline, however, were not enough to keep Jackie loyal to the president, and she joined others in urging Robert to challenge Johnson in the upcoming 1968 Democratic primaries. But he resisted, even after January 31, when Communist North Vietnamese troops launched a dramatic offensive during the Lunar New Year, called Tet in Vietnamese. While RFK sat on the sidelines, Minnesota senator Eugene McCarthy jumped into the race as an explicitly antiwar candidate and scored a surprising victory in the March 12 New Hampshire primary. Four days later, with Jackie's strong encouragement, RFK announced his candidacy in the same Senate caucus room where JFK had made his announcement eight years earlier.

While campaigning for president, RFK visited my working-class neighborhood in Darby. Word had spread that he would be driving down Main Street. There was so much excitement that you would have thought a famous Hollywood film star was coming to town. Many neighbors and family members waited alongside the road for his car to pass. Kennedy finally arrived in the backseat of a convertible, reaching out to the outstretched hands of his admirers. My aunt managed to touch him, and I remember her saying that she would never wash her hand again. Kennedy's car ran over the foot of another neighbor, and while such a misfortune would usually result in a lawsuit, the woman was simply thrilled that his car had touched her.

Millions of Americans viewed Robert as the natural heir to his brother's legacy and the antidote to all the strife and violence that followed JFK's death. It felt impossible to hide from all the turmoil in the late sixties, especially since it was broadcast every evening on the news.

It's unclear what John made of the confusing images he saw flashed on television and in the headlines: race riots, military body counts, student protests. The people who surrounded him also sent conflicting signals. He had always been told that his father was a great leader who had set the nation on a new course, but he was also learning that the nation's social fabric was unraveling, perhaps because LBJ had not followed his father's policies.

He no doubt would have sensed his mother's ambivalent feelings about RFK's running for president. Although she believed strongly that he would make a great president, she harbored nagging worries about his safety. On April 3 Jackie had dinner at the home of a friend, where they were joined by Arthur Schlesinger. At one point during the evening, she pulled the historian aside and asked, "Do you know what I think will happen to Bobby if he is elected president?" Schlesinger, apparently surprised by the question, expressed confusion. "The same thing that happened to Jack. . . . There is so much hatred in this country, and more people hate Bobby than hated Jack," she said intently. "That's why I don't want him to be president. . . . I've told Bobby this, but he is fatalistic, like me."

Those fears were surely magnified when the very next day, an assassin's bullet took the life of civil rights leader Dr. Martin Luther King Jr. in Memphis. In tapes of Jackie's conversations with Schlesinger that were released in 2011, it became clear that she was no fan of King's, describing him as "a phony" and a "tricky person" after learning that he had participated in orgies and mocked Cardinal Cushing at her husband's funeral. But at Robert's request, she agreed to attend his funeral services in Atlanta.

King's death sparked a wave of racial violence. Rioters burned twenty blocks in Chicago, where Mayor Richard Daley ordered police to "shoot to kill." The worst violence occurred in Washington, DC, where seven hundred fires burned and nine people lost their lives. For the first time since the Civil War, armed soldiers guarded the steps to the Capitol. Nationally, the death toll reached forty-six.

I have a striking memory of the riots that followed the King assassination. I was an eleven-year-old sixth grader attending a public school outside of Philadelphia. Although my grade school was located in a racially mixed, working-class neighborhood, it never occurred to me that I would be impacted by the violence in places like Washington, DC, all dominating the TV news. I went to school that day as if nothing had happened. Around midday, my teacher, Mr. Weaver, started conferring nervously with some of his colleagues who had gathered in the hallway. He popped in and out of the classroom, making a forced effort to appear nonchalant. Clearly, something was wrong.

After the third or fourth trip into the hallway, he returned and said that he had an important announcement to make. "We have decided," he said, "to give you the rest of the day off." I remember being thrilled by the news but puzzled by the decision. He continued, "If you have not had any exercise, you should run home," a statement that left me wondering why our teacher would suddenly be concerned about our fitness. He asked those who lived near the predominantly black section of the neighborhood to stay behind with him.

We lined up and proceeded down the two flights of stairs, making our way to the entrance. For some reason, I was at the front of the line and pushed open the heavy wooden door leading to the small concrete schoolyard. What I witnessed next shocked me: dozens of heavily armed police, some carrying shotguns, which until then, I had seen only on television. This was one of those rare occasions when I followed my teacher's instructions and ran home as fast as I could. It was then that I learned that a riot had broken out not far from the school, and we had been evacuated as a precaution.

Everything seemed to change after that day. Honestly, I had never given the issue of race much thought. As kids, my brother and I walked back and forth through a poor black neighborhood every day on the way to school. We often stopped to buy popsicles and candy at a small store where an older African American couple always made a big fuss over us. Now we avoided black neighborhoods, and a chill descended between blacks and whites at school.

The riots heightened the nation's sense of crisis and served as the backdrop to RFK's fight for the Democratic nomination. His campaign took a drastic turn on the last day of March, when a beleaguered and defeated LBJ revealed in a television address to the nation that he would not seek reelection. Four weeks later, Vice President Hubert Humphrey announced his candidacy. The ebullient veteran senator from Minnesota did not enter a single primary, but he quickly secured the endorsements of the party's power brokers who would decide on the nominee, whereas RFK hoped to rack up primary victories to prove that he would be the strongest candidate in November. Although Kennedy beat McCarthy decisively in the Indiana Democratic primary, McCarthy turned the tables in Oregon, setting up the following week's California primary, on June 4, as critical to RFK's campaign strategy.

Jackie made a few campaign appearances in New York for Bobby and then returned home to eat dinner in her apartment. She stayed up until three fifteen watching the results from the West Coast before going to bed know-ing that Bobby had won.

At around four o'clock in the morning, her brother-in-law Stash Radzi-will called from London asking about Bobby.

"Isn't it wonderful?" Jackie said. "He's won. He's got California."

"But how is he?"

"Oh, he's fine. He's won."

"But how is he?"

"What do you mean?"

"Why, he's been shot!"

Stash proceeded to tell her about the gunman who had been waiting for Robert in the kitchen of the Ambassador Hotel in Los Angeles.

The next morning, Jackie woke up John and Caroline, brought them to her room, and broke the terrible news. "Something's happened to Uncle Bobby," she told them gravely, "and I have to fly off to California to be with him." Caroline asked her what had happened. "A very bad man shot him," Jackie answered. Both John and Caroline burst into tears.

My brother Franny and I learned the news around the same time. My mom always woke up early to get us ready for school. She would go down-stairs and turn on the television to watch the news while she made breakfast and packed our lunches. She was so shocked by the report that she raced upstairs, shouting, "They shot the other one! They shot the other one!" We ran downstairs to follow the live coverage.

June 5 was Kathy McKeon's scheduled day off, and she awakened that morning not knowing the news. Within a few minutes, she received a call informing her that RFK had been shot and that she needed to come to the apartment to take care of the children while Jackie flew to California. Mrs. Kennedy greeted Kathy with "a puppy face and swollen eyes" and asked, "Will you talk to John and Caroline?" When Kathy expressed her sympa-thies, Mrs. Kennedy responded, "Same story all over again." She then ut-tered two sentences that she would repeat many times later. "We will all miss him dearly. He was a second father to my children." When Kathy went to John's room, she found both him and his sister crying. "Your Uncle Bobby is up in heaven looking down on you two," she consoled, though realizing that they had likely been told the same thing when their father died. "He'll always take care of you."

While it's impossible to know the emotions flowing through John's mind that morning, it's fair to speculate that Robert's death impacted him more than his father's had nearly five years earlier. It was always a source of frustration for John that he did not really remember his father. However, he had vivid memories of the time he spent with RFK. John was now old enough to comprehend the finality of death. There would be no more questions about when he would see Robert again. His mother was able to insulate him from the images of his father's assassination, but it would have been impossible for him not to have seen the photograph of his uncle lying in his own blood on the kitchen floor of the Ambassador Hotel, his head cradled by the teenage busboy Juan Romero, who'd shaken the senator's hand just as Palestinian-born Sirhan Sirhan fired a .22-caliber revolver at Kennedy, hitting him three times, including one bullet in the brain.

The complexities of John's personality must be understood in light of the repetitive traumas of his childhood. He became agitated after his father's assassination and even more restless after Robert's death. As an adult, John hungered to be perceived like everyone else, but he was always different. Few people experience the persistent and intense trauma that John endured as a child. He embodied contradictions: a man who seemed to have everything but who spent most of his life trying to process the repetitive strain of a tragic childhood. John developed coping mechanisms to deal with the many pressures that he faced. On the surface, he projected an image of casual nonchalance, but underneath he struggled with his sense of loss. Public expectations brought him yet another burden. People wanted John to fulfill his father's legacy, but he wanted to find his own identity separate from that of his family. I observed how, over time, therapy helped him come to terms with the traumas of his youth, and when therapy did not work, he exercised to release his anxiety. But the underlying restlessness never disappeared, nor did his desire to take unusual physical risks.

RFK died twenty-five hours after suffering a gunshot wound to his head. With Ethel overcome by grief, Jackie became the one to order doctors to remove him from life support. The senator's anguished press secretary, Frank Mankiewicz, made the announcement: "Senator Robert F. Kennedy died at 1:44 A.M. today, June 6, 1968. He was forty-two years old."

Later that day, RFK's body was flown to New York and transported to St. Patrick's Cathedral in New York City, where the next day mourners lined up for hours to pay tribute. At 4:25 P.M. Mrs. Kennedy made a surprise appearance at the church, accompanied by John and Caroline. They knelt at the foot of the casket, crossed themselves, and uttered a prayer. Before leaving, they placed their hands on the head of the coffin for a moment, then turned and walked solemnly away.

On June 8 John once again found himself at a sorrow-filled funeral grasping his mother's hand. This time he had to say good-bye to the only father he truly knew. He joined his sister and cousins in bringing the bread and wine for the consecration to Archbishop Terence J. Cooke, who presided over the Mass. During Communion, John offered his arm to his seventy-seven-year-old grandmother, Rose, and escorted her to the altar. For those mourners who remembered John from his father's funeral, that gesture felt too much to bear. The scene, noted *The Washington Post*, "brought quick, involuntary tears."

After the service, RFK's body was placed on a special train to Washington, DC's Arlington National Cemetery for burial a few feet away from his brother. Kathy McKeon, who accompanied the family on the trip, described John as "more wound up than usual" as they pulled out of New York's Penn Station. He found William Kennedy Smith, and the two "were soon crawling around the floor with their toy cars." Caroline, however, clung tightly to her cousin Courtney, who was also eleven years old and, like Caroline, had now lost her father. "As the train rolled through the big cities, small towns, and open fields where mourners lined the tracks by the tens of thousands to bid farewell, the two girls clung to each other and sobbed," Kathy wrote.

I was one of them. RFK's funeral train traveled on a track just a few hundred yards from my row house south of Philadelphia. My dad asked my brother and me if we wanted to go, and we both agreed. As we walked out the door, it looked as if a giant fire alarm had gone off. People were fleeing their houses to make their way up to the tracks. We stood on a trestle bridge and looked down below, waiting for the train to pass. My mind captured a picture of the poignant scene: those gathered there were old and young, men and women, African Americans and whites—all standing shoulder to shoulder. I remember a group of nuns, rosary beads in hand, lined up along the tracks beneath us. And then came the train traveling at a fairly high speed. Teddy Kennedy was standing on a platform outside the caboose, waving gently. I glimpsed the flag-draped coffin inside. What I did not know then was that someone who would change my life was also on that very train.

At one point, as they made their way down the tracks, John spied a sudden camera flash outside the window where he was sitting. He grabbed Kathy, his eyes full of fear. "Kat, is someone shooting at us?" he cried. "Are they coming to get us next?" McKeon assured him that he was safe and explained that he had just seen a camera flash and was hearing the sound of flowers hitting the train. "They're very sad that Uncle Bobby was killed, and they're throwing bouquets of flowers to show how much they loved him," she reassured him.

As they neared Washington's Union Station where they would board buses for the short trip to Arlington National Cemetery, John changed into his funeral suit and prepared for the final act of a long day of mourning his uncle. An endless procession of cars and buses transported mourners to the cemetery. The cortege snaked its way past a few buildings where RFK had served—the Senate Office Building, the Capitol, the Justice Department—before pausing briefly at the Lincoln Memorial. At Arlington, John walked up the sloping hill with six hundred other family members and friends to the graveside. The burial was originally scheduled for five thirty, but since the train was five hours late, dusk had turned to darkness, and mourners lit their own way with candles and flashlights.

After watching Bobby laid to rest, Jackie, John, and Caroline walked alone to the Eternal Flame that flickered nearby and marked the grave of President Kennedy. They knelt, said a prayer, and placed flowers on the grave site. Mrs. Kennedy then crossed herself and put her arm protectively around John.

The assassination of Robert Kennedy shocked the nation and seemed another sign that America was spiraling out of control. But for Jackie it meant even more. She had lost both her husband and now her brother-in-law to assassins' bullets. She feared for not just her own life but for the lives of John and Caroline. She grew ever more determined to find a way to shield them from harm. "If they're killing Kennedys, then my children are targets," she was reported to have said. "I want to get out of this country."

CHAPTER 4

"IF ANYTHING HAPPENS TO JOHN . . ."

In the fall of 1968, John switched from the Roman Catholic St. David's, which was a few blocks away from his mother's apartment, to the Collegiate School, a religiously unaffiliated 330-year-old boys' school on the Upper West Side. The school, which boasted one of the most demanding academic programs in the country, downplayed JFK Jr.'s enrollment, the headmaster telling *The New York Times*, "He applied, he was a bright boy, he was tested and accepted." One parent predicted that John "will be just another little boy in the class even if he does carry a great name."

Mrs. Kennedy had taken a routine tour of Collegiate in the spring of 1967. "She was obviously impressed with the school," noted an observer. "She liked the spirit of the school from the minute she set foot in it." The following week, she returned with John. It's unclear, however, why Mrs. Kennedy decided to move John to Collegiate. Some papers reported that St. David's planned to have John repeat the second grade because of his immaturity, but a faculty member there dismissed the story. "That simply isn't the reason for the change," he said. "It simply isn't a true picture. The boy is as exuberant and restless as many boys of his age."

John fit in well at Collegiate. Bruce Breimer, a popular history teacher who doubled as the director of college guidance, recalled that John "was well liked. He had a lot of friends. He was comfortable." John also enjoyed playing pranks, especially on the Secret Service agents who were assigned to protect him. "I was working late at school, and there was a track meet in Long Island," Breimer recounted. "In those days, the track team traveled in two big vans, and John switched vehicles without informing the agents.

When the van carrying John had a flat tire, the agents followed the wrong vehicle back to the school. "They were not happy, but John thought it was the funniest thing in the world."

Breimer, who was the teacher John credited with inspiring his interest in history, taught a class on the American presidency. The class, a mix of lecture and discussion, had twelve students. Since Collegiate had a trimester system, they could study only seven presidents. "We did it chronologically, and the last president we covered was his father," Breimer recalled. John, who was talkative in other sections, was uncharacteristically quiet when the topic of JFK came up.

Students were also required to write six-page papers on each of the presidents discussed in class. John had turned in good papers on all the other presidents, but "when it came time to writing the paper about his father, he gave me something that came straight from *Encyclopaedia Britannica*." Breimer sympathized with John and understood that he could not deal objectively and analytically with his father. "It was his way of saying, 'I wish I could have pulled this off but I can't. I'm accountable, and if you want to nail me for it, you go ahead and do it,'" Breimer recalled. The instructor returned the graded papers to everyone but John, who approached him after class.

"Where's my paper?"

"You know that guy Charlie Hamilton in Greenwich Village who buys all the Kennedy memorabilia?"

"Yes, I know who he is."

"Well, I sold it to him," Bruce joked. "I had to supplement my income."

"That paper wasn't worth a nickel," John responded, laughing.

Attending a new school was not the only surprise that John experienced in the months following Robert Kennedy's assassination. On October 20, 1968, the thirty-nine-year-old former first lady stunned her adoring public by donning a wedding dress and pronouncing "I do" to Aristotle Onassis, a sixty-two-year-old wealthy Greek shipping tycoon. From that moment on, she would be known as "Jackie O.," a nickname that first appeared in *Time* magazine. Her marriage to Onassis shocked the nation. "It's the end of Camelot" became a common refrain. "The reaction here is anger, shock, and dismay," declared *The New York Times*. "The gods are weeping," read a quote in *The Washington Post*. Even a German newspaper announced, "America has lost a saint."

While the wedding was a surprise to almost everyone, this was not a new relationship. Over the years, Onassis had found ways to support Jackie during difficult times. They met in the 1950s, when JFK was still a senator. After Patrick died in August 1963, Onassis invited her for a six-week Mediterranean cruise on his boat the *Christina*, a Canadian frigate named after his daughter that he had transformed into a floating palace. JFK disliked and distrusted Onassis and often dismissed him as "a pirate." In 1955 the US government had sued Onassis for removing a fleet of ships that he had purchased and promised to keep in the United States. But the president admitted it would be beneficial for his wife to get away from Washington. Onassis fell in love with the first lady on that trip, and it grew clear that Jackie enjoyed his company. She personally invited Onassis to attend her husband's funeral and asked him to stay as her guest in the White House.

Over the next five years, they arranged private rendezvous at his apartment in Paris or at exclusive dinner parties in New York. But she took care to downplay their burgeoning romance by being seen in public with other eligible bachelors, leading Onassis to refer to himself as "the invisible man." In May 1968, while on a cruise, Aristotle finally took the plunge and proposed to Jackie. She asked for time to consider his request, worried about whether John and Caroline would accept him as their stepfather. It was RFK's strenuous objections, however, that proved most central in keeping her from committing to Onassis. Robert needed Jackie's nostalgic afterglow to help fuel his campaign and pleaded for her to wait until after the election. But now that Robert was dead, she no longer felt any need to keep her relationship with Onassis a secret. "It's a tragedy for America," Onassis confided to a friend, "but for Jackie ... she's finally free of the Kennedys."

Jackie found many attractive qualities in Onassis. Although he had a reputation for being vulgar and uncouth, Jackie described him to friends as erudite and sophisticated. He held salons on his boat where he invited artists and intellectuals to discuss important topics. She was fascinated by both his charm and his extravagance. "He was a force of nature," she told her close friend Joe Armstrong. Most important, he offered her not only unlimited wealth, privacy, and security, but also warmth. She explained to a friend that she married Onassis because "I was lonely and wanted someone to care about me and someone I could care about." Onassis showered her with affection at a time when she felt vulnerable and isolated. The former first lady would say later that he "rescued me at a moment when my life was engulfed in shadows."

Apparently, though, intimacy was not part of the deal. Kathy McKeon remembered that when Onassis visited Jackie's New York apartment for the first time, two months after the assassination, she observed no sense of romance between the two. Jackie "treated him the same as she did any friend who came for a holiday," she recalled. "They relaxed in the living room with after-dinner drinks, then retired to their separate rooms each evening."

Before committing to Onassis, Jackie insisted on a strong prenuptial that would codify the terms of their relationship. Her brother-in-law Teddy Kennedy flew to Onassis's private island, Scorpios, off the western coast of Greece, to negotiate the deal for her. The marriage contract required only that Jackie and Ari spend Catholic holidays and summers together. She would be left free the rest of the time. She did not have to bear him a child, and they would sleep in separate bedrooms. In return, she received $3 million in tax-free bonds, along with a monthly allowance of $10,000 for expenses, $7,000 for medical needs, hairdressers, and makeup, and $10,000 for new clothing. John and Caroline received $5,000 a month for their education and other expenses.

John and Caroline found out that their mother was getting married the day before they flew to Athens. John once told me that whenever his mother needed to break news to him, she would take him for a carriage ride around Central Park. A few months earlier, they'd ridden around the park as she told him that she was moving him to a new school. Now they were back in the carriage, and that's where she told John and Caroline that she planned to marry Onassis. John seemed to take the news in stride, but Caroline was visibly upset.

"Could you please do me a favor and go talk to Caroline?" Jackie asked Kathy. "I just told her the news, and she's very, very upset. She's in her room crying." Kathy found Caroline curled up in her bed with her face buried in a pillow and her "small shoulders heaving with her sobs." But the ten-year-old quickly composed herself and packed her bags for the trip to Greece. Kathy noticed that John was "hanging close to his mother" and did not "seem visibly upset by the prospect of getting a stepfather."

Onassis sent a plane to fly them from New York to Athens, where a helicopter was waiting to whisk them off to Scorpios. McKeon remembered that

John was "beyond excited" to be back on a helicopter, sitting near the pilot and asking him "a million questions." Jackie and Caroline seemed "cool as cucumbers" as the helicopter lifted off, but John noticed that Kathy was nervous. "Don't be afraid, Kat," he consoled. "We're not going to land in the water, we're landing on the boat! There is a big space on the deck." Once onboard the *Christina*, Kathy, John, and Caroline spent hours exploring it, from the dining room boasting a long banquet table, to the grand swimming pool. With the mere push of a button, a floor would cover the pool and serve as a dance floor.

In October 1968, just four months after RFK's assassination, John and Caroline joined two dozen other family members to witness their mother's marriage in a tiny whitewashed chapel on Scorpios. Not everyone was happy about the wedding. Aristotle's two children, Alexander and Christina, acted openly hostile to Jackie, and the multimillionaire had to plead with them to attend. Christina bitterly referred to Jackie as "my father's unhappy compulsion."

Aristotle spent time with both John and Caroline, but he formed a special bond with his stepson. Jackie's cousin John Davis remarked that Onassis "filled a great void" in John's life. "He liked to play with the children, to take John to baseball games and to go fishing with him, and I think John enjoyed the male companionship." Caroline was slower to warm up to the new father figure in her life. She was naturally reserved; it took time for her to trust people. John had no such reticence. The way into John's heart, McKeon said, "was to get down on the floor and play with him." She described Onassis as "a good father to John and Caroline." Although he was old enough to be John's grandfather, "he paid attention to them, and they loved him."

What John enjoyed most of all was spending summers on stunning Scorpios. Onassis bought the island in 1963, shipped in sand from a neighboring island to create a private beach, planted more than two hundred varieties of trees, and constructed a large family compound. Lee Radziwill described it as "a beautiful part of the world, covered with almond and lemon trees, set in a satin sea, with a magnificent coastline."

In 1969, when they spent their first summer in Greece, Ari took them for a tour of the scorpion-shaped island in the Ionian Sea and indulged them as best he could. He treated John and Caroline to motorboat expeditions, purchased a few horses and ponies for them to ride, and regaled them with stories of his childhood. He even gave John and Caroline their own twenty-eight-foot sailing boats, requesting that John's name be painted on his. Onassis took an instant liking to John that first summer, spending hours driving him by jeep all over the island, including its heavily forested area. On a few occasions, he took John to Athens onboard a seaplane. "Ari doted on John like he was his favorite puppy," recalled Tina Radziwill, who spent summers on Scorpios. "He was really sweet with John."

The island, in addition to its natural beauty, provided the eight-year-old with space to satisfy his boundless energy. "It was John and Caroline, me and Anthony, and sometimes the Shrivers—Maria and Timmy," recalled Tina. "The day revolved around waterskiing," she recalled. "John had a tutor, and there was a lot of debate over whether he should take his lessons before or after waterskiing, because the best time to ski was in the morning when the waters were calm and before the sun got too hot." The teacher wanted to have the lesson first, but John, along with his cousins, pressured him to back down.

While Jackie and Ari lived on the *Christina*, the children stayed in what Tina described as a "functional house" with four bedrooms aligned along a terrace. John shared a room with Anthony; Tina bunked with Caroline. It was here on this deserted beach that John would form a lifelong friendship with Anthony, who shared his sense of humor and adventure. The two cousins were roughly the same age—Anthony was a year older—and they spent the school year in different countries: Anthony in England, John in the United States. Despite their physical distance, they were raised more as brothers than as cousins. "Jackie and Lee took a joint approach in raising their children," recalled Gustavo Paredes, whose mother, Providencia, had worked for the Kennedy family since the 1950s. "There was a lot of flow between the households. Jackie thought of Anthony and Tina as her own, and Lee thought of John and Caroline as hers." Even as young men, John and Anthony possessed what Tina referred to simply as "a special chemistry."

What Tina remembers most about John was his unbridled energy. He was in a constant state of motion. When he wasn't waterskiing, he was fishing or exploring the beach. He also enjoyed playing practical jokes and used to chase Caroline around, trying to spray her with a hose. It was always entertaining to watch John at mealtime. "John always felt he should have twice his regular portion," she recalled, "but most of it would remain on his plate."

Meanwhile, the children did not see much of their mother while on the island. There were people watching over them, but Jackie was never one of them. "She taught me how to waterski, but mostly she would come and see us at the end of the day when we finished swimming," Tina recalled. "She lived on the yacht with Ari and kept her own schedule. Even if she wasn't there, you knew she was around, and you felt her presence."

I learned about John's affection for his stepfather when he took me for a tour of his mother's Fifth Avenue apartment in the 1980s. As you walked down a corridor past the library, you came to a T-junction. I did not see the rooms to the right, but if you turned left, John's bedroom was on the left and his mom's on the right. On the wall outside John's bedroom, the family had hung what appeared to be a four-foot-long sheet of plexiglass over dozens of family photos—not the ones that appeared in magazines but photos they had taken themselves. Although Mrs. Onassis, John, and Caroline were among the most photographed people in the world, they, like most families, had their own private memories. I was surprised by the number of photographs showing Aristotle Onassis with John. One captured John jumping off a boat into the ocean; another depicted Onassis and John fishing. Nearly all the photos had been taken on Scorpios or the ocean. I knew so little about John's background at the time that I did not know about his memories of Scorpios. I remember asking, "John, where are all these photos taken?" He said that for a while he spent summers on Scorpios with his stepfather. "It was a magical place," he reminisced.

During the first few years of her marriage, Jackie jetted back and forth between Greece and New York. Except during summers, John and Caroline remained based in New York, where they were often left in the care of servants. According to Kathy McKeon, "[T]here were long stretches of time" when they were home without their mother. However, Jackie would call every night she was away, checking on their schoolwork. Once when his mother was gone, John developed a bad case of bronchitis, and Mrs. Onassis hired a private nurse to look after him. After John recovered, the nurse, Phyllis, invited John to a show with her son, Robert Chambers. (Shockingly, in 1988 Chambers would be convicted and imprisoned for having strangled to death an eighteen-year-old woman in Central Park two years earlier during what he claimed was "rough sex.")

John's enchanting summers on Scorpios came to an end when his mother's relationship with Onassis started to fizzle. By the end of 1972, they remained married in name only. She spent most of her time in New York, while he stayed in Greece. He began complaining about her spending habits. She regularly overspent her monthly allowance and then pleaded for more money. One time, when Jackie lost $300,000 in the stock market, which represented nearly all of her liquid capital, he refused her requests to replenish her account. Aristotle made a point of being seen in public with his former lover, opera singer Maria Callas. He started leaking stories to the press about Jackie's exorbitant spending habits. In November 1972 he even arranged for photographers to take pictures of her sunbathing nude on Scorpios—photos that made their way into Larry Flynt's pornographic magazine *Hustler*.

Neither John nor his mom knew about Ari's role in arranging for the photographs, but John was very much aware of the strains in his mother's marriage. He and his sister were still spending time on Scorpios during the summer, although less than in previous years. During the school year, Caroline, who had enrolled at Concord Academy in Massachusetts, was insulated from the angry fights between her mother and Onassis. But John, who was attending school in New York, had a front-row seat. He overheard the loud arguments and saw the screaming headlines in the New York tabloids, where his mother's marital woes were regular fodder. Ari had doted on him a few years earlier, but now he was largely absent and indifferent. It was all very confusing for a young kid who had trouble holding on to father figures. He resented the way Ari now treated his mother, but he did not hold a grudge and always maintained warm memories of his time on Scorpios.

The turning point in the relationship between Jackie and Ari occurred in 1973, when Aristotle's twenty-four-year-old son, Alexander, was killed in a plane crash. Onassis's daughter, Christina, had always resented Jackie, and she convinced her father that his wife somehow bore responsibility for Alexander's death. She called Jackie "the black widow," suggesting that she had tainted their family. "Before she came to us, she was by her American husband's side when he died," she fumed. "My unlucky father had to go find her and bring her to our shores. Now the curse is part of our family, and before long, she will kill us all."

Aristotle ultimately accepted Christina's theory that Jackie was an evil influence and began laying the groundwork for a divorce. He successfully pressured the Greek government to change its divorce laws to limit the amount of money a foreign-born spouse could receive in a settlement, and he reworked his will, leaving Jackie $200,000 per year for life, plus $25,000 per year for each child until the age of twenty-one. The bulk of his fortune went to Christina.

Ari's mental and physical health declined in the months following his son's death. He sunk into a deep depression, became increasingly unpredictable and moody, and grew obsessed with conspiracy theories that the CIA was responsible for the fatal crash. Jackie pleaded with him to see a psychiatrist, but he refused. On March 15, 1975, before he could finalize the divorce, Aristotle died in Paris of bronchial pneumonia. Jackie refused to accept his changed will and pushed for more money, declaring that she would accept no less than $20 million. Finally, after nearly two years of haggling, Christina agreed to give her $26 million on the condition that Jackie renounce further claims.

Onassis was buried next to the same small chapel where he and Jackie had been married and where Alexander was interred. John had now lost a father, a father figure, and a stepfather before his fifteenth birthday.

In 1971 President Richard Nixon and First Lady Pat Nixon invited Jackie, John, and Caroline to the White House for the public unveiling of the official portrait of President Kennedy. But Jackie found the memories of November 22 too painful and worried how her children would react to seeing the White House again. Even worse, Jackie feared, their reactions would be on full display in what promised to be a media frenzy. "As you know," she wrote Nixon, "the thought of returning to the White House is difficult for me. I really do not have the courage to go through an official ceremony and bringing the children back to the only home they both knew with their father under such traumatic conditions. With all the press and everything, things I try to avoid in their little lives, I know the experience would be hard on them and not leave them with the memories of the White House I would like them to have." She asked if she and the children could "slip in unobtrusively to Washington, and come to pay our respects to you and to see the pictures privately?"

President Nixon graciously agreed and on February 3 sent a presidential jet to fly them from New York to Washington. (Jackie requested that he not send the same plane on which she flew with her husband's body from Dallas.) Despite their political rivalry, Nixon and President Kennedy had maintained a cordial, respectful relationship. "While the hand of fate made Jack and me political opponents," Nixon wrote Jackie the day following the assassination, "I always cherish the fact that we were personal friends from the time we came to Congress together in 1947."

The evening proceeded without a hitch, except that John managed to spill his milk on Nixon's lap. After their intimate dinner, the president took them for a tour of the Oval Office before going to the ground floor to see Mrs. Onassis's official portrait. A few minutes later, they went to the Green Room, where they viewed the portrait of President Kennedy. They returned to New York that evening after a rewarding afternoon.

That night, as she came to his bedroom to say good night, Jackie explained the story behind some of the photos that hung in his room. "There you are with Daddy, right where the president was describing the great seal," she told him. "There, on the path where the president accompanied us to his car." Later, John wrote Nixon a note thanking him for the visit, though he seemed more impressed by the White House chef than by the Oval Office where his father once worked. The "food was the best I have ever had," he scribbled. "And the steak with the sauce was really good." John confessed that he had few memories of the White House. "I don't think I could remember much about the White House but it was really nice seeing it all again," he wrote.

Jackie also refused an invitation to attend the opening of the John F. Kennedy Center for the Performing Arts, in Washington, DC, later that year, despite pressure from Rose Kennedy. She told Rose that "for everyone else, this is the gala opening—but for me it is exceedingly difficult to go through another memorial to my dead husband and the father of my children with everyone staring—just like I couldn't bear to have the portrait ceremony at the White House be public. Maybe that sounds cowardly, but they are also merciless—they want you there to sell tickets and make publicity and watch to see if you suffer." Rose remained insistent that she attend the ceremony. "It is very important for you to be present at the opening of the center, dear Jackie, even though it may be difficult for you. Jack would want you there, and certainly we all do." Jackie, however, stood her ground and refused to attend.

After a 1950 assassination attempt against President Harry Truman by two Puerto Rican nationalists that left one White House policeman dead and wounded two others, Congress enacted legislation permanently authorizing Secret Service protection for the commander in chief, his immediate family, and the president-elect. The day Truman left the White House, however, neither he nor his family received any further protection. That changed in 1962, when Congress authorized six months of protection for ex-presidents, but still not their families. Following JFK's assassination, Congress extended coverage to Mrs. Kennedy, John, and Caroline for two years, and then again in 1967. It was not until 1968 that the Secret Service was required to safeguard the widow of a former president until her death or remarriage, while any minor children were granted protection until they reached sixteen years of age, unless they chose to decline protection.

Ever since election night in 1960, when the Secret Service first took responsibility for guarding the Kennedy family, Jackie seemed to resent their presence—a resentment that grew after November 22, 1963, when they failed to prevent her husband's assassination. Privately, she blamed them for the president's murder. And although Senator Bobby Kennedy was not entitled to Secret Service protection, his death made her increasingly concerned that agents would be unable to keep her or her children safe. According to Clint Hill, who had been assigned to protect her while in the White House, Jackie became increasingly fearful and distrustful—and consequently, more demanding and difficult—after Bobby's assassination. "She changed quite a bit after that," he recalled. "She was angry at everybody. She didn't trust the government. She didn't trust the United States. She didn't trust the Secret Service."

Following her marriage to Onassis, Jackie clashed repeatedly with the Secret Service. While she lost her protection upon marrying Onassis, her children did not. The correspondence between Jackie and the Secret Service, revealed here for the first time, exposed that mounting tension. Jackie was primarily concerned about John, who bristled under the tight restrictions and lack of privacy. Caroline appeared to have a good relationship with her agents and is rarely mentioned in the correspondence. It's clear that Jackie blamed the Secret Service for some of John's behavioral problems. She was convinced that not only were the agents a constant reminder of his father's tragic death but also that they made him feel trapped, prompting him to become rebellious. Jackie also anticipated that when the agents would walk out of his life at midnight on November 24, 1976, the teenager might be unprepared to confront the new reality of fending for himself. She also pointed out that the agents were used to protecting adults, but they failed to recognize that children were different. John was evolving and needed to learn the skills necessary to succeed as an adult. It was difficult for her son to build character if he was protected from any form of adversity on a daily basis. Jackie was thus trying to establish a transition phase that would make it easier for John to adjust to life without the agents.

The Secret Service, however, maintained that part-time coverage did not exist. While the agents acknowledged the legitimacy of her concerns, they insisted that they worked for the US government and not for her. By law, they were required to protect her children, and they were determined to carry out their duties despite her objections. Thus the stage was set for a series of clashes between Mrs. Onassis and the Secret Service agents assigned to John. Jackie laid down strict rules—rules that the agents believed prevented them from performing their duties.

John lived in a protective bubble for the first fifteen years of his life. Now that he was a teen, he grew restive from the constant monitoring. He traveled often—the Caribbean, Paris, Argentina, Miami, Chicago, Washington, San Francisco, London, Lisbon, Montreal—and everywhere he went, agents followed closely behind. Whether John was attending school or a weekend barbecue, a man with sunglasses and a walkie-talkie stayed within sight. When he went skiing in Utah or Vermont, a Secret Service agent skied alongside him, as did a professional skier. They lodged in vacation homes protected by the Secret Service and the local police.

While John appreciated that the agents taught him how to box, he grew increasingly annoyed by their constant presence. Instead of him taking the school bus, agents chauffeured John in a cream-and-tan Oldsmobile. One of John's friends noted that during school, the agents sat in an office "with their feet on the desk and underarm holsters, reading the *Daily News* all day." When they saw the agents looking for John, they would signal for him to hide. "It was always a game for us, trying to lose the Secret Service guys. But to John it was more serious," recalled a classmate. "He just didn't like the attention."

In November 1968, five months after the assassination of her brother-in-law, Mrs. Onassis took John on a shopping trip without informing the agents that her son would be leaving their rented home in New Jersey's Somerset

County, horse country, which the family used as a weekend retreat. She even went so far as to distract the agent at the rear of the house so that John could sneak out the front door. She later picked him up at a friend's home. An hour and a half later, Mrs. Onassis and John came back home. Agent Jack Walsh wrote to his superiors, "When they returned, I told John that he should not leave the confines of the house without an agent with him. He promised he would let us know whenever he left in the future." Walsh then addressed Mrs. Onassis, saying that "it would be appreciated if she did not take either of the children anywhere without first informing the Secret Service agent on duty." She responded that John and Caroline were her children, so she did not need to notify anyone about what they did together. Walsh explained to her that the Secret Service was responsible for protecting her children, whatever the case may be.

Reading the letter two decades later, Clint Hill believed that Jackie was "asserting her authority to let them know that she was in charge and they were going to follow her restrictions and her orders. If I had been there," he added, "I would've recommended that she decline Secret Service protection and hire her own security force." Mrs. Onassis, however, was not ready to decline protection. She believed it was possible to protect John from threats while still respecting his privacy.

Two weeks after her conversation with Walsh, Mrs. Onassis detailed her concerns in a six-page letter to James J. Rowley, longtime director of the Secret Service. The problem, she stated, was that "there are too many agents, and the new ones are not ones who are sensitive to the needs of little children." Given everything that they have experienced, she wrote, "I am sure you would agree that their peace of mind is as important as their physical security. They must think that they lead normal lives, and not be conscious of a large number of men protecting them from further violence; they must not be made conspicuous among their friends by the presence of numerous agents, or have the households in which they live thrown into turmoil by the inclusion of agents who do not care about them or understand their problems."

She instructed Rowley to establish firm guidelines for the agents. She wanted them to be with the children only during the day, "from the time they leave home in the morning until the time they return home for supper around 5:30 P.M." She maintained that she did not want agents in her apartment. "The children are secure in the apartment in New York at night." She was especially concerned about the level of protection in New Jersey on weekends. "Agents tramp outside the children's windows all night, talking into their walkie-talkies," she complained. "Cars of each agent pile up in the driveway so that our little country house looks like a used car lot."

Jackie claimed further that despite their aggressive and intrusive methods, the agents still managed to lose track of John and Caroline. She requested that the Secret Service place a trailer at the limit of her New Jersey property, where the agents could stay when they were not driving the children. She did not want them coming by the house unless specifically asked to by a member of the household. She directed them to park their cars on a road outside the property so that the children would "never see any cars but their station wagon and my own car." Finally, she requested that only one agent drive them and that protection in the evening be provided by local police, not the Secret Service.

In Greece, she saw little need for Secret Service protection. "Between the personnel on the island and the sailors on the ship, there is a force of about 75 men to enforce security," she wrote. Jackie asked that just one agent accompany the children to Greece, assisting only when they were traveling. She pointed out that they would be flying on Olympic Airways, which was owned by her husband and where "security measures will be taken." Furthermore, the one agent in Greece would have to live in a village about a twelve-minute speedboat ride away from Scorpios. "The children will never be safer than they will be on Scorpios or the *Christina*," she wrote. She asked for similar arrangements when they traveled through Europe. "The children are growing up. They must see new things and travel as their father would've wished them to do. They must be as free as possible, not encumbered by a group of men who will be lost in foreign countries, so that one ends up protecting them rather than vice-versa."

Rowley responded immediately, reassuring Jackie that he was "more than interested in satisfying your concerns and will strive to do so without compromising the security of your children." He made clear, however, that he would be the one to decide how the agents protected her children, clarifying that he would review the procedures but "will most certainly consider your suggestions in my decision."

The review resulted in a six-page point-by-point draft rebutting all of Jackie's complaints. The memo began by spelling out some basic differences. She wanted a total of four agents; they wanted eight. She called for eliminating late-afternoon and evening shifts; the Secret Service contended that "part-time protection cannot be considered acceptable." The law, it pointed out, "charges the Secret Service with responsibility for protecting the children 24 hours a day." Mrs. Kennedy was mistaken in believing that the children were safe in the apartment with her in the evening and night hours. "Anyone with serious intent to harm the children can learn at what time our security is withdrawn and act accordingly." She had requested that agents not remain at school, but the review responded that the school might appear safe, "but the function of a security precaution is to guard against more than only the obvious and the foreseeable threat." Besides, Rowley pointed out, "I would be remiss in my duties if I were to assume that security responsibility vested in the Secret Service by statute could be left to the good offices of others or omitted because of an appearance of safety."

The review went on to describe her proposed arrangements for Far Hills as "inadequate." Local zoning laws prevented them from placing a trailer at the end of her property, and her request that "agents *never* appear in the vicinity of the house except when summoned" represented "an impossible condition under which to operate while attempting to ensure that no one gains unauthorized entry to the house."

Mrs. Onassis never saw this point-by-point rebuttal of her complaints. Rowley likely feared that she would get defensive if they sent such a detailed response, so instead he sent a succinct seven-paragraph letter in March 1969. In it, the Secret Service director warned her that they were still "receiving communications from mentally ill persons who represent a potential threat to your children," and that "there is the ever-present threat of the kidnapper." He also told her that the possibility of an aircraft hijacking remained "a great concern." These reasons, Rowley argued, "we must consider in planning security for your children, and at this time these factors do not indicate that we can safely reduce security." The tactic seemed to work, because the conversations with Mrs. Onassis culminated in a meeting in her apartment on April 18, 1969, during which she assured Rowley "that she was most pleased with the detail and appreciative of the manner in which it has been functioning."

It turned out that the fears of hijacking were quite real. On July 15, 1972, the Greek government announced that security forces had arrested eight Greeks who had been planning to kidnap John. One of the suspects told police, "We could have blackmailed her for as much money as we wanted." The government claimed the kidnappers belonged to a larger plot to capture ambassadors, bankers, and other prominent people who vacationed in Greece. The goal of such hostage taking was to overthrow Greece's military regime. A Greek military tribunal sentenced two men to prison and gave six others suspended sentences. They ranged in age from twenty-three to forty-five.

"We were aware of the Greek plot, and we worked closely with the FBI and authorities in Greece, as well as authorities in New York," Clint Hill recalled. The kidnapping attempt did not, however, lead to changes in the way the service protected John. It was only the most dramatic of the many threats that the agency received. "There were many other kidnapping plots against John," he stated, "but this one was taken more seriously." Most of the threats against John consisted of people writing letters and making menacing phone calls. The agents then assessed how realistic the threat seemed. "Do they have the capability and the means to carry out the threat?" Based on the answers to those questions, the agents would then investigate and decide whether this case should go to court so that the individual could be arrested and charged. "These things happened periodically throughout the lifetime that we were responsible for John," Hill reflected.

Over the next two years, more minor incidents occurred that aggravated the relationship between Jackie and the Secret Service. In December 1972 John participated in the filming of a new monthly television show starring former *Tonight Show* host Jack Paar, who was playing with a tiger cub at a New Jersey zoo. At the time, John was accompanied by family friend Lem Billings. Agent John List insisted that John not be allowed into the area with the cub, but Billings overruled him. List then requested three animal trainers "armed with tranquilizer rifles" to accompany him and John into the cage. List also had his firearm drawn. During filming, when one of the tiger cubs attacked Paar, Agent List grabbed John and removed him from the area. John, he wrote, "was in no way alarmed or injured during this incident." But the agents felt that Mrs. Kennedy was angry with them for allowing the situation to get as far as it did, even though she had given them specific instructions to let Billings decide which activities John could participate in.

The issue of security came up again dramatically in May 1974 when John was robbed in Central Park of his $145 ten-speed, Italian-made bike and a tennis racquet while on his way to a lesson. John told the police that a boy, roughly eighteen years old, grabbed his bike and rode off into the park. The incident, which made headlines in the New York tabloids and received coverage around the country, forged a near-permanent rupture in Mrs. Onassis's relationship with the Secret Service.

That evening, with John safe at home, she sat down with Jack Walsh and explained her reaction. On the one hand, she told him she was "pleased that this happened to John in that he must be allowed to experience life." She repeated her complaint that he was "overprotected" and that "unless he is allowed freedom, he will be a vegetable at the age of sixteen" when he lost protection. "She does not want us on his heels," Walsh wrote his superiors. On the other hand, Jackie could not understand how John had escaped their protection. Her son, she felt, had the worst of two worlds: the agents swarmed around him, making it difficult for him to experience normal life, but still they could not prevent him from being robbed in Central Park. "The Secret Service is supposed to be able to follow counterfeiters all over the place without them knowing they are being followed. Why can't we do it with John?" she asked. Walsh noted that she was especially worried about all the publicity that the incident had generated. "Although she is glad John had this experience, she is displeased about all the publicity and attention it is receiving because people will think he isn't being accompanied by anyone, and there is a danger in that."

A few days later, Walsh asked Mrs. Onassis if the Secret Service could tighten protection of John. But instead of asking for more security, she rattled off instructions on how the agents needed to protect him. She concluded with an ominous warning: "If anything happens to John, I will not be as easy with the Secret Service as I was the first time."

Two weeks later, Mrs. Onassis codified her rules into a formal affidavit to the Secret Service that established the procedures for protecting John.

1. No Secret Service agents are to walk alongside John when he is traveling on foot but are to walk across the street from him or are to follow him in such a manner that their presence will not be evident to John.

2. While John is in school, Secret Service agents are to remain in their office at school and are not to enter the classroom area or school grounds.

3. No Secret Service agents are to accompany John on private aircraft or helicopter.

4. No Secret Service agents are to be present or provide protection for John while he is on the yacht *Christina* or on the island of Scorpios.

5. No Secret Service agents are to ride in taxis with John but should use a follow-up car.

6. No Secret Service agent shall ride with John in a public bus unless such agents are unknown to him. If no agent accompanies him on the public bus, the regular agents should follow the bus by car.

7. No Secret Service agents are to ride with John in the private limousine on his trips from New York City and Far Hills, New Jersey.

She concluded by acknowledging that these points were "special" and represented "a departure from the Secret Service standard operating procedures." She did not want to give up Secret Service protection but felt the agents could observe her rules while still protecting John by employing "unobtrusive surveillance traditionally employed in detective work."

Her declaration appeared to alarm the Secret Service, which no longer believed it could fulfill its mission while abiding by her demands. David R. Macdonald, assistant secretary of the Secret Service, expressed empathy for her "deep concern that your son grow up in a normal environment," but he felt that the agency had made "every effort to be as unobtrusive as possible and still carry out its function." He warned her that their mission to protect John "cannot effectively be accomplished and still comport with your perhaps higher mission of raising your children in a manner that carries on the highest traditions of a great family. The two objectives simply are incompatible." He made her aware that the restrictions she wished to place on the agents represented "a partial declination of protection."

"In other words," he concluded, "there is no way to provide the level of protection to John that the statute requires under the restrictive circumstances determined by you."

Mrs. Onassis rejected Macdonald's argument that it was her restrictions that had led to the incident in Central Park. Instead, she blamed the agency. She wrote that although the agents knew that John enjoyed riding a bike, "they have not had a bicycle of their own to follow him." She even accused the agents of being lazy and incompetent, claiming that they "simply drove to the courts and waited for him to appear. They did not attempt to follow him by car or on foot." Although they knew when he left, they were not in place and prepared to follow him. "They knew his departure time, but they were not out front; they were in the back room calling the governess," she responded. Finally, she blamed the service for not thinking of installing a bell that would allow the doorman to signal when John was exiting the apartment. "They finally did so at my suggestion," she wrote, and requested that they now "install a similar bell in the elevator."

She concluded her letter with a blistering critique of the Secret Service in general. "What I have always asked of the Secret Service, which seems a not unreasonable request of men trained in police work who should know how to 'tail' a suspect without being observed, is that they employ that technique with my children in daily events of childrens' [sic] lives when accompanying protection is unnecessary." But she charged that many of the agents were "more comfortable marching side-by-side with the child, calling 'ETA' into their walkie-talkies." This was, she concluded, "their great failing." She claimed that they made John's life "a nightmare" and prevented him "from developing the self-reliance he will need when they are gone."

In addition to writing letters, Jackie personally called Clint Hill, who was now in a senior position with the agency and with whom she maintained a close relationship. "Most of it was just the usual stuff," he recalled. "The agents are too close. They're not allowing John to be like the rest of the kids. He feels different." Hill reflected that the situation was tough partly because "the agents were frustrated." Their job was to protect John, which was quite different from running surveillance on a criminal. "In this case, you want to be close enough so that nothing can happen." In order to fulfill their duties, they needed to stick to John, but then Jackie would call complaining that they were too close. "You can't satisfy her, and you can't protect them at the same time." Hill tried to explain to Jackie that she could not have it both ways, but she refused to listen. She was, Hill admitted, "very difficult."

Macdonald asked the exasperated agents involved in the Central Park incident to respond to her letter. The agents stopped just short of calling her a liar. They *had* a bicycle, they pointed out, but did not use it because the governess had told them that John "would be leaving momentarily for his tennis lesson," and, since he was running late, she "requested that the agents transport him in a Secret Service vehicle." The agent then went to the car and waited for John, but he and his cousin William Smith emerged from the building on bicycles and pedaled into Central Park. The agent did not want to leave the car unattended while he went into the building to retrieve a bicycle, so he decided to follow as best he could by car.

As for her other complaints, they pointed out that they had installed alarms with both the doorman and elevator operator, but neither had proven reliable. "Unfortunately, the doorman, although being instructed to use it to notify the agents of John's imminent departure, does not always do so," they wrote. They faced the same problem with the elevator operator, who had been instructed to press a buzzer twice if John or Caroline was leaving the building. But the building had recently installed a self-operated elevator, making a buzzer system obsolete.

All the frustration that had been building for years now spilled over into their memorandum. The agents pointed out that Mrs. Onassis had "overruled" many of their efforts to improve security for John and Caroline. Once when she was out of town, the agents installed a sprinkler system in the apartment. Hill recalled that they thought "she would appreciate their efforts to protect her family from fire." Instead, the former first lady demanded that it be removed. Furthermore, to accommodate her, the Secret Service was using an additional team of agents from its New York City field office to provide "undercover surveillance" of John. But nothing seemed to please her. Eventually they convinced her to allow them to give the children "small portable emergency alarm systems which they could activate in the event of trouble." Clint Hill recalled that giving John the buzzer was a compromise with Mrs. Onassis: the agents would feel safer giving him more latitude if they knew he could contact them if in danger.

John once told me a story about a time when he and friends were playing in Central Park and threw rocks at an older group of teens, who then started pursuing him. John hid under a bush while they combed the area, taunting him, "We know you're in here. We are going to kick your ass!" John decided it was a good time to test his buzzer. He pressed the button and remembered sirens going off and agents rushing toward him, weapons drawn. The agents forced the teens on the ground while John stood up, dusted himself off, and strolled off toward a waiting car.

The frustration within the agency was palpable. Once again, the agent in charge never sent his rebuttal to Mrs. Onassis, but he did give it to his superiors. It's likely that she never knew the depth of the anger and resentment that agents felt toward her. He stated that he did not want to engage in "a long-range, nonproductive debate with Mrs. Onassis" but rather to document their response for their files. They were simply waiting out the clock. Caroline, now sixteen, had lost her protection at this point, and John had only sixteen months left. Macdonald responded to the agent: "I was aware of most of the facts contained in it and agree with you that any discussion of these facts with Mrs. Onassis would be counterproductive." Their response should be recorded, he concluded, "for posterity, if for no other reason." Instead, they sent Mrs. Onassis a pleasant note saying they accepted her restrictions and "appreciate the time you have taken to address yourself to this matter."

John became the focal point of a new culture of celebrity that emerged in the 1970s. The failure in Vietnam, the Johnson administration's duplicity in explaining it away, and the exposure of Richard Nixon's illegal behavior in the Watergate affair combined to erode public faith in the integrity of its elected leaders. The journalist Tom Wicker of *The New York Times* wrote that many Americans had come to view their government as "a fountain of lies." "All during Vietnam, the government lied to me," declared *The Washington Post*'s Richard Cohen. "All the time. Watergate didn't help matters any. More lies. . . . I've been shaped, formed by lies." A 1976 study revealed that 69 percent of respondents felt that "over the last ten years, this country's leaders have consistently lied to the people." Pollster Daniel Yankelovich noted that trust in government declined from 80 percent in the late 1950s to about 33 percent in 1976. More than 80 percent of the public expressed distrust in politicians, 61 percent believed something was morally wrong with the country, and nearly 75 percent felt that they had no impact on Washington decision-making.

The new skepticism found expression in the way the media dealt with political leaders. Believing they had been duped by Johnson and Nixon, reporters developed a more assertive and confrontational style, challenging the official version of events. Inspired by the example of Watergate heroes Bob Woodward and Carl Bernstein of *The Washington Post*, many journalists went in search of the next big scandal. "A lot of young reporters today are more likely to ask the right questions of the right people than before Watergate," observed an editor at *The New York Times*. Investigative reporting emerged as a major franchise in numerous newsrooms, which organized reporting teams and provided them with big budgets. This adversarial style, combined with the real corruption it exposed, reinforced further the notion that political leaders were dishonest.

Even John's father's record fell prey to the new skepticism. The 1971 release of the Pentagon Papers, a secret Defense Department study of the Vietnam War that Daniel Ellsberg leaked to *The New York Times*, exposed the failings of both JFK's and LBJ's strategy for fighting the Vietnam War. The revelations of these previously secret documents threatened the image of JFK as a pragmatic leader and cast doubt on the claim among Kennedy loyalists that the president had not been committed to Vietnam and would have pulled out after he won reelection in 1964. Revisionist historians deconstructed every dimension of Kennedy's foreign policy, accusing him of convincing the nation that it had an obligation to fight Communism in the Third World and preparing it to sink more deeply into the Vietnam quagmire.

By the mid-1970s, revelations about JFK's private life also started leaking to the public when a Senate Select Committee on Intelligence discovered connections between the president and Judith Exner, who was also involved with two prominent mob figures. In a December 1975 news conference, Exner acknowledged her love affair with JFK. Suddenly kiss-and-tell stories appeared everywhere. Historian Arthur Schlesinger once joked with me that, in light of all the revelations, it was surprising that Kennedy had had any time to get work done.

John struggled to reconcile these new exposés with the stories he had grown up hearing from David Powers. By the time I met him, John had read some of the newer revisionist books, and he was already familiar with the friendly accounts written by Kennedy partisans: Arthur Schlesinger's *A Thousand Days*, Pierre Salinger's *With Kennedy*, and Kenneth O'Donnell and

David Powers's *"Johnny, We Hardly Knew Ye": Memories of John Fitzgerald Kennedy*. John was gratified that the sordid details of his father's private life did little to dampen public support for JFK, whom Americans continued to rank as the nation's favorite president. But he always feared there would be a tipping point. What other disclosures would be revealed, and would the public eventually turn against his father? It also bothered John to learn how much his father disrespected his mother. Jackie reassured both John and Caroline that whatever their father's indiscretions, they still loved each other, and he most certainly loved them.

It seemed to John that people fell into two camps: those who wished to promote the myth and those who wanted to tear it down. Over time he was able to integrate these competing views of his father into a more coherent narrative. He would come to see his father as a man of great strength who, like all humans, was flawed. He acknowledged that his father had made mistakes, but he was also convinced that leaders should be judged by their ability to inspire the nation. He recognized that his father did not live long enough to leave a significant policy imprint, but he took pride in how his father's noble idealism had ignited hope and action in an entire generation. I think that one of the reasons John came to trust me was because I shared a similar view of his dad. I was fascinated by him, viewing him as a dynamic and inspirational leader who was constrained in office by a slim mandate and a conservative Congress. Many people wanted to focus on JFK's private life, but I felt that such titillating stories were not central to understanding his presidency.

The new cynicism toward politicians also affected the way journalists covered Hollywood stars, business titans, and other celebrities. On March 4, 1974, the first issue of *People* hit newsstands, with Mia Farrow on the cover. According to Landon Y. Jones, who joined the magazine a few months after the first issue, the editors discovered "that readers were more interested in Mia Farrow the woman, mother, and personality than in Mia Farrow the actress." They wanted to see behind the curtain and get a glimpse of the way celebrities really lived their lives. "If celebrities didn't want their problems turned into public fodder, too bad," he reflected. "It was the duty of the press to be accurate about the lives of the rich and famous. And readers demanded to be inspired and moved, but also titillated and amused."

The same formula infused Page Six, which the *New York Post* launched on

Monday, January 3, 1977. Editors wanted Page Six to revive the lost art of the gossip column. In the past, gossip columns had focused on Hollywood, but Page Six was just as likely to write about Wall Street moguls as it was about Broadway stars. Not surprisingly, the first column included snippets about John and his mom. They would be the first of hundreds of items that would appear in the paper over the next two decades.

John was acutely aware that his fame stemmed solely from an accident of birth. The public fascination with him revolved around not what he accomplished but what he represented. The tension between others' expectations of him and his personal need to establish a healthy, independent identity would become the central struggle of his life. As a result, he developed an odd relationship with the tabloid press. Like many celebrities, John complained about the intrusions on his privacy, but he also kept track of how often he was covered by *People* and Page Six. If he did not appear for a few months, it was a good bet that he would show up somewhere with his shirt off. I used to call John Superman, only instead of going into a phone booth to put on his cape, he went to the park to take off his shirt. John, who could laugh at himself as easily as he laughed at others, would always chuckle.

This cult of celebrity gave birth to a new form of photographers: paparazzi. Italian movie director Federico Fellini first used the term in his 1960 film *La Dolce Vita* to describe a photographer who chased relentlessly after celebrities and Hollywood stars. The original Italian word was usually used to describe an insect that constantly buzzed around, and the term seemed apt for the new phenomenon. By the 1970s, as more celebrities retained press agents and surrounded themselves with bodyguards, photographers found the only way to capture "authentic" pictures of their subjects was to surprise them.

On September 24, 1969, on her first day back in New York after a relaxing summer in Greece, Jackie was ambushed by a freelance photographer waiting behind the bushes. The man was thirty-eight-year-old Ron Galella from the Bronx, who claimed that he had been trying to capture "the full range of human emotions." Galella stalked Jackie at her home, hid behind bushes in Central Park, and hovered over her when she walked down the street. He bribed maids and the doorman in her building, as well as those nearby. He even dressed as a sailor once to get photos of her on Scorpios. For Galella, it was all about the money, as he got paid more for pictures of Jackie than anyone else. "The only pictures that would pay better, if anyone could get them," he said, "might be exclusive pictures of Howard Hughes," the wealthy, eccentric film producer-director, aviator, and business mogul who spent his last twenty-five years in seclusion. Jackie's "value" never depreciated. Magazines such as *Time*, *Newsweek*, and *Life* paid up to $5,000 for a cover and inside spread. Overseas, the most interest concentrated in Italy and Germany, but foreign demand also existed in Hong Kong, Japan, and Australia.

In 1971 the Secret Service filed a lawsuit against Galella on Jackie's behalf. It charged that on one occasion, he jumped from behind a stone wall and landed directly in front of John and his mother. John, in order to avoid a collision, swerved his bicycle and almost crashed to the pavement. Kathy McKeon, who accompanied John that day, recalled later that John lost control of his bike and would have "gone off the sidewalk into Fifth Avenue traffic if the Secret Service agent close behind hadn't grabbed him." On another occasion, John was at a horse show in New Jersey escorting Caroline's horse back to the stable when Galella "suddenly jumped from behind a tree in a crouched position with the camera at the ready. His action startled the horse and the horse broke free momentarily causing John to lose control." John gave what appeared to be a well-rehearsed deposition in the case. "Mr. Galella has dashed at me, jumped in my path, discharged flashbulbs in my face, trailed me at close distances—generally imposed himself on me. . . . I feel threatened when he is present."

On October 14, 1971, Jackie received a restraining order to prevent Galella from interfering with the Secret Service's job of protecting John and Caroline. He ignored the order, so Jackie took him to court in February 1972. Galella's attorney claimed the case centered on "a photojournalist's right to pursue his occupation." But the court disagreed, and, after a twenty-six-day trial, the judge ruled that Galella had to stay fifty yards away from Jackie and seventy-five yards away from the children. An appeals court reduced the distance for Jackie to twenty-five feet and thirty feet for John and Caroline.

John learned a crucial lesson from the way his mother handled Galella. Her attempts to have him arrested, in addition to the high-profile court proceeding, turned the public against her. *The New York Times* described the trial as "the best off-Broadway show in town." The public sympathized with Galella, who came off as a hardworking guy simply trying to do his job by taking photographs of "the number one cover girl in the world." Years later, when John was launching *George*, Galella contacted his office to ask permission to attend the launch and take photos of him. Surprisingly, John sent back word that he was welcome to attend.

As a child John had been small and scrawny, and even as a young teen, he had yet to grow into the heartthrob image that would soon define him. Family friend Billy Noonan, whose father had worked on JFK's 1952 Senate campaign, described John as "almost comically awkward." At the age of fourteen, John, he observed, "moved disjointedly and had no build. He had a big nose, braces, and pimples." Fashion was never a priority for John. As a teenager, he often wore an untucked button-down shirt and rumpled chinos. "He looked like an unmade bed," Noonan recalled. John became less conspicuous around the city once he lost Secret Service protection in 1976. Paparazzi still followed him, but the pressure was not as great as it would become later, when his handsome features grew more pronounced and he built his muscular physique.

There remained, however, constant reminders that John was different. He knew that my older brother was a boxer and that we grew up in Philadelphia, the home of heavyweight champion Joe Frazier. John told me that he had attended the second of three fights between Frazier and Muhammad Ali, held at Madison Square Garden in January 1974. After the bout, which Ali won by a unanimous decision, someone escorted John to his locker room. The now former champion, told that John was in the audience, had summoned him. They shared a brief conversation, and as John was leaving, Ali handed him the silk robe he had worn during his entrance into the ring. John told the story so matter-of-factly that it was as if everyone got invited back to the locker room following a momentous fight. Of course, I joked with him that Frazier had reached out to me before the fight and asked for advice on countering Ali's "rope-a-dope" tactic. "No wonder he lost," John wisecracked.

John developed close friendships with three of his cousins. He saw a great deal of both William Kennedy Smith, who lived in the city, and Timothy Shriver—the middle child of John's aunt Eunice Kennedy Shriver and her husband, Sargent Shriver, the Democratic vice presidential nominee in 1972—who was nearby in Washington, DC. In 1975 Anthony Radziwill, who had resided in London for the previous sixteen years, moved back to the United States to attend boarding school at Choate in Wallingford,

Connecticut. In the past, John and Anthony had spent some summers together on Scorpios, but now that they were living just ninety miles apart, there were more opportunities to see each other. Their friendship, already strong, now deepened.

John, however, kept his distance from RFK's kids. He remembered how they used to call him a mama's boy, and now that they were older, he felt they wore their family name on their sleeves. John also found them overly wild. He resented that Ethel allowed them to run around the Hyannis property, showing no regard for his mother's house. In many respects, he was also following his mother's wishes. "After Bobby died, Jackie deliberately kept John away from his cousins as much as she could," Rose Kennedy's secretary told author Wendy Leigh. "Ethel's children were raised wildly, with no system, no schedule, and Jackie didn't want her children to be brought up like that."

As a young teen, John seemed to possess endless curiosity and unbounded energy. In August 1972 Jackie wrote Rose Kennedy, whom she referred to as *belle-mère* (French for mother-in-law), describing their trip to London, where Caroline and John viewed the popular exhibition of priceless artifacts from the ancient tomb of the Egyptian pharaoh Tutankhamun—King Tut. "John asked so many intelligent questions," she noted proudly, that the head of trustees "got into a panic and said, 'I must send for an Egyptologist to answer all this boy's questions!'" She pointed out that John "reminded me of Jack with all his curiosity [and] intelligence."

Mrs. Onassis searched for outlets for John's energy and need for adventure. She always feared that her son would grow up "soft" because of his privileged background. So in addition to making sure he had male influences, she sought to toughen him up by organizing rugged adventures. In August 1971 she sent John and Anthony Radziwill to the Drake's Island Adventure Centre, located off the southwest coast of England. During the day, the two cousins took courses in sailing and rock climbing and explored the neighboring woods. She wrote Rose Kennedy, describing the camp as "very spartan" and "primitive." John called shortly after his arrival to complain about the living conditions. "John and Anthony sound as if they are in prison camp," Jackie told Rose. She noted, however, that "it should be good for him after Scorpios." Furthermore, Jackie wanted to ensure that the Secret Service would not try to rescue John in the event of an accident, so she instructed the agents, as usual, to be "very discreet and remain in the background." She requested that no agent be present on the island and that "John partake in the program of the island without being aware that an agent is nearby."

In 1976 John and Timothy Shriver, who was one year older, traveled to Guatemala to help victims of an earthquake there. "They ate what the people of Rabinal ate and dressed in Guatemalan clothes and slept in tents like most of the earthquake victims," recounted a Catholic priest who oversaw the relief efforts. "They did more for their country's image than a roomful of ambassadors." It was fitting given that Timothy's father, Sargent Shriver, was the first director of the Peace Corps program that President John F. Kennedy established by executive order in 1961. From Guatemala, John and Timothy traveled to Panama. The trips had such an impact on John that he would write about them in his college application. Furthermore, the fifteen-year-old enjoyed relative anonymity while traveling abroad. At one point in Panama, John and Timmy were approached by two women on the dance floor in a disco. One woman's eyes widened when she saw the *JFK* monogram on John's raspberry-colored shirt. She elbowed her friend and pointed out the initials, asking, "JFK . . . isn't that an airport?"

The following summer, Jackie enrolled John in the Hurricane Island Outward Bound School in Maine. The Outward Bound schools, like the Drake's Island experience, celebrated the idea that qualities such as tenacity, curiosity, and self-awareness could be enhanced through a rugged wilderness experience. John was enrolled in the only Outward Bound school based at sea. The basic program lasted twenty-six days and had separate groups for boys and girls, each composed of twelve students and two instructors. Half the time was spent sailing in open, ketch-rigged pulling boats. Students charted courses to dozens of islands that dotted the Maine coast. John, like everyone else, had to spend three nights alone on an uninhabited island, where he was supplied with only one gallon of water and was forced to forage for most of his food. When asked later about what he learned from the experience, John responded, "I learned I'll never allow myself to be that hungry again."

In 1978 Mrs. Onassis sent her seventeen-year-old to work on a ranch in Wyoming. Apparently, John had become more rambunctious and mischievous since losing his Secret Service protection. He continued to see a psychiatrist for most of his teen years and beyond, although it's unclear if he was on medication and, if so, for how long. Jackie feared that he would get into trouble with his antics, which included mixing five gallons of wallpaper paste and pouring it down the mail chute in her Fifth Avenue building. She contacted a Wyoming congressman who happened to be a family friend and asked, "Do you have a friend who has a ranch that John could work on?" The congressman knew just the right guy and introduced her to John Perry Barlow, owner of a large ranch called Bar Cross.

Barlow, best known as a lyricist for the Grateful Dead, recalled sitting at his desk one evening when the phone rang. Picking up the receiver, he heard that distinctive, breathy voice say, "Hi, this is Jacqueline Onassis." Barlow, not sure if he was being pranked, responded, "In the highly unlikely event that this isn't a joke, what can I do for you?" She assured him the call was not a joke and proceeded to ask if he could hire her son for the summer. A few days later, John showed up.

Barlow's first impression of John was that he was "incredibly good-looking" and possessed "a kind of thoughtless grace." He further described John as "permanently rambunctious but charming" and "physically powerful and fearless." He also used a word commonly ascribed to John by adults: *immature*. Perhaps immaturity was one of the qualities that Mrs. Kennedy blamed in part on the Secret Service for not allowing him to experience the normal bumps and bruises of childhood. Now she was determined to create those challenging experiences, both mentally and physically, that would enhance John's maturity before he went off to college. For his part, Barlow tried to toughen John by making him sleep in a partially flooded bunkhouse.

Barlow got an early sampling of John's absentmindedness. As a child, John had once nearly suffocated his guinea pig by leaving it overnight in the back of a truck, and he was notorious for losing just about everything, from keys, to books, to articles of clothing. But Barlow experienced perhaps John's most expensive act of inattentiveness. Once, he asked his new hire to drive his truck down a narrow path between two fences. They then hopped out and did some work before Barlow asked John to back the truck out on his own. John jumped into the driver's seat and, now more confident in his navigating ability, gunned the engine. There was only one problem: he had forgotten to close the doors, which were immediately sheared off when they encountered the wooden fence posts. "Is that going to cost a lot to fix?" John asked.

If Mrs. Kennedy was looking for a responsible adult who would offer John guidance and adult supervision, Barlow may not have been the best choice. According to Barlow, John had experimented with acid in the past, but Barlow introduced him to a much larger dose: 300 micrograms. When they got high, the two men would hop in Barlow's truck and go driving. They would also drop explosives down one of the uncapped gas wells surrounding the ranch. Such escapades were probably not the structured experiences that Jackie had planned for her son.

In November 1978 Mrs. Onassis threw a big party for John's eighteenth birthday and Caroline's twenty-first. The party took place on the Sunday after Thanksgiving and shortly after the fifteenth anniversary of President Kennedy's assassination. It began with cocktails at her apartment. Afterward, about 150 guests attended a private disco party at New York's chic Le Club. John spent most of his time on the dance floor. Later, partygoers enjoyed a cake with sparklers and a speech by John's uncle Teddy. By midnight, the older crowd had left, while John and his friends stayed until four in the morning, when the owner kicked them out.

Outside of Le Club, photographers, including Ron Galella, jumped from their cars to get a glimpse of John. Galella was supposed to keep his distance, of course, but he likely believed he could blend into the pack. John peered through the peephole in the red leather–upholstered door and saw the photographers waiting for their prey. He then turned and asked the manager if there was a back door they could use. There was not. The photographers knew that John would have to come through the front, so they pulled back their hoodies on the cold night, extinguished their cigarettes, and readied their cameras.

Inside, John's friends prepared for a confrontation. "Can we take them?" asked Noonan, a burly Irishman. After a night of drinking and drugs, John's friends were not clear minded. Gustavo Paredes gathered everyone together by the front door and devised their exit strategy. "This is what we are going to do," he announced. "We're going to rush out and catch a cab. And we're going to put on our sunglasses so that nobody will recognize who we are." Everyone thought it was a brilliant plan, so they all donned their sunglasses and prepared to make their getaway. "I lined everybody up," Paredes reflected in 2019. "I told Billy to take the lead."

They formed a phalanx, with Billy in front and John and his girlfriend Jenny Christian in the middle. Since there was a car parked outside the club, they needed to move left down the street in search of a taxi. "There were photographers everywhere," Gustavo recalled. According to Noonan, as he pushed forward, he warned a photographer to back away. "Fuck off, fat boy," came the response. Billy recalled that he then charged at the photographer. John tried to hold him back but got pushed to the ground in the confusion.

Paredes has a very different recollection. He said that Billy kicked a photographer in the small of his back. "I saw the pain on the guy's face," he recalled. The paparazzo handed off his camera to someone and then charged at them. But instead of attacking Billy, who was clearly the guy who'd assaulted him, the guy headed straight for John. "He blindsides John, who flips over a car hood and lands on the pavement." Paredes then grabbed the photographer by the collar of his shirt and took a swing. "I unleashed on him and lifted the guy a foot off the ground, pummeling him." In the meantime, John jumped up and wanted to join the fight, but Gustavo yanked him by the front of his coat and threw him into a cab. Jenny jumped in with John, Gustavo hopped into the front, and they made their way home.

The whole incident lasted thirty seconds, but the photos screamed across the front pages of the New York tabloids the next day. When Billy called the next morning, John said he found the whole scene funny. The only problem was that "Mummy is not happy." John tried to explain to her what happened—that he and his friends did nothing wrong—but she seemed unconvinced. "I think you should write a note," he told Billy, letting her know what happened.

John had transferred from Collegiate to the exclusive Phillips Academy Andover in Massachusetts in the fall of 1976. It would be his first experience living away from his family. The Secret Service stayed with him through most of the fall semester and then left after his sixteenth birthday. John lived in a two-story dormitory that housed twenty-seven students on Chapel Avenue, immediately north of the administration buildings. John stayed in Alfred E. Stearns House in rear room 29, located on the second floor, overlooking Rabbit Pond.

With both John and Caroline living away from home for the first time, Jackie settled into a new routine. In 1975 she had started a career as an editor at Viking Press, but she quit two years later when the company published a fictionalized account of a future assassination plot against President Ted Kennedy. She moved to rival Doubleday, where she settled into a long career as a respected editor.

Her private life had also stabilized. She dated after Ari's death, but eventually she settled down with Maurice Tempelsman, a portly, balding diamond merchant whom she had known for decades. Born in Belgium, Tempelsman fled the Nazis with his family in 1940 and moved to New York, where his father established a successful diamond brokerage. Maurice joined the family business, cultivating an extensive political network that allowed him to broker diamond deals between the United States and Africa. As a major contributor to the Democratic Party, he first met Jackie in the late 1950s and had set up a meeting between President-elect Kennedy and African mining officials.

During his first semester at Andover, John met Sasha Chermayeff, who would become one of his closest friends. He would later refer to her as the "platonic love of my life" and "coolest, least fucked-up girl I know." Both were city kids. She had attended the prestigious Dalton School while John was at Collegiate, and they had both made the unusual decision to transfer to Andover in the eleventh grade. "It was unusual," she reflected, "because most people did not go to Andover for only two years." They either went for the entire four years or, if they transferred, did so in the sophomore year. Since both of them were new to campus and did not know many people, John and Sasha naturally bonded. They ended up being enrolled in many of the same classes and could often be seen walking together from one classroom to another. "Two weeks into that first semester, we were already quite friendly," Sasha recalled. She described him as "this funny, sweet, loving guy." John, she reflected in 2018, "became like a brother to me."

It was Mrs. Onassis's decision to transfer John from Collegiate, where he was well liked and performing well, to a new school in rural Massachusetts. Partly it was to get him away from the emerging drug scene in New York. These were critical years in John's development, and his mom did not want him around the temptations of the city. John had a short attention span and was easily distracted by New York City's endless social possibilities. She likely believed that Andover's rural environment would help John remain focused on his studies. No nightclubs or other social diversions existed. But the main reason was safety. "His mother was very anxious about safety in Manhattan," recalled Collegiate history teacher Bruce Breimer. "She was afraid he was going to get hurt, that some nut was going to find him." John was about to be without Secret Service protection for the first time in his life, and everyone knew it. He would be an obvious target, and his mom felt that the remoteness of a rural boarding school offered more protection than the bustling streets of Manhattan.

On the surface, John seemed casual, easygoing, and unpretentious. Sasha described his fashion style as "schleppy," joking with him that none of his clothes ever seemed to fit. "Everything was falling off," she recalled. "He would never even dream of having a pair of matching socks." But Sasha and John engaged in long conversations, and she quickly realized that he was more complicated than he appeared. "John didn't have a carefree background," she reflected, "yet he came off like this carefree guy." She learned from their conversations "that there were difficulties in his life," and his problems became "more complex" as he got older. "That was a beautiful thing," she said. "It wasn't easy being John, but he carried his burden with such enormous grace."

In many of their evening conversations, John confided to Sasha about his identity crisis. Due to his name and family background, people imposed their own expectations on him. Even walking around the Andover campus, John noticed many students, faculty, and administrators with "Kennedy fixations." Though he understood why people treated him a particular way, he also knew that to have a fulfilling life he needed to break out of these boundaries. His family was a source of great pride, but it could also create crushing burdens. Wherever he went, the ghost of his father haunted him. Sasha noticed that John was frequently torn between doing what he wanted—camping or skiing with friends—and attending family events. His uncle Ted Kennedy was running for reelection to the Senate in November 1976, and Jackie permitted John and Caroline to make a limited number of appearances for him. John reluctantly agreed. He did not enjoy being on display, but he adored his uncle and would do anything Teddy asked of him. "He had more obligations than we did," Sasha recalled. "We could be tired and hung over, and we could do whatever we wanted, but John always had obligations."

At Andover, John's favorite distraction from such family obligations was acting. He had appeared in *Oliver!*, the musical version of Charles Dickens's *Oliver Twist*, while at Collegiate. He appeared in three more plays while at Andover: William Shakespeare's *The Comedy of Errors*; *One Flew over the Cuckoo's Nest*, based on a novel by Ken Kesey; and a production of Megan

Terry's *Comings and Goings*. "He really got into theater," recalled Andover friend Wilson McCray. "John loved acting, and if he hadn't been born a prince, I think he'd love to have gone further with it." However, Holly Owen, head of Andover's acting department, admitted that although he noticed John's obvious passion for acting, he questioned how committed he was to being onstage. "He had a facility for acting, a knack, a great deal of personal charisma," he said, "but he didn't have the inner drive for it."

While at Andover, John started dating Jenny Christian, who was regarded as one of the most glamorous women on campus. Jenny soon became part of the family and, in 1978, joined Jackie, Lee, Tina, and Anthony on a vacation to the Caribbean island of Saint Martin, where they stayed at the same luxury resort as a young, blonde actress, Daryl Hannah. John found it odd that Daryl seemed to carry a teddy bear with her wherever she went, but he also found her fascinating.

Although secluded, Andover offered no refuge from the emerging drug craze in America. In the 1960s, radical youth culture remained confined to a small number of hippies, but it became commonplace in the 1970s. "In the seventies, hardly anybody was a hippie, because everybody was," declared one observer. Emblems of sixties protest, such as long hair and casual dress, gained mainstream appeal during the 1970s. So did experimenting with drugs. Smoking marijuana became a rite of passage for young people. Meanwhile, their parents managed to get their drugs legally. The most popular drug of the decade was the tranquilizer Valium. The Rolling Stones, John's favorite rock band, poked fun at the older generation's dependency on tranquilizers in their 1966 song "Mother's Little Helper."

While at Andover, John and some friends were caught smoking pot by a campus police officer. John had to meet with a school administrator, and his mother was notified of the infraction. While some schools had a zero-tolerance policy for drugs, Andover was more lenient. John, like everyone else found with drugs or alcohol, received a warning.

Though John dabbled in the drug culture and had a serious girlfriend, his top priority remained schoolwork. History and literature were his best subjects, but he struggled with math and science. While he earned an occasional A in history, he gravitated toward Bs and more than a few Cs. Holly Owen described John as "a modest student" who had trouble keeping up with the intense academic atmosphere at Andover, which attracted many overachievers. John also had a short attention span and did not help himself by missing classes often. "He certainly wasn't at the top of his class," a faculty member told the journalist Michael Gross.

John ended up staying for a third year and graduating as part of the class of '79, because he needed another year to finish the math requirement. Andover required students to pass general exams in five subjects, including math. Normally, if a student failed any of the tests, he or she would be asked to leave. John's mother, however, worked out an arrangement with administrators that would allow John to spend an extra year at the school. "I think his mom felt that he was still a little immature," Sasha recalled. "She was a little wary of sending him off to college right away." His graduation may have been delayed a year, but that setback did not diminish Jackie's enthusiasm when he finally donned a cap and gown and received his diploma on June 7, 1979. As expected, dozens of photographers and reporters showed up to document John's every move.

Shortly after graduation, Mrs. Onassis reached out to Bruce Breimer in his capacity as the director of college guidance at Collegiate. "Is it okay if John does not go to the family school?" she asked in her breathless voice. "He doesn't want to go to Harvard." When she told him that John was planning to attend Brown University, Breimer replied, "Why not? It's not like he's going to some third-rate institution. Let him go."

Little did I know that our lives were about to intersect.

CHAPTER 5

"THE QUESTION IS, WHERE IS THIS ALL TAKING ME?"

Founded in 1764, Brown University was the seventh college established in the North American colonies. Its charter called upon the university to produce graduates who would lead "lives of usefulness and reputation." As the first Ivy League school to accept students from all religious affiliations, Brown has long prided itself on its openness. Located on College Hill, the picturesque campus of historic homes and modern buildings now overlooks the gritty working-class downtown of Providence, Rhode Island.

Considering its quirky reputation, Brown seemed like an unusual choice for John, especially given his family's close ties to Harvard. His grandfather, the late ambassador Joseph P. Kennedy, along with his father and his uncles—Joseph Jr., Bobby, and Edward—all graduated from Harvard. But John's decision to enroll at Brown highlighted his lifelong quest to establish an independent identity and to challenge expectations. Brown was also better suited to his interests and style: it was more casual than the other Ivies, its twenty-eight-credit requirement was the lowest among elite schools in the United States, and it boasted a strong theater arts department. Admitting John also served Brown's needs, as the institution sought high-profile students who could elevate its stature and help raise money. When John entered in the fall of 1979, Brown was a sleepy, second-tier Ivy League university. It was no coincidence that by the time he left, Brown had become the hottest college in America. During his four years on campus, John changed Brown as much as the institution changed him.

His time at Brown was among the happiest and most fulfilling of John's life. The press left him alone, and students grew accustomed to seeing him around campus. He formed a close group of trusted friends who stayed by his side for the rest of his life. Although he struggled academically, he immersed himself in college activities, playing rugby, joining a fraternity, and even appearing in several plays. Brown, however, failed to provide him with a clear sense of direction. After earning his diploma in June 1983, John traveled to India, which had been one of his mother's favorite travel destinations, in search of further inspiration.

What separated Brown from Harvard and other Ivy League schools was its curriculum, which emerged from the social protests of the 1960s. During this era, baby boomers—who had grown up in the prosperous post–World War II years—started flooding college campuses, determined to challenge the established political and cultural order. While the sixties did not mark the first time young Americans spoke out against the injustice and hypocrisy of their elders, social and demographic forces provided this generation with new clout. The postwar baby boom had dramatically increased the number of college-aged students in the United States. In 1965 a whopping 41 percent of all Americans were under the age of twenty. College enrollments soared from 3.6 million in 1960 to almost 8 million in 1970. And since colleges contained the largest concentration of young people in the country, they became the seedbed of youth protest.

Not surprisingly, student eruptions began just as the first wave of reform-minded youth appeared on campus. In 1962 the Students for a Democratic Society (SDS), the leading New Left organization on college campuses, wrote *The Port Huron Statement*. The founding document of the New Left, the manifesto urged universities to be agents of change in tackling the nation's problems through "self-cultivation, self-direction, self-understanding, and creativity." Two years later, students at the University of California, Berkeley, organized the Free Speech Movement (FSM), which initially protested regulations prohibiting political demonstrations before broadening its focus to blasting the "multiversity machine." The revolt quickly spread to other campuses and championed diverse causes, from opposing dress codes to fighting tenure decisions. In 1965 President Lyndon Johnson further fanned the flames of student discontent when he sent American ground forces into Vietnam, dramatically escalating what had been a simmering conflict. Student anger reached a new high the following year, when Johnson ended automatic draft deferments for college students. The threat of the draft pushed this generation of young people to protest the war on both personal and political levels.

While many campuses erupted in violence, protest at Brown remained relatively tame. In 1966, students objected to the college's loco parentis rule, which established curfews for women undergraduates (men had none) and rules restricting dorm visits by the opposite sex. In April of that year, 150 students crashed an executive committee meeting to protest the presence of the Reserve Officers' Training Corps (ROTC) on campus. In December, sixty-five of Brown's eighty-five African American students staged another protest, demanding that the university increase the number of minority students and faculty. All of this hubbub proved too much for President Ray Heffner, who stated amid his resignation, "I have simply reached the conclusion that I do not enjoy being a university president."

At Brown, the spirit of dissent was also channeled into the mandated work of curriculum reform. Brown, like other Ivy League schools, required students to take classes in English composition, foreign language, and four courses each in sciences, humanities, and social sciences. In 1967 student government president Ira Magaziner, frustrated with the perceived lack of creative thinking and dynamism in American higher education, joined forces with another undergraduate to form a Group Independent Study Project to recommend changes to the curriculum. That summer, they submitted a 418-page report, *Draft of a Working Paper for Education at Brown University*, which outlined their proposals for reform. This report, which the historian Luther Spoehr dubbed "a term paper on steroids," advocated for a "student-centered" university that would focus on creativity and curiosity, not rote learning. It advised Brown administrators to "put students at the center of their education" and seek to "teach students how to think rather than just teaching facts" through smaller courses, independent studies, and interdisciplinary efforts.

In May 1968, Brown officials, hoping to avoid the violence sweeping other universities, approved the proposals in a marathon two-day faculty meeting. The "new curriculum" represented a bold departure from traditional approaches to learning. It abolished requirements for languages, science, math, or any other particular course. The only mandatory courses were in a

student's major, and the university allowed students to create their own major. It called for replacing large lecture classes with smaller "modes of
thought" interdisciplinary seminars. To further foster individual growth,
Brown encouraged students to explore different disciplines and gave them
the option to take classes pass/fail. It did away with failing grades entirely.
Students could take a course for a grade of A, B, C, or no credit. The "no
credit" score would not show up on the transcript. Brown created a built-in
allowance for students to fail up to four courses or to take a lighter schedule,
since it required only twenty-eight courses to graduate.

Unfortunately, persistent budget shortfalls prevented the university from
fully implementing some of these reforms because it lacked the money to
hire enough professors to teach the proposed smaller classes. During most
of the 1970s, Brown was forced to borrow money from its $117 million en-
dowment, which was already the smallest in the Ivy League. By 1974, the
endowment had already dropped by $43 million. "Morale was thirty degrees
below sea level," said Sheila Blumstein, a former interim president of the
university. According to *Time*, Brown's academic reputation, despite its
high-profile reforms, "was in the basement of the Ivy League." Some referred
to it as the "doormat of the Ivy League."

In 1976, drowning in debt and facing a demoralized faculty and restless
student body, the university hired a new president. Howard Swearer, a forty-
four-year-old political scientist and former president of Carleton College in
Northfield, Minnesota, took office as the fifteenth president of Brown University in January 1977. The change in leadership turned out to be a brilliant
move, because Swearer possessed a reassuring, low-key style that made him
a perfect choice for an anxious university. He could often be seen strolling
around campus with his large tortoiseshell glasses and ever-present pipe.
More important, Swearer excelled as a compelling salesman and prodigious
fund-raiser. In the last three of his six years at Carleton, Swearer had raised
more than $15 million.

But despite the new president's masterful leadership, Brown University's
financial problems persisted. The year before John entered, it reported an
operating deficit of $721,000, nearly double what it had budgeted. The big-
gest problem came from a shortfall in tuition due to lower undergraduate and graduate enrollments. Swearer adopted a two-pronged approach to
Brown's fiscal problems: he cut costs, asking the faculty to delay expenditures

or postpone them for the remainder of the year, and he sought new revenue by increasing university fees by $500 for the upcoming 1978–79 academic year. He also announced his plan to raise $158 million in the largest fund-raising campaign in the university's history.

More than any previous president, Swearer made the admissions policy part of his development strategy, requiring Brown to admit some students largely because of their ability to raise the school's profile and improve its chances of attracting money. A February 1979 memo from the admissions office revealed that recruiters had been instructed to set aside 140 seats in the 1979 class to help with fund-raising campaigns. Howard Swearer scribbled on the memo, "Sensitive—not quotable." While development was listed as the top priority in the selection process, other spaces remained for athletes, minorities, geographic diversity, and legacies. Admissions officers wanted the administration to know that these groups made up only 18 percent of the total applicant pool but more than one-third of all acceptances. The private memorandum also pointed out that many of those admitted under these special categories did not meet the university's admission standards. Approximately 46 percent of them "clearly did not have the academic and personal growth potential as most of the 7,500" that the university would reject.

Director of Admissions James Rogers pointed out correctly that admissions was more complicated than simply picking those students with the highest grade point averages and test scores. Committee members needed to make sure that each class was balanced, including students who added racial, gender, and geographic diversity. Otherwise the entire Brown student body would consist of wealthy white kids from a handful of prestigious feeder schools. But in 1979, amid its quest for reinvention, Brown sought more than just diversity in its entering class: it also needed students with name recognition, someone who would instantly elevate the university's stature.

It was at this critical moment that John decided to apply for Brown, submitting his application in January 1979. Most of John's application materials were made public in 2017 when they were discovered among the personal items of a deceased former Brown administrator and put up for auction. He wrote his essays in longhand; his mother filled out the cover sheet, since

John was in Africa at the time. She was careful not to drop the family name, simply providing basic biographical information, such as that John grew up in New York with his mother and sister and spent "part of summer by the sea in New England with many cousins." She noted that he had attended Collegiate School, where he developed an interest in history because of an inspirational teacher, before transferring to Phillips Academy Andover. She also told the admissions committee that John participated in many extracurricular activities, including skiing and certified diving, but drama was the most significant. For his senior project at Andover, John worked at the juvenile court in New York City. "This made a deep impression on him," she noted, although she was not sure "whether or not he wishes to try for law school but hopes to decide during his years at Brown."

Finally, Mrs. Onassis pointed out that John's father's occupation was in "government" and that he graduated from Harvard with a BA, while she'd earned degrees from Vassar and the Sorbonne in Paris, and worked as an editor at Doubleday. When asked what John intended to major in, she wrote that his interest was always in "conceptual studies" and that science and math "have never been particularly interesting."

Although his mother filled out the cover sheet, the handwriting on the four-page essay clearly belonged to John. In it, he discussed the trips he had taken with his cousin Timothy Shriver to Guatemala and Panama. In Guatemala they worked for an experimental Peace Corps program helping residents to rebuild a village destroyed by an earthquake. On the morning of February 4, 1976, a 7.5-magnitude earthquake struck Guatemala City, killing more than twenty-three thousand people, seriously injuring seventy thousand, and leaving one million homeless. Many of the city's roads and bridges were destroyed, hindering rescue operations for the thousands trapped under the rubble. John and Timothy worked side by side with native peoples, creating bricks that would be used to build new houses. The entire relief effort was very primitive, he noted. Houses were constructed of mud, using the same tools and techniques that had been relied upon for the past three thousand years. They also spent time teaching "the natives" about proper nutrition and health care. John was particularly surprised by the "major role women played in the project," pointing out that they performed "the most demanding labor." Men, however, exercised complete control over the household, where women remained "subservient." During the winter, men traveled to the coast to find work, while "the women are left to fend for them-selves and their offspring. That [pressure] accounts for the soaring infant mortality rate and high percentage of malnutrition."

After leaving Guatemala, John and Timothy moved on to Panama, where they were "introduced to life at the opposite end of the social strata." The former foreign minister they stayed with introduced them to policy makers who lectured them on why Panama needed to repossess the Panama Canal. The canal, which opened in 1914, divided Panama into two parts separated by an American-controlled zone. Since then, US ownership of the canal re-mained a sore spot in the relationship between the two countries, flaring up in the 1960s with anti-American riots. In response, the two governments worked behind the scenes to try to solve the territorial issue. In August 1977 President Jimmy Carter's new administration completed negotiations for returning the canal but faced an angry backlash from conservatives at home, who saw that decision as a cowardly retreat. The Panamanian government desired a settlement that would guarantee complete sovereignty and prevent US intervention, but Carter had to appease right-wing critics by asserting America's right to defend the canal during a crisis.

Amid these tensions, Panamanian officials informed John that the canal represented an affront to their national pride. Americans living in the Canal Zone were governed by a different set of laws, did not pay taxes, and tried local citizens arrested in the American zone in their own courts. Panamani-ans, John stated in his admissions essay, "felt betrayed and bewildered by the aloofness of America, their supposedly benevolent ally to the north," which refused to even discuss renegotiating the treaty. Clearly influenced by the Panamanian perspective, John wrote smartly that the canal insulted locals, and he advocated giving Panama full ownership to help create a "self-sufficient economy independent of America." He concluded his essay by say-ing that American policy makers needed to "reflect" on their policies in Latin America, noting that his firsthand experience "made me more aware of the numerous [responsibilities] the US has and had ignored."

The application material made public in 2017 did not include his tran-scripts from Collegiate and Andover or his SAT (Scholastic Aptitude Test) scores. But it is unlikely that scores and grades would have mattered. Brown needed John more than he needed Brown. Officially, the university denied trying to recruit John. "We did not go out in search of these kids," claimed

Robert Reichley, the executive vice president for university relations at the time John was admitted. "We did not cultivate them as you might a fine quarterback. They came in over the transom." At the time, Director of Admissions James Rogers repeated the same story. Brown, he told *The Providence Journal*, had given "no special consideration" to John's application. Rather, he speculated that John chose Brown because of its flexible curriculum.

But in recent interviews, Rogers has admitted that Brown did actively recruit John, saying, "I personally, and other people in the office, worked very hard with Andover in this case." Rogers had learned in August 1978 that John intended to apply to Brown and that, if accepted, he would enroll. "How academically weak is he?" Rogers asked the Andover guidance counselor. He learned that John was "a perfectly good student, not a great student, but a fairly good student." The reality, however, is that "fairly good" students who had been held back a year in high school do not get accepted into Brown. Rogers understood acutely the power of John's name and his ability to create "buzz" for the university. "I knew immediately that this was a case where we would gain publicity," he said. "He was a national figure with reasonable grades." When asked what quality he thought John would bring to Brown, Rogers responded: "recognition." He anticipated that John "would be in the news, and next to his name would be an indication that he went to Brown." The admissions office, he conceded, went "out of [its] way to admit students that were influential and would be followed by other students."

It is not uncommon for universities to admit students with an eye to securing donations from their wealthy parents. But what made Brown unique was that it recruited students with development potential as its top admissions priority, focusing on attracting not just wealthy families but also opinion makers. In this case, opinion makers often meant the children of celebrities, who could elevate the university's prestige and stature. In addition to John, during my time at Brown, I taught William Mondale, the son of former vice president and 1984 Democratic presidential nominee Walter Mondale, and Donna Zaccaro, the daughter of Mondale's running mate, Geraldine Ferraro. Over the next few years, Brown would admit the children of two Beatles, director Steven Spielberg, and actors Marlon Brando, Dustin Hoffman, Jane Fonda, and Kevin Costner, among other celebrities.

The strategy appears to have worked. During his freshman year, when word had spread that John was on campus, the university boasted a record number of applications, marking a 4.8 percent increase over the previous year and a 31 percent increase over the previous three years. Brown received more than 11,800 applications for its 1980 freshman class, while other Ivy League schools saw no significant increases in their applicant pools. The new applicants overwhelmed the admissions office, requiring staff to work evening hours. In 1983, the year John graduated, Brown received the most applications of any school in the Ivy League. The 13,250 applicants increased 13 percent from the previous year. Meanwhile, Harvard, Yale, and Princeton Universities witnessed a drop in the number of students applying for admission. *The New York Times* declared that Brown had become the most popular school on the East Coast, reversing its image as a haven for students who could not get into more prestigious institutions. That same year, the university's five-year campaign reached its ambitious goal of $158 million, becoming the largest fund-raising drive in Brown's history.

There can be little doubt that the buzz generated by John's admission helped boost the school's profile and its popularity. Brown's decision to recruit and admit John despite his lackluster academic record accomplished exactly what the university had planned. By coincidence, I applied to Brown's Graduate Program in American Civilization the same year that John submitted his application, and we both arrived on campus in the fall of 1979. Even his acceptance earned headlines in newspapers across the country. Once he enrolled, it was impossible to talk about Brown without John's name coming up. Richard Gray Jr., who was recruited to play football at Brown the year after John enrolled, recalled that "everywhere I went, all I heard was that John Kennedy was on campus. If you told people you attended Brown, the first thing they would mention is that John Kennedy goes there."

Brown faculty and administrators bristle at any suggestion that the university's sudden popularity had anything to do with John. It is true that there were other unique features that made Brown enticing to prospective students. Publicly, the university credited "the attractiveness to students of Brown's flexible curriculum, particularly in a time when many other selective institutions are reinstating less flexible, core-type programs." It is also impossible to ignore the role that Howard Swearer played in stabilizing the school's rocky finances and improving morale on campus.

Years later, Rogers bragged that in his two decades as Brown's admissions director, his greatest contribution "was the admission and matriculation of John." He observed correctly that "people began to talk about Brown."

The summer before entering Brown, John signed up for another outdoor adventure. This time he and thirteen other students successfully completed a six-week National Outdoor Leadership School course in Kenya. The course required participants to hike sixty-two miles through the Maasai territory, surviving on dehydrated food, flour, and cheese. John's group spent the first week in dense bush country, where they managed to get lost. A member of the group remarked that John's main worry was "how concerned his family would be if his experience ever made newspaper headlines." The worried course director, Lou Awodey, sent out planes and even Maasai warriors, who found the team several days later. Awodey, impressed by John's performance, recalled, "John acquitted himself very well. He really enjoyed physical challenges of all sorts. His experiences had enough danger and adventure to hold any young person's interest, and his ordeal on the hike proved he can be counted on to keep a cool head. He took a tremendous step toward maturity during this grueling course."

On August 12 John wrote Sasha from a small café where he was amusing himself by watching a chicken digging for bugs while pooping on his foot. He joked that he spent a good deal of time going to the bathroom while on safari, earning himself the nickname "DIRTY Johnny" or "Johnny Rotten." "Food is so rough!" he wrote. And while he marveled at the interesting animals, apparently the biggest attraction for him was the "GREAT REEFER," which sold for only $2 per ounce.

On September 10, 1979, John stood in line outside Alumnae Hall, along with hundreds of other freshmen, to register for classes. Brown had made no special accommodations for him to register privately. He arrived at two o'clock, and, within seconds, photographers and reporters swarmed around him. Initially, John marched away in frustration. "Come on, you guys!" he pleaded, before a photographer offered a deal: if he posed for photos, they would leave him alone. John agreed, but as soon as they finished the photo session, a television crew arrived and began filming. *The Providence Journal* described John as "pleasant and accommodating" while fielding questions, telling reporters that he was thinking of majoring in history but had not yet settled on a career.

Adjusting to college life was demanding enough, but John also found himself pulled into the family business, as his uncle Senator Edward Kennedy was challenging President Jimmy Carter in the 1980 Democratic primaries. Amid soaring inflation and rising unemployment, Carter's presidency had hit a low point. By the fall of 1979, Teddy faced a decision that had plagued him every four years since the death of his brother Robert: whether to run for the presidency. Publicly, Kennedy declared that he expected the incumbent to win the nomination and insisted he would support him. But privately, he thought of challenging Carter in the upcoming primaries. National polls showed the senator outpacing the president by a 3-to-1 margin. Carter was not intimidated by the polls, however, telling reporters that if Kennedy ran, "I'll kick his ass."

For one day in October, the two men put aside their differences when Carter joined the Kennedy family to celebrate the opening of the John F. Kennedy Presidential Library in Boston. John sat next to his mom and sister, listening to his uncle tell the seven thousand attendees that his brother "would've loved this site and the library his family and friends and country have built to celebrate his life." Carter praised the slain president as a man who "summoned our nation out of complacency and set it on a path of excitement and hope." Then Caroline introduced John, who read a poem by the Englishman Stephen Spender, "I Think Continually of Those."

I think continually of those who were truly great . . .
Who wore at their hearts the fire's centre.

Oddly enough, this event marked the first time many people had heard John speak. "One thing that surprised us was his not having an accent," noted a photographer. "His cousin Joe and all his other cousins have Boston accents. But John didn't sound like Boston—or New York, either. His voice was flat, with no accent at all. But he was gorgeous, and everyone watching that day were stunned by his looks and his charisma."

By the time he attended Brown, John was no longer the scrawny kid whom his cousins dismissed as a mama's boy or the awkward teenager with braces. Christina Haag, who had known John in high school and was now a junior at

Brown, was surprised by how much he had changed by the time he arrived on campus. "Something about him was different," she reflected. "In a summer, he had changed. Taller, more handsome; I couldn't put a finger on it." He seemed more mature and confident. In a short period of time, his body had filled out with muscle—from working out for hours at the gym—and his face took on the handsome features that would define him for the rest of his life.

The evening before the event, John traveled to Boston with Billy Noonan and Tim Shriver. They had not made a hotel reservation, no one had a credit card, and John never carried cash, yet they still managed to scrounge enough money to afford a room for the night at the elegant Park Plaza. John did not tell anyone his last name. The concierge, who did not recognize John, was reluctant to rent a room to three teenagers paying cash, so John found a pay phone and called his mother. "Mommy, I'm here with Billy and Timmy in Boston, but the hotel won't take our cash, and I don't have any checks. What should I do?" Mrs. Onassis asked for the name of the desk clerk. John hung up, turned to his friends, and said, grinning, "Let's go back to the desk to watch this."

A few seconds later, the phone rang at the front desk. "Yes, this is Robert," the concierge answered. "Yes, I see the three boys." Suddenly his eyes snapped open. "Can you repeat that? . . . Oh, my God, yes, of course we can. . . . Yes. . . . Of course." He immediately summoned the bellhop. "Please take Mr. Kennedy and his friends up to their room," he requested, and then proceeded to apologize profusely to John's mom.

The truce between Carter and Ted Kennedy did not last for long. On November 7, 1979, at Boston's Faneuil Hall, Kennedy announced his bid for the presidency. Portraying Carter as a weak and ineffective leader who had abandoned the party's liberal tradition, he declared confidently, "The only thing that paralyzes us today is the myth that we cannot move." Teddy adopted the same themes as John's dad had when he ran for president in 1960, arguing that the nation needed new leadership to tackle the challenges ahead. Teddy also deeply understood John's charisma on the campaign trail. What better way to remind voters of the connection between the past and present than to see and hear from the son and namesake of his slain brother? Teddy wanted John to play an active role in the campaign, but John resisted. Not only was he not ready for the exposure and the rough-and-tumble of a presidential race, but he also wanted to be a "normal" college student—or at least as normal as his life could allow.

John made only a few appearances for his uncle. In December he visited Portland, Maine, where hundreds of people turned out to hear him speak. John avoided specific political issues and instead commended his uncle's leadership qualities, saying that he had the rare ability to "galvanize the nation." John also made clear that he would not take a semester off to campaign. "It's my first year," he insisted. "I think it's better if I stick it out." Many audience members did not care much about the substance of what John said. "All I can remember is the picture of that little kid saluting at his father's funeral," said a state legislator.

The following month, John appeared at a press conference in the downtown law office of a former governor serving as chairman of the Kennedy campaign in Rhode Island. John was slated to present a ninety-six-year-old woman with a complimentary ticket to the senator's $100-per-person fundraising event later that month at Providence College. Staffers for the senator told reporters that John's presence indicated that he would be taking an active role in his uncle's campaign, but John clarified that he would spend most of his time studying even as he did "a couple of things" to help the campaign. "I'm glad to do anything for my uncle," he said, adding that he would make himself available to student groups to "help make my uncle more visible and to answer questions about his positions."

This offer, however, did not always benefit John. His friend and Brown student government president Charlie King convinced John to meet with some student leaders at Providence College. While driving to the meeting, Charlie assured John that only a few people would be in attendance. "What should I say?" John asked. "Should I have prepared something?" "No, no," King promised him; it would be very casual and informal. But upon arriving on campus, they were escorted into an auditorium filled with hundreds of guests and a handful of television cameras. They both were shocked. John, furious with Charlie, stumbled through an awkward presentation. The next day, the local papers panned his performance, starkly contrasting him with his eloquent father. *The Providence Journal* noted that his speech was "unlikely to be graven in marble" and that John displayed "none of the charisma his father would have used." A decade later, when he ran into King, John confessed that his appearance that night was one of the most embarrassing of his life.

Furthermore, John's presence on the campaign trail did little to boost his uncle's presidential bid. Though launched with high expectations, Kennedy's campaign quickly imploded. It was not simply that he remained unable to articulate a clear reason for running. The 1969 tragedy on Chappaquiddick Island, Massachusetts, in which a young woman, Mary Jo Kopechne, drowned after Kennedy's car plunged off a small bridge and into a pond late at night, also came back to haunt his campaign.

At the same time, two foreign policy crises boosted Carter's stature. On November 4, 1979, five hundred young Iranians occupied the US embassy in Tehran and held fifty Americans hostage. The students were bitter toward the United States for its having long supported the oppressive regime of the Shah of Iran, who'd gone into exile after being ousted in the 1979 Iranian Revolution, replaced by the Ayatollah Ruhollah Khomeini, a seventy-six-year-old Muslim cleric and politician who blasted the United States as "the great Satan." Then, as the American hostages entered their eighth week of captivity, another crisis developed. On Christmas Day, Soviet troops invaded neighboring Afghanistan, toppling that nation's bumbling puppet regime. The American people instinctively rallied around the president during a time of international crisis. As Kennedy's campaign wilted in the patriotic afterglow, Carter secured his party's nomination on the first ballot in August 1980.

Carter was to face former California governor Ronald Reagan in the general election. The well-known movie and TV actor, who'd switched parties from Democrat to Republican in 1962, articulated a simple but compelling message: love of country, fear of Communism, and scorn of big government. Responding to fears that America's stature in the world faced decline, Reagan called for a muscular foreign policy, including huge increases in military spending. According to John's friend Richard Wiese, as of Election Day John had not registered to vote yet, but Rhode Island offered same-day registration. So that morning, the nineteen-year-old donned a Rastafarian hat and headed to the polling station to cast his ballot. Later that afternoon, and before the announcement of election results, John wrote Sasha about casting his first vote in the presidential election. Though he had voted for Carter, he felt "thoroughly stressed about the prospects." The possibility of a Reagan victory, he wrote, gave him "the dry heaves." Given Reagan's bellicose language, John worried about the prospect of war, asking Sasha if she would attend his good-bye party before he shipped out for basic training. He had reason to be worried, as Reagan trounced the sitting president, receiving 43.5 million votes (51 percent) to Carter's 34.9 million (41 percent). Carter became the first Democrat since Grover Cleveland in 1888, and the first incumbent chief executive since Herbert Hoover in 1932, to be voted out of the Oval Office.

His uncle's failed campaign further distracted John from his studies. Rob Littell, a star lacrosse player from Princeton, New Jersey, who bonded with John during the first week of school, pointed out that John "carried the schedule of two people most of his life. He got at least twice as much mail, twice as many phone calls, and three times as much unsolicited advice as the average busy person. There was always something going on, whether it was a Kennedy Library event or a cousin's campaign or a charitable obligation." John, however, compounded the problem by taking two challenging seminars. In the fall, he signed up for an intensive seminar taught by his advisor Edward Beiser, a political scientist and Harvard-trained lawyer whose classes were considered essential for anyone planning to attend law school. Beiser gave John a failing grade on his first paper, though John ultimately did pass the class. "He was really shaken," Beiser remembered. "He said, 'What am I going to tell my mother?'"

John had even less success in the spring, when he enrolled in Charles Neu's seminar on the history of the Vietnam War. John never should have been in that class, which was designed for third- and fourth-year students with some previous background in American foreign policy. Neu was also a demanding professor who never coddled students. Apparently, John told his freshman advisor that he wanted to take the class, and instead of discouraging him, the advisor took the unusual step of contacting Neu and asking him to accept John. Neu worried that even a bright, academically disciplined freshman would be overwhelmed by the material, but since the request came directly from a respected colleague, he agreed reluctantly.

Why did John lobby to get into a class for which he was clearly unprepared? He likely believed that having grown up reading about his father and listening to tales from former administration officials such as Dave Powers and Robert McNamara, he had a grasp on the war. He probably had never been exposed to the biting critique that Neu offered of his father's handling of Vietnam and especially of Defense Secretary McNamara's role in expanding the conflict. "I detest McNamara and his arrogance," Neu declared, and that contempt showed in class. Over the course of thirteen weeks, Neu dissected many of the myths that John grew up believing—namely, that his father bore little responsibility for expanding the war and that he would have withdrawn after the 1964 election.

Neu remembers John as an indifferent student who spent most of the class staring out a window. Although participation was an important component of the course, he believed that John never truly tried to engage the material. He also made no effort to write the required seminar paper that accounted for a significant portion of one's grade. "Each student in my Vietnam seminar came in to see me, to discuss paper topics. I don't recall that John ever came in," Neu revealed. "Toward the end of the semester, I ran across him on the Brown green, and he said that he needed to see me about his paper. I told him that it was far too late in the semester to begin to research and to write a twenty-five-page paper." Neu said that under these circumstances, most Brown undergraduates "would have appeared during my office hours and made a case for an extension. He never did, and he received no credit for the class."

John was placed on academic probation at the end of his freshman year. On July 2, 1980, John's mother wrote to Dean Karen Romer to acknowledge that she had received a copy of the letter sent to John informing him that he needed to complete two classes in order to remain in "good standing." However, John was in South Africa at the time and not expected home until the end of August. She promised to try to get in touch with him to see if he could return earlier so that he could start working on the classes. "I know he was upset that the professor of his Vietnam course would not give him an extension on the paper he wished very much to write." She claimed that John went to a dean to complain and was told to "leave matters as they were." Reading those words three decades later, Neu responded, "Of course he wasn't going to tell his mother that he had done little of the work for the seminar and that, in fact, he had little interest in writing a paper."

Mrs. Onassis reassured Dean Romer that John took his "academic responsibilities" seriously and that being placed on probation had "galvanized" both her and John. She said she never sought "special consideration" for her children, but she went on to state that "there was an extra burden John carried this year that other students did not. He was asked to campaign almost every weekend for his uncle." She blamed John's academic problems on his trying to do too much "rather than try to get by with as little as possible." Six weeks later, she responded in writing to another dean's message that John had failed to sign up for a required class. She promised Dean Romer that she and John were having "long discussions" about changes he could make during his sophomore year to establish some structure and discipline in his life. "I look forward to hearing that he is off probation—and to never getting another notice that he is on it."

John's summer in South Africa had been spent working for the diamond company owned by Jackie's companion, Maurice Tempelsman. The trip marked his first exposure to the injustices of apartheid. Returning to campus in the fall, he asked his friend Randall Poster, "I've got all this knowledge. Now what do I do with it?" The two decided to create a new campus organization, South African Group for Education, that would be funded by Tempelsman and designed to educate students about the wrongs of apartheid. John used his connections to bring notable speakers to campus, including Andrew Young, an African American civil rights leader who had served as President Carter's ambassador to the United Nations.

In his freshman year, John lived with other first-year students in Brown's West Quad. During his first week, he spotted Pasquale "Pat" Manocchia, a tough, muscular hockey player from a working-class family in Providence, at the other end of the hallway. "Hey, meathead!" John shouted and tossed a Frisbee in his direction. The Frisbee bounced off the wall and landed on the floor a few feet from its intended target. "First of all," Pat told him, "if you're going to throw it at me, at least get it to me." Afterward, they hopped on a bus and struck up a conversation during a field trip to Newport, Rhode Island.

The two men spent plenty of time together and decided, along with a few others, to pledge the Phi Psi fraternity. Like everything else he touched, John transformed a sleepy, low-key fraternity house full of science geeks and a smattering of soccer players into the campus social hotspot. Almost overnight, the fraternity gained a reputation for being home to the beautiful people. On Saturday nights, after a home football game, the frats competed against one another to attract the most students to their parties. "There was a sense of prestige about having more people come to your party," recalled Richard Wiese, president of Phi Psi. "As soon as John joined and his friends joined, not only did we not have to advertise—we had lines outside the door."

Before John moved into the fraternity house, he had to undergo the ritual of hazing, which consisted of pranks and humiliation. John not only participated in the usual hijinks but also seemed to enjoy them. In keeping with tradition, Wiese, who served as John's "big brother" throughout the spring semester of his first year, ordered John to fetch him food and drinks and to do his laundry. John even made Richard a paddle with a mirror and unlit stage lights around it. At one point, four fraternity brothers tried to kidnap John in the middle of a shower, but he managed to overpower them and escape. John took it all in stride, Wiese reflected. "He liked to be the butt of a joke, and he possessed a good, self-deprecating sense of humor."

Hazing ended in a ritual called "hell night." The brothers locked the twenty pledges in a room with two kegs of beer and five bottles of tequila. They then took them out one at a time and dragged them through an obstacle course in the house. Blindfolded and wearing only underwear, John was forced to drink large quantities of alcohol and swallow a live goldfish.

"Crawl, you slime!"

John slithered around on the floor, which had been littered with fish guts and dog food.

Then he moved on to another room, where he was forced to put his hand into a toilet bowl.

"Run your hand through the toilet water and grab what you find there," he was told. When he reached down, he grabbed a peeled banana.

"Thank you, sirs," John said. "That was nice."

In the last test of the night, John was placed in a room that contained an olive atop a large block of ice. "You had to pick up the olive with your ass and walk it over and drop it into a bottle," Pat recalled. "If you dropped it, you had to eat it."

After the hazing, the brothers met to vote on whom to select. As John's big brother, Richard informed him of his acceptance into the fraternity. At the time, John was in a makeup room preparing for a play. Wiese thought, "Oh my God, I can't believe that we just accepted a guy who's got a face full of pancake makeup."

In the fall of his second year, John moved into room 210 with Rob Littell, who shared his sense of adventure and mischief but who had not fully anticipated the challenges of living with John. The first thing they did was to create two sleeping lofts to free up space for their desks. Right away, issues emerged. As usual, John was rambunctious and absentminded. There were no maids to pick up after him or to make sure his clothes were washed and properly folded. Although he was always fun, he could also be the roommate from hell.

Every morning, John would jump out of bed, landing roughly on an old sofa that Rob's mother had given him. After a few weeks of what Littell described as "Tarzan-like behavior," the couch started to tear. Rob would yell at him every morning, "Hey, do you do that at home?" At another point, John decided that he wanted a pet, and not just a dog or cat, but a pig, which he purchased from a local farm. As Littell recalled, the pig "was not a cuddly, potbellied Vietnamese pet, but a fast-growing, sty-loving farm animal." John thought the pig could live with them, but Littell banished it to the basement, where it pooped everywhere. After a week, John drove the pig back to the farm.

John also showed little regard for Rob's belongings, especially his new Mazda GLC, using it to transport the pig back and forth from the farm. But that was only the beginning. He borrowed the sedan to go to Boston to visit his girlfriend Jenny. According to John, Jenny lost the keys to Rob's car. So the Mazda sat on the street in Boston for more than a week before it was eventually stolen. In a letter to his friend Sasha, John wrote, "[T]o say that I was filled with murderous rage is a gargantuan understatement." But even after Littell's car had been found and returned, John ended up totaling it in a rainstorm, though he insisted that the accident had not been his fault. All these problems, however, did little to dampen their friendship, which, in fact, would only deepen over the years and endure until the end.

John's recklessness with cars also meant that he became an avid collector of speeding tickets during his four years at Brown. In September 1981 he avoided arrest by going to a municipal court and paying $108 in overdue fines and traffic violations. The local police chief had said that law enforcement planned to fan out the next morning with a hundred arrest warrants for people who had ten or more unpaid traffic or parking tickets. In January 1983 John failed to appear at a hearing on a speeding summons, and his

Massachusetts driver's license was suspended. He had been caught in West-port, Connecticut, driving eighty-one miles per hour in a fifty-five zone on the Connecticut Turnpike. The Kennedy family lawyer who represented him in court explained that John missed the hearing because he had been traveling to Brown and most likely "became immersed in exams and just forgot the date of the hearing."

On several occasions, John's famous mom would show up at the frater-nity house wanting to see him. Wiese recalled one encounter when John had to leave for a few minutes and designated him to stand watch. "I've got to drop off a paper at a professor's house," John said. "But my mother is sup-posed to come and meet me here. If you see her, please tell her I'll be back in a minute. You know what she looks like. Black hair, black glasses." Richard found it amusing that John felt he needed to describe his mother, Jacqueline Kennedy Onassis. "I'll figure it out," Wiese replied.

When Jackie arrived, she asked Richard if she could use the phone. But there were two complications. They had thrown a party the night before, so the floors were still coated in spilled beer. "I will never forget her patent leather shoes sticking to the floor as she walked," Wiese said. The bigger problem, though, was that John and Rob were notorious for having the dirt-iest, foulest-smelling room in the house. Richard was reluctant to show her the room, but she insisted. It was, he recalled, "a disaster. You could not even see the floor." Mrs. Onassis scanned the mess, trying to find the phone. Fi-nally, she located a wire, got down on her hands and knees, and followed it. But it ended up leading to a stereo. At this point, Richard decided to rescue her by inviting her to use the phone in his room.

Perhaps it comes as little surprise that John earned a reputation for bor-rowing clothes and money from his housemates and never returning any-thing. At one dinner, John asked Richard if he could borrow a blue blazer. Wiese resisted, knowing he would never see it again. But John reassured him. "You can sit right next to me. I'll give it to you right after the dinner." By the end of the meal, the jacket sported a large spaghetti sauce stain. "Don't worry," John said. "I'll get it dry cleaned." A month later, Richard went searching for the jacket in John's room and found it crumpled in a ball be-hind the sofa. Wiese admitted that had the situation involved anyone else, he would have been mad. "It was funny because it was John," he recalled. "He could do whatever he wanted, and people still accepted him." They did so in part because he was famous, but also because he possessed genuine warmth and kindheartedness.

Pat Manocchia, who lived next door to John, had similar experiences but was less forgiving. "He would always come borrow stuff," Pat recalled. "It was so annoying." One morning John walked into Pat's room and asked to borrow a towel. "I'll get it back to you," he promised. Two days later Manocchia asked for the towel, but John said he had lost it. Pat promptly marched into John's room, took a stack of his albums hostage, and drove them to his family's house in Providence.

On another day, John knocked again on Pat's door. "Hey, man, do you have twenty bucks?" Manocchia was shocked. "Are you out of your fucking mind? You're asking me to lend you twenty dollars?" John offered to write Pat a check. "Okay, write me a check," Pat responded flatly. He then turned around and sold the check for $50 to a starstruck girl who wanted the signature, not the money. Afterward, Pat told John, "Hey, big boy, if you want to write any more checks, I'm happy to take them."

"What do you mean?" John asked, puzzled. When Pat revealed what he had done, John erupted, "You fucking asshole!" Manocchia responded that there was a simple solution to this problem: "Get your own money."

Despite these spats, John tried to attend all of Pat's home hockey games, sometimes acting like an overly enthusiastic fan. Once, as the Brown team lined up to face off in a tough game against Harvard, Pat noticed John standing behind the visiting team's goalie, screaming like a maniac. "Kick their ass! Kick their ass!" Pat just shook his head. The center forward for Harvard looked back over his shoulder at Pat. "What's up with that guy?" he asked, clearly not knowing who "that guy" was. In another game against Boston University, Pat found himself sentenced to the penalty box. He came home to the frat house to find a message from John: "Stop picking your nose in the penalty box." John told him that he had been with a girl from Harvard when they turned on the television, and "there you were in the penalty box, picking your nose."

While John could be annoying, he was also capable of acts of empathy and kindness. Pat's father died during his sophomore year, so he left campus for a week. On his drive back, he faced a snowstorm. As his car inched its way down Thayer Street, he saw someone running toward the front of his car. He slammed on the brakes, but the car slid, and the person bounced off the hood and fell to the side. Pat was terrified, but before he could turn the car to see what had happened, John's head popped up outside the window. "You're a shitty driver," John said. Pat started screaming at him, "I'm going to kick your ass!" John opened the door and jumped in the backseat. Pat, who was still angry, shouted, "You dented my car!" John then reached over the front seat, gave Pat a hug, and kissed him on the head. "I'm so sorry about your dad." Pat found the gesture very sincere—almost, he reflected, "like a dog would do it." John, he described, "had that Labrador quality to him."

For the most part, John felt safe while living on campus. Numerous girls would stop by the fraternity house unannounced to catch a glimpse of him, but their curiosity was harmless. A few security scares did happen, however, when John's housemates received phone calls from people claiming they would kidnap John. He took all this odd behavior in stride.

There were a few more lighthearted moments as well. For quite some time, a strawberry blonde kept sending him elaborate collages of photos of John in the mail. One Wednesday afternoon, near the end of the school year, she showed up at his room holding a pink suitcase and a stack of collages. John wasn't around, and Rob Littell did not find her threatening, so he sat down and talked to her. She showed Rob the many pictures of John she had cut from magazines and told him detailed stories of the times they had shared together. As she was explaining that she was John's girlfriend, John walked in, and Rob introduced the two. John pulled Rob aside. "Who the hell is that?" he whispered. John went to find campus security, while Rob entertained "Miss Crazy." Once security arrived, they escorted her out of the building and to the local bus station.

Four hours later, however, she was back. With the door unlocked and the room empty, she let herself in, took all of Rob's clothes out of the closet and dresser drawers, and stacked them in piles on the landing. When Rob returned, he found that she had showered and was in her pajamas waiting for John. Rob recalled that she looked at him as if *he* were the crazy one and proceeded to tell him that she was John's roommate. Rob slowly backed out of the room and waited for John. Once more, they called Brown security, which apologized and promised it would not happen again.

But early the next morning, they heard banging on their door, which they had finally decided to lock for the first time that year. Security, understandably fed up, threatened to escort her to the Providence police station, where she would be arrested for trespassing. The thought of her being hauled away proved too much for John and Rob. They asked the guards to leave her alone, and John called a friend, asking if he would keep her occupied. She never showed up again.

At the end of his sophomore year, John moved to Washington, DC, to work as an intern for $100 per week at the Center for Democratic Policy, a group assembled to explore the reasons for the Democratic Party's defeat the previous November. In August 1981, when the internship ended, Senator Kennedy pleaded with John to hold a press conference to let people know what he had been doing over the summer. John disliked talking to the press because he could predict exactly which questions they would ask, but he acquiesced to his uncle's request. In a packed conference, he informed reporters that he "was basically just a normal intern. I've done everything from research to stuffing envelopes." But they pressed him to reveal whether his return to Washington had some larger meaning. Was it a first step toward a political career? As usual, John deflected the question, confessing, "I haven't really thought about it. I'm not really thinking about careers at the moment. . . . I'm not a big planner. Things always sort of surprised me. I have two years of college left, so I'm fortunate enough to be able to see employment in terms of summers."

John managed to politely answer questions without divulging much about himself. In one interesting exchange, reporters asked him what it was like to be in Washington, an indirect reference to the Kennedy legacy. John responded, "I've never been here before." He quickly corrected himself, clarifying that he had no memories of living in the White House. At another point during the conference, the twenty-year-old started fiddling with his tie. "Yeah, it's pretty wrinkled," he said. "Shows I'm doing my own laundry." He then looked at the ink that stained his white shirt. "I would wear one of those plastic pocket protectors," he quipped, "but they make you look like a Republican." He then told reporters that he was staying with Sargent and Eunice Shriver and spent most of his evenings teaching himself how to play the guitar. "I don't really go out a lot," he claimed.

In his junior year, John moved off campus to a house on picturesque Benefit Street, sharing lodging with Rob Littell, Christina Haag, Chris Overbeck, Lynne Weinstein, Cordelia "Dee" Richards, John Hare, and Christiane "Kissy" Amanpour, a British-born student of Iranian descent who was enrolled at the University of Rhode Island. John's bedroom was the smallest and sat on the top floor of the three-story house. Kissy established the rules: they each had to shop and cook once a week and were designated areas of the house to clean. For the most part, John abided by the rules and even earned the prize for the most improved cook, but he did have a major blowup with Haag one time when he and Overbeck failed to buy the proper items for dinner. Also, since he was constantly losing his key, he often entered the house by climbing up the fire escape and crawling in through a second-floor window.

Among his many activities at Brown, John especially enjoyed being onstage and proved to be a talented actor. He told director John Emigh that one of the reasons he loved acting was that he believed people would cast him not because of his family background but because he fit the role best. Jim Barnhill, who taught John in a small scene study class in his sophomore year, described John as "among the best and most talented students" he ever encountered. He thought that John could have been accepted into Juilliard School or the Yale School of Drama. Don Wilmeth, the head of Brown's theater department, agreed that John was skilled but observed that he could also be unfocused. "He had great instincts and did not require a lot of direction. But he was also undisciplined," Wilmeth recalled. Rehearsing demanded an enormous time drain. Actors would spend five or six weeks preparing for a play, and rehearsals were usually scheduled in the evenings and could last up to three hours. "He did what he was supposed to do," Wilmeth said, "but often he was late to rehearsals, and on weekends he would go off to New York."

In the spring of his freshman year, John starred in an Elizabethan comedy titled *Volpone*. He played its hero, Bonario, a dashing professional soldier. "There was an open call for students to appear in the play," recalled Emigh. "John showed up and did the best reading for the part." Perhaps the director spoke truthfully, but it was probably no coincidence that John was an unmasked character in a play in which mostly everyone else wore masks. Surely Emigh understood the attention his play would garner by casting John and keeping him recognizable. However, *The Brown Daily Herald* critic gave John a gushing review: "As Bonario, John Kennedy has certainly secured for himself a firm footing in Brown theater, and to the greater extent deservedly so. Cutting a handsome figure onstage with pencil mustache and rouged cheeks, Kennedy need only loosen up a bit in his dialogue." Emigh agreed, saying, "John was wonderful."

Amid their intense rehearsals, a story appeared in the supermarket tabloid *National Enquirer* claiming that John had his gender switched at birth. The other actors kiddingly banned him from using the men's dressing room. "I don't think the women minded at all," joked Emigh. For the play's promotional materials, John posed for a photo wearing a seventeenth-century French plumed hat. His mom and sister attended opening night and teased him about the extravagant image. "That's going to follow you for the rest of your life," Mrs. Onassis said.

While John appeared in a few plays that Emigh directed, he passed on one. It was Shakespeare's *Henry IV*, which tells the story of a young man who transcends his misspent youth to become king. Even though most of his friends were in it, Emigh reflected, "John wanted nothing to do with that play. It hit too close to home."

During his sophomore year, John appeared in J. M. Synge's *The Playboy of the Western World*, in which he played the lead, Christy Mahon. The role required John to evolve from a shy, meek son controlled by his father into a strong, robust man. Critics claimed that John had been miscast because he was too attractive to play the character. According to *The Brown Daily Herald*, the role required "a metamorphosis that Kennedy is incapable of producing." But the critic blamed poor casting, not John's acting. It was difficult for Kennedy, "with his athletic frame and good looks," to come off as meek. But Emigh disagreed, praising John for transforming himself brilliantly throughout the course of the play. "John shrank into himself and pulled in his energy and then made the transformation," he explained. "He stooped his shoulders, pulled his chest, and made his voice smaller."

In January 1982 John again showed his commitment by cutting off his hair for David Rabe's play *In the Boom Boom Room*. He played the role of Big Al, a foul-mouthed street hoodlum who was dating a go-go dancer. "Kennedy's performance was really the high point of the evening," the *Brown Daily Herald* critic wrote. He brought out his "more sensitive side in a very realistic manner, all this without hardly ever succumbing to the characteristic Pacino-type movements and speech patterns so many actors feel obliged to take on."

John's final theater performance came in April 1983 for Miguel Piñero's

Short Eyes. John played the role of a child molester sent to prison with a bunch of other rough characters. "It was not John F. Kennedy and the guys," recalled Richard Gray Jr. "It was an ensemble." John, he reflected, went out of his way to be like everybody else. "It was clear in the theater community that John never wanted to get anything because of his name. He wanted to be right for the role."

Short Eyes required John to be an abrasive tough guy who used profanity freely, but sometimes the actors would stay in character outside rehearsal. One day the conversation turned to mother jokes. "Especially in the African American community, mother jokes are the building blocks upon which all your humor is built," reflected Stephen Hill, another actor in the play. One day the "mama" jokes turned on John. One of the actors referred to John's mom as Jackie O., opening his mouth wide as if simulating oral sex. John, who laughed at the other mother jokes, did not find the gesture funny. "Hey, man, don't talk about my mother. Don't talk about my mother. Don't talk about my mother," he repeated. "John was as angry as I ever saw him," Hill said. At that moment, Hill realized how fiercely protective John was of Jackie.

In one scene, Gray, as the prison guard, and John, as the prisoner, needed to fight, with Gray grabbing John and throwing him down on a table. "My mom is coming. You think you guys can tone down the language?" John asked. "Yo, man, I don't care," fellow actor Kenneth Robert Jones II told him. "We have to do the play the way we know how to do it." But Gray did ultimately modulate his part. In the scene where John fought another prisoner, Gray was supposed to push him to the ground and say, "I will fuck you up, man. I will slap you down with my dick." Gray thought, "I can't say that with Mrs. Onassis in the front row." So instead he said, "I'll slap the hell out of you."

John was one of the few white actors in an ensemble that included African Americans from backgrounds very different from his own. Jones credited John with changing his views of race relations in America. The two men had grown up in vastly different worlds. John lived amid wealth and privilege, while Jones confronted a gang-infested, black and Hispanic neighborhood in South Phoenix, Arizona. "Yet John was the most genuine, open, and nonjudgmental person I ever met," he reflected. Jones never felt that he was treated any differently than John's rich, white Andover friends. "He never showed there was a line between us," Jones stated.

John was color blind, and Jones noticed another quality that John tried to nurture in himself: he never wanted to appear weak. "He thought that people believed he was soft because he was a president's son and was raised by his mom," but Jones was convinced that John did not want to be perceived that way. He pushed himself physically, participated in sports, and enjoyed outdoor adventure because he felt he needed to constantly prove himself.

Jones also discussed with John whether he planned to enter politics. "My family business hasn't done well for us," John responded. "We don't have much longevity in our family business." When Jones pointed out that people sometimes saluted him when he walked by, John snapped, "Do you think that makes me feel good? It actually reminds me of a terrible time." John stated that he wanted to do something completely different with his life. Although he wasn't sure exactly what his occupation would be, he insisted to Jones that "it definitely will not be politics."

Mrs. Onassis, who attended the opening-night performance of *Short Eyes*, gave them rave reviews, telling the actors, "This was as good as anything on Broadway." Stephen Hill recalled that John's famous mother "radiated this glow of friendliness and warmth. I remember how proud she was of John, how happy John was to be with his mom and introducing her to all of us. It made me realize Jackie Onassis is just another proud mother."

Many people have written that John wanted to be an actor and that his mom objected and forced him to pursue a more traditional legal career. Christopher Andersen quoted a friend as saying, "His mother laid down the law. She told John in no uncertain terms that acting was beneath him, that he was his father's son, and that he had a tradition of public service to uphold." But not all close friends shared that opinion.

"I really think that's just myth," reflected Sasha Chermayeff. "I think he enjoyed acting. But he had no intention of pursuing acting professionally, ever. I never ever heard him say anything seriously about wanting to pursue it as a real life's work." Although director Emigh claimed that John confessed he liked the theater because he would be evaluated based on his talent and not his family name, John was not so naïve as to believe such neutrality existed. He knew there was no escaping his past—not even when he was pretending to be someone else.

As previously mentioned, John once told me that he was actually two people. He was forced to play the role of John Fitzgerald Kennedy Jr., the son of the dynamic president who had inspired our nation. He understood what he represented to millions of people, and he was willing to carry that burden. But he never confused his public role with his private identity. At his core, he remained just John, a typical guy who happened to be the scion of a famous family. People wondered why John loved acting so much. Like Sasha, I agree that he never wanted to make it his career. Instead, I suspect it was largely because he had been acting his whole life, brilliantly playing the part that the country had imposed upon him.

By the time I taught John in the spring of his sophomore year, he had evolved into a respectable B student. In the history department at Brown, most professors lectured twice a week. The class was then broken down into smaller discussion sections of roughly twenty students each, and my job as a teaching assistant was to lead two of these sessions a week to help students synthesize the reading and lectures. I was also responsible for grading exams and papers. Back in the day before computers, the teaching assistant would post a piece of paper with the times of our discussion groups, and students would sign up. It was all very random.

In the class on modern American political history for which I was his teaching assistant, John alternated between engagement and indifference. He logged more than his share of absences, and even when he was present, his mind appeared to wander elsewhere. But once in a while, John came alive and could be passionate about discussing topics, especially civil rights. We spent a session talking about his father's presidency, a potentially tricky situation, but John referred to his father almost clinically as "President Kennedy." He did not try to offer unique insight into his father's thinking or become defensive when other students criticized his father's administration. Students were surprisingly not intimidated by his presence. One young woman even said that JFK was overrated and that people admired him because of the tragic way he died.

Every student was required to write a short review of a book from a preselected list of options. John chose Paul Goodman's *Growing Up Absurd: Problems of Youth in the Organized Society,* a classic text from 1956 that blamed the oppressive nature of corporate capitalism for the growing restlessness among young people. I don't remember much about the paper other than that it was a rather standard B. John failed to adopt a critical voice and seemed more interested in championing the author's cause than in placing it in its appropriate context and exposing flaws in Goodman's thinking.

Students submitted their reviews near the end of the semester; when they finished writing the in-class final, I handed them the graded papers. As John approached, I pulled his paper from the stack. He thanked me and then left the room. A few minutes later, he marched back in and confronted me, asking why he did not get an A. I explained to him that if he wanted to contest the grade, he needed to write a response explaining why he found it unfair. He never responded.

My experience with John was similar to that of Mary Gluck, who taught John in her European intellectual history lecture class in his junior year. He also earned a respectable B in that class, then signed up the next year for her capstone seminar on the same topic. Over two years, she had an opportunity to observe him closely and to evaluate his academic work. "There was a sweetness about him," she recalled. "He possessed a spirit of generosity, engagement, and respect. It was very hard not to like him." She also noticed that he could be very naïve. In one instance, an attractive young woman, one of the brightest students in the class, asked John if he could help with her presentation. She clearly did not need help, but John went to Gluck and asked if she would mind if he helped his classmate. "He seemed oblivious to the larger motive," Gluck said.

John enrolled in Gluck's seminar in the final semester of his senior year, needing to pass the class in order to earn the twenty-eight credits required to graduate. At no point, Gluck recalled, did anyone from the administration inform her that if John did not pass her class, he would fail to graduate. John did not meet the deadline for submitting his twenty-page research paper. On the last day that Gluck could submit grades, John rushed into her office with a copy of his paper on William Wordsworth, a poet who launched the Romantic Age in English literature. Gluck described the paper as "competent" and assigned a grade of B+. "He never had enough patience to sit down and do the work," she reflected. "He liked ideas. He was interested but not that good at exploring complex concepts. He was not a scholar by temperament. But he was an observer of culture and history. John had the social skills and intellectual skills, but he lacked the technical skills to excel."

In the last meeting, Gluck asked John what he planned to do after he graduated and whether he intended to enter politics. "A wall went up," she said, a reaction that surprised her because they had developed a relationship over the previous two years. After a moment, John ventured an answer. "I've been involved in my uncle's campaigns, and it is a very hard life." Because John saw the challenges of political life at a young age, he knew the sacrifices involved, and he was not prepared to take that leap until he felt certain about wanting to join public life. If and when he made that move, he would do so with his eyes wide open.

Though sensitive to his character and weaknesses, Gluck went out of her way to avoid showing John special treatment. She even placed him on the wait list for her seminar and accepted him only after other students dropped out. Yet, in retrospect, she believed that in the effort to treat John the same as everyone else, she ended up handling him differently. Oftentimes students would come to her office hours and talk about their lives and futures. Few people were willing to have that conversation with John, she reflected, "because they feared they would be prying into his life. We censored ourselves. We knew there are places you could not go."

I taught John in the spring of 1981 but had little contact with him the next fall and spring of his junior year. I did, however, have my first exposure to the way the media treated John and his friends. John once described November as "hunting season" on the Kennedys because newspapers and magazines tried to unearth something new and shocking about his father's assassination. It was always a difficult time for him and especially for his mom. Beginning in late October, a reporter from *People* magazine started leaving messages for me with the department secretary, saying that she needed to speak with me. I ignored them, but one day I walked into the building to pick up my mail and found her waiting for me.

She told me that she had talked to John's classmates, who described him as "dumb and disruptive." She wanted to know if I agreed with that assessment. It was not true, and I immediately felt the need to stand up for John. I was too naïve to believe that a reporter would invent stories, and she seemed nice enough. Most important, she offered to buy me lunch at one of the nice restaurants lining Thayer Street, which graduate students on a small stipend could never afford. While stuffing a week's worth of calories in my mouth, she disclosed all the allegedly bad things students were saying about the class. I knew that I could not discuss anything specific about John, such as what grades he earned, but I did need to defend him. I recall saying that John was "bright, intelligent, and articulate." But I was horrified when the issue came out over Thanksgiving. The story quoted me as saying, "I heard that John was a dummy" who "was more interested in sex than in school. But he was very articulate and intelligent." The reporter used me as a prop, substituting her own thoughts for mine. Since it was Thanksgiving, John was away from campus. One day after classes had resumed, I saw him walking toward me, but before I could apologize for my stupidity, John grabbed me, put his arm around my shoulder, and said, "Stevie, I'm so sorry that I put you in that position. Don't worry about it. They do that to lots of my friends. Now you have a sense of what I put up with all the time."

I often saw John around campus that year, but it was not until his senior year that we started spending a considerable amount of time together. I was a frustrated former baseball player, and, since I was now working out with the Brown varsity baseball team, the coach granted me access to the weight room. Beginning in the fall of 1982, I went dutifully every day at three o'clock. John had been playing rugby, but because he'd hurt his shoulder, he started showing up in the weight room around the same time as me. Initially, we said hello to each other, made some small talk, and then went about our individual workouts. But after a few weeks, John started asking me to spot him on the bench press. Soon we were working out together, grunting and sweating, competing to see who could lift the most weight.

One evening I was sitting in the lounge outside the second-floor reading room of Brown's John D. Rockefeller Jr. Library—"the Rock"—when John strolled up to me. "Stevie," he said, "we need to add some cardio to our workouts. Let's find a place around here that has racquetball courts. All Brown has are squash courts, and squash is for pussies." Turning to the Yellow Pages, I discovered a sports complex in Seekonk, Massachusetts, about a twenty-minute drive from campus. On a Friday evening, I hopped into John's Honda hatchback and we drove to the gym. A membership official explained that the gym had both an initiation fee, which I believe was around $90, plus a small monthly charge of around $20. But he said they had a special deal beginning the next day in which they would waive the initiation fee. John knew that I was living off a $5,000 stipend and that it would be difficult for me to afford the initiation fee. Before I could say anything, he thanked the guy and told him that we would return the next morning. He did not want to embarrass me by offering to pay, nor did he want to put me in the position of asking, so he volunteered. He picked me up the next morning, we signed up, and worked out at our new gym for the first of many times.

It was not until we traveled off campus that I witnessed the frenzied way the world reacted to John. He lived a fairly sheltered life at Brown. While there were the usual head turns when he walked down the street, students grew used to seeing him on campus. But every time we went to the gym, there would be five or six very attractive and well-dressed women standing behind the front desk, waving us inside with big smiles. Once, John, who struggled all his life with holding on to keys, lost his locker key while we were working out. "Let me check at the receptionist desk," I told him. "Maybe someone found it and turned it in."

I explained to the woman—the numbers had thinned once we had passed—that my friend had lost his key, and we were wondering if anyone had brought it in. "No, they haven't," she responded excitedly, "but don't worry. We will find it." She hopped onto the intercom, calling all the other attendants to the front desk. Within minutes, a handful of women were crawling around on their knees searching for the key while John and I continued our workout. After a few minutes, one popped up, shouting, "Found it!" She then rushed over to personally hand it to John, who thanked her before continuing with his set of curls.

John never met a mirror he did not like, and he enjoyed showing off his body, even in rather inappropriate ways. Our routine was to lift weights before engaging in intense games of racquetball. Afterward, we would put on our bathing suits and sit in the hot tub or take a steam. There was a sauna in the men's locker room, but the "wet" area with the steam room and hot tub was coed. One day John forgot his bathing suit, so he put on his stretched white underwear and started walking out to go into the hot tub. "John," I said, "you can't go out there like that." He responded, "Stevie, why are you so modest for me?" I wasn't sure what he meant, but we went anyway. There were two older, gray-haired women sitting in the hot tub when John came out and plopped right next to them. They were so startled they practically ran into the women's locker room. We would then take showers and enter the men's sauna wearing only our towels. John would often strip away the towel, inspect his private parts in full view of other people in the room, or get down on the floor to do pushups. Remembering it now, all I can think is how lucky John was that he grew up in an age without cell phone cameras.

It was always curious to me that a guy who was so private would be such an exhibitionist. During touch football games, John would divide the teams into Skins and Shirts. John was always Skins. (Thankfully, he chose me for the Shirts.) It was not difficult to see the photographers with their long-distance lenses peering at him from afar. While he revealed little about himself to the press, he seemed to enjoy exposing his body to the world. It always seemed to me that his body was the one aspect of his life over which he felt some control. His good looks were genetic. His family name was a birthright. But he, and he alone, was responsible for transforming himself from an awkward, scrawny kid into an Adonis. He had spent long hours laboring at the gym, working with trainers, pushing himself to his limit to build muscle mass and burn fat. Years later, when he was living in New York and working on *George*, John would have memberships at more than a dozen gyms. He took great pride in his body and what it represented to him, and he wanted the world to see what he had accomplished without the help of his famous family.

By the time we finished in the evening, the cafeteria at Brown was closed, so John and I would get something to eat on the way back to Providence. A fancy new fast-food restaurant called Wendy's had just opened up, and we probably ate there once a week. Of course, John never had money, so I usually had to spring for dinner.

It was during these many hours that we spent together that I bonded with John. He shared with me stories of his colorful life, and he asked me just as many questions about mine. John was fascinated by people raised under circumstances different from his own. And mine was very different.

When we were young, my dad worked two jobs and still managed to attend school three nights a week to earn an associate degree in engineering. My loving mom stayed home and took care of us—my older brother, Franny, and younger siblings, Mike and Karen. I had been an indifferent high school student, ranking in the bottom 20 percent of my high school graduation class and managing to fail three subjects during my senior year. I'm too embarrassed to mention my SAT scores. I received one honor at graduation: my classmates voted me class clown. (Apparently, the vote was unanimous.) For most of my youth, I dreamed of one day becoming a major-league pitcher, even though I only had a seventy-mile-per-hour fastball, and that was with hurricane-force winds at my back.

After graduating high school, I applied to a handful of local colleges and ended up attending Widener College, only a few miles from our family home. Widener bragged about its strong commitment to a liberal arts education, small classes, and dedicated faculty. But truthfully, I ended up at Widener because it was the only college that accepted me. I tried out for the baseball team and made varsity as a freshman. I thought I was well on my way to playing for my beloved Phillies, standing on the same pitching mound as Steve Carlton and Jim Bunning. But a remarkable thing happened along the way. In my sophomore year, I took a class in medieval history. It wasn't that I had any real interest in medieval history; I did not even know what it was. To me, everything before World War II was medieval history.

As it turned out, however, that class changed my life. It was taught by Dr. Lawrence P. Buck—a young, dynamic professor who was genuinely interested in students and who clearly loved to teach. One day he opened the class for discussion. I remember sitting in the back of the room listening to my classmates and thinking, "Why can't I talk like that? Why can't I articulate my thoughts that way?" At that moment, I realized that I would never be a professional baseball player, and that if I was going to succeed, it would have to be with my untested brain and not my tired right arm.

At the end of class that day, I walked out of the room, went to the gym, and turned in my baseball uniform. I then took out a campus map, discovered that the big white building next to the football stadium was the library, and entered its doors for the first time. Over the next few years, I discovered both a love for history and a passion for learning. Although Widener had admitted me on academic probation, at graduation I managed to win the Faculty Prize, awarded to the undergraduate who earned the highest grade point average (GPA) in their junior and senior years. My next decision was partly influenced by Gordon Wood's *The Creation of the American Republic*, which I thought was the most brilliant book I had ever read. I saw that Wood taught at Brown, so I applied to its graduate program, hoping that he would accept me as his student. But though I went to Brown to study colonial American history, I quickly gravitated to modern America, which I found more accessible.

My love of learning was only one reason I ended up in graduate school.

The other was my fear of dying if I chose the other alternative: doing manual labor. I spent my summers during college making toilet paper at Scott Paper Company in Chester, Pennsylvania. The work was tough. I was required to not only rotate shifts every week but also spend a long time around heavy machinery and sharp objects. My first time on night work, I was given a sharp blade and told to take a large roll of defective toilet paper (roughly five feet in diameter and eight feet long), slice through several layers at a time, and then toss the paper into a churning vat, where it would be turned into pulp and sent back to the mill. I made the first few slices just fine, but suddenly the blade lodged itself into my left thumb. Oddly enough, there was no blood, but I knew I had done serious damage. I casually walked to the nurse's station, where a young woman with one arm in a sling started to examine me. I was playing tough guy until I looked down and saw that I had cut all the way to the bone. Suddenly all the blood rushed out of my body. The nurse struggled to keep me upright while I searched for a safe landing spot on her shiny linoleum floor. Fortunately, a few guys from my crew who were walking by helped lay me on a bed until a security guard took me to the hospital.

I returned with about six stitches and a large bandage wrapped around my thumb. Since it was now five in the morning, and the shift ended in two hours, I assumed the supervisor would either send me home or allow me to rest. I was wrong. He was furious because he now had to fill out a bunch of paperwork. "Gillon," he growled, "I'm going to give you a job that not even you can fuck up." Just to make sure I understood my new duty, he demonstrated it for me. It involved picking up small rolls of paper, about three feet in diameter with a solid cardboard core, and then placing them on a small metal pipe jutting from the floor. Once the roll was securely resting on the device, I needed to press a pedal to shoot the pipe upward and knock out the core, which got tossed into a bin while the paper went back into the vat for reuse. Since I tend to be the curious type, I placed the first roll on the metal tube and, wanting to see how far up the pipe shot, leaned over the device and pressed the pedal. Turns out the pipe came up to my top front teeth, which were now scattered across the metal floor. I was stunned for a few seconds. When I looked up, I could still see my supervisor, who had stopped to talk to someone about thirty feet away. Fearing that I would lose my job, I continued working and kept my mouth closed so no one could see my jagged teeth. By the time the night finally ended, I had shattered my teeth and almost sliced off my thumb.

When people ask me why I chose to be a historian, I always tell the story about being inspired by a dynamic professor. While that is true, it is also only part of the story. I chose my career path because I was too clumsy to do anything else.

John loved hearing about my older brother, Franny, who was a former Philadelphia Golden Gloves champion, an all–Marine Corps titleholder, and, along with future heavyweight champion Leon Spinks, the interservice winner. "Are you sure you and your brother came from the same womb?" he used to tease me. He marveled over people who worked in factories and listened intently to my stories of summers spent making toilet paper. John had completed Outward Bound and had recently finished the Outdoor Leadership course in Kenya, but he had no experience with factory life. He was, however, relentlessly curious.

We also spent a great deal of time discussing politics, and John often expressed surprising views on current events. Although he voted for Jimmy Carter, John came to respect President Reagan out of admiration for presidents who, like his father, could galvanize the nation. He once said, and would repeat a few times later in life, that "politics was about giving people hope. It was about making people believe that the future would be better than the past." He felt that Reagan's eloquence and stature inspired confidence. Liberals snarked about Reagan's lack of knowledge about policy, but John found that critique mistaken. Reagan, he argued, appealed to values, invoked themes, and identified myths that many Americans embraced. That storytelling ability was what made him such a great communicator. He did not agree with Reagan's conservative agenda, but, for him, policy represented a secondary concern. The real purpose of politics was to motivate people, and he felt that Reagan, more than any president since his father, accomplished that goal.

John's political views were difficult to discern, largely because he had yet to settle on an overarching philosophy. But his approach to politics was more like his father's—practical, nonideological, and skeptical of both Left and Right orthodoxies—than those of his uncle Senator Edward Kennedy, who had emerged as the most outspoken leader of the liberal wing of the

Democratic Party. John loved his uncle Teddy, but he did not share Teddy's unquestioned commitment to the liberal agenda. I recall a discussion in which John agreed with the concern of many conservatives that welfare provided a disincentive for people to go out and find jobs. His uncle was the leading critic of that viewpoint, claiming that structural problems in the economy—the lack of employment or effective training—represented the main source of poverty. Therefore, the federal government needed to spend more, not less, to help the poor. But while he may have disagreed with his uncle on specific policies, John did share a deep commitment to equality and an empathy for those less fortunate than him.

I witnessed almost every day how gracefully John handled the expectations placed upon him, and often with a healthy sense of humor. In 1983 John decided he wanted to watch a professional boxing match that would be broadcast over a new network called HBO. In those days, before widespread use of cable television, you needed to go to a bar to watch a fight. John had found a place in South Providence that was showing the event, so we drove there. As we walked into the bar, I saw two pictures on the wall: Jesus Christ and John's dad. Both still had the palms that had been placed on top of the frame the previous Palm Sunday. I knew this night was going to be interesting. The bar was in a working-class, largely Puerto Rican neighborhood, not the usual place for Brown students, who literally lived atop a hill overlooking the city of Providence.

We were standing in the middle of a large crowd watching the fight when I noticed patrons parting in front of us. A little guy, who could have been Danny DeVito's brother, gently pushed me aside and stood a few inches away from John. His arms dropped to his side as he stared upward. "You're John," he uttered in disbelief. "You're John." Understandably, such moments were often uncomfortable for John. He was accustomed to people coming up and shaking his hand or calling out to him on the street. "John-John" some would say, to which John would firmly respond, as usual, "One John is sufficient." But this situation was different. This man was completely mesmerized. After a pause, John muttered, "Yes, I am." The guy lifted his arms and hugged John without inhibition. "I loved your father," he gushed. "I loved your father." He then released his grip on John's torso and started walking away, but not before announcing to the waitress, "Free drinks for my special friend." (I soon discovered that I was not his special friend as well. John drank for free; I had to pay. Fortunately, I drank only soda back then.)

A few minutes later, I saw the crowd parting once again. I turned to John and warned him that he was about to have another visitor. Before he could respond, the Danny DeVito look-alike had returned, this time dragging his wife behind him. "Marilyn," he proclaimed proudly, "I want you to meet my old friend, John Kennedy."

"Old friend? Really?" I thought. They had just met about ten minutes earlier. But John did not miss a beat. "Hi, Marilyn," he said. "I've heard a lot about you. I'm glad to finally have the chance to meet you." Her face lit up immediately, and the two walked away, totally satisfied.

On the way home, I asked John what had just happened and why he pretended to know this random fan. He dissected the scene the way I used to dismember frogs in my high school biology class. The guy owned the bar and had probably told people he was friends with the Kennedy family, John said. He lived in the apartment upstairs; he simply left and brought back his wife. "What harm was done?" he asked. "I made two people very happy tonight." I was oblivious to the dynamics taking place in front of me, but John had an instinctive ability to read a situation quickly and know exactly what to say. In that moment, I realized that John, despite his professed disinterest in public life, had politics embedded in his DNA.

We played our last game of racquetball while at Brown a few days before John's commencement. It was a rather typical afternoon, except that John had to hurry back to campus to meet his mother. He dropped me off at the student union, where I sat on a deck overlooking the serene campus green. After several minutes, I caught a glimpse of a mob of reporters and cameramen moving slowly across the other side of the green. As I looked closer, I saw John in the middle of the scrum. For a second, I thought, "Why are all these people bothering John?" before realizing that he had transformed into John Fitzgerald Kennedy Jr., strolling confidently across campus with his famous mother.

On Saturday, June 4, I joined seven hundred people in a packed auditorium to hear Senator Edward Kennedy speak at a forum on nuclear disarmament. "Instead of lavishing our treasure on first-strike weapons, let us spend it on first-class schools and first-class colleges for students," he thundered.

But the most memorable part of his speech came at the beginning when he spoke of John. "I know how much my brother Jack cherished John's future, and how proud he would be to be here today," Kennedy said, his voice faltering.

That evening, John and his roommates threw an all-night party. John's roommate Rob Littell recalled that the party left them "exhausted and hung over" on graduation day. Still drinking beer at seven thirty in the morning, they quickly showered, changed into clean clothes, and then joined the procession beginning at eight thirty. Students lined up on the campus green before walking through the historic East Side district of Providence as parents, friends, and family watched. Photographers were on the lookout for John, although he was not easy to identify, since the cap covered his distinctive mop of curly brown hair. When they finally spotted him, they rushed toward him with their cameras clicking. Some photographers complained that his friends tried to shield him, but most of his friends were used to the prying eyes of cameras. More likely, the people around John hoped to squeeze into one of the pictures. Littell recalled how one classmate "glued himself unnaturally to John's shoulder as the seniors marched up College Hill, obviously determined to be in the news photos."

The general commencement consisted of all 1,400 graduates on the campus green, where they listened to speakers and witnessed the awarding of honorary degrees. The graduates then headed to their home departments, where they received their degrees. Before the general ceremony ended, a small plane buzzed overhead, skywriting the words, "Good Gluck John." Many assumed that the misspelling was a silly mistake. The Canadian newspaper *Globe and Mail* viewed it as a sign of the problems plaguing the American education system. In fact, the message referred to a playful family joke about how John would not have graduated had he not received a passing grade in Mary Gluck's class. The timing was off, however. The plane was not supposed to start writing until after the general ceremony had ended.

Many of the departments held their ceremonies outside, but the history department broke with tradition and handed out degrees in the safe confines of St. Stephen's Episcopal Church, a 119-year-old stone structure just a few steps away from the green. It offered a small, intimate setting free of reporters. No one seemed to notice that John, his sister, and mother, along with his cousin Anthony Radziwill and Jackie's companion, Maurice Tempelsman, occupied the room. After all the diplomas had been awarded, families posed for pictures. At one point, John handed me a camera and asked me to take a picture of him with his family. Afterward, police and security officials escorted John and his family into two black limousines parked a few feet from the church entrance.

Though John's graduation marked his emergence as a mature young man, for many Americans he still remained that fragile young boy gesturing at his slain father. "The image of a small boy saluting his father's flag-draped casket outside a Washington, DC, cathedral remains vivid in the minds of millions of Americans who were numbed in 1963 by a senseless tragedy," wrote the UPI. But John, the news agency acknowledged, was "no longer the imp who played hide-and-seek beneath his father's Oval Office desk." The challenge for John would be to establish his own identity, freed from the haunting images of his past.

Two months after graduation, John decided to join a treasure hunting expedition with an old friend, Barry Clifford. Among his many other activities, John enjoyed scuba diving. In 1979 and 1980, Clifford and John dove together off the coast of Martha's Vineyard exploring shipwrecks. On one occasion, they and another diver, John Beyer, descended deep into the bowels of a World War I freighter when Beyer's regulator broke, leaving him unable to breathe. "Kennedy immediately gave Beyer his regulator, and they buddy breathed," Clifford recalled. "But it wasn't just a simple buddy breathing where you had to get to the surface. We had to go through these passageways that were falling—like going through a maze—to get out of the ship. But John didn't even blink. There was no panic. It was just cool, calm, collected, business as usual."

During their dives, the two men decided to search for the remains of the *Whydah Gally*, originally a slave ship that had been captured by pirates led by Samuel "Black Sam" Bellamy. In 1717 a violent storm sunk the ship off Cape Cod, killing all but two of the 146 men on board. The *Whydah* was loaded with the plunder of fifty ships, worth an estimated $400 million. "It's like finding a department store on a shipwreck from the eighteenth century," Clifford said. The captain of a research vessel called the *Vast Explorer,* which was leading the expedition, was a rough, old-school, six-foot-ten, 325-pound guy nicknamed Stretch. John wanted to go on the treasure hunt, but Stretch was not enthusiastic about having an inexperienced Ivy League preppie on his ship. Clifford pleaded John's case. "Look," he told the captain, "I've been diving with this guy for years, and he's good. He's a good diver and a helluva athlete, and you can depend on him, believe me." Relenting, Stretch allowed John on his ship, but from the very first day, he did everything he could to force John to quit. He gave him the dirtiest jobs, ordering him to crawl into a little section of the ship to paint the rudder posts. "Kennedy," Clifford recalled, "was breathing engine fumes and wearing lead paint," but he never complained. His efforts eventually earned Stretch's respect, and he welcomed him as part of the team.

At one point, as John and Clifford were searching for what they hoped were the ruins of the *Whydah*, John found himself trapped under an avalanche of sand. "It was like being buried alive," he told Clifford. Fortunately, John exercised his skills as a diver and managed to escape by holding his arms to his side, keeping his body rigid, and moving his fins with just his ankles. After this incident, John became convinced that he had found the ship's cannons, drawing pictures of them as proof. But the archeologists dismissed his claims. The following year, however, Clifford went diving in the same spot and found the cannons. In 2007, when divers began the process of removing the cannons that John had identified, they found a plastic compass bearing the initials *J.F.K.* attached to one of them. Clifford speculated that the sharp metal had ripped the compass from John's wetsuit as he tried to free himself.

In October John traveled to India, where officially he planned to study food production, health, and education under the direction of a professor at Delhi University. It seems more likely, however, that John wanted to escape, immerse himself in a mysterious place, and spend time thinking about his future. According to his Brown roommate and future girlfriend Christina Haag, John believed that spending time in India represented "an invaluable opportunity to have distance from home, friends, family, and country, and he was excited to live in a place where everything from government to food to sex was considered in a completely different manner." John grew up hearing stories about the exotic beauty of the nation from his mom, who traveled there as first lady, as well as from family friends, especially the famed economist John Kenneth Galbraith, who served as US ambassador to India during the Kennedy administration.

John recorded his travels in a diary, which the family controls, and much of his time there remains undocumented, but he did write letters and post-cards that offer a glimpse into his six months abroad. I had the sense that John did not maintain a diary when he was in the United States. But India was different. It was the first time that John was free from the media circus for an extended period of time, living in a different culture and experiencing unique situations. It made him very contemplative. He told me later that he spent a lot of time sitting in a tree, smoking pot, and contemplating "the meaning of life."

The Indian government coordinated with the US embassy to protect John's identity. Instead of staying at the embassy, he moved around New Delhi, sleeping on floors and occasionally staying at the embassies of other governments or in dingy hotels in the city center. At a wine and cheese party at the Irish embassy, John met the Indian journalist Narendra Taneja, who was surprised to learn that the famous son of a famous US president was spending nights in a sleeping bag on the floor of an embassy official's home. Taneja had just moved to the Indian Institute of Technology, where he was staying in a four-room house, so he offered to share the space with John.

The next morning, an official from the American embassy visited Taneja and warned him not to reveal John's identity to anyone. A professor, how-ever, discovered that John was on campus and invited them to his house for tea. "I hesitated but agreed, telling him no one else should know about him staying here," Taneja told his son, who later wrote about his father's experi-ence. When they arrived, they found twenty people gathered in the living room waiting for them. "We decided to stay even though I had asked him specifically not to let anyone know," Taneja said. After a few minutes, the professor asked John, "So, do you remember when your father was assassi-nated?" Taneja described John as "aghast" at the question, and the two im-mediately left the house. Taneja apologized to John as they headed home. "It's okay," he replied. "It's just that no one ever asks me that."

While in Delhi, John wrote Sasha, telling her that he was studying under inspiring professors as well as interviewing locals about life in India. He confessed to being lonely but said the solitude was manageable. He was not impressed by New Delhi, which he described as "soulless and nonrepresen-tative." Much of his time was spent dealing with more practical matters. He struggled with the Indian practice of eating with the right hand while "the left is saved for foreplay and wiping your ass." Since he was left-handed, John wondered what "proper Indians" thought when he plowed "into the communal rice ball with my, as far as they are concerned, fetid, freshly soiled left hand." Like many Westerners who travel in India, John often described the challenges of adjusting to Indian food. He told Sasha about having to submit stool samples to check for intestinal worms. Not only did he have to use the restroom every two minutes, he wrote, but he had to "drop a little sample of one's own in a Dixie cup and trundle it over to the laboratory, look the lady straight in the eye, and ask her to poke through it for you."

At one point, John joined Taneja on a trip to Tundla, a small, remote town in the state of Uttar Pradesh. Getting there required using third-class accommodations on crowded trains. "He not once complained throughout his stay about anything," Taneja wrote. "In fact, he even took up some typical Indian traits, such as haggling with the *tuk-tuk* driver over the price of the journey." Not only did John not complain, he told Sasha that it was impossible to understand what it was like to be poor in India without traveling third class. Spending twenty-four hours "in frantically crowded trains with families and all their belongings (from food to plows to chickens in boxes) is a great opportunity to indulge in a bit of in-depth study," he wrote. He observed that many Indians who work hard to have the opportunity to travel first class could not understand "why this crazy Westerner is trying equally hard to be poor."

While in Tundla, John had his hands examined by a palm reader, who seemed startled by what he found. "This man is the son of a king," he said. "You have to be the son of a king. Who are you?" Later that day, John insisted on returning to meet the palmist, but this time alone. He spent more than two hours with him.

John stayed with Taneja for a week before moving on to Calcutta, later named Kolkata, where he roomed with another journalist at the request of the Indian government. "He stayed with us for a week," his host recalled. "It was great fun having him. I remember that women used to line up around the staircase of the building as he ran up and down, bare bodied, for eight floors whenever there was no electricity and the lift would not work." While in Kolkata, John visited Mother Teresa's Missionaries of Charity headquarters, where he met with the nun herself. He later said that Mother Teresa made him believe in the existence of God, a comment that would have shocked his devoutly Catholic paternal grandmother.

John and I corresponded a few times during his travels through India. He was fascinated by the upcoming 1984 presidential election and frustrated by the dearth of information available to him. He said that his "soul was in America" and that he was desperate for news about the primaries that did not come from British papers. President Ronald Reagan was running unopposed for the Republican nomination. Meanwhile, former vice president Walter Mondale, who had secured the endorsements of most major Democratic Party leaders, found himself fighting for his political life when Gary Hart, a youthful senator from Colorado, defeated him in the crucial New Hampshire primary. Hart fashioned himself as a new JFK, calling for "new ideas and new leadership," and "a new generation of leadership [for] a new generation of Americans." Hart embraced Arthur M. Schlesinger's "cycles of history" argument that every three decades, the nation experienced a burst of new ideas, beginning with FDR in 1932 and President Kennedy in 1960. John found the argument intriguing. "But Stevie, what about Gary Hart?" he asked. "Are we hitting another thirty-year peak, as he claims? What about JFK overtones? What the fuck is going on?"

John had plenty of free time in India to ponder what he should do when he returned. Initially, he considered a graduate program in public affairs. I remember telling him that graduate education, which was tightly regimented, was not an ideal place to figure out what you wanted to do with your life. He wrote later that he received similar advice from his Brown advisor Edward Beiser, who cautioned, "It's a basic mistake to go there [graduate school] and think it will somehow help you figure out what you want to do with yourself."

But John's self-exploration went beyond debating practical steps about whether to attend graduate school or law school. John faced an existential crisis. He needed to discover his place in the world and establish an identity separate from his famous family. While still at Brown, John contacted John Perry Barlow, the Grateful Dead lyricist and essayist, whom he often turned to for advice. "You know, this is going to sound incredibly arrogant," he said, "but it would be a cakewalk for me to be a great man. I'm completely set up. Everyone expects me to be a great man. I even have a lot of the skills and tools. The thing is, I've been reading the biographies of great men, and it seems like all of them, my father included, were shitheads when they got home. Even Gandhi beat his wife." John confessed that the real challenge for him "would be to set out to become a good man." But first he needed to define precisely what it meant to be "a good man."

John had hoped that by escaping the pressures of celebrity at home and throwing himself into a challenging new environment, he would get closer to grasping the substance of a good man. He likely anticipated that spending six months in India would help him discover his calling and guide him toward a career path. But that inspiration never materialized. As he prepared to return home, he told Sasha that he learned a great deal during his time abroad. But, he wrote, "The question is, where is this all taking me?"

CHAPTER 6

"I'M NOT MY FATHER"

In 1984, after returning from India, John and former Brown roommate Rob Littell decided to live together again. John insisted that they find an apartment near Central Park, so they leased a two-bedroom, two-bathroom unit on West Eighty-Sixth Street, a few blocks from the park. The only issue with the apartment was that it contained a master bedroom larger than the other. John proposed that they switch rooms every six months rather than pay different rents.

In many ways, John could be regarded as the most visible metrosexual of his time: an urban, straight man who spent a great deal of time and money on grooming. Naturally handsome, he possessed his mother's aquiline face and her dark hair and eyes. He enhanced his natural features by getting facials long before such luxuries were fashionable for men. I knew John from the time he was nineteen years old and rarely saw a skin blemish. He continued to work hard maintaining his toned physique. By his midtwenties, John stood six foot one and weighed 187 pounds of solid, sculpted muscle.

John was a man constantly in motion. He simply had trouble sitting still for any length of time. When not lifting weights or playing racquetball, he headed to Central Park to toss a Frisbee or play touch football. The activities did not end there: he also enjoyed swimming, surfing, skiing, snorkeling, kayaking, hiking, and camping. He flew as a passenger in F-15 fighter jets and parachuted out of airplanes. The more danger, the better. John explained to his friend Billy Noonan why he was so committed to physical activity: "If I stop to think about it all, I would just sit down and fall apart."

The challenge for his friends was to look beyond his status as a national icon and accept him simply as "John"—a real human being with the same emotions and struggles as everyone else (and a few more). I realized this truth early on. One evening, as I was getting out of his car after spending a few hours together, I felt that I needed to say what I thought about him. "You know what, John? When I remove all that stuff that revolves around you because of your family and just look at the person sitting in front of me right now, I see a really good guy. Someone who is warm, kind, gentle, thoughtful. I just want you to know that." He seemed genuinely touched. And I meant what I had said. John was simply a very likable guy: warm, funny, down-to-earth, and unfailingly polite. He could be careless and absentminded, but never intentionally rude. In fact, it was part of his charm and provided endless fodder for teasing. He exuded boundless energy and love of life that magnetized those around him. He had an ironic sense of humor and loved telling stories. He made fun of everyone, including himself, and was a great mimic. He used to imitate Barbra Streisand complaining about the paparazzi right before breaking into the chorus of "People," from the musical *Funny Girl*. He could leave you rolling on the floor with his impersonations of family members, especially his uncle Ted Kennedy and Arnold Schwarzenegger, who was married to his cousin Maria Shriver. But he was also the person from whom you would seek serious advice. In private he could be sad and pensive, but he would never allow the public to see that side of him.

John loved New York, and the city loved him back. He could be seen cheering loudly for the Knicks at Madison Square Garden or rooting for the Mets at Shea Stadium. Rob Littell claimed that going out with John in the evening was "like having a key to the city. He was invited to everything. Doormen bowed and velvet ropes fell when he stepped out of the cab." John knew the most popular clubs in the city and the best nights to visit them. He could waltz into the busiest restaurant in New York and be ushered quickly to a table.

Unsurprisingly, John's presence tended to generate overenthusiasm. "John was absolutely attacked by a crowd of mostly over-seventy-year-old women," observed a bystander at a local market. "They were climbing over the lox counter to get to him." Most often, people would stare, point, and whisper. Some would shout out his name. I can't tell you how many people I have seen trip over curbs or walk into telephone poles while doing a double take. Oddly, it was usually men who embarrassed themselves. Women had no trouble stopping in their tracks to stare, but men who did not want to get caught checking out another guy tried with limited success to walk and glance simultaneously.

Over the years, John had developed methods for dealing with this kind of adoration. He was always late, especially if meeting at a public place such as a restaurant. This unpunctuality was mostly strategic, as the last place he wanted to be trapped was standing in line in full view of other patrons or passersby while waiting for a table. When walking down the street, he kept his head down to avoid eye contact. On all but the hottest days, he would wear either a stocking or a wool hat over his head to disguise his easily identifiable curly hair. He would occasionally take the subway, but he preferred to get around town on his bike, which afforded him maximum freedom and enabled quick getaways if followed by the paparazzi.

Despite (or perhaps because of) such efforts, the tabloids continued to document his every move around the city. The widespread use of handheld camcorders made every citizen a potential filmmaker and fed new tabloid television shows that were ready to hand over bundles of cash for any images of John in a compromising position. The two most popular tabloid shows each had a ten-year life-span. *A Current Affair* went on the air in 1986, followed by *Hard Copy* three years later. Nearly every time John was spotted with a different woman, a story would appear on Page Six of the *New York Post* or on tabloid TV.

John's busy social life provided gossipmongers with plenty of fodder. The tabloids salivated when John briefly dated actress Sarah Jessica Parker, who would later star in the popular TV show *Sex and the City*, and pop singer Madonna. While the public seemed to know every detail of John's private life, I remained willfully ignorant. It was complicated for me. For the first decade that we were friends, I had a secret: I was living in the closet. Actually, I was living in a closet inside a locked vault. It's a long story, but coming to terms with my sexuality was a long and difficult struggle. Certainly in the 1980s and early 1990s, I was not ready to discuss it, except with a few very close friends. My fear was that if I asked John questions about his personal life, then mine, too, was fair game. He was clearly curious. Occasionally, he would delicately probe.

"Stevie," he would ask, "what do you do for fun?" Or: "Stevie, do you ever go out on weekends?"

I would quickly, and often awkwardly, change the subject. John, whose emotional IQ was off the charts, clearly picked up on my discomfort and, much to my relief, stopped asking.

But the interest in John's personal life was impossible for anyone to ignore. Jackie's friend Joe Armstrong recalled staying with her on Martha's Vineyard in the summer of 1993. One day after sailing, they walked into a small country store, where she spied a magazine with John's picture on the cover. She let out a sigh and said, "They're going to do to him what they did to me." Jackie, who knew what it was like to be hounded by photographers, be the subject of scurrilous gossip, and sacrifice any semblance of privacy, worried that John would suffer a similar fate.

Like his mother, John always had a love-hate relationship with the tabloids. His mom used to send people to purchase them for her, and she'd read just about everything written about her. Similarly, as much as John disliked being followed by paparazzi, he remained an avid reader of New York's gossip rags. "He was funny because he hated the tabloids, but he loved gossip," recalled a close friend. "He hated being mobbed, but you could sense that if enough time went by and he hadn't gotten any attention, he would do something like take his shirt off or rent a convertible, when the car he was driving wasn't getting him the attention."

The tabloids also loved the fact that John often juggled more than one girlfriend at a time, but it was actually a conscious strategy on his part. John was neither as monogamous as some friends claimed nor as promiscuous as the tabloids suggested. John always needed to appear to be dating because if word spread that he was single he would be "barraged" by dating offers. "John described receiving messages from distant contacts in his father's administration and members of far-flung aristocratic families proposing introductions, which he gracefully sidestepped," recalled friend Barbara Vaughn. John would be monogamous for long periods of time, but once he felt the relationship was fizzling out he would search for a replacement before breaking up.

Unfortunately, that meant there was often overlap, which could lead to awkward moments. One evening he was in bed with a woman when the phone started ringing. He waited for it to stop and then took the phone off the hook, resting it on the table to avoid being interrupted again. John then rolled over and continued what he had been doing. What he did not realize, however, was that he had lifted the receiver prematurely and ended up answering the call. The girlfriend on the other end of the phone listened while John made love to someone else. She started yelling into the receiver. After a few minutes, John realized his mistake and quickly hung up the phone. For most cheating men, that moment would have marked the end of both relationships. But people rarely held John accountable for his actions, and both women forgave him.

In 1985 John started a serious relationship with actress Christina Haag. The two had met as teenagers on New York's Upper East Side, attended Brown together, and even lived in the same Benefit Street house. They did not become romantically involved until they both moved to New York and appeared together onstage in six invitation-only performances of Brian Friel's *Winners* at Manhattan's Irish Arts Center, which was directed by fellow Brown graduate Robin Saex. John thought it would be fun to perform in a play with Christina, and he tamped down any speculation that he would become a professional actor. "This is definitely not a professional acting debut by any means," he told reporters. "It's just a hobby." But the romance with Christina was real. While rehearsing for the play, they traveled to Mrs. Onassis's country estate in New Jersey, where John kissed Christina for the first time. "I've been waiting to do that for a long time," he told her.

John was smitten. "I'm obsessed with you," he told her at one point. "You make me an emotional person, and I'm not." He told Rob Littell that Haag was "the girl I'm going to marry." And Christina was equally enamored of John. "He had his faults, like anyone," she admitted, "but never arrogance, never meanness, never snobbery. What he aimed for, and succeeded some days entertaining, was a remarkable equipoise of humility and confidence that is grace." She introduced John to Cumberland Island off the coast of Georgia, where they stayed at the same inn where, ironically, John would hold his wedding to a different woman a few years later. It was here that John professed his love for Christina for the first time.

Christina also got a taste of John's attraction to danger when they took a kayak trip near Treasure Beach while vacationing in Jamaica. They set out on the two-person kayak with three sandwiches, a mango, and a liter of water. The water seemed calm, so they kept paddling farther. They then moved through a stiff current to reach Pedro Bluff, where they stopped, ate lunch, and watched the dolphins frolicking nearby. John insisted on testing their limits by paddling even farther out in search of a secluded beach. As they inched closer, the gentle swells had turned into angry waves that were breaking on a coral reef just off the shoreline. John spotted a possible opening in the coral just wide enough for the kayak. "If we are going to do this, I need you with me," he pleaded. "And I need you to paddle hard, so we can pull ahead of the break. I can't do it alone. What do you say: Are you game?" Christina nodded. They were only a few yards from the beach when they saw a large boulder blocking the narrow entrance to dry land. She was convinced they would hit it and get thrown into the jagged coral. But just as they approached, a wave lifted them up above the boulder and carried them safely to shore.

The encounter left both John and Christina shaken and too scared to speak. John, who rarely showed fear, paced the beach muttering, "Don't tell Mummy, don't tell Mummy." Christina said that he appeared to be in a trance. His hands were shaking. "I had never seen him like this—not skiing down the chute during a whiteout in Jackson Hole or nearly colliding with a gray whale in Baja." Just as with other dangerous situations John had put himself into, he managed to extricate himself and walk away unscathed. Maybe that was one of the reasons that John remained so careless until the end. He always managed to survive.

After graduating from Brown, Pat Manocchia spent two years playing professional hockey in Spain. In the spring of 1985, he returned to New York and spent a few days living with John and his mom at their New York apartment. Even though it could be intimidating for his guests, it was not uncommon for John to invite friends to stay at 1040 Fifth Avenue, sometimes for extended periods of time. The experience gave Pat unique insight into John and his relationship with Jackie.

"His mom was a character," Pat reflected. On the first night, just the three of them ate dinner together. "When you play hockey, you learn not to be intimidated by people no matter how big they are," Pat said. But Mrs. Onassis was "the most intimidating person" he had ever met. His nerves soon calmed, however. Jackie thanked Pat for inviting John to his house for Sunday dinners while at Brown. "It's good for a mother to have another person's mother taking care of him," she said. Pat responded, "It was fun. And he was reasonably well behaved."

As they chatted, Marta Sgubin, the cook, brought out the dinner of spaghetti and meatballs. John went berserk. "You can't do that!" he shouted. "You can't make that for him! His mother has the best meatballs in the world." Manocchia tried to defuse the situation by pointing out that he would take meatballs any time he could. "I'm not a gravy snob," he assured Mrs. Onassis. "Yes you are!" John retorted. Pat found the situation disarming, and it helped lighten the mood for the evening.

Over dinner, "Mrs. O" talked about the surprising similarities between Pat and John. "You both chose to go to Brown, and you both decided to live abroad. You both are back in New York. Both lost your fathers at a young age. And now you're both discovering how hard it is to find a job." Pat was initially shocked by the suggestion that his friend was having trouble getting a job. "It's a little more complicated than you might think," she said, smiling. Manocchia realized quickly what she meant: everybody wanted to hire John F. Kennedy Jr., but not necessarily for the right reasons.

"At that moment, I really understood how hard it was for him," Pat reflected. "It was difficult for John, or just about anyone else, to know whether people wanted him for his qualifications or for his name. He never knew who was using him."

A few years later, when Manocchia began working daily as a private trainer, he got a glimpse of John's forgetfulness. John had been hounding him to come visit Martha's Vineyard. One day Pat came home from work and found a plane ticket for that Friday taped to his door. The note read, "Just show up." Pat decided to take John up on his offer. He called in sick and used the ticket that John gave him to fly to the Vineyard. He landed at the island's airport, expecting John to be there waiting for him. But no John. Pat called the house, and Mrs. O answered the phone.

"Hi, Mrs. O. This is Pat."

"Are you coming to visit us?" she asked.

"Yes, I'm actually here."

Dead pause.

"Where?" she asked.

"I'm at the airport."

Dead pause.

"John's not there?"

"No, he's not here."

Dead pause.

"Wait there." A few minutes later, Jackie arrived, driving a red jeep and wearing her distinctive kerchief and extra-large sunglasses. "I'm so sorry," she said. "I don't know where he is."

She handed Pat the keys and said she needed to stop in town to grab a few things. They pulled up in front of a small market, and as they walked into the store, two elderly ladies started to approach her. "She looked at them, and they stopped dead five feet from her and walked away. She froze them like nothing I've ever seen."

Shortly after they arrived at the house, John came sauntering up from the beach. "Did you forget that your guest was here?" his mom asked. Pat, never missing an opportunity to tease John, repeated her question: "Yes, did you forget that your guest was here?" "You were supposed to come later," John responded. Pat reminded John that he was the one who bought the ticket, so he should have known what time the plane would land.

In 1989 Manocchia, an avid mountain climber, invited John to join him with a few others to scale Mount Rainier in Washington State. Although John had completed Outward Bound, he had no climbing experience. But as usual, he threw himself into the adventure. They went with a group of hard-core climbers who worried about having a novice climber in their ranks and had to be convinced to allow John to join them.

On the first day, they reached ten thousand feet and decided to camp for the night. The next morning, the party woke up early hoping to reach the summit. They eventually made it to a ridge of solid ice positioned at a forty-five-degree angle and a three-thousand-foot drop to the bottom. As they started making their way across the ridge, the wind picked up, and the guide decided that it was too dangerous to proceed. "We're going back," he announced. John, though the least experienced, exploded.

"I didn't come all the way here not to climb the mountain!" he screamed.

Pat, who usually delighted in poking fun at John, was not impressed by his temper tantrum. "Okay, Mr. *People* Magazine, get the fuck back to the camp!"

As they descended the mountain, events took another unexpected turn. They came across a young girl sitting on a bench in the middle of nowhere. "I knew you were coming here, so I came up because my prom is tonight," she told John. John sent the others down to the camp and spent a few minutes talking to her. When John returned, he told them that the girl had climbed halfway up Mount Rainier just for the opportunity to meet him.

The story did not end there. The next day, they boarded a plane from Seattle to New York for the trip home. As usual, John went wandering around the airport and had to rush to get on the plane before the doors closed. He was supposed to sit in the aisle seat in front of Pat but spied two empty seats farther back and plopped down there. A few seconds later, a woman boarded the plane, saw John, and asked if she could sit in the empty seat beside him. About forty-five minutes into the flight, John signaled to Pat that he needed to talk. They went to the back of the plane near the bathrooms. "You gotta rescue me," John begged. "She is a flight attendant who is from New York. She found out my itinerary and flew today from New York to Seattle to be in the seat next to me for the flight back to New York. When she saw that I had switched seats, she followed me." John told him that the first words out of her mouth were, "You know, my ex-boyfriend said you would not even talk to me."

Pat got a huge laugh out of the situation and told John that he was on his own. John returned briefly to his seat, told the woman that he needed to talk with his friends, and then maneuvered back to his original seat.

After arriving in New York, they headed to the baggage claim, where they found a well-known actress in a full-length mink coat (and nothing else) waiting for him. Manocchia refused to name the actress, but other sources identified her as Sarah Jessica Parker. It was not the first time that Parker had appeared in a similar outfit while waiting for John to retrieve his luggage. She scooped up John, and the two jumped into the backseat of a waiting limousine. Later, John told Pat that he had gone mountain climbing to escape the constant dating and women seeking his attention. "That really worked out for you," Manocchia wisecracked.

Family obligations continued to call. In March 1985 John and his sister, Caroline, met with President Ronald Reagan in the Oval Office. Teddy Kennedy had arranged the visit so that the two of them could ask Reagan to participate in a fund-raising drive for the JFK Library. The Kennedy Library faced a unique challenge because it did not have a living former president to help raise money. Reagan wrote them a follow-up letter saying he would be "delighted" to join them and that he would "stand ready to help in any way I can."

The president kept his promise. On June 24 Reagan joined 250 people for a fund-raising event at Ted Kennedy's home in a high, heavily wooded bluff overlooking the Potomac in McLean, Virginia. The cost amounted to $25,000 a couple. A Reagan speechwriter noted, "This is a great time for Ronald Reagan to take the high road and not discuss party differences but unity, patriotism, the office of the presidency."

The themes of the night centered on patriotism and nonpartisanship. In a symbolic gesture, John presented Reagan with an eagle that had adorned his father's desk in the Oval Office. In his remarks, Ted Kennedy welcomed the president and thanked him for being "extremely kind and generous and hospitable" to members of the family. "You remind us anew of the enduring truth that we are Americans first and only then are we Democrats or Republicans. That we can disagree, we can debate, we can campaign, but beyond that, we treasure a mutual respect and civility towards each other in a shared heritage of freedom." He acknowledged that although President Kennedy would have disagreed with Reagan on many policy issues, "he would have admired the strength of your commitment and your capacity to move the nation." When Reagan began speaking, he praised JFK as a man who "seemed to grasp from the beginning that life is one fast-moving train, and you have to jump on board and hold on to your hat and relish the sweep of the wind as it rushes by." The president described John's father as "self-deprecating yet proud, ironic yet easily moved, highly literary yet utterly at home with the common speech of the workingman."

According to one news report, John "looked contemplative and somber" as he listened to the speeches. The tone and tenor of the evening impacted him hugely. During the 1980s, Teddy Kennedy had emerged as the leading voice of liberalism and a tough critic of President Reagan's conservative agenda. Reagan entered office promising to dismantle many of the social programs that John's uncle had championed for the past two decades. Yet they managed to unite for a common cause, acknowledging their differences while embracing the core values they shared. A few years later, as he contemplated starting a magazine centered on politics and culture, John would recall that pivotal evening.

The following year, on a sunny July afternoon, the entire Kennedy clan gathered at Our Lady of Victory Church in Centerville, Massachusetts, five miles from the Kennedy family compound, to celebrate the marriage of twenty-eight-year-old Caroline to forty-three-year-old Edwin A. Schlossberg, a conceptual artist with a PhD in literature and science from Columbia

University. Caroline had graduated from Radcliffe College at Harvard, worked in the film department at New York's Metropolitan Museum of Art, and had recently completed her first year of law school at Columbia. A crowd of more than a thousand people stood in the heat to catch a glimpse of America's royal family. In a thoughtful gesture, Ed asked John to be his best man.

John and Caroline were as close as brother and sister could be, their bond forged by adversity. In personality and temperament, however, they could not have been more different. Caroline was reserved, distant, and protective of her privacy. For understandable reasons, she fretted that people used her family to sell books and magazines. She was also disciplined and focused, a first-rate student at both Harvard and Columbia Law School. Meanwhile, John managed to create a sphere of privacy while still remaining open and accessible. He had an outgoing and gregarious nature but lacked the discipline to be a good student. While much of the public attention focused on John, he always believed that Caroline faced a harder situation because Jackie insisted that her daughter be perfect in every way. She wanted her to wear designer clothes, maintain an ideal figure, and develop the same refined sensibility that she herself possessed.

Caroline was not interested in such frivolities. Like John, she was fiercely independent and wanted to craft her own identity. As a teen, she rebelled. She wore torn jeans and T-shirts, ate pizza, and enjoyed thick milkshakes. When Caroline was eighteen, Jackie sent her to London to study art history at the famous Sotheby's auction house, but soon the British tabloids were filled with pictures of her late-night antics. John used to say that he felt sorry for his sister because everyone expected *him* to "be a fuckup," while Caroline had to attain perfection.

After the wedding, the family and guests retreated to the compound, where a white tent large enough to accommodate a small circus covered the reception area for four hundred guests. John delivered a moving and heartfelt toast. "All my life, there has just been the three of us: Mummy, Caroline, and I," he told an eclectic group of family, friends, and celebrities. Rob Littell remembered being "surprised at the depth of John's emotions, because I hadn't spent much time around him and his sister."

Except for large family gatherings such as this one, John kept a healthy distance from most of his cousins, but he remained close with Tim Shriver,

William Kennedy Smith, and Anthony Radziwill. In 1982, after graduating from Boston University with a degree in broadcast journalism, Anthony moved to New York, where he and John were now able to spend more time together. Over the next few years, while Anthony pursued a career as a television producer and John attended law school, the two men became constant companions, meeting for meals, playing sports, and traveling together. Most people who knew them remarked on the easy friendship they shared that allowed them to constantly needle each other. It was also clear, however, that they were bound together by mutual bonds of affection, respect, and trust. Anthony was perhaps the only person whom John trusted with his innermost secrets.

At the same time, John did not have much of a relationship with RFK's children. In a sense, he was continuing the practice that his mother started after JFK's assassination, when she moved her family to New York. She always worried that RFK's unruly horde would leave a bad influence on John. Though John did not harbor the same worry, and empathized with his cousins' struggle to emerge from their famous father's shadow, their relationship was always complicated. He found them immature; they found him arrogant. He felt they wore their names and their privilege on their sleeves; they were jealous of the media attention he received. "Don't tell me about the fucking family," he occasionally complained.

Indeed, John resented being lumped together with his cousins. I always sensed that John thought of himself as the first among equals and that the Kennedy legacy was his by birthright. It should be passed to him. It bothered him that so many of his cousins were entering politics and running on the Kennedy name. RFK's two oldest children had entered politics. Kathleen Kennedy Townsend had lost her bid for Congress in the Baltimore area (but went on to serve as lieutenant governor of Maryland for eight years), while Joseph Patrick Kennedy II overcame a troubled youth to win a House seat formerly occupied by John's father—a seat he held for twelve years. Ted Kennedy's youngest son, Patrick, was a state representative and, later, congressman from Rhode Island. Though not ready to throw his hat in the ring, John still resented his cousins for trying to seize control of a legacy he felt belonged to him.

John clashed occasionally with his aunt Ethel as well, who he felt intruded on his space in Hyannis and acted rudely to his girlfriends. In January 1987 John and Christina were scheduled to spend time at the family mansion in Palm Beach. He booked the house in advance through Joseph P. Kennedy Enterprises, which handled the family's extensive investment portfolio. They spent the first night of their vacation at the Breakers Hotel because Ethel was using the house and asked to spend an extra night. But when they arrived the next day, his aunt was still there and occupying John's favorite room near the pool. Although annoyed, John told the Irish housekeeper to bring his bags to his grandfather's room. He and Christina then went to the beach for the afternoon. When they returned, they discovered that Ethel had moved Christina's bags to his grandmother's suite. John let it go. "She's difficult, but she's still my aunt," he told her. But in the kitchen one morning, Ethel brought Christina to tears by refusing to acknowledge her presence. That coldness proved too much for John, who confronted his aunt and warned her that if she did not treat Christina with respect, he would ask her to leave.

His friendship with William Kennedy Smith was also put to the test after Smith was accused of raping a woman at the Palm Beach estate. On March 30, 1991—Good Friday—Smith and Senator Ted Kennedy, who had divorced his wife, Joan, in 1982 and was now single, picked up two women during a night of bar-hopping. Afterward, they returned to the Kennedy estate, where one of the women, Patricia Bowman, would accuse Smith of raping her. John demonstrated his loyalty to William in November 1991, when he joined his cousin in a West Palm Beach, Florida, courthouse for the jury selection. John sat on a wooden bench in the first row of the courtroom, directly behind Smith and his defense team, occasionally jotting on a legal pad. John denied any effort to influence the outcome of the trial. "William is my cousin, and we grew up together. . . . I thought I could at least come down and be with him during some difficult times."

In 1984 John accepted a $20,000-a-year position in the Office of Business Development for New York City. Here he would meet Michael Berman—an encounter that would change the directions of both their lives. Berman, who grew up in an affluent family in Princeton, New Jersey, was three years older than Kennedy. In 1979, after graduating from Lafayette College, Michael settled in New York, where he took a job working for a division of a global advertising company. He quickly became disenchanted working in a large corporate environment and decided to explore his entrepreneurial instincts. Over the next few years, he formed a number of companies in marketing and communication and started handling several big clients, including Pfizer, Hallmark, and Johnson & Johnson.

At the request of a client, Berman volunteered to work pro bono at the Office of Business Development. One day he arrived at the office and was introduced to its newest employee: John Kennedy Jr. Shortly afterward, John invited Michael to a small birthday party of "close friends and family" at his mother's apartment. Instead of finding an intimate formal dinner, he walked into what appeared to be "a glorified frat party in one of the most rarefied apartment buildings in Manhattan." A few weeks later, John asked Michael to join him at a small music club in Manhattan to watch one of his favorite bands. Over the next few years, John would introduce Michael to his eclectic musical taste, inviting him to concerts by Sinéad O'Connor, Bruce Springsteen, the Rolling Stones, and Patti LaBelle.

After a few months, John invited Berman to lunch. He revealed that his uncle Teddy was pressuring him to participate in a few events that would involve talking with reporters. John expressed ambivalence. "I'm willing to do it if I can set some parameters," he told Michael. "I don't want to talk about myself personally, I don't want to talk about my family legacy, and I certainly won't talk about my father." Michael's advice was simple: "Then stay home."

But John continued to struggle with either alternative, so Michael asked why he was reluctant. "That's a good question," John responded. "It makes me uncomfortable. I just don't want to." Berman explained that it was possible to grant interviews "without giving away your deepest, most personal feelings." He told John that he could merely give them a glimpse of himself. "When you speak to a reporter, you need to tell the truth, but you don't have to tell your entire truth," he said.

John asked Michael to serve as his informal publicist. Berman was surprised that John was coming to him with this request, since they hadn't known each other very long. He assumed his family had already set him up with a team of advisors. But instead, it just seemed like he was sent out without out a net; he had no professional support group. John also had never really had much formal media training. "His default position had always been to say no," said Berman. There was no handler, no fixer, no strategist. And there was certainly no tutorial for being John F. Kennedy Jr.

The two men quickly bonded, forming a close friendship and a mutually respectful professional relationship. "When I watched John and Michael, it was more like watching siblings than watching friends," recalled Nancy Haberman, a powerful public relations expert who had been friends with Michael for many years and would later serve as the publicist at *George*. Both were quick witted and shared a similar sense of humor. Haberman remembered being with them one evening and telling John that he had almost single-handedly transformed Brown University into a hot college, noting that nearly half of her daughter's high school graduating class of 105 had applied for admission there. John responded in a voice loud enough to get Michael's attention, "How many applied to Lafayette?" But it was also their differences that contributed to the special alchemy that created their friendship. John could bring attention to any issue with his high-powered celebrity, and it was not lost on Michael that being associated with John helped his business. Furthermore, where John was scattered and unfocused, Michael was disciplined and detail oriented. John trusted Michael, convinced that he would respect his privacy.

John relied on Berman to handle his public image and empowered him to negotiate all his media appearances. From Michael's perspective, it seemed obvious that John, who had always protected his privacy, was inching into the public realm. He would show up at Michael's apartment with lists of topics he wanted to cover at his media appearances. He constantly received requests for interviews from local tabloids and occasionally *The New York Times*. If John held a dinner party, reporters would call Michael and ask for the guest list. Berman also had the unenviable job of managing bad press. John was photographed more than once buying pot on a street corner. Berman would implore reporters not to print the pictures, emphasizing that John was a private person, and the pictures would "ruin his life." Surprisingly, reporters acquiesced.

In 1988 Teddy Kennedy asked John to introduce him at the Democratic National Convention in Atlanta. John was apprehensive but could not say no, so Berman enlisted a media coach named Michael Sheehan to train John for his brief speech. Sheehan recalled seeing John enter the media training room escorted by Teddy, and he was stunned by how handsome John was.

"I said, 'Just go out there and look up. The rest will be easy.'" Sheehan realized the minute he saw him that, with his good looks and his association with his father, there would be an automatic emotional bonding between John and the audience. "He's going to get more applause than you are, so don't be disappointed," Sheehan joked to the senator.

Sheehan described John as cooperative and eager to learn but not especially happy to be present. "It was like he had to ski down a very dangerous hill," Sheehan reflected. "He did not want to be there, but he did not want to disappoint his uncle." Giving a speech in a convention hall had numerous challenges. "They have to get used to the size of the room, the noise, and the visual input, which is overwhelming." The trickiest part was using the teleprompters, one placed on either side of the podium. Without a center prompter, speakers needed to learn how to move back and forth so as not to get stuck reading from one prompter. Despite these difficulties, Sheehan gave John rave reviews. "He was the best person I ever worked with. He had every justification to be a jerk. But he was unfailingly kind and gracious. I would want my sons to grow up to be like him."

The Democratic Convention, held in Atlanta from July 18 to July 21, ended up being a fairly dull event, as the party rallied around its nominee, Massachusetts governor Michael Dukakis, and his running mate, Senator Lloyd Bentsen of Texas. Dukakis, who lacked both a governing philosophy and passion, had secured the nomination after front-runner Gary Hart, who had so fascinated John back in 1984, was caught allegedly having an affair and withdrew from the race.

On the day of his speech, John was pacing around backstage with Andrew Cuomo, the thirty-year-old son of the governor of New York, Mario Cuomo, and his friend Jeffrey Sachs. Both were helping him with his delivery. John was supposed to cut his long hair before appearing on national television, but he was so nervous that he and Cuomo went running on the roof of the convention center in hundred-degree heat. By the time he returned, no time remained for him to get his hair cut.

John ascended the podium at 9:10 P.M. on the second day of the convention. The crowd roared and sprang to its feet, giving him an ovation that lasted longer than a minute. As he tried to speak, delegates gathered near the podium to take his picture. "Over a quarter of a century ago, my father stood before you to accept the nomination for the presidency of the United States,"

he said in a voice that bore little resemblance to either his father's or his uncle's. "So many of you came into public service because of him, and in a very
real sense, because of you he is with us still." He continued, "I'm not a political leader, but I can speak for those of my age who have been inspired by
Teddy to give their energy and their ideas to their community and not just
to themselves.... He has shown that our hope is not lost idealism but a realistic possibility." The thunderous applause nearly drowned out his introduction of Uncle Ted.

John's appearance marked one of the most passionate moments of a
largely passionless convention. UPI noted that John drew "misty eyes from
a charmed" crowd. Conservative activist Richard Viguerie commented, "I
can't remember a word of the speech, but I do remember a good delivery. I
think it was a plus for the Democrats and the boy. He *is* strikingly handsome." All the reports about John's appearance referred to the famous image
of him saluting his father's coffin. Maureen Dowd, writing in *The New York
Times*, noted that the "little boy whose picture saluting his father's funeral
cortege was seared into America's consciousness 25 years ago" was now
grown up. Indeed, the nation could remember him in almost no other way.
This moment marked the first time many saw him again, especially in such
an overtly political environment. His image had appeared in magazines for
years, but there was no matching the power of television. "I remember his
speech at the Atlanta Democratic Convention in 1988," said William Schneider, a political analyst at the conservative think tank the American Enterprise Institute. "It was a success the minute he showed up onstage. There was
an audible gasp. I'm not sure anyone remembers one word of what he said."

Inevitably, speculation arose, much of it encouraged by Senator Kennedy
and his staff, that John's appearance signaled a new desire to get involved in
politics. "It's his debut before the party," claimed a Kennedy spokesman.
Teddy told reporters that he believed John would be involved in public affairs. "Not necessarily running for office but trying to make some sort of
contribution." Cousin Bobby Kennedy Jr., Robert and Ethel's third oldest,
also echoed Teddy: "He has a tremendous sense of duty and responsibility.
Whenever any of the cousins need help on one of their [charity] projects,
John always participates."

The convention speech signaled a turning point for John. With Berman
as his guide, John started assuming a bigger public profile. "He went from

ignoring requests to controlling them," Berman recalled. "He liked participating in things every once in a while, but on his own terms. I think the
understanding that he could take control is what freed him to be able to
participate more. At first, he was tortured by it all, and would often agree to
things and then cancel at the last minute. But once he became more comfortable with the process, it was easier for him. It became yet another sport."

As a child, John felt trapped by the constant presence of the Secret Service; now, as a young adult, he needed to gain greater control over how the
public would see him. He used to complain often, "Don't box me in." He
liked to do the unexpected. For instance, he once posed for an Annie Leibo-
vitz photo in *Vogue*, which "was one of the last places you'd expect to see
him, but it seemed like an easy way to promote a project for the John F. Kennedy School of Government at Harvard University he was working on," said
Berman. "He hosted a six-part documentary, *Heart of the City*, on New York
City's unsung heroes, and while he basically had an open invitation to appear on network TV any time he'd like, he opted for the local PBS station
instead. It was his way of giving back to his adopted city." The documentary
served two purposes: it allowed John to brag about the city he loved while
also gaining more experience in front of the camera. In November 1989 a
division of Random House released an audiobook of John reading his father's *Profiles in Courage*, which earned him a Grammy nomination. He also
appeared one Christmas on *Good Morning America* to read a book to a gathering of children.

These baby steps toward assuming a bigger public profile were dwarfed in
September 1988, when *People* magazine named John "The Sexiest Man Alive."
Many celebrities actively solicited the title, but John knew nothing about it.
Unlike previous selections, which included actors Mel Gibson, Mark Har-
mon, and Harry Hamlin, John was clearly not a professional actor. For the
most part, John got a kick out of the label. His mother worried that it would
make it more difficult for people to take him seriously, but John, who was
proud of his good looks and muscular body, saw it as a badge of honor.

Years later, he said of the story, "It got me my life." While obviously an
exaggeration, it's true that the designation did add luster to his appeal. He
was both a figure of some historic importance and now like a Hollywood
star: a perfect mix of power and celebrity. From then on, it became even
more difficult for him to go unnoticed, and random people would stop him

on the street. "He would be cordial, graceful, and sometimes, depending on his mood, he thanked them," recalled Christina Haag. "Most of the time, he would just let them talk."

In November 1988, one month after the *People* magazine milestone, John got an early taste of the appeal of being the sexiest man alive. He went to Bloomingdale's department store to sell boxes of Christmas tree ornaments designed by disabled people from six developing countries. He was acting on behalf of a program called Very Special Arts, started by his aunt Jean Kennedy Smith in 1974. Other members of the Kennedy family were also present, including cousins William Kennedy Smith and Edward Kennedy Jr., along with actress Lauren Bacall. But virtually everyone who attended the event came to see John. As he walked onto the balcony wearing a blue blazer, red tie, and corduroy trousers, a collective roar erupted: "My God, it's him!" Some of the younger women screamed as if Elvis Presley had appeared. The crowd eventually grew so big that the store had to cut off elevator service to prevent more people from reaching the floor.

"I'm here to sell boxes," John insisted as flashbulbs went off. But clearly, no one was interested in the boxes or his words. They simply wanted a photo. "Turn this way, John! Smile, John!" The newspaper *Newsday* took detailed note of John's appearance: "So here is a young man who must cause the hearts of political kingmakers to throb, their palms to sweat. He has the profile of a matinee idol, and crowds seek him out and bestow on him such precious gifts as attention, respect, and even awe."

A few years after the *People* headline, Berman and his wife, Victoria, were spending a weekend in East Hampton, where they had been invited to a large party. John was also staying in the Hamptons, and he asked Michael if he could join them at the event. "It was one of those early-nineties celebrity-heavy Hamptons parties where most people seemed to be a well-known bold-faced name," Berman recalled. They were used to being the center of attention. But once John walked into the room, all eyes turned to him. "It had to be apparent to everyone there that if there were a hierarchy of celebrity, there was John and then there was everyone else."

In 1989 the Kennedy family had established the John F. Kennedy Profile in Courage Award to honor political figures who adopt unpopular positions for the common good. The award's name came from JFK's 1957 Pulitzer Prize–winning book, the same one that John had recently narrated, which recounted the stories of eight US senators who risked their careers by embracing unconventional causes that they believed would benefit society. "Throughout my life, people have come to me and said, 'I got into government because of your father,'" John stated. "I feel a great pride in that. So, as my father tried to do in his book and in his life, we want to recognize and encourage not only excellence in public service but also rare courage: people who have sacrificed something, taken a position that is politically unpopular and stuck to it because it's the morally right thing to do."

In 1992 John and Caroline decided to promote the award by appearing on *Good Morning America* as well as sitting down for an interview on ABC's news program *Prime Time Live*. The award winner that year was Connecticut governor Lowell Weicker, who had enraged many of his constituents by raising taxes. By this point, John had finished law school, started working for the Manhattan District Attorney's Office, and failed the bar exam twice before passing on the third try.

The extended TV interview would be John's first, so Berman reached out again to Michael Sheehan. They set up shop in Berman's apartment and spent three full days prepping. First, the media consultant guided John through a series of straightforward questions. He taped John's responses and played them back so that he could analyze them. John, he recalled, was "not enthusiastic" about watching the tapes, but he "was willing to learn."

Once John reached a certain comfort level with the process, Michael moved into more sensitive topics that were likely to be asked in the televised interview. The most obvious was the clip of John saluting his father's casket. "What's your reaction to this?" Sheehan asked. "Look," John responded, "there are things I remember and there are things I don't remember. I really don't remember that." Next, John deflected a question about the many books that had been published digging into his father's infidelity: "People had this idea that we spend all of our time at Hyannis running around the house singing the score to *Camelot*." John made it clear that he possessed an identity separate from his family and did not feel the need to explain or justify the actions of other people, including his father. Finally, Sheehan warned him, "We have to get some really shady questions, because you will be asked them." He raised the topic of *People* naming him "The Sexiest Man Alive." John's quick-witted response, referring to his failed bar exam: "It beats the headline in the *New York Post*, 'The Hunk Flunks.'" After three days of rehearsal, Sheehan judged John ready. "He got a gentleman's B," Sheehan said. The biggest problem was that he appeared stiff, uncomfortable, and not expressive enough. "Don't be so rigid," he told his pupil as a final word of advice.

This training came in handy, for as much as John and Caroline wanted to talk about the Profile in Courage Award, the host kept returning to their father and his assassination. "You've heard the stories about your father," asked ABC's Jay Schadler in an obvious reference to JFK's sexual peccadilloes. "Do you think that had that been dealt with by the press, do you think it would have tarnished the image we have of him?" John replied, "I think the real question is whether or not, given the tenor of the times, my father would have gone into politics at this point." The host repeatedly tried to provoke John and Caroline into saying something newsworthy about their father. But both of them remained firm and focused. John told Schadler that he and his sister "view my father's administration through the colors of others and the perceptions of others and through photographs and through what we've read. It's difficult for us to discern much about him independently of what other people's impressions are."

When pressed about what he believed happened on November 22, 1963, John responded, "There are people—historians, filmmakers, etcetera—who are going to take money and time studying that. Whatever they find, whatever they decide, it is not going to change the one fundamental fact in my life, which is that it won't bring him back." When asked about the Warren Commission's lone-gunman theory, he deflected again: "I'll leave it to people to quarrel about or discern or analyze . . . and just walk away from it." Though the interview rambled, John received his first initiation into the world of answering questions on television. He performed well, steering the focus to what he wanted to talk about and sidestepping questions he did not wish to answer.

That fall, John had an opportunity to run for office when Congressman Ted Weiss died of heart failure at sixty-four. Weiss, who represented one of the most liberal districts in Manhattan, had just won the Democratic Party's nomination for reelection a few days earlier. The party had to name a successor to serve out his unexpired term and run for a new term beginning November 3. John got a call from Uncle Teddy.

"I'll get you that seat," Teddy promised him. "It's yours. It's your way to

Washington without having to break a sweat." But after thinking about it for a day, John said he was not interested. It was not just that he didn't believe himself ready; he also didn't want to do what was expected. He felt that although he might decide to enter politics someday, he first needed to accomplish something meaningful before joining "the family business."

Although they rarely talked about John entering politics, Berman always felt that John would have made a great mayor of New York. New York represented a major part of his DNA. "He took greater advantage of the entire city than anyone I knew. He had favorite haunts in every borough. He created excitement everywhere he went, and the entire city was always wide open to him. No restaurant was ever booked, no bike path off-limits, no concert sold out. . . . If there was a golden ticket, it was his."

Indeed, Berman witnessed firsthand how dramatically John's presence could defuse a tense moment. In April 1992 riots tore through many American cities after a predominantly white jury in a Los Angeles suburb acquitted four white police officers accused of savagely beating an African American motorist, Rodney King, after stopping him for a traffic violation and being led on a high-speed chase. The jury arrived at the verdict despite the existence of a videotape showing the officers delivering numerous blows to a seemingly defenseless King.

John and Michael were on their way to the airport in John's convertible when they got stuck in Harlem traffic and heard the broadcast of disturbances breaking out. Instead of hunkering down in his car or fearing that he might be a target, John put down the convertible top and stretched so that he was almost standing up in the car. At some level, John knew that his presence could serve as a calming influence. "You have to understand," Berman reflected, "people were petrified. Everyone else had their windows rolled up. But John gets up to stretch in the middle of this chaos and fear." When other drivers recognized John, they started honking their horns. Even African American pedestrians shouted to him. "Hey, John!" said one. "Can you save us from this?"

Berman was stunned by what transpired in those few minutes on Second Avenue. "I knew that day that I had seen something truly extraordinary," he reflected in 2019. Berman knew John well by the time of this incident and thought of him mostly "as just a more privileged, sought-after, better-looking version of the rest of us." But what he witnessed that day changed his perception of John and the power of his appeal. "I saw someone—just because of who he was—who was able to lift spirits, elevate the human condition, and bring a sense of calm to a terribly fractured environment."

Before graduating from Brown in 1983, John had decided to attend law school and, while still in Providence, signed up for a review course to prepare for the Law School Admission Test, or LSAT. John always struggled with standardized tests, and this one was no different. Although he'd earned Bs at Brown and scored only modestly on the LSAT, John applied to some of the most competitive law schools in the country, including Harvard. Roommate Rob Littell said that the only time he saw John "truly dismayed" was when he opened the thin letter from Harvard announcing that he had been rejected. He retreated into his room and did not come out until the next morning.

Before applying to law school, John spent a day with me at Yale University, where I was now an assistant professor of history. He wanted to take a tour of the Yale School of Organization and Management, which had a dual identity as a public policy and business school that attracted people interested in entering the public sector. I sensed that John was still searching for an alternative to law school. The School of Organization and Management offered a prestigious degree, and its admissions standards were lower than those of a traditional business or law school. At the end of the day, however, he chose not to apply.

As the law school rejections began piling up, John wondered whether he might have a poison pen letter in his file—that is, a purported letter of recommendation that turns out to be critical. I was skeptical. John simply did not come close to meeting the statistical requirements for a top law school. While universities do consider a student's background in order to create a diverse class—and John certainly had a unique upbringing—those factors do not always compensate for mediocre test results. Most likely, in the view of many admissions officers, John was just another rich kid from Manhattan, but he seemed oblivious that places like Harvard would be a long shot. I did not share this with John, but I was teaching bright, ambitious students at Yale who were at the top of their class and had near-perfect test scores, and some of *them* were being rejected from the same schools. Finally, after a few more rejections, John received a thick letter from New York University welcoming him to the class of 1989.

When he entered NYU Law School in September 1986, Mrs. Onassis suggested that it was time for John to find his own place, sans roommates. "Our extended fraternity run was over," Littell recalled. Apparently, they left the apartment in a shambles, and newspapers made sure to cover the story. "Somebody put a fist through the wall," complained the owner of the complex. The landlord sought legal action, and John settled the case out of court. Littell admitted they had not been model tenants, but their infractions, he claimed, were not "the kind of offense that rated national coverage."

John moved briefly into a hotel before taking over the top floor of a renovated town house on West Ninety-First Street. His mother called Bloomingdale's and had the entire apartment tastefully decorated. The place was an odd choice, given that the school was located south of Fourteenth Street in Greenwich Village. On nice days, John would ride his bike roughly eighty blocks to Vanderbilt Hall at the south end of Washington Square Park. On other days, he would take the subway.

The first year of law school is always the most challenging. "First year is grueling," observed Gary Ginsberg, an old friend from Brown who graduated from Columbia Law School, "because that's when you're first exposed to the Socratic method of teaching and forced to come to class prepared lest you're called on and exposed. It's a numbing, out-of-body experience being called out on the spot and forced to defend yourself before a professor and your fellow students." The first year is also when students compete for the all-prestigious law review, positions that are determined by a combination of grades and writing. Only those who make the law review have any chance of securing a clerkship with a judge. John struggled, as did many of his classmates. "You have no idea," he confessed to Christina. "It's like another language." An NYU professor later described John's performance as "unremarkable," saying that he showed little "evidence of ambition, drive, and vision."

Although John struggled in the classroom, he made friends quickly. Faith Stevelman, who met him on his second day, said that he "turned out to be completely different than I expected." She claimed that the press made him appear like "a narcissistic celebrity brat," but he was actually authentic and down-to-earth. Another classmate noted that John was "interested in school, but he takes things in stride. He's not one of those guys with the load of books, running around worrying that he's going to get a bad grade."

John found at least one familiar face among the sea of students at NYU.

Brown classmate Charlie King was in his third year when John arrived on campus. They played together on the law school's championship flag football team, Capital Punishment. More important, they created an organization, the City Policy Group, that met monthly to discuss relevant topics. At each meeting, one of the fifteen members would pick a topic, do research, and then present to the rest of the group, followed by discussion. Everyone promised confidentiality, which was largely for John's benefit so that he could express his opinions and not have to worry about them appearing in the *New York Post*.

The first meeting took place at John's mom's apartment. The issue that John had framed for the day was "the people's right to know versus an individual's right to privacy." This topic was obviously dear to John's heart. King distinctly remembered John being "adamant" that there existed "a sphere of privacy for everyone." He was struck by the contrast between John's strongly held views on privacy and the gracious, gentle way that John dealt with those who invaded his privacy daily on the streets of New York. "Even though he felt fiercely that people had a right not to be bothered," King reflected, "you could never know from the way he acted in public."

Law students fight for a handful of coveted internships that are usually awarded based on grades, class rank, and participation in the law review. Although John met none of these criteria, he received a string of prestigious assignments. During the summer after his first year, John won one of six competitive spots to work in the Civil Rights Division of the Reagan Justice Department. Ironically, he worked for William Bradford Reynolds, who was leading the administration's rollback of long-standing desegregation policies in housing, education, and hiring.

At the end of his second year, John took a $1,100-a-week summer job as an intern at the Los Angeles law firm of Manatt Phelps & Phillips. Charles Manatt, Teddy Kennedy's college roommate, had just finished serving as the chairman of the Democratic National Committee. Partly because of these connections, many in the firm resented John. "They give him all the easy work," one lawyer griped. "Shit, I just worked my ass off on a fifty-page brief that bored me to tears, and he gets to iron out a minor contract dispute" involving a rap group. Another complained, "He is so dumb, they can't afford to give him anything important." Such criticisms were unfair, as John was certainly a competent law student and likely not the only intern that summer with powerful political connections.

After attaining his law degree in 1989, John received another plum job working in the Manhattan District Attorney's Office headed by Robert Morgenthau, whom John's father had appointed US attorney for the Southern District of New York in 1961. John was among sixty-nine new prospects chosen from a pool of one thousand applicants. They each earned $30,000 a year during a three-year stint.

But before he could accept the post, John had to take care of some housecleaning: $2,000 in fines for outstanding parking tickets. He almost jeopardized his job in July, when, on his way to Kennedy Airport, he was pulled over for driving sixty-three miles per hour in a fifty-mile-per-hour zone at three in the morning. His car was unregistered, uninsured, and uninspected. He was issued four summonses, and his car was impounded. "He had to clear himself of all judgments in order to qualify for the DA's office," explained Judge Bertram Shair, who heard John's case. For John, that meant paying all his tickets.

John soon discovered that working in the DA's office was anything but glamorous. "You did your own typing," John's new coworker Owen Carragher Jr. told the *New York Daily News*. "You would have the courthouse dust on your cuff links." Carragher, who'd been at the DA's office for a year before John arrived, saw at least one immediate benefit: because of a prior dispute with the cleaning lady, the office hadn't been cleaned in months. But with the addition of his new office mate, "suddenly she made the most intrepid visit. She was cleaning under the lightbulbs, she was there for hours on end. I had the cleanest office in the building."

Brian Steel worked with John on the late shift, from five in the afternoon until one in the morning, at the Early Case Assessment Bureau (ECAB). On his first day, John strolled into the office and introduced himself as he always did, "Hi, I'm John Kennedy." The small office, which Steel described as "bleak," consisted of two metal desks and four chairs. Their job was to process complaints. A police officer would come in with a complaint (the legal document the prosecutor uses to decide if the defendant will be charged), and John's job was to review the document to see whether to process it as a violation, a misdemeanor, or a felony. "We would read the complaint in front of the officers, ask questions, figure out how to charge it, look at the penal law, and make sure that everything matched up," Steel explained. Occasionally they would cross-examine the police officer, trying to determine if witnesses had been present. They would also question defendants, to make sure they had been read their Miranda rights.

Even while working in the DA's office, John found a way to get outside and throw a Frisbee or organize a lunchtime game of touch football. Steel soon became a regular in John's touch football gatherings in Central Park. He was also daring enough to go kayaking with John on the Hudson River. Once, John called him around midnight and asked him to kayak to the George Washington Bridge. On another occasion, John decided to play chicken with a large ship that was making its way to the Atlantic Ocean. Steel watched in horror as John tempted his fate with the steel hull of a cargo ship.

John was later assigned to the Special Prosecutions Bureau, where his team cracked down on fraud and white-collar crime. He spent most of his time doing legal research and investigation rather than litigation. Everyone gave him high marks. "He's a team player," said one of the supervisors. "He's someone who wants to keep busy and have a variety of cases. He recently had a case requiring a lot of nights and weekends here, and he really did a good job." Morgenthau described him as "a hard worker and a great kid. His performance has been excellent and is very professional. I think he has the makings of a good lawyer."

It was while working at the DA's office that John experienced his highly publicized struggles with the bar exam. He took it for the first time right after law school and learned in the fall that he had failed. In public, John appeared nonplussed. He did not shy away from the hordes of photographers and reporters who showed up outside his office. But privately, the misfortune ate him up. He felt embarrassed and humiliated, and the tabloid headline "The Hunk Flunks" only poured salt in the wound. Christina Haag said that John cried in her arms when he failed. "He was upset because he thought he was disappointing the people in his life," recalled Pat Manocchia. "He cared less about himself than he did about the people around him. He didn't worry about whether it was going to crash his opportunities. He wasn't above embarrassment, but he would just keep working at it."

On May 1, 1990, it was announced that John had failed the bar exam a second time. The New York tabloids had a field day, with the *Daily News* screaming: "The Hunk Flunks . . . Again." John knew that he would have another chance to take the bar, but if he failed a third time, he would lose his job. "All assistants get three chances. It's a long-standing office policy," said a spokeswoman for Morgenthau. This was one bar that John could not surmount based on charm and hard work. But John was not alone. According to the DA's office, fifty-eight members of the most recent class of sixty-five recruits passed the bar on the first round. Of the seven who failed, two passed the second time.

Once again, John's public demeanor revealed none of his inner turmoil. "I'm clearly not a major legal genius," John openly told reporters who had amassed outside his office. But John was truly devastated and did something unusual: he disappeared for days. He drove alone to an upstate motel with a bottle of whiskey and several self-help tapes to drown away his sorrows. Many friends believed that failing the bar for a second time sparked what Rob Littell called "a crisis of sorts regarding his father." A few days after John's second miss, an older colleague in the DA's office pointed out that by the time his father was the same age—twenty-nine—he had already written a bestseller, won a Purple Heart, and been elected to Congress. John was not amused by the comment. "I'm not my father," he snapped.

Michael Berman watched the two failed bar exams take a psychological toll on John, so he offered to help. He was surprised that no one had ever asked that John be allowed to take the test privately. The New York State Bar Association made special provisions, but only for people who were physically handicapped or had severe learning issues. When Michael suggested to John that he ask his tutor about the possibility of taking the exam alone, John was told there was no category to allow that to happen.

"Let me see what I can do," Berman said, and he reached out. "I know there's no special category for the overprivileged," Berman told the tutor lightheartedly, "but this isn't just about John." Berman said that he "understood there have been paparazzi lining the entrance to the exam as if it were a red carpet, and the photographers were pressing their cameras against the windows to get a shot of him while everyone is supposed to be concentrating. It's unfair to him, but it's equally unfair to everyone else taking the exam at that location. It's putting all of them at a disadvantage." Several days later, John heard that he would be allowed to take the exam privately in an off-site location.

For the previous eleven months, while he was working in the DA's office and studying for the bar, John also handled a few cases in the courtroom.

The first case that he tried occurred after he had failed the bar exam twice. The police called the defendant the "sleeping burglar" because he had been found asleep in the victim's locked apartment with her jewelry in his pocket. John prosecuted and won the case in August 1991, and it marked a significant achievement, even though journalist Murray Kempton noted that it was a carefully selected case that was almost impossible to lose. Still, John managed in that one case to acquire more trial experience than his uncle Bobby had when he was appointed US attorney general in 1961.

On July 23, 1990, John took the bar exam for the third time. He received the results on November 3. "The Hunk Finally Does It!," exclaimed the front page of the *New York Post*. John invited some people to his apartment to celebrate. Berman was out of town and couldn't make it, but when he returned a few days later, John had dropped off a couple of bottles of wine with his doorman with a note reading: "From one bar expert to another. Cheers!"

John won all six cases that he tried. In his first case since passing the bar, John tried Venard Garvin, who'd been accused of selling heroin. A *New York Times* reporter sat in the courtroom during jury selection and the trial. "Mr. Kennedy's articulation," he wrote, "in a pleasant but unremarkable baritone, had been a bit halting in jury selection. But his opening statement was clear, and his direct examination of three police detectives and a police chemist was to the point." He pointed out that John "lacked the theatrical flair of his rival," but his summation was "well organized and persuasive." The journalist said that "the Mr. Kennedy who was famous never got in the way of the Mr. Kennedy who is a prosecutor. The jury stuck to the evidence. The verdict: guilty."

John lent his name to numerous charitable causes while in law school and working in the DA's office. He sat on the boards of the John F. Kennedy Library Foundation and the Institute of Politics at the John F. Kennedy School of Government at Harvard. "He's very intent on doing only things he's qualified to do," said a colleague at the institute. "He really wants to be involved." He served on the board of Naked Angels, a creative theater group founded in 1986. He was also a board member of the Robin Hood foundation, created in 1988 to provide financial support to programs that targeted poverty in New York City.

But John made his most significant and unique contribution by founding

Reaching Up. In 1989 John's aunt Eunice Shriver held a competition among the cousins to devise proposals that would contribute to the field of intellectual disabilities. Eunice's interest in people with special needs stemmed from the experience of her sister Rosemary, who suffered from cognitive and developmental deficits, which Joseph P. Kennedy hoped to correct by approving a lobotomy. The surgery failed, and Rosemary, permanently incapacitated, spent the rest of her life in an institution, dying there in 2005 at the age of eighty-six. John spoke about his idea to his friend Jeffrey Sachs, who had served as a health care advisor to New York governor Hugh Carey. "I want to help disabled people, but my real interest is in helping the working poor," John told him. Sachs responded logically, "Maybe there's something that helps both the developmentally disabled and poor people."

Over the next few months, Sachs arranged meetings with several leading thinkers and practitioners in the health care field. All eagerly shared their ideas, but John found most of them generic and too patient focused. Finally, in their last meeting, they sat down with Michael Goldfarb, a New York health care advocate. They listened to what he had to say, but his ideas initially sounded like all the others. As they started to leave, Goldfarb shouted, "Come back!" He explained that the biggest problem facing the developmentally disabled was the amount of turnover among their professional caregivers who were trapped in low-paying jobs with no upward mobility. "There's no chance for them to get ahead," Goldfarb noted. Most of the people caring for the disabled were poor and often left those jobs to flip hamburgers at McDonald's because they could make more money there.

John knew instantly that he had found an idea he could sink his teeth into because it focused on health care workers, not patients. John's proposal won the family competition, which awarded him a $25,000 grant. He used this money to lay the foundation for a new nonprofit organization, Reaching Up. The goal was to provide a career ladder and advancement in higher education for direct care workers. John met with the chairman of the board at City University of New York (CUNY), who was the father of a child with developmental disabilities. John wanted to offer opportunities and scholarships for health care workers to take classes at CUNY, possibly even earning a degree in their field. "He realized," reflected Bill Ebenstein, the executive director, "that you could not have good services for people with intellectual disabilities, the vulnerable elderly, or challenged children unless you had a strong workforce that was respected and educated and that had a chance to get ahead." John, he said, "was ahead of his time."

John, Ebenstein, and Sachs worked together to tackle the many obstacles that stood in their path. The first challenge was to create coursework at CUNY in the field of developmental disabilities. The great irony is that universities, which are designed to foster new ideas and creative thinking, are among the most ossified institutions in the country—burdened by layers of bureaucracy and overlapping jurisdictions that make change nearly impossible. Reaching Up also had to contend with faculty arrogance. "Should these workers be coming to the college?" some asked. "Will they lower our standards?" Initially, CUNY wanted to create just a certification program, but John insisted that the only way for students to advance their careers was to receive college credit.

Success would also require forming unorthodox partnerships with unions representing the workers and the employer, along with state and city officials. "John was very involved in setting it up," recalled Ebenstein. "He used his clout to bring people to the table. Everyone wanted to meet with him: the unions, state government officials, private nonprofit organizations, and the advocacy groups." This collaboration was the way John liked using his celebrity status—as a magnet to bring people together in pursuit of a cause he cared about deeply.

One of the first people he contacted was Dennis Rivera, the powerful head of the three-hundred-thousand-member SEIU (Service Employees International Union). "He was very interested in the plight of working people," Rivera recalled. "A large sector of our members were poor, from minority communities, and John wanted to find a way to help them. He had a sense that we should help people who help others." Rivera claimed that John's ability to pick up the phone, get anyone on the line, and then convince them to support his effort was "unparalleled." John, he reflected, "chose to cast his lot with a group of people who wanted to better their lives so they can better their families. He brought the spotlight and the attention to that issue."

Over the next few months, John met with representatives from various constituency groups and convinced them all to participate. In its first year, Reaching Up chose ten Kennedy Fellows to receive $1,000 scholarships every semester. It gradually expanded the program by adding ten to twenty fellows each subsequent year. John was involved in every step, meeting individually with each fellow. "He paid attention, he was involved, he knew us by name," said Kennedy fellow Getulio Rodriguez, who went on to earn a master's degree in social work at Manhattan's Hunter College. "I was promoted twice after I became a Kennedy fellow," he reflected in 1999. "The fellowship is more than money. It is also mentoring, networking, and being inspired to fulfill your potential." Damian Crocevera, who was earning a master's degree in forensic psychology, concurred with that assessment, claiming that John "was always attentive." He admired John's "interest in people like me, the direct care staff. I admire his vision that to make the system better we, the hands-on people, needed a chance to become better."

Reaching Up remained a relatively small program, but the idea of providing a career path for low-wage health care workers persisted. Dennis Rivera expanded the concept to include all low-wage, dead-end jobs in health care, including child care workers, nurse aides, and home care workers. It later extended to include paraprofessionals working in special education. Today there are undergraduate and master's programs in disability studies.

Reaching Up was John's greatest and most unheralded achievement. "He helped create a whole field that did not exist before," said Ebenstein. "Reaching Up was the leading edge of that movement." John worked below the radar to establish the program and help it expand. He never took credit for Reaching Up. Rather, he showed genuine compassion for many of the workers in the program and would often spend time with them outside the classroom as well. Sometimes he would show up unannounced to classes. This venture modeled how John wanted to use his celebrity: as a force uniting different stakeholders and encouraging them to invest in his vision. "He understood how to put together a coalition that benefitted the working poor," said Rivera. "He had that secret ingredient that could make it work."

In May 1999, just two months before his death, John delivered the commencement speech at Washington College in Chestertown, Maryland, which honored him for his work at Reaching Up. He told the graduates that over the previous ten years, "Reaching Up" had awarded scholarships to four hundred caregivers. Of those, two hundred went on to receive a bachelor of arts or master's degree; fifty earned associate in arts degrees; and 95 percent were still working as caregivers. "What this means," he declared, "is that the most vulnerable people in our society receive better support, their families feel more secure, employers experience less turnover, and caregivers are better trained, better compensated, and better appreciated."

Since returning to New York following her marriage to Onassis, Jackie had lived quietly with her companion Maurice Tempelsman. When not working as an editor at Doubleday, she was fighting to preserve historic buildings, including New York's Grand Central Terminal, and spending time with her grandchildren. Caroline and her husband, Ed, had three children: Rose, born in 1988; Tatiana (1990); and Jack (1993).

Though perhaps the most famous woman in the world, Jackie resembled any other mother. "His mother looked at him like my mother looked at me," recalled John's Brown classmate Richard Wiese. John shared a special bond with his mom. "They both were big fun. And each one of them had such a spirit of fun and sparkle about them," recalled Jackie's friend Joe Armstrong. "Jackie liked John's carefree spirit, and John gave her joy because he was fun and always had an original way of seeing things and people. They both had a great sense of humor, they loved to laugh, and possessed a playful streak that could be hilarious." She understood John's penchant for being independent and unpredictable, and she chose not to let it worry her. When Armstrong asked Jackie if she worried about John bicycling all over Manhattan in intense traffic and without a helmet, she responded: "I do not worry about things that I can't do anything about."

Although much has been written claiming that Jackie micromanaged John's life, forbidding him from becoming an actor and forcing him to attend law school, the reality was always more complicated. Pat Manocchia recalled that Jackie offered general guidance but did not dictate individual choices, once advising him to "do something with your name." At dinner one evening, she offered both of them the same advice: "You have been given great opportunities. You have to do something worthwhile." John's struggle was trying to discover a path that he found not only personally rewarding but also "worthwhile" on a larger scale. He attended law school not because Jackie insisted but because of the future opportunities it promised—as well as the three-year delay in having to make a firm career choice.

Jackie, however, did not shy away from letting John know how she felt about his girlfriends. She approved of Christina Haag but grew concerned when he started dating Daryl Hannah, a tall blonde actress who had starred in the 1984 hit movie *Splash*. Just a month after the *People* magazine article dubbing him "The Sexiest Man Alive," John was spotted on a date with Hannah. They had actually been set up by her billionaire stepfather, Chicago businessman and film producer Jerrold Wexler, a major contributor to both the Democratic Party and John's uncle Ted. Their first meeting occurred in the early 1980s while vacationing separately in Saint Martin with their families, but they met again at the 1988 wedding of John's aunt Lee Radziwill to film director Herb Ross, who had worked with Hannah on *Steel Magnolias*.

Both John and Daryl were still in relationships when they quietly started dating. Officially, John remained linked to Haag, and Hannah was nearing the end of a contentious ten-year relationship with singer-songwriter Jackson Browne. In 1989 paparazzi spotted them over Memorial Day weekend on a fifty-six-foot yacht at Smith Mountain Lake in Virginia, then later at various places around New York City. Initially, Daryl was unwilling to leave Browne without a commitment from John that they would be exclusive. In the meantime, John, who had broken up with Christina Haag in 1990, was seeing various other women, including Jackie look-alike Julie Baker, an actress.

Their unofficial relationship changed on October 1, 1992, when John flew from New York to Los Angeles to retrieve Daryl, who was upset over an altercation with her ex-boyfriend at their home in Santa Monica. Thereafter, John and Daryl began seeing each other exclusively. In August 1993 John was seen with the actress on a scuba diving vacation in Palau, a scenic island in the South Pacific. Eventually he moved into Hannah's apartment on Manhattan's Upper West Side.

The relationship had been rocky from the start. It is often said that every successful relationship has a flower and a gardener: one person needs to be tended, while the other loves to nurture and support. However, according to Rob Littell, both John and Daryl were flowers. One of John's close friends recalled that Hannah possessed "these self-absorbed neurotic qualities that she couldn't see beyond. She was a movie star, she was a bombshell, and she was all about her most of the time." John quickly started to notice the insular, narcissistic nature of her world. "She was on a little hamster track of her own stuff that she may not ever face and grow out of," remembered a friend.

Charlie King recalled having lunch with John a few weeks before the thirtieth anniversary of his father's death in 1993. He noticed that John appeared uncharacteristically quiet and withdrawn. "He seemed really distracted," King reflected. When he asked him what was going on, John responded, "I got into a fight with Daryl, and I'm living in the basement of a friend's house, and my mother doesn't really like Daryl all that much. It's the thirtieth anniversary of my father's death so I'm not really watching television. It's a difficult time. This Daryl thing has me thrown for a loop."

The next month, Mrs. Onassis discovered a lump in her right groin. A doctor mistakenly diagnosed it as an infection and ordered a round of antibiotics, but a few weeks later, she developed a cough, swollen lymph nodes in her neck, and stomach pain. She flew back to New York from the Caribbean where she had been vacationing, and she was diagnosed with an aggressive form of non-Hodgkin's lymphoma. "This is the good kind," she assured John. "We can beat this."

Initially, both doctors and Jackie expressed confidence that she would make a full recovery. In January 1994 Joe Armstrong found her in very good and determined spirits when he met her for lunch as she began her chemotherapy treatments. "I have to face this head-on and get through it. Then I'll be okay by summer," which was her favorite time of the year.

Her optimism seemed warranted. Yet by March, scans showed that while the lymphoma had disappeared from most of her body, it had spread to the membrane covering her brain and spinal cord. To treat the issue, doctors gave her radiation therapy.

John suspected that his mom's illness was more serious than she admitted. "John seemed resigned to her fate, outwardly stoic, and relying, I think, on her strength to carry him through," Littell observed. "He didn't like talking about her illness. We stopped referring to his mother in conversation. The only thing John enjoyed during those sad months was his mother's company. It was a special time for both of them, as she tried to prepare him for a life without her, and he immersed himself in the life she still had. Among the most important things she told him then was not to be afraid of his name."

On Saturday, May 14, Armstrong, who had not seen Jackie for a month, met with her and singer Carly Simon for lunch at Simon's Upper West Side apartment. "My heart just sank when she walked in," he reflected. "She was as cheerful and warm as ever, but she was so thin and without eyebrows, without eyelashes, and a wig that didn't really fit. I could never let her know that seeing this was breaking my heart." Jackie gave Armstrong a ride home, and as he got out of the car she said, "Joe! Four more weeks, and I get my life back." They talked on the phone the next morning, and then later that day, she collapsed and was admitted to New York Hospital–Cornell Medical Center.

John could not be with Jackie that weekend because Daryl insisted that he deliver the ashes of her dead dog and attend its funeral in Los Angeles. John longed to be with his mother, but he agreed to his girlfriend's request anyway. When he arrived at the dog's funeral, Hannah became distraught because John had placed the ashes in a simple box rather than something more elaborate. John was angry at himself for not being home with his mother the entire weekend, but he did not want to deal with the media fallout over a breakup while he should be focusing all his energy on his mother.

John returned to New York after the weekend, and on Tuesday evening he, Caroline, and Ed joined Anthony Radziwill and his fiancée, Carole, for dinner. Earlier that day, they had learned the gravity of the situation and the likelihood that Jackie would die. John was both furious that he had been at a dog's funeral thousands of miles away and devastated that he was losing the most important person in his life. At one point, he excused himself from the table and locked himself in the restroom. When he returned, his eyes were red. He did not want to break down in public, so once again he hid his grief.

On Wednesday, everyone's worst fears were confirmed. A CAT scan showed that the cancer had spread to Jackie's liver. The doctors stopped all treatment, and she decided to die at home. A health care worker told *The New York Times*, "She had an aggressive cancer that was treated aggressively and that initially responded to therapy, but it came back in her brain and spread through her body."

Joe Armstrong was scheduled to have lunch with John on Thursday, May 19, but John called in the morning to cancel. "It's like a car speeding down the highway and the pieces are falling off," he said. Later that afternoon, Jackie's cook and assistant, Marta, called both Joe Armstrong and Carly Simon and asked each of them to come say good-bye. The family held a quiet vigil around her bed, where Jackie lay with a bright-colored scarf wrapped around her head. She looked peaceful, with her hands folded over her stomach and her eyes closed. Joe did not think it appropriate for a man to enter her bedroom, so he waited in the living room with John while Simon paid her respects. When John walked Joe and Carly to the door, he said, "Mummy loves you two so much," and broke down in tears.

That evening, Jackie lapsed into a coma after receiving the last rites of the Catholic Church and died at ten fifteen, with John and Caroline by her side. She was just sixty-four. "It's a strange procession," John told Billy Noonan. "First come the doctors, then the lawyers, then the funeral director. It isn't simply a death but a series of steps in death."

The next morning, John went downstairs to address the dozens of reporters and cameramen clustered outside the apartment building. He revealed that his mother had died, "surrounded by her friends and her family and her books and the people and the things that she loved. She did it her own way and on her own terms, and we all feel lucky for that, and now she's in God's hands." He thanked the public and said, "I hope now we can have these next couple of days in relative peace."

On the day of the viewing, John grew restless and needed some exercise. He went roller blading with Hannah past St. Ignatius Loyola Roman Catholic Church at Park Avenue and Eighty-Fourth Street, where the funeral would be held on Monday the twenty-third. John staged his appearance with Hannah for the press. In his mind, the relationship had already ended, but he did not want rumors of their impending split to distract from his mother's death. In private, the two were barely talking. "It was very awkward," recalled a family member. He left the apartment at one point to play football in Central Park, pursued by nearly a dozen photographers and reporters. "It's his mother!" his former roommate Christiane Amanpour shouted at them. "Leave him alone!" His friend Chris Cuomo, younger brother of Andrew and a future TV news personality, checked in to see how John was holding up. "I need this right now," John responded, referring to his desire to get outside and run around in the park.

That evening, John and his sister, followed by four dozen photographers, arrived for Jackie's wake. By six o'clock, nearly eight hundred people had gathered outside the apartment. Sightseeing buses stopped occasionally to allow tourists a chance to take pictures. Strangers dropped bouquets of roses at the doorway, while dozens of reporters, photographers, and television camera crews camped outside. At one point, John stood on the balcony and acknowledged the onlookers with a wave. "Can you believe this?" he said, incredulous, to Billy Noonan. "They've been there for days. All for Mummy." Jackie's body lay inside a closed coffin, draped with an antique cloth. Once the many guests had left, a small group of family members and close friends

gathered for a buffet-style dinner. A clueless Daryl made small talk by telling
another guest about how she had met Jackson Browne.

St. Ignatius had been Jackie's childhood church; she had been both baptized and confirmed there. Once again John did not want to reveal his grief
to the public. "It's just going to be really hard for me because I am not going
to cry," he admitted to Sasha. "I'm not going to cry in front of fifty million
people." Although TV cameras were not permitted inside the church, the
CBS, NBC, and CNN networks all broadcast the audio of the funeral service.

Rising to the pulpit, John told the one thousand mourners that "choosing
the readings for these services, we struggle to find ones that captured my
mother's essence. Three things came to mind over and over again and ultimately dictated our selections. They were her love of words, the bonds of
home and family, and her spirit of adventure." His uncle, Senator Edward
Kennedy, remembered John's mom as someone who "made a rare and notable contribution to the American spirit. She was a blessing to us and to the
nation. No one ever gave more meaning to the title of first lady." Jackie,
Teddy concluded, "was too young to be a widow in 1963 and too young to
die now."

Her body was carried by private plane to Washington National Airport,
where thousands of people lined the roadside to observe the hearse make its
way to Arlington National Cemetery. There, on that hot afternoon, Jackie
was buried near the same Eternal Flame that she had lit thirty-one years
earlier during another moment of national grief. The brief ceremony lasted
a mere fifteen minutes and was attended by only a hundred family members.
"May the flame she lit so long ago burn ever brighter here and always brighter
in our hearts," President Bill Clinton proclaimed. John and Caroline knelt
in silent prayer before the casket. Caroline placed a white lily on the bier,
then kissed the casket. John went next, pausing first to gently reach down
and touch the simple bronze grave marker for his father.

John was left "emotionally wiped out" by his mother's death, but he kept
such feelings to himself. "I learned from my family that you don't wallow in
death," he told Gary Ginsberg. "You move on. You hold it inside."

John elaborated on his thoughts about death six months after his mom
passed, when he learned that his friend Charlie King had lost his father. John
sat down and penned a remarkably thoughtful letter about life and loss that
revealed a great deal about the way he had learned to deal with death. "I

heard through the grapevine of your loss and wanted to just let you know that I know what you're going through," he wrote. "It's hard and it sucks and there's really nothing that folks can say especially those who didn't have the pleasure of knowing your father." He went on to say that his own experience had taught him to "let yourself steep in the whole experience of loss, it's as much a part of life as birth, laughter and marriage and so it has its own meaning and purpose that must be considered." Too often, he continued, "we look at death as some shocking anomaly and thereby blind ourselves to the many revelations and epiphanies it can bring. So explore the meaning of it all, it's there and you'll grow enormously from it." He told Charlie that his mother once told him "that 18 months after she lost my father she would smile when she thought of him instead of cry and that made all the difference. That's starting to happen to me now," he admitted. "And I hope it comes soon to you."

Apparently, one of the revelations that John had while dealing with his mother's passing was that he was now on his own. In an odd way, Jackie's death proved liberating for John. "It left him unequivocally an adult, the bearer of his parents' legacies," Rob Littell wrote.

Following the funeral, John and Daryl spent the weekend in Hyannis with Sasha, who recalled, "Daryl was upstairs freaking out because another one of her dogs was sick. She was going on and on about her dog." John, who was returning to Hyannis for the first time since his mother had died, remained overcome with grief, repeating, "I just didn't want her to die." He could not understand how his "girlfriend" seemed more concerned about her dog than she did about him. "I felt so bad about him that all she cared about was her dog," Sasha reflected.

The loss of his beloved mother gave John the strength to finally end his dysfunctional relationship with Hannah shortly afterward. The breakup was easy for him, as he had already started seeing another beautiful blonde—the one who would eventually become his wife.

CHAPTER 7

"WHAT ABOUT A MAGAZINE ABOUT POLITICS?"

In 1988 Michael Berman and John started talking about pursuing a business venture. Michael had been serving as an unofficial advisor for the past few years, during which the two men developed a close friendship. John felt it was the right time for him to take risks. While he relished taking physical risks, his professional life had followed a conventional route until this point. After graduating from Brown in 1983, John went to New York University Law School and then spent four years working in the Manhattan DA's office before leaving in early 1994.

John often told me about how his grandfather Joseph P. Kennedy's business acumen and entrepreneurial spirit had primed the family for financial security and allowed future generations to pursue careers in public service. Aside from the inspiration from his family's past, John found creating and owning a business attractive on other, more personal levels. He could not envision himself working as a cog in a large bureaucracy, and it was clear to me that after four tiresome years in the DA's office, he knew he did not want to practice law long term.

Berman seemed like the ideal partner. John enjoyed Michael's quick mind and dry humor, while Michael understood John and made sure not to exploit his celebrity. John's contribution to any venture seemed obvious, as his fame could open doors that might otherwise remain closed in addition to providing access to people normally unavailable. Furthermore, pairing John's reputation with Michael's keen public relations skills would hopefully lay the basis for lasting success.

They formed a corporation, appropriately named Random Ventures, to pursue whatever ideas came to mind. John's first idea grew from his love of outdoor adventure, specifically kayaking. Long before the sport became popular, John had purchased a custom-made kayak from a company in Maine, which produced, in his words, "the Rolls-Royces of kayaks." This superior model, John believed, could be made more accessible by selling kits that would allow people to build independently. Berman thought John raised an interesting question: "Could you mold these kayaks and mass-produce them in a way that was affordable?" Berman and Kennedy traveled to Maine to meet with the owner and inspect the kayaks. After looking at the numbers, however, they both came to the realization that people who wanted custom-made kayaks would not buy a mass-produced version.

John then transitioned to the idea of creating a rent-a-dog business. In his mind, the typical customer might be a lonely, recently divorced father or a family of young children who could not care for a dog full-time. "A lot of people say to me, 'I would love to have a dog, but I can't take care of one,'" John said. "It would be good for the dogs because they could provide at least a temporary home for strays." He also noted that having a dog often served as a way to meet and bond with others. John, who could sometimes be oblivious to his fame, pointed out that whenever he took his dog Friday for a walk, strangers would approach him, oftentimes bringing over their spouses and kids. As they petted and admired the dog, they would strike up a conversation. Berman nixed this idea, too, pointing out that the dog was probably not the object of their attention.

Neither of these initial ideas panned out, obviously, but over the next few years, the two of them toyed with other initiatives. The challenge was that both had day jobs—Michael at a public relations firm and John at the Manhattan DA's office—so they met infrequently. Michael turned to his friend and publicist Nancy Haberman as an additional soundboard for ideas. In 1993, shortly after Arkansas governor Bill Clinton became president, Michael approached her with a new proposal. "I have this idea for a magazine that will be a mix of pop culture and politics. What do you think?" Nancy was initially unimpressed, but when Michael added that he intended to ask John to join the venture, she responded, "It just got a little better in my mind."

One evening over dinner, Michael pitched the idea to John, enticing him with the prospect of a multifaceted magazine integrating the popular with the political: "We could be what *Rolling Stone* is to music and *Vogue* to fashion."

Much of the motivation behind this vision had been inspired by the current political landscape. They agreed that the 1992 presidential race, especially Bill Clinton, had electrified nearly everyone they knew, even those who had been apolitical in the past. The excitement that the forty-six-year-old Clinton had been able to drum up reverberated with John, who had already been fascinated by the charismatic candidate. John admired politicians like his father, who could inspire and motivate people regardless of their political affiliation. In the 1980s, he admired President Reagan for many of the same reasons. Gary Ginsberg, who worked on the Clinton campaign, recalled John picking his brain about all aspects of the race.

John saw obvious similarities between his father and Clinton. Both were engaging, young, and energetic. They offered a fresh alternative to a tired, old establishment figure. Clinton spoke often of how JFK had inspired him to pursue a life of public service, and his campaign never let pass an opportunity to show a 1963 photo of a sixteen-year-old Bill Clinton, who was in Washington as a delegate to Boys Nation, an American Legion program, shaking the president's hand in the Rose Garden. One of Clinton's themes from the start of his political career was to emulate JFK's call for mutual responsibility, urging citizens to give back to their country. John's mom, who usually avoided endorsing politicians other than family members, came to Clinton's aid in the critical New York primary, where former California governor Jerry Brown was running a spirited campaign after having won the Connecticut primary two weeks earlier. Mrs. Onassis appeared at a public event and allowed the governor to claim himself as the rightful heir of the Camelot legacy. The day before his inauguration, Clinton traveled to Arlington National Cemetery to lay a wreath on the graves of JFK and Robert Kennedy, and once in office, he had photos of both men displayed prominently in the White House.

Creating a new magazine, especially one that combined politics and popular culture, was risky. There had been a boom in new magazines over the previous two decades. Since the 1970s, celebrity magazines such as *People* had gained in popularity. Women's magazines like *Cosmopolitan* and teen magazines like *Seventeen* also flourished, as did fashion publications, especially *Vogue* and *Harper's Bazaar*. Each targeted a very specific audience, since magazines depended on advertising dollars to survive. In 1995 there were few gender-neutral magazines. Men flocked to *Sports Illustrated* and

Car and Driver; women read *Vanity Fair* and *Cosmopolitan*. Fashion and cosmetics advertisers filled the pages of magazines focused on women, while car and alcohol ads flowed into men's magazines. The conventional wisdom was that female readers did not read about politics, and without female readers, John's proposed new magazine would not have a viable advertising base. Nina Link, who served as the CEO and president of the Magazine Publishers of America (MPA), noted that there was always risk in launching a magazine. "There was, however, a greater risk with *George* because it was creating a different category."

Despite the obvious challenges, they knew what they were getting into and were willing to take the plunge. John attended a two-day seminar called "How to Start Your Own Magazine." On the first morning, the instructor cautioned the earnest faces before him that they could launch a successful magazine on any subject—except religion and politics. John then heard the statistics that seemed to doom his venture before it had even started: 90 percent of all start-up magazines fold, and no commercially viable political magazine had existed in the entire twentieth century. John left before the first coffee break. He and Berman decided to look on the bright side instead. "If everyone said that you can't launch a successful political magazine, at least we won't have any competition," Berman said.

In retrospect, they underestimated the depth of the problem and overestimated their ability to solve it. Some of the most experienced veterans in the magazine business had tried and failed to find ways of bridging the gap between male and female advertiser preferences. But John and Michael were two novices in the worlds of both publishing and business: neither had run a magazine before, let alone created one. But they did have a secret weapon in the power of John's celebrity. Would his appeal transcend the gender divide and allow them to create a new genre of magazine publishing?

I spoke with John several times about his ambitions for *George*, and my crystal ball was no clearer than his. What struck me was his willingness to take on such a risky venture, a quality that I had recognized years earlier when he was still a student. During his last semester at Brown, he chose to enroll in Mary Gluck's extremely demanding course on European intellectual history, despite knowing full well that he was required to pass all his classes. Now, as he was starting his professional life, he resolved to do what no one else had accomplished: launch a successful political magazine designed to reach both men and women. Again, he seemed undaunted by the challenge. I remember thinking, "You can do anything. Why not take it step-by-step? Take a job at *Rolling Stone*, establish a reputation for being a good editor, learn about the business, and then launch your own magazine." But I was always reluctant to offer John advice about anything other than history, because I knew that his life was often far too complicated for me to understand.

The greatest complication was that John felt he needed to prove himself— and fast. Most of us climb ladders in our careers: we start at the bottom and work our way up gradually. John had the means to start at the top, and he preferred it that way: hurrying and skipping steps that others lingered on. Perhaps it was the frequent comparisons with his father and what he had accomplished at a similar age that accounted for John's rushed approach. Like many of his generation, John had enjoyed a prolonged adolescence. He spent three years at law school and another four years working in a field he knew he did not plan to pursue. Now in his midthirties, he felt the need to make a decisive career move. He wanted something identifiably *his*, a venture that he could own and expand into a successful business. He keenly understood his strengths and weaknesses, and he longed to be taken seriously for his own merits and not just because of his family name. If he launched a successful magazine, he could prove to the world that he was a man of substance.

John's lack of direction had troubled his mother, who'd asked her close friend Joe Armstrong to meet with him to discuss career options. Armstrong had been a successful magazine publisher who went on to work at ABC News. Joe recalled spending a week with Jackie on Martha's Vineyard in the early 1990s, and she told him that John was bored working in the District Attorney's Office and was restless; he knew he had no interest in practicing law, but he had no idea what he wanted to do next. "Joe," she asked, "would you have lunch with John and just talk with him?"

On this occasion and many others, John was not aware that his mother was reaching out to her vast network of friends to provide him with direction and opportunities. She was a "hidden-hand mother," pulling strings behind the scenes, asking people to contact John and offer him plum summer jobs, internships, or, in the case with Armstrong, career guidance. She wanted John to think that he found these opportunities on his own, when, in fact, she had set them up for him. "She often planted seeds for options to come his way," Armstrong recalled. "She knew that he could be very casual about things." He would forget to put in an application for school or a job. She, on the other hand, "was totally disciplined, and strategic, and such a responsible person."

Armstrong does not remember the details of what he and John discussed over a handful of lunches, but he had a vivid memory of the most telling comments that John made. He told Joe that the Clinton White House had offered him a Labor Department post organizing after-school programs for disadvantaged children. But he turned it down. "Joining the new administration is too predictable and what people would expect me to do," John said. "I want to do something unexpected. All I know for certain is that I don't want to do what people expect."

A year later, John called Joe to tell him that he and Michael Berman wanted to start a magazine. Armstrong, who had served as publisher for ten magazines, was just the right person to guide them. John explained the concept, then asked, "Is this viable?"

Armstrong sincerely loved the idea and encouraged them to pursue it. "Joe was very kind at a time when most people we spoke with didn't think we stood a chance," Berman reflected in 2019. "He was a magazine insider and very well connected in the media world. He had a wide network that he was happy to introduce us to. He didn't come from a large corporation like Time Inc. or Condé Nast or Hearst. He was more of a renegade and that appealed to us. He'd worked for start-ups like *Texas Monthly*, *New York*, and *Rolling Stone*—all scrappy, independent publications, working with small, smart staffs and limited budgets that somehow managed to break out and become important voices in the cultural zeitgeist. That's what *George* aspired to be. And while he was soberingly realistic about the challenges we would face, not once did he say it couldn't be done."

Armstrong also offered valuable advice. "First thing you do," he said, "is to tell no one. Neither of you has any experience in magazine publishing, so people are not going to take you seriously until you prove yourself and prove that you know what you are doing." He then asked a series of pointed questions: "What writers will you get to write for you? What kind of stories will you publish? How are you going to find your audience? How can you prove to potential investors that there will be interest and support for this magazine?

How can you prove that there will be reader and advertiser support, so that investors will see solid evidence that the potential is real? What advertisers will be in the magazine, and how can you prove to them that they can't find readers in other ways?

"Political magazines have always had small audiences and small ad support," he continued. "How can you give confidence that your publication will be the exception?"

They could not answer a single question. "They knew nothing about publishing a magazine," Armstrong recalled. "I told them again that their one chance would be destroyed if they didn't keep this secret until they knew the answers to my questions, and until they could give potential investors confidence that they knew what they were doing, and until they could make a powerful case for a way to success." Kennedy and Berman, he said in 2019, needed to prove that the business was viable and that they were smart enough to run it. "Otherwise the media would have torn them apart as unqualified and unprepared" and would destroy their ability to find investors.

John and Michael took Armstrong's lecture to heart and set out to answer the questions he'd asked. "They were determined and rolled up their sleeves and worked hard," Armstrong recalled. Over the next year, Armstrong, in addition to helping them write a business plan, introduced them to the top magazine designers in the business and to circulation professionals, so that they could perform direct mail testing to prove their concept to investors. "I helped them create mock-ups as well as advertising and circulation and editorial plans," Armstrong reflected. John and Michael did not always accept Joe's advice, but they appreciated his enthusiasm and his encouragement.

Armstrong wanted John to meet other people in the business, so he managed to get him a coveted seat at the 1994 Gridiron Club dinner, an annual event where the media performed satirical skits and the president was expected to engage in self-deprecating humor. "John," Armstrong said, "would you like to go to the Gridiron dinner?" "What is that?" John asked. Armstrong was surprised that someone who was launching a political magazine had never heard of the event. "Well," Joe told him, "you should think about going because you can see the whole Washington power structure. You can meet people at the cocktail hour. You can plant some seeds to build relationships."

As they settled into their seats, the emcee began the event by saying, "We have in the room today a man who every woman wants to have *dress* them: Ralph Lauren." The fashion designer stood and welcomed the round of applause. "And," he continued, "we also have in the room the man who every woman wishes would *undress* them: John Kennedy Jr." As a spotlight shined on him, John sheepishly lifted himself from the chair, giving a brief wave before sitting down.

The next day, Ralph Lauren offered to fly the two men back to New York in his private jet. He suggested they stop at his estate in Bedford, New York, for lunch, and then he would arrange for cars to take them into the city. "Let's do it," John said. He was curious to see Lauren's famous mansion, but he was even more excited to ride in his private jet. John's childhood fascination with the military had long since faded, but he never abandoned his love of flying, although the object of his affection was now planes, not helicopters. He spent the entire flight in the cockpit with the pilots. "That was when I realized how much he loved flying," Armstrong recalled.

As his first real professional project, John saw *George* as a way of forging a new identity. He'd spent his whole life up to now trapped by the image of himself bleakly saluting his father's coffin. John longed for the public to recognize him for his accomplishments as an adult. Rather than conjuring up dusty images of a kid romping around the White House or bidding his father farewell, John hoped they would see an accomplished editor and a successful businessman.

John also wanted to disprove the public perception that he was not bright. He had failed two bar exams. Being a district attorney should have put those concerns to rest, but no one could seem to forget John's most publicized case, in which a man robbing a house fell asleep before escaping. He won, but how could anyone have lost? Now, at nearly thirty-four years old, he felt he lacked any professional accomplishment, and he feared any success he achieved would be attributed to luck. He told me that if he was appointed to a high-profile job, especially in politics, people would assume that his family connections had worked their magic. But founding and growing a business seemed different. He was convinced that if the business proved successful, no one could dismiss it as mere good fortune.

By this point, all of us who knew John realized that he was gravitating toward a life in politics and envisioned *George* as his stepping-stone. While he had long avoided getting pulled into the family business, I began noticing a gradual change in his views. It became most obvious to me one night while dining together at the New York Athletic Club in downtown Manhattan. It was a moment so jarring that I can still recall John sipping from his bowl of steaming-hot tomato soup. He told me that he had spent the day ice-skating with underprivileged kids in Harlem. He noticed how excited they were to see him; how they clung to him as he circled around the rink.

"What they need is hope," he said. "They need to know that tomorrow will be better than today." He then paused and put down his spoon. "I can do that. I can give them that hope." I was stunned. Never had I heard him state so clearly his intent to enter the political arena. But he said that he had to make his magazine a success first, adding, "I can't fuck this up." Over the next few months, John and Michael engaged in long discussions, trying to articulate a clearer message and meaning for their vague concept. Together they produced an early working document that they planned to present to wealthy individuals and publishers to gauge interest.

Both viewed Clinton's election as a turning point in American history, like that of Franklin Roosevelt in 1932 and John F. Kennedy in 1960. Their own observations convinced them that the 1992 election was significant, and they turned to history to support their belief. They found useful evidence in a theory developed by famed historian Arthur Schlesinger Jr. The former Harvard professor and advisor to both JFK and RFK held that US politics was cyclical and repeated itself every thirty years. Each cycle allegedly began with a transfer of presidential power, which was animated by a desire for change and renewed public involvement in national affairs. Eventually that initial energy would fade and give way to a preoccupation with private affairs. Just as Roosevelt and Kennedy had inaugurated new eras in American life, so had Clinton's election signaled the beginning of another. John and Michael pointed out that citizens turned out to vote in record numbers, including more than one million newly registered voters under twenty-five. Minority participation spiked despite the absence of a prominent black candidate on the ticket. The number of women voters also increased significantly. On election night, ABC, CBS, CNN, and NBC posted prime-time ratings that jumped from a 34.8 share in 1988 to 46.3. These figures, they argued, showed that voters "were once again wholly vested in the political process."

John and Michael also marveled at how technology was transforming the way that politicians communicated with the public. John's father had been the first to use television to project his image into American living rooms. Now the emergence of cable television and twenty-four-hour news cycles was redefining the nature and experience of publicity; CNN and C-SPAN delivered unedited political news almost immediately as it occurred. Given the force and reach of this new media, politicians needed to adapt accordingly. In the most famous example, Bill Clinton played Elvis Presley's "Heartbreak Hotel" on his saxophone, while wearing hip dark shades, during an appearance on *The Arsenio Hall Show*. President George H. W. Bush appeared on MTV, and third-party candidate Ross Perot announced his bid on *Larry King Live*. Vice President Al Gore's appearance on *Late Night with David Letterman*, just two months into the Clinton-Gore administration, produced the show's highest-rated program. "Al Gore!" John would say incredulously, given the vice president's reputation for being stiff and pompous.

Michael and John observed another significant trend: the line between entertainment and politics had blurred beyond recognition, as politically themed films proliferated, and politicians became regarded as heroes. They used the example of the hit movie *Dave*, a 1993 political comedy about a man who bears such a striking resemblance to the commander in chief that the Secret Service recruits him to fill in while the real president lies in a stroke-induced coma. But it turns out that the substitute president is everything the original is not: honest, decent, and incorruptible. Berman and Kennedy believed the movie was important not only because it had a positive message, reaffirming that good people could still change a corrupt political system, but also because it highlighted the convergence between Hollywood and popular politics.

That convergence began with John's father, who turned to Frank Sinatra and his Rat Pack—Dean Martin, Sammy Davis Jr., Joey Bishop, and JFK's brother-in-law Peter Lawford—to reinforce his image as a celebrity politician, and peaked in the early 1990s. Ronald Reagan may have been the first Hollywood actor to become president, but his policies were too conservative for most stars in the entertainment community. It took the campaign and election of Bill Clinton to consummate the marriage between Washington power and Hollywood celebrity. Each had what the other desired. Celebrities wanted access to power. No longer content to hand over cash at star-studded fund-raisers, they insisted on sharing with those in power their views on everything from protecting the environment to promoting the arts. Politicians, who had seen their status decline since Watergate, understood that stars could not only fill their campaign coffers but also boost their stature and generate buzz. A picture taken with Robert Redford, Sharon Stone, or Richard Gere would land in newspapers and magazines and get more attention than any campaign event or commercial. It was no surprise that two A-list producers, Harry Thomason and Linda Bloodworth-Thomason, produced *The Man from Hope*, the schmaltzy Clinton biography that debuted at the 1992 Democratic Convention.

Once Clinton won election, a steady stream of celebrities flowed into the White House. Some commentators quipped that Barbra Streisand spent more time at the White House than members of the president's Cabinet. "The Clinton White House is extravagantly starstruck," complained *The New York Times*.

Now convinced that the federal government was in capable hands, Hollywood's elite turned out films that presented politicians in a more sympathetic light. John and Michael, however, believed that consumer demand accounted for Hollywood's sudden eagerness to make big blockbuster films about politics. "We the people are insisting on more information about the personalities who shape the issues and ideas that define our times," they wrote.

John's determination to create a magazine went beyond a celebration of celebrity for its own sake. He grew up listening to stories of the "good old days" when the public looked up to its leaders and the media focused on meaningful issues and not personal peccadilloes. Like many members of his family, John harbored a certain nostalgia for his father's presidency. Former advisors Kenny O'Donnell, Dave Powers, and Robert McNamara regaled him with glorious tales about JFK's administration—how his dad used his star power to rally the nation to fight the Communist threat globally, jumpstart the economy, and advance civil rights. Of course, they did not tell him that his father had also exaggerated the Soviet threat or that he had been slow to address civil rights violations. By the time John and I were having these conversations in the 1980s, he was well versed in the critical literature about his father, but he clung to the basic notion that had his father lived, the nation could have avoided much of the turmoil that shaped the 1960s.

I experienced this nostalgia firsthand when I helped John prepare a short speech about Robert McNamara, the US secretary of defense under both JFK and LBJ. In March 1998 *Time* magazine celebrated its seventy-fifth anniversary with a gala at Radio City Music Hall to honor those who had graced its cover over the decades. The event included political leaders such as President Clinton and Mikhail Gorbachev, the former leader of the now-defunct Soviet Union; Hollywood A-list celebrities (Tom Cruise, Sean Connery, Tom Hanks); and dozens of journalists, including NBC anchor Tom Brokaw. John was asked to deliver a speech honoring McNamara. He asked me to help him write the tribute, so we went to dinner at a small Italian restaurant not far from his apartment.

"I understand that McNamara made a mistake in Vietnam," he said, "and I don't want to ignore that, but he was loyal to my father and to my family. That counts for something." As we talked about walking that tightrope, John made a passing comment that his father would have pulled troops out of Vietnam had he lived. I questioned that assumption, pointing out the political blowback he would have received had he allowed South Vietnam to fall to Communism. The longer we debated, the more I realized that he had learned just about everything he knew about Vietnam from the surviving members of his father's administration. (No wonder he failed his Vietnam seminar at Brown!) The next day, John called me at home to say, "I talked to Bob McNamara last night, and he said you are completely wrong." I surrendered, not because John had convinced me but because I knew the issue was deeply personal for him. We were, after all, talking about his father.

Over the next few weeks, John faxed me drafts of his speech, which I would edit and then send back. We finished the day before the event, and I felt confident about the speech. But the content of the speech John delivered was completely different, and much better, than the one I had worked on. Clearly, he had called in the pros at the last minute. Taking a cue from his father's *Profiles in Courage* book, which honored senators who had made politically risky decisions, John spoke about McNamara's character. He wisely chose not to relitigate the Vietnam War, instead describing the courage that McNamara had shown by later admitting his own mistakes. However, one sentence did remain constant throughout each draft: "I would like to thank him for teaching me something about bearing great adversity with great dignity."

John was too well read and too sophisticated to accept the myth of Camelot, but he retained his father's ideals, his sense of public service, and his desire for change. I remember talking with him about the influential article and, later, bestselling book "Bowling Alone: America's Declining Social Capital," written by Harvard social scientist Robert Putnam. Published in an academic journal in 1995, the article used a wealth of statistical data to chart the decline of civic culture in the United States. Americans, Putnam pointed out, were no longer civically engaged—they were less likely than other generations to attend public meetings, go to church, or even participate in local sports. Americans, as Putnam reported memorably, were even bowling alone.

John found the argument wholly convincing and very disturbing. It appealed to him because it offered a new perspective that did not fall neatly into tired liberal and conservative orthodoxy. It underscored for him that the nation needed to find ways to get people—especially young people—invested in their communities and to care about political decisions that impacted them. An older generation may have grown too cynical to change, but John saw *George* as reaching young people who had yet to be tainted by the poisonous atmosphere in Washington. Most of the magazines that covered politics, such as *The New Republic* and *National Review*, were ideologically driven and written for political junkies. While John did want those in Washington to read the magazine, his true ambition lay in extending his reach beyond the Beltway.

In short, John intended to take a different approach to politics and journalism, promising that their venture would "be informational, not ideological." Both he and Berman believed that politics did not simply involve exercising the franchise; it was also about the colorful personalities and off-beat stories that helped voters to understand the human side of the political process. John was particularly sensitive to the necessity of humanizing politicians. He saw how his uncle Ted had been turned into a caricature by his conservative opponents. What if they could see Ted the way he did? This treatment should work both ways, John believed: liberals, too, needed to gain a deeper understanding of even the most controversial figures on the right, such as Alabama governor George Wallace and South Carolina senator Strom Thurmond. "*George* is a magazine that understands culture is more powerful than politics," John and Michael opined. Their goal was to "showcase politics as engaging, exciting, and hip" by combining "policy wonk" topics with "stylish, provocative reporting and writing."

They had the concept; what they needed next was a name. They tried to get away from names that included the word *politics*, since it made the magazine sound too much of an inside-the-Beltway production. But nothing worked. At the time, John was still dating Daryl Hannah, and the name *George* was the brainchild of her brother-in-law Lou Adler, the founder of Dunhill Records who was responsible for signing and recording such groups as the Mamas & the Papas and the comedy duo Cheech & Chong. "Yours is the first postpartisan magazine," he said. "Why not name it after our first president?" Both John and Michael loved the idea; more important, their testing showed that potential readers also responded warmly.

Not everyone had a clear idea of the magazine's vision, though. When John described the concept to his dying mother, Jackie asked, "John, is it going to be the *Mad* magazine of politics?" Her friends recall her making similar comments. But her concerns ran deeper. "John has never shown the slightest interest in the magazine business before," she told the author Edward Klein. "And he has no experience in journalism. Why would he want to start the kind of magazine that snoops and pries into people's private lives?" Mrs. Onassis was understandably sensitive about the prospect that her son would join the ranks of the paparazzi—the same people who had tormented her. But that was never the type of magazine that John planned to publish, as he explained to her on a number of occasions. Nevertheless, she was happy that John had not only found some career focus but also revealed a passion and dedication that was normally reserved for sports.

I had never seen John so passionate as when he was talking about *George*. After all, the concept of creating a magazine that used pop culture to generate interest in politics was both bold and innovative. I knew nothing about the magazine business, but I appreciated the power of John's charm and knew that he possessed the brains and perseverance to pull off such a daring feat. Over time, however, I came to question some of the assumptions upon which this enterprise rested. Most troubling was their belief that the country stood on the brink of entering a postpartisan age in which ideology no longer mattered. During his campaign, Bill Clinton had fed this notion by abandoning many traditionally Democratic positions, declaring himself a "new

Democrat" who remained tough on crime and aimed to "end welfare as we know it." He managed to win the 1992 election by maintaining the loyalty of the party's traditional constituencies—labor, African Americans, city dwellers, the poor—while also luring back the rapidly growing white, largely suburban middle class that had abandoned the party in the 1980s.

John's position becomes more understandable when viewed in relation to the mistakes of his father. JFK, along with many liberals of his generation, assumed that prosperity had muted ideological differences. "Politics," Kennedy said with a typical flourish in 1962, needed to avoid "basic clashes of philosophy and ideology" and be directed toward "ways and means of achieving goals." He could not have been more wrong. Ideological clashes defined the 1960s. The decade witnessed violent battles over race relations, bitter debates over the Vietnam War, and the emergence of a generation of radicalized, militant students who joined groups on opposite ends of the ideological spectrum.

There was a window in the mid-1990s when reasonable people could again believe that the nation was headed for an age of peace and prosperity devoid of partisanship and ideology. The end of the Cold War, the great ideological struggle that had defined President Kennedy's generation, seemed to usher in a new age of liberal democracy—a "new world order," as President George H. W. Bush declared. With the collapse of the Soviet Union, the United States stood as the world's sole superpower, prepared to spread its values across the globe. The political scientist Francis Fukuyama went so far as to proclaim "the end of history," pronouncing, "there are no serious ideological competitors left to liberal democracy." A similar sense of optimism infused thinking about America at home. Technological breakthroughs promised to increase productivity, a global economy dominated by the United States offered the prospect of ever-rising living standards, and the coming-of-age of the baby boom generation, the largest and best educated in history, conjured hopes of unending prosperity. Unburdened by history, and by the threat of global recessions, Americans decided to focus their energy on private pursuits, and politicians clashed more about culture than about the substance of policy.

We now know that optimism was misplaced. The technology bubble that burst at the end of the decade was a precursor to a global crash less than a decade later. The 9/11 attacks on the World Trade Center and the Pentagon in 2001 underscored the persistence of radical ideologies that threatened the global order. Globalization, it turned out, enriched a few and left many behind, producing a massive wealth gap in America.

While no one at the time could have anticipated these events, it was possible to see that John had vested too much significance in the 1992 election. Shortly after the Democratic Party reclaimed the White House after twelve years, Arthur Schlesinger Jr., the same historian whose ideas shaped John's thinking about *George*, asked me to write an essay on the election for a series he was editing on the history of presidential elections. Given all the hype and excitement surrounding Clinton's victory, I assumed I would find evidence revealing an important shift in voting patterns. I was disappointed. Clinton won with 43 percent of the popular vote in a three-way race. Businessman Ross Perot, who ran as an independent, did not win a single vote in the Electoral College but did claim almost 19 percent of the popular vote—more than any third-party candidate since Theodore Roosevelt in 1912. Some signs of change were apparent. Voters sent six women to the Senate and forty-eight to the House of Representatives. California became the first state to elect two women senators—Barbara Boxer and Dianne Feinstein—and Illinois elected the first African American woman to the upper chamber, Carol Moseley Braun.

Like Kennedy and Berman, many Democrats hoped and believed Clinton's victory set the groundwork for a realignment like Franklin D. Roosevelt's revolution of the 1930s. But much to my surprise, I learned that Clinton's victory did not, overall, deviate from recent elections. From 1980 to 1992, four separate Democratic nominees won between 40 percent and 45 percent of the popular vote. The Republican range was much wider, swinging from 59 percent in 1984 to 38 percent in 1992. Clinton received the same percentage of the electorate as Hubert Humphrey in 1968. His 43 percent was lower than Dukakis's 45.6 percent in a two-way race in 1988. Only 38 percent of Independents voted for Clinton—the same number who voted for Walter Mondale in 1984. Only 10 percent of Republicans crossed over to vote for him. Voter surveys showed that economic discontent and a desire for change spearheaded the Democratic victory. The election represented a rejection of the Bush presidency, not a new mandate for reform.

Even as Berman and Kennedy were fine-tuning their nonpartisan pitch,

American politics was taking a disturbing lurch to the right. In the 1994 midterm elections, Georgia firebrand congressman Newt Gingrich, who had been pushing Republicans to adopt a highly partisan, take-no-prisoners approach to politics, led his party to take control of the House. That year, not a single Republican incumbent for Congress or governor lost. Republicans seized control of both houses of Congress for the first time in forty years. In Senate races, they won all nine open elections and defeated two sitting Democrats. The day after the election, Senator Richard Shelby of Alabama switched to the Republican Party, increasing the GOP's edge to 53–47. Republicans also scored well in the states, where they controlled the governor's mansion in eight of the nine most populous states. Democratic gubernatorial stars Mario Cuomo of New York and Ann Richards of Texas went down to defeat. For the first time in history an incumbent House Speaker, Tom Foley of Washington, was defeated.

The election represented the culmination of a process that began at the end of World War II, when the Democratic Party began inching toward support for civil rights, a process that accelerated once Lyndon Johnson signed the Voting Rights Act of 1965. While the white South voted solidly Republican in presidential elections, it continued to support Democratic candidates on the local and state levels out of habit. But that tradition changed in 1994, heralding a new era of conservative politics. Nineteen of the forty-nine House seats Republicans garnered came from thirteen southern states: the eleven states of the Confederacy along with Kentucky and Oklahoma. Most of the seats came from districts that tended to vote Republican in presidential elections but had continued to elect Democratic congressmen. For the first time since the post–Civil War Reconstruction—the twelve-year period from 1865 to 1877—Republicans controlled most southern governorships, senatorships, and congressional seats. In less than a generation, the Republicans turned the solidly Democratic South into the securely Republican South. Texas, home of Speaker of the House Sam Rayburn and Lyndon Johnson, now had two Republican senators and a Republican governor. Republican members of Congress outnumbered Democrats by 2 to 1 in Florida, Georgia, Kentucky, North Carolina, Oklahoma, and South Carolina.

Although not apparent at the time, the same technology that Berman and Kennedy celebrated as the vehicle for mobilizing disenfranchised voters was also a double-edged sword. Radio did marshal voters, but it was not the apathetic liberals who responded to the agitation. In 1960 only two radio stations had talk formats. By 1995, there were 1,130. The most popular hosts were overwhelmingly men, and nearly 70 percent of listeners were conservative. By 1994, 20 million Americans were tuning in to hear right-wing conspiracy monger Rush Limbaugh on 659 radio stations. In addition, his late-night television show was syndicated to 225 stations, and his two books topped the bestseller list.

The optimistic ideas that informed *George*—that Bill Clinton's campaign and election signaled the beginning of a new postpartisan age, and that the merger of politics and popular culture would lead to more educated and engaged voters who didn't depend as much on parties for their political identity—were the product of America's unique environment in the 1990s. Unfortunately, many of those assumptions would prove false.

Berman and Kennedy labored quietly for two years, but the initiative picked up after Jackie's death in May 1994. Since leaving the DA's office earlier that year, John spent most of his time working out of Joseph P. Kennedy Enterprises on Forty-Second Street in Manhattan. He rode his bike from there to Michael's Manhattan office a few times a week for meetings. The weekend after Jackie's funeral, John called Berman and asked if he could move into Michael's office. "I need to focus on this, and I can't have everyone telling me how sorry they are every day," he explained. "I can't deal with the sympathy in the Kennedy office."

Berman and a partner, Will Steere, had formed a public relations firm called PRNY, and Berman hired a tough-talking woman from the Bronx, RoseMarie Terenzio, as his assistant. Since they handled many celebrity clients, Rose was not surprised when John started showing up at the office. According to RoseMarie, by the spring of 1994, John, accompanied daily by Sam, his "slightly demented rescue dog," visited the office every day. Michael never told Rose why John was coming to the office, but she did notice they had several "spirited" meetings during which John would gesticulate wildly. No one ever knew what they were talking about, and they always were careful to take whatever papers they had brought with them.

A few days after Mrs. Onassis's burial, RoseMarie arrived at work only to find John and a stranger placing her possessions in a cardboard box and moving them out of her office. "What are you doing?" she shouted. John explained that Michael had offered Rose's office to him. Rose shouted for Michael, who then explained to her that he and John were now working together. "Let's be realistic," he said. "You really think I'm going to give him the smaller office?

"You're going to be just fine," he added, reassuring her that her job was safe but that she simply was being dislodged from her office.

RoseMarie remained so angry that she ignored John every time he entered the office. He would greet her with a pleasant "good morning" as he walked past her small office, but she refused to reciprocate. On a few occasions when she heard him coming down the hall, she would pick up her phone and pretend to be talking. This act continued for about a month, until one day John decided to stick his head in her door and say, "Good morning, Rosie." It marked the first time that he referred to her by name, and no one outside of her family ever referred to her as Rosie. He then stared at her to see how she would react. At first, she extended her middle finger but then started laughing. John's gesture broke the ice. He did not know it at the time, but it would also gain him a trusted assistant and a dear, lifelong friend.

Over the next few months, each man spent $150,000 of his own money to hire consultants and develop business plans. During long, sometimes contentious sessions, and after conversations with dozens of consultants, paid and unpaid, they refined their vision for the magazine. Joe Armstrong convinced them that they would be in a better negotiating position with an investor or partner if they proved their concept through a direct mail campaign. "You buy ten thousand names from the mailing lists of fifteen magazines," he told them, "and send out a mock-up of the magazine." He hooked them up with George Lois, a legendary art director who'd produced iconic covers for *Esquire*, to help with the design. For every hundred samples sent out, the hope was to get 3.5 responses from random consumers who claimed they would pay for a $24 subscription. "*George* is to politics what *Rolling Stone* is to music. *Forbes* is to business. *Allure* is to beauty. *Premiere* is to films," the editor's letter read.

They mailed two test batches: one with John's name on the masthead, and one without. "If the test without you is successful, then we have a business," Berman told Kennedy. "Otherwise we have a business about you, and that's not good for either of us." The responses to both batches proved quite positive. Not surprisingly, they scored a 5.7 response rate with John's name visible. But what was surprising was that the one without his name earned an impressive 5.1 response.

"This is a go," they declared.

John's personal life was also in transition. In 1990, while still dating Daryl Hannah, John met Carolyn Bessette, a personal stylist catering to celebrity clients at the Calvin Klein store in Manhattan. Carolyn told model Michael Bergin, her boyfriend at the time, that she had originally been introduced to John at a charity event. Afterward, John visited the Calvin Klein store to purchase three suits and Carolyn served as his stylist. Although Carolyn admitted to Bergin that she knew John, she downplayed any hint of romance, telling him that she had been "under-impressed." In reality, that first encounter led to a brief romance. In the summer of 1990, Carole Radziwill recalled staying at a house that John and Anthony shared in East Hampton, when Carolyn came bouncing out of John's bedroom.

John was clearly smitten with Carolyn—and for understandable reasons. She was stunningly beautiful: tall (five feet, ten inches) and slender with long blonde hair, blue eyes, and broad shoulders. But it was not just her looks that John found attractive. When she wanted to be, Carolyn was also charming, engaging, almost mesmerizing. John preferred surrounding himself with friends—and girlfriends—who were not spellbound by his fame. He gravitated toward strong, independent-minded women who were not afraid to voice their opinions. "Most women sort of became tongue-tied around John," said Brown fraternity brother Richard Wiese. "But not Carolyn. She was very strong-minded, knew what she wanted, and had absolutely no difficulty speaking her mind." John once told Carole Radziwill that on one of their first dates he scored tickets to a play, but Carolyn got stuck at work and never showed up. (This happened before cell phones and instant messaging.) "John was shocked that she stood him up," Carole recalled.

Carolyn Jeanne Bessette was born on January 7, 1966, in White Plains, New York, to kitchen designer William Bessette and public school administrator Ann. She had two twin sisters, Lisa and Lauren, who were older than her by two years. When Carolyn was six, her parents separated. Carolyn blamed her father for the breakup of their family and rarely spoke to him after that. In 1973, Ann married Dr. Richard Freeman, the chief of orthopedic surgery at a White Plains hospital, and the family moved to tony Greenwich, Connecticut.

Carolyn spent two years at Greenwich High School before transferring to St. Mary's High School. She graduated in 1983, the same year that John finished at Brown. Her classmates voted her the "Ultimate Beautiful Person." A story recounted by a fellow student offers evidence of why she received the honor. "When I was a freshman and she was a big senior, she was incredibly sweet to me," recalled Claudia Slocum. "I remember I burst into the girls' room one day, just sobbing, probably over some lip gloss that my friends had made fun of or something. And she was there with her friends. And she came right over. She dried my eyes and tucked my hair behind my ears and talked me up. And after that, she always smiled and said hi to me in the halls."

That fall, Carolyn entered Boston University, where her reputation— unlike in high school—was less than stellar. No one at Boston would have voted her the "Ultimate Beautiful Person." Friends attested that Carolyn did not join clubs or play any sports and never made the dean's list. She did, however, enjoy an active social life, dating influential men on campus, attending parties, and going out to local clubs.

During this time, Carolyn worked at the Calvin Klein store in the Chestnut Hill Mall, near the Boston College campus. It was here, in 1988, that she met Grace (a student at Boston College who does not want her last name used), who was shopping for a dress when she struck up a conversation with Carolyn. They became fast friends. "We were interested in similar things such as fashion, art, and photography," Grace told me in 2019. "We both liked the same designers." During one of their chats, they shared their romantic fantasies. When Grace asked who Carolyn's "dream guy" was, Carolyn responded, "John Kennedy Jr." "I'm going to get him," Carolyn insisted. "I'm going to move to New York and I'm going to get him." Grace was shocked by the intensity of Carolyn's focus on John. Carolyn's comments suggest that her later encounter with John at a charity event may not have been by chance.

That obsession was not the only disturbing revelation about Carolyn. When Grace asked her what she wanted to do with her life, Carolyn stated, "I want to be famous. Maybe if I hook up with the right guy I will be famous." Grace observed that Carolyn had a knack for getting to know the most important people on campus. "She had to be with the guy of the moment." She dated fashion empire heir Alessandro Benetton, as well as John Cullen, a

Canadian-born hockey star who later became a professional player for the Tampa Bay Lightning. Furthermore, it did not matter if the man she desired was already in a relationship. Another female classmate who wishes to remain anonymous recalled how Carolyn waged a campaign to steal her boyfriend, who was also a star hockey player. And yet another student told Christopher Andersen that "Carolyn was sort of known as the campus man-eater."

In the end, Grace realized that even after spending months hanging out with Carolyn, "I did not know her true self. On one occasion, she would be stoic and reserved; on another, she would be wild and crazy. She would pretend to be humble and then turn around and be a complete snob when she was hanging out with fashion people. I felt that she was always acting."

It took Carolyn an added semester to earn her degree in elementary childhood education at Boston University. After graduating, she continued to work at the Calvin Klein store while also doing marketing for That's Entertainment, a company that owned a number of nightclubs in the area. Joe Verange, who hired her, remembered her as "a good schmoozer, a good networker," capable of organizing parties at a variety of clubs. But Verange also told *The Boston Globe* that "she was obviously looking for more than a life of hanging out in nightclubs."

That opportunity for a wider life came when Susan Sokol, president of Calvin Klein's women's collection, spotted Carolyn while visiting the Boston store. She was impressed by Carolyn's looks and style and invited her to move to New York, where she would have a job accommodating celebrity clients. "She wasn't intimidated," Sokol recalled. "She had a wonderful ease about her. She was comfortable with anyone, and she had a lot of self-confidence, aside from looking great."

With that new job, Carolyn finally landed in John's orbit. But their brief romance ended when Daryl Hannah moved to New York to try to mend her relationship with John. Carolyn continued dating Michael Bergin. John, however, made sure to keep tabs on her. He would always inquire about her from mutual friends. "It was often the first question out of his mouth," recalled one friend. According to Carole Radziwill, "He always had one eye on her."

By the time Jackie died in 1994, John had already been planning to ditch Daryl. He started seeing Julie Baker, whom he had dated briefly before meeting Daryl. But Carolyn still lingered in his mind. Although she had clearly made it her goal to be with John, Carolyn now played hard to get. If John did something to upset her—like canceling dinner at the last minute—she would scream at him, "Fuck you! I'm going off with Michael!" She would claim to mutual friends that she was not going to wait for John, but she would actually remain home and listen for the phone to ring.

Even as he pursued their relationship, John tried to gather more information about Carolyn from others. He had heard rumors that Carolyn liked to party, so he asked a friend who had connections in the Manhattan nightclub scene to investigate and report back to him. The friend, who wishes to remain anonymous, recalled that he did not deliver a "flattering" report. "She does a lot of blow, she stays out late, she knows how to reel in guys and play guys, she dated the star football player in high school, the captain of the hockey team in college. Be careful." John not only ignored this advice, he also told Carolyn everything he'd heard. She never forgave the friend.

Yet for now, John tried to keep his relationship with Carolyn under the radar, partly because most of his time was occupied by the launch of his new magazine.

Over the next eighteen months, the two partners arranged meetings with wealthy investors, many of them friends of John's mom, along with a handful of publishing houses. "Every door was open to them," said a friend of John's. "But that was good news and bad news. Did these people believe, or did they just want to meet John?" At one point, John and Michael joked that they could fund the magazine simply by charging people $1 million to meet with John.

Their initial meetings did not go well. Even if Michael and John attended a meeting together, it would become clear that everyone wanted to see and hear from John. The two men were invited to make a presentation to a large publishing house. Michael did all the talking, and John sat largely silent. When the publishing executives were asked afterward how the meeting went, one said, "We were pissed. We had no intention of giving them any money. We just wanted to hear from John, and all we got was Berman. We could not kick them out of the office fast enough."

Some potential investors found them unprepared and unfocused. One of those they approached described it as "very much amateur hour." The president of a small publishing company said that John came to him with only a vague idea about his magazine's direction. "He gave me his feelings about the marketplace, that young people are interested in politics, but we don't realize it and it doesn't show up in the stats," he recalled John explaining. He then asked John about a magazine article suggesting that only 15 percent of any generation find government or public affairs interesting, but John dismissed the observation. "It was the worst presentation I have seen in my business life," the executive stated. "He was like, 'I'm JFK, so there you go.' He just knew he had this perfect idea; he was so worked up."

Even close friends of the family rejected him, including Jann Wenner, whose negative response especially disappointed John. He initially thought that Wenner, the founder of *Rolling Stone* magazine, would at least offer constructive comments. Instead, John complained afterward, "He shit all over it." "Politics doesn't sell," Jann told him bluntly. "It's not commercial." He then proceeded to offer John a job at *Rolling Stone*. John suspected that Wenner simply did not want the competition. "John was hurt and felt betrayed by Jann," a colleague recalled.

They also set up a meeting with David Koch, an oil billionaire from Wichita, Kansas, who donated heavily to both the Republican and Libertarian Parties. But Koch seemed less interested in buying the magazine than he did in purchasing Mrs. Onassis's apartment, which he'd seen and wanted a second look at even though potential buyers were allowed only one visit. "I am planning to get married, and I'm looking at your mother's apartment," he told John. "Your mama was a lot like mine. Neither one of them likes spending a penny. That apartment is a mess." John was taken aback by Koch's bluntness and his lack of interest in the real purpose of the meeting, but he arranged for the billionaire to see the apartment again, and Koch eventually bought it. "We received no investment from him," Berman recalled with a laugh. "But John got $9.5 million."

John and Michael did manage to snare about a dozen investors, mostly Europeans, who were willing to offer between $500,000 and $1 million each. The total sum added up to roughly $10 million, which fell well short of the $20 million they needed to launch. A large portion of the money needed to be directed toward circulation, publication, and sales, three essential elements that a publishing company would already have in place. But no publishers expressed interest. Worse still, John and Berman feared that many of those who put up money did so for the wrong reason: they just wanted to be in business with JFK Jr. "It was like buying a racehorse," Berman claimed.

By the end of 1994, it appeared that *George* was dead. "We were a little dejected at the time," Berman recalled. Little did they know that they would soon find an unlikely ally.

David Pecker was born in 1951 in the Bronx, the son of a bricklayer. After graduating from Pace University, he worked as an accountant for the prestigious firm Price Waterhouse. In 1979 he secured a position as a bean counter at CBS's magazine division, then quickly ascended the ranks to become company vice president. Eventually the magazine division was sold to Hachette Filipacchi Magazines, which named Pecker its new president in 1990. He rapidly cultivated a reputation as "the bad boy of magazine publishing." His critics dismissed him as a "used car salesman" and a "bottom fisher" who presided over a "bargain basement" empire. He had raised Hachette's profile in the United States by buying failing magazines, cutting staff to reduce costs, and offering big discounts to advertisers. Sometimes he tailored the editorial content of his magazines to suit advertisers. His tactics, however unconventional, worked. He made *Elle* the number two fashion magazine behind *Vogue* and ahead of *Harper's Bazaar*. He was also central to the success of *Metropolitan Home* and *Car and Driver*.

Pecker, with his slick black hair and thick mustache, relished his bad-boy image in the industry. He was a larger-than-life figure who swaggered around the office and did little to hide his ruthless ambition. He thought there was nothing that money and success could not buy. John used to tell the story about a conversation he overheard between Pecker and his wife. Pointing out that they did not have children, she asked him, "Who will mourn us when we are dead?" Pecker responded: "We will hire people."

Hachette's president was not the kind of person John ever imagined being in business with; in fact, for most of his life, he had studiously avoided celebrity hounds like David Pecker. But facing a string of rejections, John probably realized he could not be picky.

Kennedy had approached Pecker at a benefit dinner in June 1994. According to Pecker, after John introduced himself, he immediately started detailing his idea, but other people came between them, and they never finished the conversation. When Pecker returned to the office, his director of communications mentioned that John had also pitched him his magazine idea at the event. "I was really interested," Pecker recalled, but for the next few months, his calls to John went unanswered. Now running low on options, John finally decided to return the call. "I just want you to know we have a lot of interest, and not just in having lunch with John Kennedy," Pecker told him.

A few weeks later, Pecker made a dinner reservation at an Italian restaurant on East Sixtieth Street in Manhattan. He arrived first and watched as John pulled up on a bicycle, despite the frigid December night, with a briefcase slung over his shoulder. John confided that he had approached several other publishers, but none believed in the concept. Pecker knew that under normal circumstances, a magazine combining politics and pop culture could never work. John and Michael had conducted a successful test showing there was interest in the concept even without John's name attached. But attracting advertisers would be the challenge. Could John's fame and celebrity overcome this obstacle and make such a combination plausible? Pecker planned to find out, using John to sell not only *George* but also the other magazines in his stable. Most important, he intended to raise Hachette's national presence and to elevate his own profile. According to Wenner Media executive Kent Brownridge, "every fucking publisher in New York" had turned John down, but Pecker "instantly saw the world's greatest ad sales machine was standing right in front of him."

John made it clear, however, that he did not want his celebrity to overwhelm the magazine. "I want the magazine to speak for itself," he said. The conversation at this first meeting set the tone for the next few years, with Hachette desperately trying to commercialize John's celebrity and Kennedy resisting. This tension was never resolved.

Pecker inquired whether John was developing the magazine on his own. John told him about Berman and his background. "You should be the editor, and since Berman is a PR guy, he should be the publisher," Pecker stated. They agreed to hold a follow-up meeting that would include Berman as well as members of Pecker's team. "Look," Pecker said, "I love your idea. I love your concept. I appreciate the research you have done already. But I am going to put together a little SWAT team."

They worked over the next week to produce an executive summary, a white paper, and a business plan showcasing the magazine. The new blueprint was far more ambitious than anything Berman or Kennedy had imagined. Their initial proposal aimed for a circulation of 150,000, whereas Pecker had his sights set on more than double that: 400,000. It would require an initial investment of $20 million, but Hachette estimated that *George* could turn a profit in two and a half to three years. The first year, it would appear only on newsstands. The plan was to publish twice in 1995 before going bi-monthly in 1996, with the possibility of switching to monthly later that year to provide coverage of the upcoming presidential election.

Pecker hoped that John's celebrity would allow him to make a big splash in the magazine world. "The original plan has changed one hundred eighty degrees," he told the trade magazine *Mediaweek*. "This is more of a *Vanity Fair* type of launch." *Vanity Fair*, with its celebrity writers and renowned photographers, exercised enormous influence and was considered the grande dame of magazines. Now, with John in tow, Pecker dreamed of adding to his stable a magazine that could compete against the venerable *Vanity Fair*.

Pecker relished John's celebrity stature and rarely missed an opportunity to exploit it. Several *George* editors complained that the publishing executive used Kennedy for his own benefit. "He treated John as a possession," said one. "He was like a toy. He was like a shiny object that he could tout to these advertisers and potential advisors and people he wanted to rub elbows with." Pecker's memories of working with John are filled with images of hysterical women, surging crowds, and flashing cameras. Reflecting on their trip to Paris to sell the concept to the French, Pecker said, "John was a rock star. From the time we got into the Charles de Gaulle Airport and walked through the airport to get our bags, to the time we arrived at the hotel, people were screaming as if he was Mick Jagger."

The day after their arrival in Paris, they sat down with the French execu-tives. The session could not have begun more awkwardly. Pecker had warned CEO Daniel Filipacchi that under no circumstances was he or anyone else to refer to their guest as John-John. But as soon as they walked into the room, Filipacchi greeted him that way. "He was pissed," Pecker recalled. "He was clearly pissed." Apparently, the French were as starstruck as Pecker, who described John's presentation as "mesmerizing." Despite the uncomfortable start, the French left the meeting convinced.

At Berman's suggestion, they announced the partnership on February 22, 1995: Washington's birthday. Since he believed that he had more experience, and, frankly, was the more reliable partner, Michael wanted 51 percent con-trolling interest of their share of the business, but John balked at the idea, and they ended up splitting their 50 percent share equally, while Hachette controlled the other 50 percent. Neither man put any of his own money on the table. They both considered John's celebrity status as their investment. The contract called for a salary plus a performance bonus that could potentially pay each of them $1 million a year.

That evening, Pecker organized a special dinner at Rao's in East Harlem, one of the most exclusive restaurants in the city. The upscale setting seemed the perfect place to celebrate two years of hard work and sacrifice. David brought his wife, Karen, and Michael's wife, Victoria, joined in the celebration. John came alone. Even Madonna and actress Sharon Stone, who were sitting at an adjacent table, decided to join them for the festivities.

With the contract signed, *George* moved into the Hachette Building, a forty-eight-floor skyscraper constructed of black glass and steel and located at Broadway and Fifty-First Street. They set up camp on the forty-fourth floor, in a windowless conference room containing three metal desks, three computers, two phones, and no watercooler. "I couldn't believe we were stuck in such a shabby hole," RoseMarie Terenzio reflected. But John was composed. "This is the life," he said.

At this point, *George* magazine consisted of only three people: John, Michael, and RoseMarie. But it soon became apparent that John and Michael would not be treated as equal partners. Within a few weeks, someone from Hachette arrived to escort them to their individual offices. John received a large, beautiful corner office with two waist-to-ceiling windows that offered sweeping views of the Hudson River to the west and Central Park to the north. Michael, on the other hand, got a small cubicle. "It was predictable, and almost laughable," he recalled. But it also reminded him that even though he and John had begun this enterprise jointly, Berman would always be overshadowed by his celebrity colleague. John found the whole arrangement ridiculous and rushed to Michael's defense, "Look, if you want me to go up and talk to them, I am happy to do that." He did exactly that, and Michael was switched to a more appropriate space.

But a much bigger problem than office space arose on that first day. Up to that point, everyone had theoretically agreed about the magazine, its name, and its purpose. Now Hachette argued unexpectedly that the magazine should be more akin to *People*, revolving around John's life. The company's editorial director, Jean-Louis Ginibre, wanted the magazine to write puff pieces about the powerful celebrities and politicians they needed for their covers, and he insisted that John write as many as seven articles per issue. He even proposed a different name—*Crisscross*—since the magazine would operate at the intersection of power, money, and culture.

Upon learning of the plan, John erupted in anger. "He was furious," recalled Berman. "He was beyond furious." Both men felt betrayed. During early negotiations, there had been no ambiguity about the magazine's name or about John's role in it. Suddenly, on the first day, Hachette derailed all of their carefully developed plans. "It was amateur hour," said Berman. "John was freaking out." Berman assured John that he would handle this latest setback himself. John gave him clear instructions: "Look," he said, "we are going to walk out right now. We couldn't have been any clearer about what this magazine was about. And you know this is not a John Kennedy fan magazine. I am the editor, and that's all. If they think they got me in the door so that they could compete with *People* magazine, then they are completely wrong." Berman delivered the message. Pecker quickly apologized and dropped the issue. "It was," Michael recalled, "a very unpleasant first day."

The incident highlighted an important dimension of John's leadership style. John preferred to remain above the fray, avoid conflict and confrontation, and have someone he trusted play the role of bad cop. "Suddenly the struggle over the direction of the magazine is very serious," an anonymous source told the author Michael Gross. "There are different conceptions. John is smart, but he lacks an edge. He's one of the least assertive people you'll ever meet; he's never had to assert himself—he's John Kennedy! Now, suddenly, he's in a huge corporation. He wants a magazine of ideas with a sugar coating. They want a political *People*." For the first time in his life, John found himself thrust into the brutal and often uncompromising style of corporate politics, and, for now, he trusted Berman to protect his back.

Along with these early struggles over the new magazine's scope, they also needed to recruit advertisers. Hachette had close ties with General Motors, which was not only a major car manufacturer but also the largest advertiser in the world, spending $1 billion on media every year. Pecker and John traveled to Detroit to meet with Linda Thomas Brooks, an executive vice president whose team handled strategic planning and buying across all General Motors brands. Thomas Brooks found both the magazine and its celebrity editor intriguing. Here was a publication that aimed to appeal to a younger demographic while demonstrating the same quality control, thoughtful editorial tone, and meaningful content of more traditional magazines. "It was just different from everything else out there," she recalled. "We saw things all the time that were either the same or just slightly different from what already existed in the market. When John brought this in, I didn't realize what a hole in the market existed. But it was there, and John found it. That's why I thought it was interesting."

Unlike his very first attempts to court investors, John impressed Linda and the members of her team. "He had assimilated enough of the publishing business to have a meaningful understanding of the business," she recalled. "He learned the game." They had worked with celebrity editors before, but John appeared different. "He had obviously got himself schooled in what it really meant and how it worked." He had become an expert on the interplay between politics and culture. He spoke passionately about how young people hungered for more information about the political process but had nowhere to turn. *George*, he said, was designed to locate future "thought leaders"—those who wished to have an impact on communities at home and abroad. There were, however, still unanswered questions: What was the editorial going to include? In essence, they needed to develop a unique style and voice that would distinguish *George* from other magazines and then assign articles that would communicate their distinctive message to readers.

Linda asked John to return to Detroit later to meet her boss, Michael Browner, who had met his wife while campaigning for John's father in 1960. Browner, GM's executive director of media and marketing operations, eagerly welcomed John, who explained the magazine concept and asked him to place an advertising order. "I didn't know whether or not *George* was going to be a big success," Browner reflected, admitting, "I did not immediately fall in love with the concept." But he hoped that John's personal charisma and celebrity, along with the backing of a professional media company such as Hachette, would enable this unconventional magazine to both survive and thrive. What impressed him most was how John talked about politics, without malice: "It wasn't left-wing politics or right-wing politics; it was how interesting the subject of politics could be." Browner always thought of politics as a clash between two parties, but "John talked about it in a way that transcended partisanship. I was extremely impressed by him."

Most advertisers, along with Hachette executives, viewed John as a convenient tool to sell more magazines. John, however, longed to be taken seriously as an editor and as a businessman. He faced a delicate balancing act: he wanted to contribute just enough of himself to attract attention to the magazine, but he never wanted the magazine to be about him. In his meetings with both Thomas Brooks and Browner, John insisted that the new publication must succeed based on its quality, not his celebrity. "He did not want to turn it into a JFK Jr. magazine," Browner reflected. While Browner believed that the magazine would have had a greater chance of success had John included more of his personal life in its pages, he admitted that "it would not have been the magazine that John wanted to edit."

But for all John's inner conflict, no one could fully ignore the realities of his fame. Toward the end of the Browner meeting, a staff member came into the conference room and asked Linda to leave. "We have to take him out the back way," she said. Word had spread that John was in the building, and the lobby had filled up with curious bystanders and reporters. They ended up smuggling John out through the freight elevator and into a car behind the building.

After the meetings with Thomas Brooks and Browner, General Motors became the first company to make a major commitment to the magazine. "We committed to multiple pages in the initial schedule of issues," Thomas Brooks recalled. But they made sure to structure the deal to minimize their own risk. They received the best rates, and the contract stipulated that if the circulation didn't reach the agreed-upon targets, their rates would be reduced. If, however, the magazine struck a major chord, General Motors would have the first option to remain the premier advertiser.

A few weeks later, John returned to the Motor City for a third time to speak at the Adcraft Club of Detroit, the largest association of advertisers in the country. The club rarely invited editors of start-up magazines, but it knew that John would prove to be the main attraction. Throughout the day, people lined up along the hallways of the Renaissance Center's Westin Hotel hoping to snare one of the 1,900 tickets available for the event. Television cameras loomed everywhere. "It was more like something for a rock star," said Adcraft Club spokesman Bill Jentzen. One magazine publisher told the *Los Angeles Times* that the "advertising world went nuts for this guy. It was bizarre. I can't think of anyone else in this country who could have drawn the range of interest that he did. Everyone wanted to see the guy. Everyone."

Whether intentional or not, organizers scheduled the event on Secretaries Day, so hundreds of young women packed the audience. Pecker remembered how much John resembled a Greek god, striding down the center aisle while women in the audience shrieked. As he took his seat on the dais, dozens of women rushed to the stage to take his picture before being told to return to their seats. After introducing John, Michael Browner announced that he had committed to becoming the magazine's largest advertiser.

John understood the importance of this presentation, and he skillfully played with expectations by handing out small nuggets of personal information—just enough to make people feel they knew him, while still protecting his privacy. "I'm well aware of the expectation that sooner or later I would be giving a speech about politics," he said. He talked about his career and his hopes for making the right choices in life. "I'm speaking not as a politician, but as a magazine editor," he said. "And if I do that right, I hope someday to end up as president [*long pause*] of a very successful publishing venture."

But despite John's efforts to turn the focus to more meaningful issues, he remained the spectacle. During the question-and-answer session, many audience members used their index cards to convey home phone numbers and lipstick kisses instead of hard-hitting questions. John, always the showman, jokingly put one of the cards in his pocket, but he maintained his professional manner. The only bit of his private life that he revealed was, in response to a question, that his childhood idols were Mick Jagger and Muhammad Ali.

Following the Adcraft event, both Berman and Kennedy watched with surprise as advertiser interest in the magazine grew steadily. Their original proposal had budgeted only thirty pages of ads, but now they faced overwhelming attention. To help deal with the advertising deluge, they recruited Elinore Carmody, who boasted fifteen years' experience in the world of magazine publishing, including stints at *New York* magazine and, most recently, at Hachette-owned *Tell* magazine. The timing could not have been more perfect, as Elinore had just taken some time off after getting married. Pecker hadn't wanted to completely cut ties, so he told her, "Go get married, come back, and I will have something for you."

A few months later, when Elinore read in the *New York Post* about John's fledgling magazine, she informed Pecker she would love to be involved in the venture. Not only did she know that the magazine would attract plenty of attention because of John, but also she liked the unique concept. Elinore arranged a meeting to discuss coming aboard. "My first impressions were very positive about both John and Michael," she reflected. "I thought they were smart guys who did their homework, conducted research, and had clearly worked closely with consultants."

At that meeting, they asked Elinore if she could estimate how many advertising pages the magazine would attract. "It's not a question of how much; it's a question of how much you can handle," she said. John and Michael seemed shocked when she told them they could have at least a hundred pages of ads, probably more. Elinore's confidence came from an informal survey she had conducted among her advertiser friends. The two founders had not realized how much the fashion industry would embrace *George*. Professionals in the advertising world associated Hachette with automotive, liquor, and other brands. But not fashion. However, Elinore called a friend, the marketing director at the fashion house Giorgio Armani, and asked, "I am going to call on you. What are you going to say?" Her friend promised to fax the offer to headquarters in Milan, Italy, and assured Elinore that Armani would instantly agree. At that moment, Elinore sensed that *George* would draw a wider range of advertisers, from both female-driven fashion and male-driven automotive industries, than most other magazines.

Elinore insisted that the magazine produce a prototype to present to advertisers. "I knew from experience that advertisers need to see something, they need to look at something, they need to touch something, they need to have the sense of the feel of it, the look and feel of it," she said. Pecker, unwilling to spend the money, resisted, but John and Michael agreed. The prototype ended up being a huge hit, boosting their confidence that they truly had "a real magazine" on their hands, something that did not depend solely on John's cult of personality. "It legitimized the adventure," Elinore recalled.

Soon enough, all the major fashion brands hopped on board. Elinore requested all advertisers to purchase the same number of ads, at the same price, in the second edition. Their top advertisers included the biggest names in fashion: Armani, Ralph Lauren, Tommy Hilfiger, Gianni Versace, Gucci, Louis Vuitton, Dolce & Gabbana, Calvin Klein Fragrance, Abercrombie & Fitch, Isaac Mizrahi, Donna Karan, Ellen Tracy, Nautica, Neiman Marcus, Reebok, and Anne Klein. At one point, the roster grew so long that they had to stop selling advertising space. "We were getting near to close," she remembered; there wasn't going to be enough editorial to support any more advertising." Demand was outstripping supply at such a rapid rate that Michael told Elinore, "I know this sounds crazy, but you got to stop selling."

These many advertisers had different motives for buying into *George*, ranging from the idealistic to the practical. Some hoped that *George* would grow into a successful crossover magazine, just as John and Berman envisioned. "It's different than being in a purely fashion magazine. Maybe it's the next *Vanity Fair*," explained Sam Shahid, head of an agency that placed ads for Abercrombie & Fitch in the first two issues. Tommy Hilfiger embraced the concept, saying: "People in my age group are certainly interested in learning about politics from a younger angle. I think it will go beyond politics. I think it has a really good shot." Others had more immediate reasons, simply buying into the buzz surrounding the magazine. "Isn't exposure the whole point of advertising?" said Donna Karan, while according to Ann Richardson, vice president of advertising at Neiman Marcus, "Part of our thinking was it will be a launch that will get a lot of publicity and generate an exceptional amount of interest. We figure it will reach an educated and affluent audience, which is right for us." She added, "Down the road, we'll see if the interest stays past the first few issues."

One of the fashion advertisers who expressed interest in the magazine was Valentino, whose full name was Valentino Clemente Ludovico Garavani, a favorite designer for socialites and Hollywood royalty, including Elizabeth Taylor, Audrey Hepburn, and John's mom. In 1964 Mrs. Kennedy ordered six black-and-white dresses, which she wore during the year following JFK's assassination. Valentino also designed the dress that she wore when she married Aristotle Onassis in 1968.

John wasn't sure why Valentino needed to meet with him personally, but Berman knew exactly why. "He wants to meet you," he said. They were eating lunch at Valentino's Fifth Avenue apartment with a few other people when the fashion designer interrupted the conversation. "John, may I ask you a question?"

"Yes, of course. Ask me anything."

"I know that when your mother died, you sold off many of her things."

"Yes, we did. She lived differently than my sister and me. We thought other people would enjoy her, and that would have made Mummy happy. They are bringing joy to other people."

"Your mother's clothes . . . what happened to your mother's clothes? I notice you didn't auction off any of those. During your mother's lifetime, I must've designed her a hundred beautiful custom dresses that I was so proud to make for her. I would like to buy those dresses from you. They are among the most beautiful I've ever created."

"We don't have the dresses."

"You don't have the dresses? You sold the dresses?"

"No, we couldn't bear the thought of walking down the street and seeing people in her clothes, so we gave them away."

At this point, Valentino was practically gasping for air. "You gave away my dresses? My beautiful dresses? Who did you give them to?"

"Well, Mr. Valentino, sir, we gave them to a convent in Rhode Island."

"You gave my dresses to a convent? Why?"

"We just thought it was a good home for them. Just think how happy those sisters are when the lights go down at night and everybody has gone home, and they turn up some music and are twirling around in your clothes."

Valentino was just one of many potential advertisers whom John met personally. It seemed that two or three times a week, John found himself attending an event or dinner. He understood that he needed to get advertisers to buy space in his magazine, but he resented the way Pecker seemed to be putting him on display. Pecker had one of the biggest celebrities in the world in his stable, and he planned to use him. He dragged John to all kinds of events, even some unrelated to *George*. On one occasion, Pecker was being honored by a Jewish organization in Manhattan and asked John to attend. As usual, John was late and came strolling down the center aisle wearing a tuxedo after everyone else had already been seated. The event, however, was not a black-tie dinner. John sat down at the head table next to GM's Michael Browner, leaned over, and said, "Am I the only jerk wearing a tuxedo?" Michael looked around the room and said, "No, the waiters are wearing tuxedos." Without missing a beat, John took his napkin, draped it over his arm, and went around the table taking drink orders.

John's nursery in the White House.

At the controls of the presidential helicopter, Marine One, during a weekend at Camp David.

Playing with the typewriter in the office of the president's personal secretary, Evelyn Lincoln.

ST-A4-70-62. Cecil Stoughton. White House Photographs, JFK Library.

John and Caroline playing together in John's nursery in the White House.

ST-A4-75-62. Cecil Stoughton. White House Photographs, JFK Library.

Nanny to the Kennedy children, Maud Shaw, holds John in his nursery.

In May 1965, John traveled with his family to London for the dedication of the JFK Memorial at Runnymede. Here he is clowning around with cousin Anthony Radziwill while photographers look on. Anthony's sister, Tina, is in the background.

Getty Images / McCabe

John spent a great deal of time onstage while at Brown. This photo is from a Brown University production of *The Playboy of the Western World*.

Here he is acting in Shakespeare's *The Tempest*.

John and sister, Caroline, attend the dedication of the John F. Kennedy School of Government at Harvard University in 1978.

On the thirtieth anniversary of his father's assassination, John agreed to let friend Barbara Vaughn shoot this portrait. Notice the date on the calendar in the far left of the photo.

© Barbara Vaughn

Playing around with girlfriend and, later, close confidant Julie Baker.

© Barbara Vaughn

John with his trusted friend and executive assistant, RoseMarie Terenzio.

RoseMarie Terenzio

John announces the launch of *George* magazine at a packed New York City news conference in September 1995. Seated are business partner Michael Berman (left) and Hachette's David Pecker (right).

One of John's greatest accomplishments was the creation of Reaching Up, which offered health care workers the opportunity to advance their careers by earning college credits. Here he is with the "Kennedy Fellows" selected for the program.

There was little John enjoyed more than playing Frisbee in Central Park. He divided teams into shirts and skins. John was always skins.

At her wedding, a joyous Carolyn hugs John's cousin and best friend, Anthony Radziwill, while Carole Radziwill looks on.

John thought that he could reason with the paparazzi. Shortly after returning from their honeymoon, he escorted Carolyn out of their apartment building where he pleaded with about two dozen photographers to respect Carolyn's privacy. The plea fell on deaf ears.

Getty Images / Lawrence Schwartzwald

Anne Marie Fox

John in his office at *George.*

Clinton Presidential Library, photographer Ralph Alswang

President Clinton takes John and Carolyn for a White House tour where they stop to admire President Kennedy's portrait.

In May 1997, John offered to sit down with me for a History Channel special to talk about his father's legacy on what would have been JFK's eightieth birthday.

Provided courtesy of A&E Television Networks, LLC

Keith Stein

One of the last photos of John, taken with businessman Keith Stein in Toronto four days before the crash. John, still on crutches, flew in with an instructor to discuss a possible investment in *George*.

CHAPTER 8

"LADIES AND GENTLEMEN,
MEET *GEORGE*!"

Having built a firm foundation of advertising revenue, John and Michael turned their attention to hiring editors who could help realize their vision of a magazine that used pop culture to make politics more accessible. Over the next three months, they interviewed numerous candidates to fill important roles on the team. John wanted smart individuals with experience in journalism, but he had an additional criterion. He would often say, "Would you want to see this person every day, and could they be your friend?" It was not that John was hunting for new friends; rather, he remained concerned about his privacy. He would now be surrounded daily by people working closely together in an intense environment. Apprehensive about being so exposed, he wanted coworkers who were not only smart but also trustworthy. According to senior editor Elizabeth "Biz" Mitchell, he also cared about the work environment, "and he really believed you needed a place to work where you were happy every day to see the people there."

Mitchell, twenty-eight, had originally been considered for the position of executive editor. As an editor at *Spin,* she ran investigative features on subjects ranging from the Irish Republican Army to the opium trade in Myanmar. Mitchell had graduated with honors from Brown and had planned to leave *Spin* to enter a program at Cambridge University to study political history, but she put her academic career on hold when she learned about the opportunity at *George.* Her own writing, which found homes in varied publications such as the *New York Observer, Glamour,* and *The Guardian,* made her an ideal fit for *George.* She did not want her colleagues at *Spin* to know that she was interviewing for a new job. The first few times that John called Biz at work, she received messages that John Kennedy from *George* called, so she asked him to use an alias when he contacted her at the office. One day she got a message that "Steve Kennedy" was on the line. "You have to come up with a better disguise than that," she told him. Also on the short list was thirty-eight-year-old Eric Etheridge, who had held jobs at *The Nation, Harper's,* and *Rolling Stone* before becoming executive editor of the *New York Observer* in 1994.

In the end, both Berman and Kennedy believed they needed a more seasoned editor than Biz. Since neither John nor Michael had any experience in publishing, they required someone who could handle the nuts and bolts of running a magazine. More important, their ideal executive editor would be capable of sending a clear message that the magazine should be taken seriously. Based on this calculation, they offered the position to the highly experienced Etheridge and brought on Biz as a senior editor.

Etheridge then recruited Rich Blow, a thirty-year-old editor of the recently defunct Washington-based business magazine *Regardie's*. Blow had sterling academic credentials. After earning an undergraduate degree in history at Yale, he entered a highly competitive and demanding PhD program in American Civilization at Harvard. Although he completed all the required coursework, he left before writing a dissertation because he felt that he had found his calling in journalism, not academia. Despite his academic pedigree, Blow, whose father had been an editor at *Reader's Digest,* "always felt a kinship with outsiders and the less than powerful."

Since *George*'s distinctive mark would be as a serious but nonetheless eye-catching glossy magazine, John knew he needed a top-notch creative director. To fill that position, he hired Matt Berman (no relation to Michael), who worked for *Elle,* another Hachette-owned magazine. Matt bore a striking resemblance to actor Matt Dillon, and often bragged about his ignorance of politics, but he possessed a creative mind and a clear sense of what fashion advertisers wished to see in a magazine. John repeated his slogan that *George* would exist at the intersection of politics and pop culture, empowering Matt to discover how to represent that relatively vague concept in visual terms.

Gary Ginsberg, John's friend since their days at Brown, came on board as a senior editor and legal counsel. John not only trusted Gary's journalistic instincts but also enjoyed his company outside of work. The two men were

as comfortable battling each other on the racquetball court as they were debating story ideas in the office. Early on, Michael Berman instructed Gary
to require every staff member to sign a nondisclosure agreement in case any
disgruntled staff members decided to sell a story to the tabloids or write a
book about their experiences at *George*. Gary went to all the staffers and told
them it was important to John that they sign the agreement.

Ginsberg's request ignited an early confrontation with a few of the editors. Biz Mitchell signed after Gary amended the agreement so that it applied only to John's personal life. Richard Blow held out the longest, claiming
that the nondisclosure agreement allegedly violated his First Amendment
rights. Eventually John delivered an ultimatum: "If you don't sign it, you are
gone." Blow agreed reluctantly, but apparently he never intended to honor
the agreement. Two years after John died, Blow penned *American Son*, an
insightful and sympathetic account of John's time at the magazine, but one
that could only have been based on meticulous note taking.

By the end of May, the staff had filled out with the addition of three associate editors: Rachel Clark (who came from *Esquire*), Manny Howard
(*New York*), and Hugo Lindgren (*Metropolis*). Not one of them had worked
for a political magazine before. But John believed that each understood his
vision and possessed the creativity to execute it. "I'm trying to create something different," he told them, "and your nonpolitical background will be an
asset." When Matt Berman confessed that he knew nothing about politics,
John said he possessed the ideal qualifications because "you are going to be
working on a magazine for people who don't know much about politics."

Now they faced the seemingly insurmountable task of producing the inaugural issue in just three months, because it had to be shipped to the printer
by the beginning of August. That challenge required the small staff to develop story ideas, designate writers, edit pieces, and prepare for publication.
"I had something like six features to assign and edit, and they were not simple features," reflected Mitchell. "It was grueling." The staff worked forty
days straight, many of which extended well past midnight. Following one
day off, they returned promptly for another forty uninterrupted days.

What impressed the staff was that John remained there with them, laboring in the trenches day and night. "Whenever we thought we were working
too hard, we would look over and see John slaving alongside us," recalled a
senior editor. "Here is a guy who could do anything he wanted, but he is

sweating along with the staff." Sometimes John would take a break in the afternoon, watching a movie at a nearby theater or going to the park to toss around a Frisbee. In the evenings, he often ate at a popular Brazilian restaurant, Rice 'n' Beans, before returning to the office to continue late into the night.

John's office reflected his varied interests and links to the past. On any given day, there might be a stack of books surrounded by half-eaten meals and sweaty gym clothes. On his wall hung a black-and-white picture of Mick Jagger in Hyannis and a photo of John as a boy on his father's shoulders. Other reminders of his dad were scattered around the office. There was the American flag that had been planted on the moon in 1969 and then returned to Earth and given to his family to honor JFK for daring the nation to accomplish this feat by the end of the sixties.

Directly behind his desk hung the frame containing the signed portraits of every president from Washington to JFK. I had first spied the frame years earlier when it was hanging in John's bedroom. I immediately appreciated its value, realizing that many of these signatures, especially those of George Washington, Thomas Jefferson, and Abraham Lincoln, were rare, and for them to be together made this a valuable historical document. When I had asked him how he got possession of it, John told an interesting story. He said that in the days after his father's assassination, Lyndon Johnson invited him to the Oval Office. Before John left, Johnson took the frame off the wall and handed it to him, and he'd had it ever since. (It's a story that I have tried but failed to verify. But if true, that rare piece of history probably belongs to the US National Archives and Records Administration.)

As suggested by the contents of his office, John's greatest problem was that he was pulled in many different directions and easily distracted. In addition to his usual family demands and his need to exercise, John performed dual roles at the magazine. He served as an editor but also often found himself on the road meeting with potential advertisers. "He was a combination of highly attentive and then sometimes not," Mitchell said. "He would be very engaged at certain times, but his focus was difficult to maintain because of his other commitments."

Throughout the day, John faced constant interruptions. Hachette executives needed to see him, while staff from other Hachette publications found excuses to roam the *George* floor, hoping for a JFK Jr. sighting. According to RoseMarie, young women from *Elle* "turned John spotting into an ongoing contest." Maintenance workers visited their floor to change unburned lightbulbs or fix the unbroken thermostat. Celebrities wandered the hallways searching for him. It was not unusual to spy supermodel Cindy Crawford, or rapper Sean Combs (Puff Daddy), or actress Demi Moore coming out of John's office. On one occasion, John invited Muhammad Ali, his childhood idol, to visit him. In the early stages of Parkinson's disease, the three-time heavyweight boxing champion had tremors but was able to communicate. Since there were no African Americans among the senior staff at *George,* John sent word to the largely black maintenance staff that Ali was in his office and invited them to meet him. For an hour, the *George* space, normally home to young white professionals, was overwhelmed by older, largely African American representatives from cleaning crews, clerical staff, and maintenance workers who managed to meet two of the most famous people in the world.

One occasional visitor was Kellyanne Fitzpatrick, an aspiring Republican consultant who performed stand-up comedy at night. She could often be seen roaming the office handing out free passes to her shows. She would later get married, change her name to Conway, and become a White House advisor to President Donald Trump. Even John's friends and family, especially his sister, popped up unannounced.

Initially, there were so many interruptions that it was hard getting work done during regular business hours. "We were like a new toy," RoseMarie reflected. Thus, the real work of putting together the magazine didn't start until night, when all the distractions disappeared. The cost-conscious Hachette did not help matters by turning off the air-conditioning every evening at five o'clock, when the executives fled the building, leaving the people who produced their magazines stuck in sweltering offices.

Privately, John faced another potential distraction in the summer of 1995. According to FBI files declassified as part of my lawsuit against the US Department of Homeland Security to secure FBI and Secret Service files related to John, the ruthless Colombian drug lord Griselda Blanco de Trujillo, who went by many names—"Cocaine Queen," "the Godmother," and "Black Widow"—was believed to have threatened to kidnap John. It was not uncommon for the FBI to receive threats against John. One example occurred in May 1985: while he was working for the City of New York, someone called the Herndon, Virginia, police department and "stated to the effect that he and seven other individuals intended on kidnapping John Kennedy that evening at 8:00 P.M." Since the caller was identified as "an apparent intoxicated white male," there seemed little urgency to deal with the threat, although the FBI did attempt, unsuccessfully, to contact John.

But this time, the FBI took the threat seriously. Trujillo, who was part of the Medellín Cartel, initially established her foothold in the cocaine business in Miami before moving to New York, where she took on the Mob and murdered anyone who got in her way. In 1994 she had been convicted of three counts of drug-related homicide and sentenced to federal prison. The hundreds of pages of FBI files are heavily redacted and difficult to follow, but this much is certain: in July 1995 someone contacted the FBI's San Francisco office claiming that "he had information concerning a plot to kidnap John F. Kennedy Jr. in New York City." Two associates of Trujillo planned to abduct John while he rode his bicycle and then use him as a bargaining chip to get her released from jail.

The San Francisco office sent out a priority notice to the FBI director and to the New York office. Given her violent history, the FBI knew that Trujillo had the ability to carry out such a threat. On July 20 the San Francisco office filled in more details from its informant. The kidnappers would travel from Colombia to New York, grab John while he was riding his bike, and then take him to a private residence. Although all the identifying information has been removed, it was clear that the FBI conducted a background check on the owner of the home. Prison officials agreed to track all visitors to Trujillo's jail. The informant also said that "he never heard any statements from anyone who suggested that Kennedy would be harmed."

The following year, on May 9, 1996, an FBI agent interrogated Trujillo at the Federal Correctional Institution in Marianna, Florida. "De Trujillo was questioned regarding her knowledge of a plot to kidnap a prominent individual," one document noted. "De Trujillo was then advised the FBI had received information [of] a plan to kidnap John Kennedy Jr." At that point, the agent noted, she "became very defensive, saying this is not true and terminated the interview." Shortly afterward, the FBI contacted the private company that provided security for the Kennedy family. It, in turn, informed John of the threat. (Trujillo was assassinated in 2012 in Medellín, eight years after she was released from the US prison.)

This plot, the most serious since the 1972 attempt by eight Greek nationals, had little impact on John. He had grown immune to potential threats on his life. He often said that he refused to live in fear. If he cowered in the face of every possible threat, he would never leave his house. I never saw John maneuver to avoid a crowd or show any trepidation when walking the crowded streets of New York or entering a packed subway car. For the most part, he had a fatalistic view: if someone was going to try to harm him, there was nothing he could do about it. I also felt that he believed he was strong enough to fight off any potential kidnappers, at least until help arrived. There is no evidence that John took extra precautions on this occasion, either, and he could still be seen riding his bike around town and back and forth to the *George* office. He was preoccupied with launching his magazine and nurturing his relationship with Carolyn. Everything else was clutter.

Although they created the magazine, neither John nor Michael had a clear vision for how to turn this somewhat vague concept of mixing politics and culture into printed words on a page. While most start-up magazines struggle with their identity, *George* faced this challenge acutely. John and the staff confronted a central question: "What is a *George* story?" They could find no clear answer. Some people envisioned *George* as the *Rolling Stone* of politics, but Hachette told editors they saw the magazine as a political version of *Vanity Fair*. Meanwhile, John told a reporter that he thought *George* should look like the Hachette-owned *Mirabella*, which was a smart women's magazine. Even the tagline—"Not Politics as Usual"—described the magazine by what it was not, begging the question: How did *George* plan to cover politics? Since the magazine could be characterized only in relation to other magazines, editors struggled to produce stories that made *George* unique. Each editor proposed his or her own ideas. "It was hard to get people to buy in to John's vision, and as a result, the magazine never found its true identity," recalled associate editor Hugo Lindgren. "We tore up the magazine over and over again before the launch."

In terms of the editorial content, John was attracted to stories that were unconventional and counterintuitive. He liked lists—such as "The Ten Most Powerful Women in Washington"—and would later oversee publication of a *George* book of lists. According to associate editor Ned Martel, John found articles in political magazines like *The New Republic* "tedious and overbaked."

When he talked to the reporters who wrote those stories, he discovered that many of the more interesting tidbits of information had been edited out to make the piece sound more authoritative. "No," John would say, "that's useful intelligence for somebody who wants to evaluate political candidates and political ideas on their own terms." The material left on the cutting-room floor of highbrow political magazines, he believed, was ideal for the first-time, consumer-oriented reader that *George* was trying to reach.

John was inspired by the people he read about while doing research for the annual Profile in Courage Award, which recognized political figures who took controversial positions despite obvious political risks. They chose only one recipient a year, but he knew there were dozens of stories about people standing up for principle. Those were the kinds of people he wanted in the magazine, and if *George* did write an article about a well-known political figure, he searched for a unique angle for presenting the story—one that would emphasize human qualities more than political positions.

While John found meetings with advertisers tedious, he did pick up valuable information that he planned to incorporate into *George*. He learned, for example, that women made decisions differently than men. Men were loyal to certain brands, while women were more likely to evaluate products and choose those that were best for their families. The same was true for the way they bought cars and groceries. As a result, he wanted the magazine to provide women with more information about politics and the political process. John wanted to demystify politics by finding stories that explained in clear language how the Electoral College worked or how gerrymandering shaped elections.

Unfortunately, Eric Etheridge, the magazine's executive editor, had his own ideas, and the two often clashed, partly because they had different understandings of their roles. "Eric thought that John was going to be a celebrity editor and a figurehead, and that *he* was going to make all the decisions," Lindgren recalled. "Under the cover of John Kennedy's glamor, he was going to make a nerdy magazine." Etheridge thought "it was his magazine," Lindgren observed, "and it turned out that John wanted to be the boss," adding that the executive editor assumed that John "was going to open doors to get them access and then get out of the way."

Furthermore, Etheridge came to *George* with a conventional view of how to cover politics, proposing stories that could have appeared in any other magazine. "John found a lot of things that Eric was pitching him to be boring," Lindgren recalled. In Kennedy's opinion, the types of articles that Etheridge pushed were too reverential toward authority and lacking a sharp journalistic edge—akin to what John referred to as "kissing your sister."

But developing story ideas was only part of the challenge. Since they were starting from scratch, the staff also needed to figure out the structure of the magazine. Hachette refused to pay for focus groups, which were commonly used, and since there was no clear model, they made it up as they went along. They decided there would be longer features followed by shorter stories under the categories The Art of Politics and The Politics of Art. John was involved in every decision and every story. "Nothing went into the magazine without John's approval," claimed a senior editor.

The finished product contained both serious pieces (a long profile of FBI chief Louis Freeh) and conventional ones (an article about White House photographer David Kennerly). But it also showcased the offbeat in a distinctive way. Instead of adding to the mountain of stories already written about House Speaker Newt Gingrich, George featured a piece about his lesbian half sister, while John's friend John Perry Barlow sat down for an interview with the Speaker himself. Saturday Night Live comedian and future senator Al Franken wrote a piece about reducing the budget. Pointing out the millions of dollars that motorcycle daredevil Evel Knievel had received for his failed attempt to jump over Idaho's Snake River Canyon in 1974, riding atop a sort of rocket bike (more rocket than bike) called the Skycycle X-2, Franken proposed putting an elderly person in a rocket every Sunday and then "[firing] it over the Snake River and [putting] it on pay-per-view. The revenues go straight to reducing the debt." Further highlighting the link between celebrities and politics, John commissioned a story about actress Julia Roberts's humanitarian trip to Haiti.

One of the shorter pieces that John created and enjoyed the most was "If I Were President." This quirky and playful feature captured the essence of what it meant to combine politics and pop culture by having politically minded celebrities discuss important issues. John wrote to Madonna and pitched her two ideas: designing "an ideal voting booth" that would be "provocative futuristic" and attract a younger crowd or writing an article about what she would do if she were president. Madonna passed on the voting booth idea but agreed to pen "If I Were President." In the essay, which bore the title "A Political Virgin Takes a Romp Through the White House," she promised to pay schoolteachers more than movie stars, sentence right-wing radio host Rush Limbaugh and ultraconservative North Carolina senator Jesse Helms "to hard-labor work camps for the rest of their lives," and allow gays and lesbians in the armed forces to come out of the closet.

John knew that the most important piece in the magazine would be his Editor's Letter, since it would, finally, define for readers what *George* was all about. Most of the letter rehashed what he and Berman had been saying for two years: that politicians were using new methods to reach voters and that the line between politics and entertainment had blurred. *George* differed from conventional political magazines, he claimed, since it aimed to illuminate "the points where politics converges with business, media, entertainment, fashion, art, and science." Furthermore, it defined politics "extravagantly," encompassing everything from elected officials to ordinary Americans. "If we can do just one thing at *George*, we hope to demystify the political process, to enable you to see politicians not just as ideological symbols but as lively and engaging men and women who shape public life."

If David Pecker and others at Hachette expected John to use this forum to specify his own political views, they were sorely disappointed. The only glimpse John offered was to describe himself as a "lifelong spectator of the giant puppet show that can turn public people into barely recognizable symbols of themselves." The letter, which became a regular and popular feature in the magazine, accompanied a photograph of John reaching over a desk to shake hands with former Alabama governor George Wallace. Even that detail almost did not make it into the magazine. "What editor has his picture taken with the person he is interviewing?" John fumed. Reluctantly, he agreed, but only because it was the first issue.

George differed from other magazines not just in terms of content and approach; the atmosphere at the office had no parallel. Matt Berman, the creative director, called the *George* offices "a circus." While Blow described the staff as "a motley but enthusiastic crew," other staffers offered more critical assessments. "It was very much like a junior high school yearbook," an anonymous editor told *Spy* magazine in 1998. "Everything there was junior high." The one common feature was youth. Etheridge, at thirty-eight, was the oldest, and except for John and Michael, both in their midthirties, everyone else, including senior editors, was in his or her twenties. The staff discovered that most also shared another unique characteristic: nearly all were the youngest children in their families.

It was also clear from the first day that John was the sun around which everyone else revolved, but not always in a healthy way. Young staffers imitated him by wearing their wallets on pickpocket-proof chains. Senior editors hung on to John's every word and tried to interpret his expressions and body language. "If John cleared his throat, all heads pivoted in his direction," Blow recalled. "If we were debating an idea, everyone would monitor John's expression. Was he frowning or nodding in agreement?"

Many of the editors competed for his attention and time, and securing lunch with John became a combat sport. "There was a lot of jealousy and infighting," reflected a senior editor. "There was always someone looking to stab you in the back," especially if it got the person a step closer to John. It was not an unfamiliar environment for John. Since he was a child, he noticed that people around him fought and jockeyed for his affection, bragging that they were friends with him. Over the years, John had learned how to weed out celebrity hounds who courted him because of his fame. Outside his small group of close friends, he tended to categorize and compartmentalize acquaintances based on the roles that they played. However, that strategy did not work amid the intense office environment at *George*, where he had to deal with the same people all the time. In response, John made it a point to schedule individual lunches with all the editors to make sure they felt loved.

But he also tried to keep them at a distance, relying on RoseMarie to limit unwarranted intrusions on his privacy. Despite their rocky start, John grew increasingly close to his assistant. He valued her loyalty and enjoyed her irreverent sense of humor. Meanwhile, Rose relished the opportunity to play the role of the "Bronx badass." Never known as quiet or unassuming, Rose magnified her foul mouth, often launching dozens of F-bombs in a matter of minutes. "I wanted them to be a little scared of me," she recalled, "but I also did it for John, who loved my Bronx-y façade. When I strung together four or five curse words by way of an answer, he found the sassy street attitude charming."

Most of the editors, especially those educated at elite schools, were put off by RoseMarie's style. One editor dismissed her as a "dumb girl with a Bronx accent." They did not realize that John wanted someone tough to protect him from the constant barrage of requests—including from them. On one occasion, John, who had been told that the staff was going out for lunch, returned to the office from a meeting and discovered Rose at her desk.

"Oh, you didn't have to wait for me to get back," he said. "You could have gone to lunch with everybody else."

"I wasn't invited," she responded.

"What? Why?"

"They never invite me."

Clearly annoyed, John invited her to join him for lunch. He took her to the same restaurant where the staff was eating and requested a nearby table. "I didn't need to look over at their table to know they got the message," she recalled.

Although John worked long hours, he insisted on exercising every day. On most days, John barely could contain his energy and needed a variety of outlets. He would pull out a Frisbee or a football and start tossing it around the office. To help blow off steam, he even invited the staff to Central Park for an afternoon game of Frisbee, where he was disappointed to learn that not everyone in the office shared his appreciation for competitive sports. He continued his usual exercise routine, slipping out late afternoons to go to the New York Athletic Club for brutal games of racquetball and intense weight lifting sessions.

I had just moved to Oxford, England, the previous January, so I was not around much that summer, but I recall meeting him a few times. This had been our routine for more than a decade, but I noticed something different about John that summer. He seemed to be trying harder but achieving less. I even managed to beat him on the court, something I had not done in quite a few years. He labored to match his typical number of reps on the bench press. He looked thinner. I said nothing to him, because I was enjoying a brief period of physical dominance. Only later did I discover that he suffered from Graves' disease, a thyroid disorder that required him to drink a disgusting concoction of iodine and seltzer. Apparently, anxiety only aggravated the problem. He was having trouble sleeping, often waking up at five o'clock, leaving him completely drained at work. "By midafternoon on many days, he would be slumping in his chair, looking mystified by his body's betrayal," wrote Blow. Fortunately, John's condition was easily treated with medication, and soon the debilitating symptoms disappeared.

Despite his exhaustion, John built loyalty, trust, and admiration among those who worked with him. "He was an incredibly charismatic leader of an embryonic organization," said Ginsberg. With his usual discernment, John excelled at identifying talent and encouraging individual improvement. "He did a good job of caring and being involved while allowing people to do their own thing," Ginsberg claimed. Even those staffers who had originally been starstruck—and many were—found John to be unpretentious and down-to-earth once they got to know him. "John treated everyone the same," Lindgren recalled. "He was not one of these people who was your best friend one day and then ignores you the next. I remember being amazed by that." He exhibited a dry sense of humor and enjoyed mimicking famous people. Everyone's favorite continued to be his imitation of Arnold Schwarzenegger bragging about a recent sexual conquest.

Perhaps because he had such a young staff, John took time to encourage and nurture their talent. "He told me something I use all the time now with people I manage," Ned Martel observed in 2018. "You are going to need my approval on a lot of day-to-day issues," Martel recalled John telling him. "Try to think of the one thing that nobody else knows that you really want for yourself and for your career, and I will help you get it." He went on to say, "You don't need to darken my door to win small battles, because we will have this one goal that you and I are working to achieve together."

Because he took care to hire people who would work well together, John preferred a casual atmosphere at the magazine. On weekends, he would stroll into the office wearing shorts and a T-shirt. He would sneak his dog Friday, a black-and-white Canaan, past security in a duffel bag and allow him to run freely around the offices. He also demonstrated enormous generosity, handing out courtside seats to Knicks games and even calling New York Yankees owner George Steinbrenner to secure thirty tickets to a sold-out playoff game. Fashion designers sent him clothes all the time in hopes that he would be photographed wearing them. On one occasion, John sent a memo to the staff: "Re: Fine neckwear. Due to oversupply and under-demand (too many ties and not enough neck), I am parting with some fine neck drapery. If you are interested in acquiring any of said booty, it's hanging in the back-hall closet."

John could still be absentminded, but he now had a support system in place. RoseMarie organized his life, constantly reminded him of appointments, and, for the most part, kept him on time. John often carried around the office a leather binder where he kept reminders to himself. It was also where he kept track of ideas that popped into his head or recorded important points made by the staff. *George* meant a great deal to John, and he was determined not to allow his bad habits to get in the way of success. John was probably just as forgetful in his thirties as he was in his twenties. The difference was that he recognized his limitations and deliberately tried to compensate for them.

Over time the staff bonded with John not because he was famous but because he was a decent and kindhearted guy. When he learned that Ned Martel had turned thirty, John announced that he was hosting a party for him that evening after work. He invited everyone from the magazine, along with a handful of Ned's friends, to join him at a lounge in New York's trendy SoHo neighborhood, where they drank champagne and told funny stories.

John's sensitivity toward his colleagues mirrored his hands-on approach as editor. "He would try to read everything in the magazine and give editorial comments," Biz Mitchell reflected. If editors submitted pieces to him at an early stage, they could expect extensive and comprehensive comments. He would have sessions with front-of-the-book people, who were responsible for shorter features, and often added novel ideas. Because of his broad and eclectic interests, he could not only pinpoint stories with good potential but also identify missing elements or flip pieces around to create a more interesting structure.

In addition to developing stories that highlighted the magazine's mix of politics and pop culture, John needed to find images that would grab reader attention. He and Matt Berman struggled extensively with whom to put on the cover of the inaugural issue. The cover was key, since it would offer the first glimpse of John's brainchild. It needed to instantly captivate while also conveying the message that *George* stood apart, enticing the reader to venture inside and see if the articles lived up to the hype. To help strategize, John invited Matt to his apartment one night to meet the famed photographer Herb Ritts. Over dinner at a local restaurant, the three of them began to list as many celebrities as they could. Berman noted that the person who graced the cover "had to be [as] American as apple pie but with an edge." John suggested President Clinton, but Matt and Ritts nixed the idea. Then Ritts proposed, "What about Cindy?" The photographer, who was on a first-name basis with the biggest models in the world, was referring to Cindy Crawford. "That settled the issue," Berman recalled.

Now that they had chosen their cover model, a new question arose: the cover concept. Ritts suggested dressing Crawford as George Washington, and John loved the idea. However, many senior editors were not impressed, complaining that the cover would diminish the magazine's effort to be taken seriously by the mainstream media. John disagreed and stuck with the peculiar idea. By superimposing a political icon on a popular star, he was "announcing to the world that *George* was not a typical political magazine," reflected Matt Berman.

Although they had nailed down the cover, John continued to struggle with many of the articles. He expected the first feature piece to be an essay by Gore Vidal about George Washington, expanding on the cover theme. Everyone was delighted at the prospect of having an author of Vidal's stature writing for the first issue. But Vidal turned in what amounted to a prolonged assault on the nation's Founding Father. Blow, assigned to edit the piece, faxed a letter asking for revisions. Vidal responded with a phone call: "People don't edit my work. They either use it—or they don't." John killed the piece.

As mentioned, John's regular Editor's Letter and his interviews were among the magazine's most popular features. Although he would have preferred to be a behind-the-scenes editor, John knew that Hachette wanted him to appear in the magazine—ideally, photographed with his shirt off. He thus searched for a way to reveal part of himself without distracting from his main role as editor. The solution was for him to write a letter and conduct an interview of some historical figure for each issue. Most intriguing, he wanted to create historical tension by interviewing leaders who had butted heads with his father, thus highlighting lingering questions from JFK's presidency. At the top of the list was George Wallace, the pugnacious segregationist Alabama governor known for blocking the schoolhouse door to prevent the desegregation of the University of Alabama in June 1963. That act of defiance led John's father to give one of the most memorable speeches of his presidency. On June 11 JFK went on national television to declare "civil rights" a moral cause and introduced national legislation that paved the way for the Civil Rights Act of 1964.

John spent days preparing for the Wallace meeting. "We took it very seriously," recalled Ginsberg, who traveled with John to conduct the interview in Montgomery. Although John was already well read on his father's presidency, he doubled down on books that focused on civil rights. He also met with Nick Katzenbach, the assistant attorney general whom his father had dispatched to Alabama to confront Wallace back in 1963.

Although John knew that Wallace was in bad health, he was shocked by how enfeebled the seventy-five-year-old former governor had become. "He couldn't hear; he could barely speak," recalled Ginsberg. "He was in severe pain the entire time we spent with him." Most troubling, Wallace's memory was fuzzy, his answers incoherent. Because of Wallace's hearing problem, Ginsberg and Kennedy had to shout their questions to him, often to no avail. Eventually they needed to write down the questions so that he could read them. On the last of the three days they visited him, they conducted their interview at Wallace's home. The former governor was still suffering from the physical trauma of a failed 1972 assassination attempt that left him paralyzed from the waist down. He suffered from so much pain that he was lying in a hospital bed set up in the middle of his living room. Kennedy and Ginsberg stood at his bedside and peppered him with questions, but Wallace was too incapacitated by powerful painkillers to offer useful answers.

That evening, two friends of the governor invited Gary and John to dinner at a quiet roadside restaurant. As they approached, they saw a hundred cars packed in the parking lot and along the road leading to the restaurant. "I'm not doing it," John said. "I'm going back to the hotel." He realized that he had been set up. The supposedly private dinner had turned into a public event. "He was really debilitated by his thyroid condition," Ginsberg recalled, "and had lost a lot of weight. He was clearly both physically and, to some extent, mentally, just feeling exhausted." Ginsberg, however, managed to convince John to enter the restaurant. If not, he warned, "you are going to disappoint a lot of people, and you are going to embarrass our host. As pissed as you are about it, you can't take it out on the people who have traveled, presumably, long distances." John realized that he had to switch into his John Fitzgerald Kennedy Jr. role. He exited the car, strode into the restaurant, and turned on the charm. For two hours, he enchanted everyone, signing pictures of his father, posing for dozens of others, and listening to stories of people who claimed a connection to his extended family.

The two men returned to New York believing they had pulled enough information out of Wallace to submit a piece. They were wrong. The transcript of their interview was incomprehensible. John dispatched Ginsberg and Blow to go back and try to obtain a few coherent sentences. They found Wallace propped up in bed wearing striped pajamas. On his lap sat an ashtray holding seven cigar butts. They needed to extract useful material from the ex-governor, but Blow called the experience "ghoulish, as if we were pilfering loose change from beneath a pauper's mattress." Ginsberg and Blow scribbled their questions on legal-sized paper and placed them in front of Wallace. "Do you think there will be blacks in heaven?" Blow asked. A fiery Wallace shot back, "Of course there will." The question, however, never made it into the published interview. John nixed it, judging it too confrontational and something he never would have asked.

While preparing to launch the magazine, John arrived at another important decision: to marry Carolyn. Their relationship had deepened in the year since Jackie's death, and John had grown convinced that Carolyn was the one for him. He considered her the first girlfriend who could see beyond the veneer of his fame and celebrity. She teased him and stood up to him because of her independent, passionate personality—qualities that John found attractive. Naturally, their relationship veered between extremes of emotion. Sometimes, they could not seem to take their hands off each other, while at other times, they fought with equal intensity. "They were fiery," recalled Ariel Paredes, a mutual friend. "They would love hard and they would fight hard but they were very much a couple."

In November 1994, John officially introduced Carolyn to his only remaining immediate family members—his sister, Caroline, and her husband, Ed. Carole Radziwill, who was there with her husband, Anthony, described the encounter as awkward. Caroline hugged John "warmly" but hesitated for a moment before greeting Carolyn with, "So nice to meet you." A few weeks later at Christmas, Carole and Anthony shared dinner with Caroline and Ed and began trading New Year's resolutions and predictions. "I think John and Carolyn will get married," Carole said. As soon as she made that statement, the room fell silent. "No, he won't," Ed insisted. "Caroline doesn't even know her." This exchange was the first indication of what would be a rocky relationship between Carolyn and her in-laws.

The possibility of marriage became more likely that spring when Carolyn moved into the 2,600-square-foot penthouse co-op in Tribeca that John had purchased shortly after his mother died. At the time, it was a large industrial space, so John hired an architect to add a kitchen, two bathrooms, and one bedroom. According to Carole Radziwill, although John spent hundreds of thousands of dollars on the design, it still looked like "the ultimate bachelor pad." Carole and Carolyn gave it a nickname: "Home Depot, the warehouse."

Over July 4 weekend in 1995, they went to Martha's Vineyard, and John invited Carolyn to go fishing. "I wanted to go fishing like I wanted to cut off my right arm," Carolyn later told RoseMarie. John took her out on the boat, knelt down on one knee, and said, "Fishing is so much better with a partner," as he pulled out a platinum band sparkling with diamonds and sapphires— a replica of the ring his mother had worn.

Oddly, Carolyn did not say yes, although she wore the ring and told friends they agreed they would eventually get married. The truth was that she was in no hurry. It's possible that Carolyn, who had obsessed over John since at least 1988, came to realize that marriage with him would be very different from fantasizing about it. Carole Radziwill had the impression that Carolyn would have preferred to remain secretly engaged forever without having to actually get married. "I'm only twenty-nine years old," Carolyn confessed to RoseMarie. "I don't think I'm ready to settle down." Furthermore, she rightly worried about the expectations that would be imposed upon her by marrying the heir to the Kennedy legacy. At one point, she confessed to him, "I can't be like your mother. I'll never be the person she was. I fear that is the standard by which I will be judged."

Carolyn's reluctance puzzled John. Women had fawned over him his entire life and he could have married just about anyone he wanted—famous celebrities, beautiful models, celebrated actresses. But he chose a stylist from Calvin Klein who now seemed less than enthusiastic. He assured her that he lived an independent life separate from his family and that he wanted to marry her, not his mother. From his mistaken perspective, the public and the paparazzi would lose interest and stop hounding him once he was no longer an eligible bachelor. While John wanted to marry Carolyn because he loved her, he also saw marriage as the route to a more normal life.

They managed to keep the engagement a secret from all but a few friends until the *New York Post* ran a story before Labor Day showcasing a close-up shot of Carolyn's left hand with the engagement ring. Suddenly, their engagement became hot news. For Berman the timing could not have been worse, coming mere days before a press conference announcing *George* to the world. Michael feared that every question at this conference would now revolve around the engagement news, overshadowing the introduction of the magazine that they had spent the last year putting together.

Initially John wanted to ignore the story, but Michael convinced him that it would distract from the *George* launch and potentially sink their business venture. John agreed that he needed to publicly deny the engagement, but neither he nor Berman wanted to be the one responsible for lying to the press. So they dumped the job on Rose, who then called Carolyn to tell her what was happening. Carolyn was not pleased to have to deny their engagement but she understood the compromises involved in having a relationship with John. She also insisted that Rose make the announcement. "If anyone is going to make a statement about my personal life, it should be you. You're the only one I fucking trust."

Later that day Rose released a statement: "Once again, John Kennedy seems to be bearing the brunt of a slow news day. The story circulating regarding an engagement is untrue. He is not engaged. While it is not our habit to comment on John's personal life, the story seems to have taken on a life of its own, and we feel it necessary to respond."

Michael and John debated how they should announce the magazine to the world. Michael insisted that they hold a large press conference and invite all the major news organizations. John resisted the idea, fearing that it would degenerate into a feeding frenzy on his private life. But the other option was even less attractive: an endless number of satellite interviews with major news outlets. The staff knew that given his short attention span and inability to sit still for long periods of time, John would perform well for the first two or three and then get bored, and that would be a disaster for him and for the magazine. Over time John warmed up to the idea of a single press conference. Michael convinced him that they could manage the event so that the press would stay focused on the magazine. Blow recalled John saying, "Public relations is what you do, so if you think a press conference is a good idea, I'll do it. But everything I know tells me not to."

Their top choice for holding the conference was historic Federal Hall in downtown Manhattan. The site of Federal Hall has played a significant role in American history for centuries. In the 1700s, before it became Federal Hall, it functioned as New York City's city hall, where John Peter Zenger was tried and acquitted of libel for exposing government corruption in his newspaper, an event considered an early victory for freedom of the press. It was also here, in October 1765, that the Stamp Act Congress gathered to protest "taxation without representation." After the American Revolution, the Continental Congress assembled at city hall under the Articles of Confederation. Following the US Constitution's ratification, it was renamed Federal Hall and served as the first Capitol of the newly created United States. The First Congress met there to draft the Bill of Rights, and, most fitting of all, George Washington was sworn in on its steps as the first president of the United States on April 30, 1789. While the original building had been demolished in 1812, it was rebuilt in 1842 as the current structure. In 1939 it became classified as the Federal Hall National Memorial in recognition of the historic events that have occurred at that location.

Berman and Kennedy, along with publicist Nancy Haberman, went to scope out the space and meet with the hall manager charged with deciding who could and could not use the facility. John, who lived on North Moore Street, within walking distance, decided to use the occasion to walk his dog, Friday. Upon trotting inside, the Canaan promptly lifted his leg and relieved himself. The official called for the custodian to clean up the mess. John shook his head. "My dog," he said firmly. "I will clean it up; please just get me some paper towels." The manager was in a "huff" over the incident, but later that afternoon he called Haberman, saying, "It's fine. I have gotten approval." He added: "Please leave the dog at home."

John spent weeks preparing for the conference. Michael Sheehan reprised his role as media trainer, offering suggestions for ways to handle the press. The night before the event, Ginsberg and former Clinton advisor Paul Begala went to John's apartment to conduct a "murder board," asking John the toughest, most challenging questions imaginable. Ginsberg did not waste any time.

"John," he began, "you failed the bar twice. Was it because you were too lazy to study or just too dumb to pass it?" John roared with laughter.

But Gary did not relent. "Are you going to use your magazine to do investigative pieces?"

John answered, "It's not my focus, but I would not rule it out. It's more of a lifestyle magazine."

Well, then, Ginsberg retorted, "will you use it to look into who shot your father?"

Begala recalled that the question seemed to suck all the oxygen out of the room.

"No," John responded calmly. "As you can imagine, I thought about this a lot. I have come to realize that I could spend the rest of my life on that question, and it would not change the central operative fact that I don't have a father."

On the morning of September 8, 1995, John's limousine pulled up to the curb, and six private security guards whisked him through a side door. Waiting for him inside were 160 reporters, photographers, and television camera crews from around the world—an extraordinary assembly. "I did presidential events," reflected Ginsberg, who had organized campaign events for Clinton in 1992. "I know what campaign events look like, and it was no different than a general election event by a major party nominee within a month of an election."

The moment had finally come for John to introduce himself and his magazine to the world. Older Americans knew him mostly as the poor little boy saluting his father's casket. A younger generation had marveled at his stunning good looks and his reputation as the world's sexiest man. Now the world would see John in an entirely different light: a grown man of substance. "The launch was an opportunity to define who we were," Ginsberg reflected, "to introduce *George* in a way that was befitting of the magazine, with John—front and center, charismatic, magnetic, and embodying the excitement and electricity of the magazine itself."

John, Michael, and Pecker gathered in a small room on the second floor. "For the first time, I saw John Kennedy a little anxious," Haberman recalled. Shortly after ten in the morning, surrounded by Doric columns in the rotunda of Federal Hall, John ascended the stage, accompanied by Berman and Pecker. "I never knew you were such a big draw," John quipped to Michael as they stared out at the world's media. After they took their seats, Berman noticed John looking toward him and then pointing at the crowd. "What the hell are you pointing at?" Berman thought, before John started laughing. "I'm giving the photographers a shot, you idiot! You are such an amateur!"

John may have had more experience, but even he was overwhelmed. Pecker spoke first, then Berman, who delivered one of the best lines of the event. Being John Kennedy's partner, he said, "is a little like being Dolly Parton's feet. I'm sure they're perfectly nice, but they tend to get overshadowed." The people in the crowd laughed, but they clearly were not there to see either Pecker or Berman. John, wearing a fitted, double-breasted navy suit, white foulard, solid navy tie with a shadow stripe, and black shoes, rose from his chair and walked to the podium amid a flurry of flashbulbs and a round of enthusiastic applause.

"Ladies and gentlemen, meet *George!*" John announced. The crowd clapped as John revealed a giant blowup of the first cover, featuring Cindy Crawford dressed as George Washington, sporting a powdered wig and a bare midriff. The idea of putting the magazine cover on a mounted display that could swing around was the brainchild of Robert Isabell, a renowned event planner who organized many Kennedy family events. "It was the single most important piece of advice we got," said Haberman.

Following the unveiling, John held his first press conference as founder of *George.* "I haven't seen so many of you in one place since they announced the results of my first bar exam," he quipped in a well-rehearsed opening. The self-deprecating humor seemed to disarm the reporters. "Politics isn't dull," he said, turning serious. "Why should a magazine covering it be? Politics is a drive. It's about trial and loss, the pursuit of power, and the price of ambition for its own sake." Richard Blow noticed from his seat in the balcony that "flashbulbs illuminated the room in such a constant stream that it appeared someone had turned on a strobe light."

After he completed his prepared remarks, John opened the floor to questions. But first, once again he charmed the reporters with his humor:

"Yes. No. We're only good friends."

"None of your business."

"I've worn both."

"Maybe someday, but not in New Jersey."

The "answers" were in response to the obvious questions he expected about his private life, including his new relationship with Carolyn Bessette, his rumored affair with Madonna, whether he wore boxers or briefs, and if he planned to run for the Senate in New Jersey. John's tactic, which Blow described as "transparently manipulative," worked. He made it harder for the reporters to be rude and easier for them to write about his modesty.

Fortunately, most of the questions remained respectful and focused on the magazine. Asked if he could really be nonpartisan given his family's close ties to the Democratic Party, he quipped, "My uncle Ted said, 'If I'm still talking to you by Thanksgiving, then you're not doing your job.'" The crowd loved it. When asked whether the magazine would cover the sex lives of politicians, John said, "It would be disingenuous to say that I don't have some sensitivity to the seamy side of issues." He made clear that the magazine would address the private lives of politicians only if it related directly to political affairs. Another reporter asked him whether his mother would approve of his new project. "My mother would be mildly amused, glad she is not standing here." After a pause, he said, "She would be very proud."

That evening, John and Berman attended the US Open. John had not received feedback from the press conference, but he received rave reviews among those at the tennis tournament. Berman recalled that people were coming up to him unsolicited and offering congratulations. The two men had a running joke that if they obtained something because of John's celebrity, it counted for one point. If it was *despite* who he was, it was worth two. "What do you think about today? One or two?" John asked Michael on the ride back into the city.

"Today was a three," Berman answered, "and, my friend, you'll probably never hear me ever say that again!"

Berman was right, because the next day, John's performance received uniformly positive reviews. "He displayed an engaging candor and easygoing nature with the media—not unlike the style of his father," observed *Newsday*. "He now has a forum that is both a business venture and a touchstone to the political world that may be his next career." The *New York Daily News* described John as "articulate and funny." The *New York Times* praised him as "confident and relaxed, fielding questions and making a persuasive case for his magazine."

After the magazine launched, John went into Michael's office. "You know, I got this really nice note from your father wishing us well." John thought it was a thoughtful gesture. "Unfortunately," he cracked, "you're not going to get one of those back."

The media response to the magazine varied wildly. *The Philadelphia Inquirer* hailed it as "revolutionary fun. Not to mention zippy." *The New York Times* praised the first issue as "a blend of substance and fluff with dashes of irreverence and wit." *U.S. News & World Report* magazine described the inaugural issue as "a playful romp that merges the seamy and the serious," and *The Detroit News* deemed it "a political gem." But not everyone was impressed. *The Wall Street Journal* dismissed the editorial content of the magazine as "an afterthought." *The Boston Globe* blasted its "disappointingly vapid" material, while *Harper's* editor Lewis Lapham referred to *George* as "the political magazine from which the politics had been tactfully removed." Maureen Dowd, a columnist for *The New York Times*, questioned the magazine's celebration of celebrity, which, she argued, distorted "democracy by giving the rich, beautiful, and famous more authority than they deserve. And the last thing politicians need is another instrument of public relations."

Whatever the media's assessment, *George* proved to be a huge hit with the general public. The original print run of five hundred thousand sold out within days of hitting newsstands. An additional order of one hundred thousand copies disappeared quickly as well. Soon after publication, John went on a media blitz and managed to secure a coveted ninety-second slot on the popular TV sitcom *Murphy Brown,* starring Candice Bergen as a hard-nosed TV news anchor and investigative journalist. Berman and John pitched the idea and scripted the scene. "They barely changed a word," Michael recalled. In the scene, John stops by to personally deliver Brown a one-year subscription to his new magazine as a wedding present. Brown is not impressed. "Gee, I hope you didn't have to sell the compound," she mutters as she searches the gift box for something more.

"Okay, fine, if that's your attitude. But don't come crying to me when you have to pay full newsstand price," John says as he turns and walks toward the elevator.

While critics sneered at his appearance and made the predictable comparison with his father, John dismissed the criticism. He thought he had made an important step in freeing himself from the burden of his past. Besides, the free scripted advertisement reached thirty million viewers, whereas paying for a commercial would have cost $2.5 million.

Two days after the *Murphy Brown* show aired, John traveled to Washington to talk with CNN host Larry King. Media coach Michael Sheehan spent hours preparing him for the interview. King sat at a desk, with his guest seated directly across from him, which meant John needed to ignore the cameras and maintain eye contact with his host. Once King asked a question, John could look up toward the ceiling or even down at the table for a few seconds to collect his thoughts, but he always had to finish his answers looking at King. By this point, John anticipated that he would get the usual questions about his father and his childhood. King tried different ways of posing the familiar questions, but John stuck to his standard and well-rehearsed responses. When the host asked if it was complicated being the son of a legend, John responded that "it makes for a rich and complicated life" that was "part of the puzzle to figure out in my life." And when King asked him the obligatory question about whether he remembered saluting his father's coffin, John explained his own confusion: "What happens is you see an image so many times that you begin to believe, remember the image . . . but I'm not sure I really do."

What the audience did not know was that the King interview almost never happened. John was scheduled to fly from New York to Washington to tape the show live in the CNN studios, but he failed to anticipate the traffic on the way to LaGuardia Airport and missed two flights. Fortunately, CNN was covering the O. J. Simpson murder trial, which pushed back John's interview to later in the evening.

A few weeks later, Larry King called Pecker and asked if John would consider sitting in for him while he went on vacation. The network had narrowed it down to two favorites: General Colin Powell and John. CNN president Tom Johnson also contacted Pecker, pleading with him to convince John to take on the role. Much to Pecker's disappointment, John refused. Pecker believed that John lacked confidence and was "unsure" of himself. "He wouldn't take that extra step like an editor should," Pecker stated. "I think that he didn't feel comfortable in his own skin." In fact, just the opposite was true: John knew exactly who he was and had no desire to become a television host. He saw no need for extra exposure, agreeing to appear on *Larry King* in the first place only to promote his magazine, not himself.

John also sat down with CBS News anchor Dan Rather, who seemed to be trying to discover John's passion in life. When asked how much his mother influenced the decision to start a magazine, John replied that he "grew up in a household where words and books and magazines were always around, and we weren't allowed to watch television too often, but we were allowed to read magazines. So it's an area where I'm comfortable." Rather had done his research and likely surprised John with a question about his acting career. The newsman told John that nearly everyone he spoke to said that John's "real passion was to be an actor." John pointed out that the myth had somehow become perceived as reality. If something "is repeated enough" and went unchallenged, John responded, "it becomes the truth." He went on to say that he enjoyed acting at Brown, "but it was never even remotely a career option for me." It was not, John said, something that he "was passionate about pursuing for the rest of my life."

Apparently, the media attention produced a new threat against John's life. On September 21 a woman called the JFK Library in Boston and, after initially pretending to be a member of the family, became agitated, claimed that John "had publicly insulted her," and demanded an apology. According to a declassified FBI report, she proceeded to say that "she was going to shoot John F. Kennedy Jr." Later that day, she left two additional messages. While the messages are partially redacted in the FBI memo, she demanded, "Who gives you the right to fire me, John?" followed by "John . . . you owe me." The FBI informed John of the threat. He told them he was not familiar with the name of the caller. It's unclear from the available documents what, if any, steps were taken in response to the threat.

There was little time to relish the success of the first issue because they needed to get out the second by December 1995. Director Oliver Stone had just released a new movie about the late Richard Nixon, who died a month before Jackie in April 1994, and it was generating a lot of buzz. It seemed like an ideal fit for *George* to produce a cover depicting a blockbuster Hollywood movie about a controversial American president. But it turned out to be a poor decision. In 1991 Stone had directed another blockbuster, *JFK*, which managed to incorporate in two hours nearly every harebrained conspiracy theory about the assassination of President Kennedy.

A clueless Eric Etheridge suggested that John meet with Stone to discuss the content of *JFK*. John was shocked. Anyone who knew him understood that his father's death was off-limits. When a friend who had seen the movie told him how entertaining it was, John replied bluntly, "It's not entertainment for me." I spent many hours talking with John about his father and his presidency, but we rarely broached how he died. He made only two cryptic comments. On the thirtieth anniversary, in November 1993, considerable news coverage rehashed the assassination. "Why are people so fascinated by my father's death?" John asked, clearly not wanting an answer. I always assumed that he did not believe in the countless conspiracy theories, but as previously mentioned, he once said enigmatically, "Bobby knew everything," and he said it in a way that made me think perhaps Bobby knew things that the public, and maybe even the Warren Commission, did not.

Nixon seemed so ideal for *George*, however, that John could not pass up the opportunity. He asked Berman to make it clear to the director not to raise anything about the assassination. "Look," Berman told Stone, "we are happy to meet with you, happy to do it, John's happy to promote your movie, but you can't bring up anything about his father's assassination." Stone agreed. Berman and Kennedy then flew to Los Angeles, meeting Stone and his agent for dinner at the Buffalo Club in Santa Monica. Beforehand, though, Michael and John worked out a signal in case Stone reneged and started talking about the events of November 22, 1963: John would politely excuse himself from the table to use the restroom, and, while he was gone, Berman would end the dinner.

According to Berman, the four of them enjoyed a pleasant dinner, discussed the Nixon film, and the new information Stone had discovered about the disgraced former president. With time running out, the director made his move just as dessert arrived. "You know, John," he said, "I just have to ask you. I am knee-deep in all of these conspiracy stories about your father, and you know the reality is it could not have been one bullet." On cue, John excused himself.

As John walked away, Berman turned to Stone. "You crossed a line, and we can't go back. John's going to return to the table. We will ask for the check and then casually walk out. It was very pleasant, but the dinner is over."

John fumed on the way out. "I'm not promoting his movie. He went back on his word, and I'm not doing it." When John returned to the office the next day, he told the staff, "I just couldn't sit across the table from that man for two hours. I just couldn't."

John's decision to cancel the Nixon cover and scrap his interview with Stone threw everyone into chaos. They scrambled to find a replacement. Michael suggested Robin Williams, but they could not find an obvious connection between the comedian and politics. At the last minute, someone proposed Robert De Niro, who was then starring in the Martin Scorsese epic *Casino*, which would allow them to make a connection between gambling and politics. "We had fallen from the possibility of a home-run cover to the reality of a ho-hum one," Blow recalled.

Worse still, John's Editor's Letter lacked punch and had clearly been cobbled together at the last minute. He opened by quoting Bill McKay, the fictional California Senate candidate played by Robert Redford in the 1972 film *The Candidate*, who has just won the election in a surprising upset: "What do we do now?"

"My sentiments exactly," John quipped. "After all the bells and whistles surrounding the launch of our first issue, the realization that we had to do all that heavy lifting again and publish yet another issue so soon came as something of a shock—at least to me." The letter mentioned three new Hollywood movies that dealt with politics in some capacity: *The American President, Casino,* and *Nixon.* But the most embarrassing aspect of the letter was the accompanying picture showing John standing next to De Niro wearing his George Washington costume. The caption read: "Meeting with Robert De Niro at the cover shoot." The only problem was that John did not attend the cover shoot. Matt Berman faked a photo by merging two separate images.

The original plan was for John to interview Anthony Hopkins, who played Nixon in the Stone movie, but they searched for an alternative and settled on Warren Beatty, who in addition to being an A-list actor was a partisan Democrat who had once campaigned for Robert Kennedy during his 1968 presidential campaign. The first exchange exposed some of the complexity of trying to publish a political magazine that was relevant to the current conversation while also trying to anticipate future trends. John asked what it was like for a "political partisan" to be interviewed "by a magazine that believes party affiliation alone no longer defines political identity." Beatty responded that it was not difficult because "the Democratic Party and the Republican Party aren't that far apart." Neither of those statements has stood the test of time. John had convinced himself that the nation was entering a postpartisan age, and Beatty asserted there was no difference between the parties, when there was growing evidence of a massive partisan realignment where party affiliation, and the opposite directions the parties were moving in, mattered more than anything else.

This issue also hit the *George* sweet spot, highlighting its nonpartisan approach to politics. If anything, the issue leaned right and included articles about a conservative federal judge, former singer and now Republican congressman Sonny Bono, along with a look at Republican grassroots politics in Iowa and New Hampshire. A long profile of Jesse Jackson's son stood as the sole representative of voices on the left. The choice of articles highlighted the challenge facing John's vision of a postpartisan magazine. Featuring voices from across the political spectrum did not add up to a postpartisan point of view; it simply pulled together, under one cover, highly partisan figures.

Overall, John was happy with the final product but knew it could be better. Part of the issue was his continuing battle with Etheridge over the magazine's substance and tone. In editorial meetings, John would listen to Eric pitch his ideas and say, "Yeah, yeah, yeah, good, good, good." But once the meeting ended, he would pull aside another editor and complain, "Can you fucking believe this? This guy does not get what we are trying to do."

Eric's imperious style also grated on John. Etheridge rarely held full staff meetings where editors could pitch and debate ideas. John would suggest story ideas to him, but the executive editor would either drag his feet on seeing them through or dismiss them altogether. Shockingly, Etheridge even tried removing John's cofounder title from the masthead of the first issue. John found out and had it restored. From that point, Eric's days were numbered. Adding fuel to the fire, Etheridge, a few weeks later, sent a mailing to all 535 press secretaries on Capitol Hill announcing the magazine and affixing John's name to the letter without getting permission. John did not like firing people, but he later told a colleague that he "enjoyed" dismissing Eric.

After firing Eric in February 1996, John promoted Biz Mitchell, but he did away with the title of editor in chief and made himself the magazine's top editor. Promoting Biz was easy. John genuinely liked her enthusiasm and can-do attitude, and he respected her talent. He knew that she would be a good partner and had no agenda of her own. "My general position was that I wanted the magazine's content to be truly fun when it was fun and important and serious when it was serious," Mitchell reflected later. Making himself the top editor was more problematic, especially since he had only a few months of experience in the magazine business. It did, however, send a clear signal that he had no intention of being a figurehead. Hachette would have preferred it if John had simply handed over the reins to Biz so that he could spend more time making television appearances and meeting with advertisers, but he had no such plans.

Still, the publisher was thrilled with the success of the first two issues, and for good reason. Its first issue sold 97 percent of the 500,000 copies published. The December issue sold 78 percent of 600,000 copies. The average newsstand sale for Hachette's twenty-six other magazines was 44 percent. Pecker assumed that the magazine would continue to sell at the same pace.

There were other hopeful signs. Because Hachette refused to conduct a subscription drive, which would have involved using its sales force to contact potential readers, *George* was forced to recruit subscribers by asking them to return a form inserted in the magazine. Berman and Kennedy had expected this old-school method would bring in maybe 7,500 subscriptions with the first two issues. Instead, they received 97,000. The first two issues also set an advertising record for a new magazine, with 175 total pages. Pecker was so thrilled that at the end of January 1996, he announced that *George* would begin publishing monthly in the spring.

John and Michael had plenty to celebrate as the year ended. They had devised an original idea for a business, developed it despite the naysayers, and launched it amid great fanfare. Along the way, John demonstrated tenacity and skill. He made strategic use of his celebrity status but kept the focus squarely on the concept and not himself. But John felt partially unsatisfied with what he and his team had produced. "The death of any magazine is that it doesn't stimulate or provoke people," John told the trade magazine *Advertising Age* in 1996. He remained unconvinced that the first issue rose to that standard. He expected the buzz but questioned its motivation: Was it because readers hoped to get a glimpse of him or because *George* contained a story that stimulated or provoked them?

The venture began as the product of a partnership between Kennedy and Berman, with each man contributing passionately to its early success. "I could not have asked for a better partner," Michael recalled in 2018. That sentiment did not last long, however. Soon the two became entangled in open warfare, threatening the very survival of the magazine.

CHAPTER 9

"SHE'S ACTING CRAZY"

M om and Dad are fighting again," editors whispered when Michael and John erupted during one of their many spirited battles. Once the shouting began, editors quickly closed their doors and muffled their phones' mouthpieces so that people on the other line could not hear the commotion. "Michael would quietly but intensely provoke," recalled a senior editor. "John would resist. John would eventually not be able to take it any longer. He would then yell. Michael would gleefully engage in the fight then." Those who witnessed the fights blame Michael for provoking John, pointing out that Kennedy was never a hothead with the staff. A senior editor also noted that John "never harassed an employee. But Michael did." The fights were shocking even to the few veterans on the staff. "I heard and saw some behavior between the two of them that I had never seen in business before," reflected Elinore Carmody.

Their fights only grew in frequency and intensity during the magazine's first year, unnerving everyone at *George*, and for good reason: such behavior was highly unprofessional and inappropriate. One employee recalled that they "were both dilettantes on some level. They never had to have a real job. They did not know that you don't go in and start screaming at the top of your lungs. Maybe that happens some places, but it never happened where I worked."

John and Michael had spent two challenging years developing the idea for the magazine, pitching it to advertisers, getting a buyer, and building a staff. Now, after less than a year in business, they unleashed heated battle after battle on the office floor. What happened? It's difficult to analyze the evolution of their falling-out, since of the two people who knew the details, only one is alive. But in-depth interviews with Berman, who spoke on the record for the first time, along with other *George* editors and staff, create a clearer picture of the major issues that came between them.

From the very first day, when Hachette provided John with a corner office offering views of the Hudson and assigned Michael to a small, windowless cubicle, Berman realized that he would never be an equal partner with a celebrity of John's stature. His famous colleague simply sucked all the air out of the room. Numerous minor insults followed the first. For example, when *The Washington Post* requested a photo of John for a story about *George*, Kennedy insisted that Michael and David Pecker be included. The *Post* agreed but then blurred out the other two so that only John was visible. Berman had been handling John's public image for a decade, so he understood that John F. Kennedy Jr. would be the face of the magazine, but it proved difficult to accept the feeling of being sidelined.

After the first two issues, Berman grew critical of the entire editorial staff and their choices about which stories to publish. Channeling feedback from advertisers and reader surveys, he charged that the magazine was "too formulaic." Since it lacked quality control and clear editorial direction, *George* seemed to be reinventing itself with every issue. Berman did not believe that simply plunking a celebrity on the cover dressed as George Washington could adequately sustain the magazine. Rather, they needed to produce must-read stories that would attract people and ad dollars to the magazine. "Nonpartisan politics doesn't mean politics light," he insisted, and "the magazine was becoming very light." Thinly disguising a model for the cover, whether it was Cindy Crawford, Robert De Niro, or basketball star Charles Barkley, was interesting at the outset but quickly became gimmicky. It is worth noting, however, that while Berman was always ready to criticize John and his editorial staff, no one at the magazine recalled him ever offering an alternative direction.

John nixed the few ideas that Berman did offer. In one case, Michael suggested that John interview First Daughter Chelsea Clinton, then sixteen, a move that he thought would represent the kind of unique perspective that *George* could bring by having one presidential child talking to another. John rejected the idea. He had not forgotten his mother's counsel: when Hillary Clinton asked Mrs. Onassis for advice on how to raise a child in the White

House, Jackie suggested never allowing Chelsea to talk to the press. At another point, Berman proposed that they create an advisory board composed of editors and writers who could make suggestions. "Absolutely not, absolutely not," John responded. "I don't need other people. I have enough people weighing in. I don't need more."

The early conflict highlighted one of the many questions facing the young magazine. Michael had come up with the original idea of a publication that blended politics and pop culture, John quickly grasped the possibilities, and together they had successfully sold the concept to Hachette. But they had still not solved the problem that plagued the magazine from the very beginning: a clear strategy to identify the intersection between culture and politics, and to strike the balance between hard-hitting, newsworthy stories and lighthearted, gossipy fare. They struggled, as any magazine would in the early stages of life, to populate *George* with stories and photos that drove home to readers the true purpose of the magazine. But Berman blamed John for failing to provide the staff with sufficient guidance to ensure that they stayed true to the original concept. He thought the first issue came close to fulfilling this innovative concept, but then *George* quickly lost its way. "Over time," he complained, "it became very inconsistent. It became what others thought a political magazine would be." It missed the types of stories that grabbed headlines. "The magazine lacked a clear vision," he concluded. "And I blame him for that because that's what he should have provided."

Berman's criticism angered John, who found the comments biting and the tone harsh. Those who observed their exchanges described Michael as "taunting" and "disrespectful." For multiple reasons, the two men found it impossible to sit down and have a measured, professional discussion of their differences. Many of their arguments spilled outside their offices. Even if a quarrel began in Berman's office, it would intensify as Michael furiously pursued John down the hallway. One editor recalled Michael walking a few feet behind Kennedy, belittling him in a voice loud enough for bystanders to hear, "Who's going to save you now that your mother's not here?" John would try to ignore him, but Michael persisted: "You're nothing. You're a loser." Eventually John would lose control, leading to shouting, angry recriminations, and shoving.

Michael's tone was regrettable, and most of those who worked at the magazine blamed him for instigating many of the arguments. But there was some truth to his criticism. The sales and ad buys for the first two issues were unique, driven by the media buzz surrounding John's entry into the business and propped up by Carmody's decision to require advertisers to buy the same number of ads at the same price for both the first and second issues. Michael knew that beginning with the third issue, they would have to renegotiate ad prices, and he was hearing grumbling from advertisers about the future direction of the magazine.

There was another problem plaguing their relationship that likely prevented them from engaging in meaningful conversations. Those who observed John daily noticed an evolution as he finally became more confident about his own instincts. He no longer needed Michael to manage his public image, nor did he feel it necessary to consult Berman about whom he planned to interview or whether he intended to do a radio interview or talk-show appearance. He also found other people to assume some of the responsibilities that Michael had adopted in the past. Berman, who for a decade had played the "bad cop," now found his role usurped by the tough-talking and fiercely loyal RoseMarie. She had become the person who said no to requests and who took the blame for John's mistakes. John knew that Rosie, as he called her, had no agenda other than to protect him.

While John appreciated Michael's advice and trusted his intuition, he came to resent his partner's efforts to micromanage him. He felt that Berman was no longer just offering advice; he was issuing demands. That aggressiveness did not sit well with John. "There was nothing John disliked more than being managed and being put into a box," recalled RoseMarie.

Berman had reasonable concerns about the magazine's direction, and as a cofounder, he had every right to share his ideas with John. But the more Michael complained, the more John retreated. After the fourth issue, John told Berman to stop attending editorial meetings because he felt Michael was undermining staff morale and challenging his authority as the editor in chief. "If you want to talk to me about it, we can have a meeting," John said to him. Berman agreed, and they decided to touch base twice a month, usually every other Tuesday at twelve thirty. One meeting would be to discuss editorial, the other to review reader surveys. At their first meeting, John became defensive when Berman criticized editorial, and they ended with no progress made. For the next scheduled meeting, Berman invited John to lunch in a more informal atmosphere. "Oh, I can't have the meeting today," John said about ten minutes beforehand. "I have a doctor's appointment." Berman went to a restaurant across the street from the office only to find John having lunch with a staff member. "Basically, he totally shut me out of the editorial," Michael recalled.

The tension between the two became so intense that John moved his editorial meetings to a nearby hotel, seeking refuge from the office drama and making sure that Michael did not pop in unannounced. "Matt and Biz, come over," John would say, calling from the hotel, "so we can go over pages."

On occasion, the two men, who had been friends for more than a decade, could find some humor in their situation. One day, after listening to them argue, an employee asked jokingly, "How did you guys ever wind up going into business together in the first place?" Berman responded drily, "Because I didn't know Amy Carter"—the daughter of former president Jimmy Carter. John laughed hysterically, and the next morning, he pasted a mimeographed photo of Amy on the back of Berman's office chair.

Berman found himself increasingly isolated, convinced that the star-struck staff had been blinded by John's celebrity. "No one ever said to me, 'You're right,'" Michael reflected. Berman understood John's magnetism, but he assumed mistakenly that behind the closed doors of a magazine he co-founded, the staff would treat them as equals. In his mind, he never received that treatment, even when it was unequivocally deserved. "I could have looked out the window on a sunny day and said, 'Oh, it's beautiful out.' And John would have said, 'It's starting to rain,' and the staff would always side with John. 'You are right, John. It's raining. It's not beautiful. He doesn't know what he's talking about.'"

Berman believed that the staff was not only ignoring his advice but also undercutting his authority by trying to force a wedge between him and John. "I have never been in a work environment where employees thought it was okay to insinuate themselves between two partners. There were only two partners. There were a lot of employees—wonderful, talented people—but there were only two partners." Berman would occasionally pull aside editors and lecture them about their responsibilities. "You have the right to object to both of us," he would say, "but you can't come between me and John." But his grievances again went unaddressed.

There was some truth to Berman's complaints. In any office, it is common for staff to jockey for access to the boss, and John's celebrity status only intensified the infighting. "It was made more dramatic because it was John who was the boss," reflected Matt Berman. John recognized that dynamic and went out of his way to encourage the staff to disagree with him. "Tell me what you really think," he once pleaded with Matt. "Don't blow smoke up my ass. If you don't like my ideas, tell me."

Initially, the staff had nothing against Michael. Over time, however, even those who would have been his natural allies turned against him because of the way he treated them. "I gravitated away from Michael because he scared me," said Matt Berman. "He forced us to choose sides." Most senior staff members described Berman as arrogant, abrasive, and controlling. They complained that Michael, feeling cut off from the natural flow of information, circled the floor quizzing editors, trying to ascertain whether they were loyal to him or to John. When Michael could not find John, he would confront editors, barging into their offices and asking, "Truth time, truth time! Where's John? Where is he? Tell me where he is." On one occasion, a senior editor was holding a job interview when Michael tried forcing open her door, demanding information about John.

However, the problem went far beyond personality clashes and staff intrigue. More fundamentally, John and Michael had different expectations about how their relationship should evolve now that they were running the magazine. Michael wanted their roles to remain the same, in which he and John would get together and make all major decisions, even though many more people would be in the office. He even had his title changed from publisher to president, assuming that the new role would justify his involvement in all aspects of the magazine.

John, on the other hand, wanted Michael, regardless of his title, to shoulder all the responsibilities of being the publisher, while he took control of editorial. This was an arrangement common at most magazines. "It was the standard church-versus-state conflict," noted a senior editor. "John did not tell Michael how to sell ads, and he expected him to stay out of his side of the business." Berman assumed that he would continue to be the gatekeeper, controlling access and the flow of information to John. He also planned to continue his role as John's handler, overseeing every detail of his public life. Unlike the new editors, who were willing to ignore John's short attention span and his nonchalant handling of important issues, Michael insisted on asserting that authority even further. "I knew many of John's strengths and his weaknesses," he recalled, "and I believed that together we could have controlled the direction of the magazine had it not been for all the other voices weighing in."

While Michael miscalculated just how much John would submit to being managed, he was right about a key point: it was impossible to separate John's private life from the life of the magazine he now led. Michael had the unenviable task of reminding John that any negative stories about him would distract from their ability to get the public to take *George* seriously. Meanwhile, John believed naïvely that he could continue to maintain a wall between his private and public lives. But nothing demonstrated the fragility of this wall better than his very public fight with Carolyn in Washington Square Park.

On February 25, 1996, John and Carolyn got into a loud, physical dispute, all of it captured by a *National Enquirer* photographer who snapped eleven photos and a videographer who recorded the entire scene. They were walking their dog and holding hands when the argument erupted suddenly. According to the *New York Daily News*, Carolyn stopped in her tracks and started yelling at him. They continued walking, but a scuffle broke out. John was captured yelling at her, pointing his finger in her face while she grabbed the back of his neck. According to a witness, "He got hold of her wrist with his left hand; they are wrestling with each other. His right hand is between them; he could be lashing out or he could be protecting himself." John then tried unsuccessfully to rip Carolyn's "friendship ring" from her finger. When she appeared to leave with Friday, John shouted, "You've got my ring! You're not getting my dog!" A photo showed John sitting on the pavement, his arms crossed and his head bowed. Carolyn went to his side and tried to console him. They spoke for a few minutes before John got to his feet. Then, as if nothing had happened, the two walked away holding hands. On March 3 the *New York Daily News* story "Sunday in the Park with the *George* Editor" hit the newsstands with a scandalous eight-photo spread.

The cause of this infamous fight, and the many that followed, stemmed from Carolyn's ongoing complaint that John let people walk all over him. A few weeks earlier, the couple had attended a wedding. If John accepted every invitation to the wedding of a "friend," it would have been a full-time job. Couples whom he knew only casually did not just invite him to their wedding; they even asked him to be the best man. "Can you believe this?" John complained to his friend Sasha Chermayeff. "I barely know this guy, and he wants me to be his best man." On this occasion, John and Carolyn agreed reluctantly to attend, only to find themselves seated next to the society page editor of *The New York Times.* Carolyn surmised instantly that the bride wanted to get the *Times* to cover her wedding and was dangling John as an incentive. She may or may not have been right, but she was furious at John for not making a statement by walking out. It was a familiar argument, one she had belabored frequently in private, but this time it leaked into public view.

After the negative publicity, most of the editors went about their business and did not raise the topic with John when he returned to the office. Except for Michael. "He was furious that John hadn't told him about the brawl before its public screening," RoseMarie recalled. Berman had been in Milan, Italy, when he learned of the incident and heard that photographs existed of the shoving match. Worst of all, rumors were circulating that John had hit Carolyn. Coming so soon after the launch, and while wrapping up the third issue of the magazine that would hit newsstands in February, Berman feared how the public would react, especially after the video footage revealed the truth. "This could be the end of the business. A wife beater?" he fretted. "America's heartthrob is a wife beater?" Meanwhile, John remained unconcerned and instructed Michael firmly to stay out of his private life.

"This is personal," he told Berman angrily.

"Which part of this is personal?" Michael shouted back. "I'm sitting here in Milan meeting with advertisers, and I know nothing about this, and you're doing nothing to clean it up. This is not just personal—this is the point where your personal life and your professional life mesh in ways they don't for other people. There needs to be a response from our company." No one had yet seen the video that was scheduled to air the following week. "Let them show it," John said. "It will show that she was the aggressor, not me." In Michael's eyes, though, it was not so much about who had been the true aggressor. Had he been informed ahead of time about the video, he would have softened the blow by arranging a photo op with a smiling and still-very-much-in-love couple.

Berman was right to feel that the fight could not have come at a worse moment. After publishing two highly successful editions, ad sales crashed for the February/March 1996 issue, which had basketball star Charles

Barkley dressed in Revolutionary War garb on the cover. Everyone warned John of the unfortunate reality that, based on research, placing an African American on the cover of the magazine would hurt sales. But he insisted, saying that he wanted his magazine to highlight the achievements of a diverse group of people. As predicted, sales dropped, and critics pounced. "The magic appears to be wearing off for John F. Kennedy Jr.'s magazine venture," noted the *New York Post*. And it was not just advertising dollars that declined. Newsstand sales also dropped. While the first issue with Cindy Crawford on the cover sold five hundred thousand copies, the March issue plummeted to fewer than three hundred thousand.

In many ways, the magazine was a victim of its own success. Berman and Kennedy originally planned to start small and gradually expand. They had anticipated no more than thirty to forty pages of ads in the first issue. Pecker, however, decided to engineer a big splash, and his calculations worked. But Hachette failed to follow up with a subscription drive that would help the magazine sustain its numbers. Since *George* had required advertisers to purchase the same number of ads in the first two issues, it was natural that ads would decline for the third. "When we had a hundred pages in the third issue, which was an extraordinary feat, it looked like we were losing all our ads," said Berman. Most magazines would have been thrilled with those numbers, but *George* had set the bar so high with the first two issues that its third issue could not be perceived as anything other than a disappointment. "It was the beginning of where I started to see how *George* was going to be judged differently than other magazines," recalled Elinore Carmody.

For Berman, the sales drop provided further proof that the magazine was drifting and needed to return to its original mission. He argued that what made *George* different from all the other magazines was John's unique perspective. He never thought of *George* as a way for readers to know John better. Instead, it was a way for people to understand politics better, through John's eyes. "It was to me the beauty of *George*, and why he could be a great editor. It was not because of his editing skills, but because he had this unique perspective and could share it with the world." Berman did not want *George* to be a *People* magazine about the intimate details of John's life. Rather, he wanted John to infuse more of his voice into the magazine's content. "Anna Wintour herself is not on every page of *Vogue*," he said of the fashion bible's longtime editor in chief, "but her perspective on fashion and culture is."

At the same time, David Pecker was pushing John in the opposite direction, complaining that advertisers thought the magazine had lost some of its creativity after the first two issues. "They felt that the content itself, the features that were being written, did not really deal with pop culture or take the risks they were expecting the magazine to take," Pecker reflected in 2018. Advertisers warned Pecker they felt the magazine "was floating." "What you need is consistency," Pecker told John. "You need the wow factor on the cover, you need the wow factor on the pages, and, as editor, you need to make your voice heard." John repeated to Pecker that he did not want the magazine to be about him and that he refused to commercialize himself.

"You are running a commercial venture," Pecker retorted, "and you must give readers what they are looking for, and in the case of *George*, what they were looking for is you." Clearly, John gave the magazine its uniqueness. "It's the uniqueness that the advertisers are going to invest in," Pecker insisted. By now, John must have been tired of this argument, believing that he had already settled it on the first day. But as sales declined, then advertising pages, Pecker decided to raise the issue again.

Both Pecker and Berman misjudged John, who had made it clear at the outset that he would neither appear in the magazine as Pecker suggested nor be the voice of the publication as Berman wanted. Berman assumed that John, because of his family history, possessed a rare and unconventional view of politics and culture. But to be honest, I never saw anything like that. Like many other bright, highly educated, and cosmopolitan members of his generation, John was knowledgeable about big issues. Because of his family background, he had a sense of public-mindedness programmed into his DNA. However, he did not possess a singularly unique view of politics or of its relationship to pop culture, and his political ideas were not yet fully formed. While he had good instincts about story ideas, he always wanted the magazine to speak through the voices of its many talented writers and editors. John preferred to work behind the scenes: pitching story ideas, guiding editors, offering his comments to writers, and, when necessary, using his stature to open doors and provide writers with access. But as hard as he tried, that didn't seem to be enough, especially for Berman.

John grew increasingly puzzled and annoyed by his partner's behavior, which seemed a total departure from what he had witnessed the last two years. Even when they had argued angrily in the past, they had always managed to cooperate and share responsibility. But now that they were running a large, complex organization with many employees, John continued to maintain it was best to divide responsibility, a decision that did not sit well with Berman.

A staff member remembered having prolonged sessions with John dissecting Michael's behavior. John, who spent years in therapy, was skilled at analyzing motives and understanding why people acted the way they did. He wanted to maintain at least a respectful relationship with Michael, partly because a highly publicized spat would be damaging to the magazine, especially at such an early stage. But as much as John hoped to salvage their bond, he struggled to understand Michael's motives. "Where is this coming from?" he asked. "Why is he shooting himself in the foot like this? What does he want that he is not getting?"

While it is possible that Berman and Kennedy could have worked through their personal and editorial differences, there was no way around the conflict over Carolyn's role in the magazine. It was obvious to observers that John hungered for Carolyn's approval. John rarely revealed self-doubt, but he recognized that he had no experience in journalism and that he needed the magazine to be successful, especially if he planned to use it as a launchpad for a career in politics. Matt Berman recalled once sitting in John's office reviewing logos for the magazine. After offering a few comments, John leaned back in his chair and confessed, "I'm kind of bad at this stuff. Which one do you guys like?" Always self-aware, John could recognize his weak spots; but now he had Carolyn, who could fill in where he had weaknesses, especially when it came to fashion and photography. On another occasion, Matt and Carolyn were eating pizza when John walked into Matt's office and asked her abruptly, "What do you think of the magazine?" Matt sensed a certain amount of fear in his voice. But Carolyn reassured him, "John, it's exactly what it *should* be." Carolyn, not Michael, was rapidly becoming John's closest advisor. Even Pecker noticed her growing sway over John. "Carolyn had a tremendous amount of influence," he recalled.

Berman, struggling to maintain control and increasingly sensitive to any slights, immediately identified Carolyn as a threat. "Michael had a lot of influence over John, and John had been very dependent on Berman for a lot of decisions," recalled RoseMarie. "He trusted Michael. But when Carolyn came along, John started to rely on her counsel and her opinion. In the process, it changed John's relationship with Michael, who no longer had the access that he used to have. He wasn't John's main go-to person anymore." Berman viewed Carolyn as a "roadblock," RoseMarie continued. "He used to have direct access to John all the time. Now there's this person who John sees as protecting his best interest and starts listening to her."

Berman felt as if he could barely control his current partner; by no means did he need a second one added to the mix. As she became a regular presence around the office, Michael stewed. When Carolyn was not home phoning staff members, she was wandering in and out of the offices, usually settling into Matt Berman's office to make small talk and smoke cigarettes. She delivered baby clothes to a pregnant senior editor. She joked and told stories. She would often invite editors for drinks after work and treat them to dinner. Berman saw only sinister motives behind her actions, but there was actually a much simpler explanation. The *George* offices were one of the few places outside her apartment where she felt safe, and she trusted most *George* employees because John had already vetted them. Initially, Carolyn was not there to undermine Michael's authority. She was there to relax and find an outlet for her energy, two things she could rarely do anywhere else, and she had every reason to believe that the staff appreciated her contributions.

These simmering tensions exploded on the night they were putting the first issue to bed, as Carolyn sat in Matt Berman's office, tinkering with the cover. Michael was furious. They had already settled on the cover, and here was Carolyn, potentially holding up production. "She kept changing already approved cover colors, fonts, and other things in the issue. Each extra minute was costing us printing overtime charges we could ill afford, and everyone was exhausted," Michael recalled. Berman's wife was a famous interior designer, known professionally as Victoria Hagan. Around three in the morning, Berman said to John, "Please tell your [girlfriend] to go home. People pay my wife handsomely for her color advice, and she's not here. So ask [Carolyn] to go home." John responded with an uncomfortable laugh and went to Matt's office to ask Carolyn to leave.

Unlike Michael, neither Matt Berman nor Biz Mitchell minded Carolyn's presence that night. "She had worked for Calvin Klein," reflected Biz. "She knew what those advertisers were looking for in the magazine. She had a lot to offer, and most of her suggestions were very helpful." Matt especially appreciated Carolyn's input and enjoyed her company. "She always made me feel good about what I was doing, and when she showed up at the office, I felt like someone had my back. She didn't know so much about politics, either, but when she looked at the work and gave her approval, it was with such confidence that it always sounded like I found the perfect solution."

Although the staff did not agree with Michael's wholesale opposition to Carolyn, it was inappropriate for her to be involved so directly in important decisions impacting the magazine. As the girlfriend of one of the founders, she overreached the moment she started injecting herself into internal debates at *George*. Michael Berman was not a big fan of celebrity covers and felt the magazine needed to reduce its emphasis on popular culture. Matt Berman, on the other hand, found the magazine too content heavy and envisioned more photographs, graphics, and celebrities. When Michael nixed some of Matt's ideas, the creative director complained to Carolyn, who, in turn, argued his case with John. As a result, a tug-of-war emerged, with Matt and Carolyn lobbying for more creative content and less dense stories, and Michael prodding the magazine in the opposite direction.

Carolyn seriously complicated Michael's already difficult relationship with John. After the initial success of the Herb Ritts photo of Cindy Crawford, John and Michael agreed that they would try to re-create the same excitement for the second issue by asking Ritts to do the cover photo again. Herb agreed but cautioned that he was under contract with the publishing giant Condé Nast, so John and Michael would need to get permission for him to work for *George* a second time. A few weeks before the scheduled meeting with Condé Nast, John and Michael traveled to Florida to talk to advertisers. Carolyn accompanied John on the trip. At one point, John approached Michael and said ominously, "I need to talk to you." Berman braced himself for the worst.

"Carolyn thinks that it would be better if I went to Condé Nast by myself because they might be more inclined to say yes if it's just me alone than if you were sitting there, too," John explained. "Let's face it, they are taking the meeting because they want to see me." Surprisingly, Michael agreed to the idea and suggested that they come up with something they could offer Condé Nast in return. John cut him off. "Well, I am not being totally honest. I already had the meeting, and it didn't go well. They said no." Berman went ballistic. "How do you have the nerve to look me in the face and tell me that? What kind of partnership is this?"

Infuriated, Berman returned to his room, where he received an unexpected visit from Carolyn. "Honey, honey, I am so sorry. Don't blame John," she pleaded. "It's not his fault, it's my fault. I thought I was doing what was right for the magazine, and I am so sorry, and you know you can't be mad at him." She then asked for sympathy, claiming that John was in the bathtub, crying. "You have no idea, he's so volatile." Berman was taken aback by her sweet and complimentary tone. "She didn't say one bad thing," he observed. Michael was also puzzled as to why John, who had been ignoring his advice and doing his best to create distance between them, would now be so distraught about having offended him. Michael did not believe that John was upset, and his instincts were proven right the next morning when both John and Carolyn seemed in high spirits.

For understandable reasons, Michael resented having to negotiate with the girlfriend of his cofounder. Sensing Michael's hostility, Carolyn tried to charm him the same way she did everyone else. She worked to establish a relationship with Michael and Victoria by flattering them and inviting them to dinner. Initially, her behavior could border on the flirtatious, suggesting that she and Michael shared insider knowledge. "Honey," she would say, "you and I, we are the only ones that really understand John. He relies on us. The rest of these people, they are freaks and sycophants."

But the charm offensive did not work, nor did it last very long. As Michael's relationship with John soured, Carolyn reverted to the role she relished most: a fierce protector of her boyfriend. "She hated him," recalled a senior editor. "She wanted Berman gone." One of her friends told the author Edward Klein that Carolyn "thought Michael wasn't on the up-and-up and that he had a vested interest" in her boyfriend. The friend went on to say that she intentionally "poisoned" John's relationship with Michael. "I don't believe Michael's your real friend," she told John. "The only reason he's close to you is because you're John F. Kennedy Jr."

Meanwhile, John found himself trapped between a troubled girlfriend and an angry business partner. Realizing that their conflict was hurting the magazine, John could have pulled them together into a room and imposed a truce. But he never did. In fact, as the battle escalated, he remained largely passive. It's hard to know why John chose not to act. Most likely, he was more concerned with placating Carolyn and preserving his relationship than he was with defending Berman. Maybe he also hoped that these tensions would die down on their own.

But such a resolution would never happen.

Beginning in the spring of 1996, Carolyn escalated the conflict by harassing Michael over the phone multiple times a day. On one occasion, she screamed at him, telling Berman that he had no idea how difficult life was with John. "He's irresponsible! He doesn't give a shit about me. He doesn't give a shit about anybody but himself!" she shouted into the phone. She shared embarrassingly private details of their sex life before turning her ire on Michael.

"All of you enable this," she snarled. "Why don't you tell him to get home? You just want to be around him. You don't care about his magazine. You just want him around your office. That's all you want." She was just warming up. "And it's not just you, it's everybody—everybody wants him there." She then proceeded to attack John's friends, seeing them as part of a conspiracy to keep John away from home. Berman listened patiently to the tirade but could not understand why she was telling him all these things. "It made absolutely no sense," he reflected.

Some of the calls came in the middle of the night. "Stay the fuck out of my life!" she shouted on another occasion. "No one in the office wants to deal with you. You're bringing down the business and you're bringing down John. Why don't you go away?" Michael demanded that she stop calling him. "Carolyn, I really can't have this conversation with you," he recalled saying. "You have to stay out of the business. You're causing trouble and friction between the two of us and between me and the rest of the staff. And with me and Hachette. Don't call me again."

When John arrived at the office the next day, Michael revealed what had happened and asked his partner to talk to Carolyn. "She's acting crazy," Michael told him. Berman was floored when John later repeated everything he had said to Carolyn. "Yeah, yeah, I told her that Michael Berman says you are crazy, and that you should stay out of the office." John naturally defended his girlfriend, saying that she admitted to calling, "but she says some of the things were somewhat misrepresented. She was just upset." Any chance of reconciliation between Berman and Carolyn, however slight, ended that day.

And the calls kept coming, just as frantic and frequent as before. Berman recalled being on a business trip when the phone in his hotel room rang at two in the morning. A "hysterical" Carolyn screamed, "You should leave! John could be so much more successful if you weren't there! John can't stand you!" Berman responded firmly, "Carolyn, I can't listen to this anymore. You can't call me anymore. You just can't do this. I am going to tell John." "Go ahead," she challenged. "John's right here."

In some cases, specific incidents set off Carolyn's rage. Once, she had a conversation with an executive at Condé Nast who complained that John had canceled lunch with him three times. When she asked John about it, he said he never had a lunch scheduled. She discovered that Michael had made the appointments, promising John's attendance, and then canceled.

On another occasion, John and Michael had scheduled an eight o'clock breakfast meeting with a major advertiser, who called Berman an hour before and switched restaurants. Berman contacted John to notify him of the switch, but John had changed his number and had not given Michael the new one. Berman went alone, while John showed up at the original location. "It was embarrassing for me because the advertiser wasn't coming to see me," said Berman. "I had met with him many times before." When Berman returned to the office, he found John irate. "Why didn't you call me?" John shouted. "You made me look bad! Why did you do this?" Berman told him, "I did honestly call your number, but it's disconnected." John shot back bitterly that they'd had the number disconnected because "Carolyn doesn't want you calling our house." Actually, John changed his number often to stay one step ahead of paparazzi, who somehow managed to get hold of it. Besides, Berman insisted that he called the house only when he could not find John in the office or needed to reach him in the evening.

Carolyn saw Berman the same way she viewed many others in John's life: clinging to his fame and offering little value. "He's a fucking schemer," she told John. "He's using you." But while Michael may have been overzealous in his efforts to manage John and offensive in the way he treated him, what he wanted most was to publish a successful magazine. Had he been so enthralled by John's celebrity status, he would not have risked his professional relationship with critiques and fights. In his eyes, it was Carolyn who deserved blame for interfering in his business relationship with John by undermining his authority.

Although John and Carolyn had denied they were engaged, by the summer of 1996 they were actively planning a secret September wedding. Neither wanted a media circus. They preferred an intimate celebration with only a handful of close friends and family. But organizing such an event and keeping it secret would prove challenging, considering that they were two of the most photographed people on the planet. John made it clear that he did not want to follow his sister's example, holding the ceremony on Cape Cod with an elaborate reception at the family compound in Hyannis Port. New York, the media capital of the world, was also not an option. Instead, they searched for places that would be private and inaccessible to the press but also peaceful and romantic. At RoseMarie's suggestion they traveled to Nova Scotia, but soon after they arrived, Carolyn called RoseMarie. "Honey," she said, "what the fuck are you doing to me? This is the most depressing place in the whole world. I'm not getting married here."

With Nova Scotia scratched off the list, John suggested Cumberland Island, where he had once vacationed with Christina Haag. Georgia's southernmost barrier island, located twenty miles off the coast, offered both isolation and romance. Fewer than thirty-five people lived on Cumberland for just part of the year and it was accessible only by ferry, private boat, or helicopter. "If Mr. Kennedy wanted privacy, this was a good place to find it," Newton Sikes, chief of operations for the National Park Service, which owned most of the island, told *The New York Times*.

No landlines existed on the island, only a radiophone for emergencies, and there was only one place to stay, the Greyfield Inn. The Southern Colonial–style inn, which had been constructed for Andrew Carnegie in 1900, had fewer than twenty rooms. John rented the entire space for the weekend of September 21, even buying out the reservations of those who had already booked rooms. He also booked a few private homes nearby for guests who could not be accommodated at Greyfield.

Carolyn and RoseMarie handled the logistics in the months leading up to the event. So as not to trigger any suspicions, they sent everything needed for the wedding—wine, plates, glasses, silverware, tents—in a series of small shipments, making them appear as routine supplies for the inn. RoseMarie had travel agents create fake itineraries showing John and Carolyn traveling to Ireland that weekend. No one on the island, including the caterers and hotel staff, was allowed to leave that weekend, and they were required to sign confidentiality agreements. In case an industrious photographer managed to make it to the island, they hired a small security force to guard the entry to the ceremony. To help identify intruders, a security guard handed each of the guests an Indian Head nickel to keep with them at all times.

Devising the guest list proved tricky. John had many friends and a large family, leading to some difficult decisions about whom to exclude. In addition to his sister and her husband, Ed, John invited one member to represent each branch of the extended Kennedy family. He chose Anthony Radziwill as his best man. John also cut a few friends who he feared could not keep a secret, later admitting that Carolyn had nixed the friend who had delivered the critical report about her. The week before the wedding, John called each of the guests to invite them to an unspecified party on Cumberland Island. He asked them to make plane reservations and say nothing. Many of those traveling there had no idea they were attending a wedding.

John rented a Learjet for the weekend, and he and Carolyn flew to a small airport in St. Marys, Georgia, accompanied by Billy Noonan and his wife, Kathleen; and Rob Littell and his wife, Fran. According to Rob, John and Carolyn giggled the whole way down. Once they landed, they climbed into an old fishing boat and motored across the bay to Cumberland Island, reaching the Greyfield Inn just in time for the rehearsal dinner.

Friday night's rehearsal dinner on the veranda was a "boisterous and lighthearted" affair, interrupted only by the toast delivered by Carolyn's mother, Ann Freeman. No one seems to remember exactly what she said, but the message was shockingly clear. With John sitting a few feet away, she openly questioned whether he was the right partner for her daughter. According to Littell, her remarks left John "visibly stung."

That same night they headed to the beach, where a bar had been set up under a giant tent and a bonfire blazed nearby. Their guests stayed up until the early-morning hours, but John and Carolyn turned in early. The following afternoon, John invited a number of friends to his suite and handed out wedding party gifts. Instead of more traditional gifts, such as cuff links, John gave everyone a pair of blue silk boxer shorts, with John's initials embroidered on the right leg, and his guest's on the left. "Wear them well, my friends," he said. "Think of me when you wear them."

The ceremony was scheduled for Saturday at dusk at the First African Baptist Church, which had been founded by slaves in 1893. Since the church was on the northern end of the island, John and Carolyn arranged for jeeps to shuttle guests from the inn. It was a reflection of John's unpretentious style and down-to-earth manner that he—one of the wealthiest, most famous people in the world—held his wedding at a rustic church in the middle of a muddy field filled with pig dung.

Not surprisingly, John arrived late to his own wedding. Some accounts say that he could not find his tie; others, his shirt. Either way, the event began rather uncomfortably, with guests gathered outside, swatting away swarms of mosquitoes and watching dusk turn to dark before the bride and groom finally appeared. Because of the oppressive heat inside the church, the doors stayed open to catch a breeze while everyone clustered in the eleven weathered pews. Since the church had no electricity, the guests used candles and a few flashlights to observe the service. Standing at the altar before a cross made of sticks and twine, John, thirty-five, and Carolyn, twenty-nine, exchanged vows.

When the ceremony ended, everyone hopped back into the open-top jeeps for the reception at the inn. Even a light shower did not dampen the celebratory mood. Back at the Greyfield, they had set up two large tents near a giant mangrove tree for the DJ, dance floor, and bar. The occasion proceeded joyously. People drank, some to excess, and an abundant supply of marijuana and cocaine was available for those who wanted it. The highlight of the evening, however, was Anthony's Radziwill's heartfelt toast to his cousin and best friend. "We all know why John would marry Carolyn," he announced at dinner. "She is smart, beautiful, and charming." But, he continued, "What does she see in John? A person who over the years has taken pleasure in teasing me, playing nasty tricks, and, in general, torturing me. Well, some of the things that I guess might have attracted Carolyn to John are his caring, his charm, and his very big heart of gold."

Now married, John and Carolyn assumed that the paparazzi would lose interest, taking only a few pictures before leaving them alone. Precisely the opposite happened. They became even more relentless and aggressive. Every

day, between eight and twenty photographers could be found hanging outside their apartment. "This is out of hand," John told Rose over the phone.
"I'm going downstairs to give a statement, and then Carolyn and I will take
a few pictures." Carolyn, however, did not favor this strategy. She pulled the
phone away from John. "I don't want to go down there," she insisted. "I'm not
sure this is a good idea." Rose reassured her that she should trust John's instincts. "They just want a shot of you two together, the newlyweds. And then
they have it. I think it's a good idea. You don't have to say anything or even
smile. Just stand there."

After the phone call, John and Carolyn went downstairs holding hands
and, standing on their building's steps, asked the photographers to respect
their privacy. According to paparazzo Lawrence Schwartzwald, the photographers appreciated John's gesture and remained polite and respectful as he
spoke. But the truce lasted the length of John's statement. As soon as John
and Carolyn started walking toward their car, the cluster of photographers
"broke rank" as everyone scrambled to get the "money shot"—the one picture that no one else could capture. The scene petrified Carolyn. After that
moment, she realized that there would always be another "first" photo—the
first time wearing black shoes or red shoes; her hair up or down; walking
the dog; going to the deli. The pursuit would never end. "It was very demoralizing," recalled Carole.

Michael Berman remembers watching clips of the press conference that
night on the local news. He thought to himself, "What is he thinking? They
just made it so much worse for her. He's asked the paparazzi to leave her
alone? It will just entice them even more." Despite his many clashes with her,
Berman empathized with Carolyn's plight and blamed John for not doing
more to protect her. "He knew better," Berman reflected in 2019. "He certainly understood how important it was to have someone run interference
for people in the public eye. He left her on her own, and that seemed ill-
advised and very unkind to me."

Over the next few months, the paparazzi swarmed Carolyn like locusts.
As she walked down the street, they would get in her face and shout, "You
whore! You ugly bitch!" Oftentimes, she would call RoseMarie and reveal
some of the things they said to her. "This is ridiculous," Carolyn lamented.
"If I don't leave the house before eight A.M., they're waiting for me. *Every*

morning. They chase me down the street." Carolyn grew more reclusive, less willing to leave the apartment. But the paradox is that the more mysterious she became, the more the public yearned to know more about her.

For the paparazzi, money drove the entire operation. Victor Malafronte, who stalked John for years, claimed they could demand $500 to $1,000 for an exclusive picture of John and Carolyn. While that amount may not sound like much, a photographer could sell a photo to multiple newspapers and magazines, both in the United States and around the world. Therefore, he could end up making between $15,000 and $20,000 with a single picture. Malafronte remained unapologetic about hunting John and later Carolyn. "It's hard to feel sorry for a guy who is so rich, good-looking, and a Kennedy," he said matter-of-factly.

Not all the press that Carolyn received was negative, however. In November, she and John stepped out for their first formal function at the Whitney Museum's thirtieth anniversary gala, an event that prompted the *New York Post* to crown them New York's "king and queen." A woman said, "She's a lot like Jackie. Not the looks, exactly, but the bearing. She has a presence—gracious, warm, but with that Jackie aura that gently reminds you not to get too close." More often, however, stories appeared from "reliable sources" claiming that she and John were breaking up or that Carolyn was pregnant. The *New York Post* even announced that if they had a son, they planned to name him John F. Kennedy III; if a daughter, Jacqueline.

What worried Carolyn most of all was what journalists might dig up about her past. She had led a private life, but now everything that she did or had done long ago seemed to show up in print. Her alarm increased when, only a month after their marriage, the *New York Post* ran a story claiming that she was illegally subletting her $600-a-month East Village apartment to one of her friends.

Michael hoped that John and Carolyn's marriage in September 1996 would ease hostilities. Perhaps Carolyn would be more secure once she was John's wife. She would likely get involved in charity events and maybe even set up a foundation. But none of those possibilities materialized. She actually seemed less happy after the wedding than before. "This is not what I signed up for," she complained to a *George* colleague, referring to the constant presence of paparazzi scrutinizing her every move. If anything, the pressure caused her to spend more time at the magazine and immerse herself even deeper in office politics.

Things grew so strained that even Christmas became a source of tension. As the 1996 holiday season approached, Michael and John agreed to follow their usual pattern, giving modest gifts to the staff and writing checks to a handful of special people. A few weeks before Christmas, Michael had his assistant tell John that they needed to pick out gifts, but he never heard back. Soon after, he saw John and Carolyn handing out lavish gifts to the staff. Carolyn had spent thousands of dollars trying to find the perfect gift for each employee: engraved pens, boutique handbags, expensive clothing, and jewelry. RoseMarie received stacked boxes and garment bags on her desk, along with a check for $5,000. Adding insult to injury, they even handed out gifts to Michael's staff. They had excluded Michael from the process entirely. "It was just an effort to undermine me," he reflected. "I was furious."

After the Christmas debacle, the two men were barely on speaking terms. The final straw came a few weeks later, in January 1997, over Michael's handling of ancillary income streams. He and John had always believed that *George* could not sustain itself solely as a magazine and that they needed other revenue sources. "*George's* paradigm on politics has long been applicable to television," John told advertisers. "*Martha Stewart Living* has demonstrated television remains a potent means of selling subscriptions and extending the brand." All the major networks expressed interest in striking a deal. Furthermore, if Hachette had its way, the company would have moved John over to television not only to generate more income but also to nudge him out of the editor's chair in order to become more visible. Berman was in the process of negotiating book deals and television rights, but he knew that John wanted to limit his time in front of the camera.

John understood that he would be a big draw, but he still wanted to be taken seriously as an editor and not as a celebrity. He told Berman that he would be willing to make a brief appearance at the beginning and end of a show, but that was all. When the networks asked if John would participate, Michael's response always remained the same: "Yes, but in a small way." According to Berman, they struck a deal with NBC in which John would introduce a one-hour *George* special and then reemerge briefly at the end. "He would say hello and good-bye," Berman said. "He had full approval of everything he would say. His name would not appear in the title. He would not be asked to promote it."

As clear as these conditions seemed, misunderstandings arose over what exactly John's role would be. Berman saw his partner's role as limited, no more intrusive than his appearance on *Murphy Brown* to promote the first issue. But John worried that he was being pitched as the host of the show. "We can do a *George* television show," he told RoseMarie, "and I will promote it, but I am not Jerry Seinfeld. I am not going to host a TV show. It's not what I want to do."

One day in February, John marched into Michael's office and grabbed the folder on his desk containing all the documents related to the deal. He then declared, "We are not doing any of this." As they struggled over the folder, John tugged at Berman's shirt and ripped his cuff. "This is it!" he shouted at Michael. "I'll be the editor, and you can be the publisher. That's the way it's going to be." Berman retorted that John had better come up with a good reason for canceling the negotiations. "I took care of it," John stated coldly. "I told them that you were doing this behind my back." With that, all of Berman's frustrations with John and Carolyn boiled over. "When you come in the office, you're unrecognizable!" he hollered. "You're exhausted. You're unfocused. Whatever your problems, keep them at home. Don't let them spill over into the office. That's all I ask." Michael then ripped into Carolyn, repeating his familiar refrain, "Get her the hell out of the office."

John, caught off guard by Michael's accusations and seemingly unrelated attack on his wife, rushed to her defense. "You have no idea!" he shouted back. "That's not true. Don't say that about her. She has legitimate friends in this office." He told Berman that he was jealous because they liked her but did not like him. "She's the best thing that ever happened to me. Why would you try to ruin that? I can't tell her what to do."

Berman snapped. "Her behavior is deplorable!" he shouted.

Stunned, John turned and ran out of Michael's office, but Berman followed close behind. Of all the fierce arguments that Michael and John had had in the past, this one was by far the loudest and most intense. To those who witnessed the scene, Berman appeared out of control. He stood outside John's office, roaring, "Open the fucking door! Open this door!" He then grabbed a letter opener from RoseMarie's desk and tried picking the lock. Michael claims to have no recollection of what happened after failing to gain entry into John's office. But according to multiple sources, before Berman fled the area, he confiscated John's appointment calendar from RoseMarie's desk. "Do you fucking believe this?" Michael grumbled as he passed by Matt Berman. "He ripped my shirt!"

Somehow John pulled himself together and immediately returned to business as usual. He called to have the lock changed on his door and then, as if nothing had happened, held an editorial meeting with Rich Blow and Biz Mitchell a few minutes later. While they talked in his office, the locksmith started removing the old lock cylinder and installing a new one. Suddenly Michael reappeared and instructed the locksmith to change *his* lock too. John managed to get his lock changed with a simple phone call; his cofounder was told he needed to submit a work order. Michael stomped away, only to return a few minutes later to plead his case to the locksmith. "Why can't you just do it?" he asked. "Why can't you just change my lock?" The man held his ground, emphasizing again that he would need the proper paperwork. "Maybe I'll call David Pecker, then," Michael threatened. According to Blow, "John's face was filled with rage." He dared Michael to make the call, knowing that such a move would only make Michael appear small and petty.

Meanwhile, RoseMarie was pacing nervously outside the office, searching for John's appointment book. She confronted Michael, who denied taking it. After a few minutes, though, he showed up holding it. "Here. You left this in my office," he muttered before tossing it on Rose's desk. It's unclear why Berman would have needed John's calendar. Perhaps seizing his calendar represented a last desperate effort to assert control over John. Or perhaps Michael felt so enraged that he acted impulsively.

Berman retreated to his office, knowing that his friendship with John was now officially over and that he could no longer remain at *George*. Elinore Carmody contacted Hachette and complained that the fight between the cofounders had created a threatening work environment for the other employees. "Nobody can function like this," she told Pecker, who then intervened and found Berman a job in another division of the company. As if to mark the end of their partnership, John bought out Michael's 25 percent share, thus assuming half ownership of the magazine.

Not everyone was happy to see Michael leave. "You cannot underestimate the impact of Michael leaving," reflected Elinore. Jean-Louis Ginibre, who served as the editorial director for Hachette, called "the divorce" between John and Michael "fateful," adding, "When Berman left, something was lost in the mix." Blow observed that Michael's absence significantly hurt ad sales. "His relationship with John may have been deteriorating," he claimed, "but Michael could articulate the vision of *George*, and he was a hell of a salesman." These assessments were right. John and Michael had gone into business a decade earlier because they complemented each other: Berman, the professional businessman who, because of his background in public relations, was pitch perfect in making sales calls; John, the ubercelebrity who could open any door and dazzle people with his presence. As time went on, however, John became more comfortable in his editor's role and began to trust his own journalistic instincts, even if the results continued to be mixed. But no matter what, he still needed someone with Michael's talent for articulating the magazine's message to advertisers. He needed more, not fewer, people in his inner circle who were not overpowered by his celebrity.

Both men were embarrassed about the way they had behaved. Two days after their falling-out, John delivered to Michael a new shirt along with a handwritten apology. He seemed surprised, not just that Berman had left but that he had stayed away. So many people clamored for inclusion in John's life, and few ever walked out completely. Several months after Michael left *George*, John had a conversation with publicist Nancy Haberman. "At this point," John said to her, "I really don't remember what the issues were between us, and I think maybe it's time we could go back to being friends." Haberman, who was close to Berman, laughed and told him, "You're out of your mind." John made a similar overture to another mutual friend. "I really think we're past this. Do you think Michael feels the same way?" Perhaps John hoped for Berman to return, but the colleague, knowing the emotional damage the incident had inflicted on Michael, doubted a reconciliation would ever happen. And the colleague was right. Michael never spoke with John again.

Looking back two decades later, Berman wishes that he had responded to John's efforts to reach out. "I regret having lost control that day. I certainly knew better—we both did—but my professional life had just come crashing down," he reflected. "John reached out a number of times over the next couple of years, but I never responded. I was still too angry." Berman went on to have a very successful career as an early investor in a number of lucrative content-based digital platforms and, later, as the president of a boutique private equity firm. Berman quietly remembered the magazine around the twentieth anniversary of its founding by endowing an initiative for journalism students at a major American university to explore the intersection of politics and popular culture. "I wanted to give back by encouraging a new generation to be able to build on our initial premise," he reflected. Now he teaches his sons not to hold on to anger, "since time is a luxury you don't always have." He believed that John, having suffered so much loss in his life, instinctively understood that lesson. "Having allowed that to be our final interaction haunts me to this day," he admitted.

Despite their differences at the time, Berman today is gracious and generous when recalling Kennedy. "John started out as a good partner," he reflected. "He intuitively understood the intersection of politics and pop culture better than anyone I have ever known. He worked hard and challenged the status quo. He provided tremendous value well beyond his name. *George* foresaw what now constitutes an inherent aspect of twenty-first-century American culture. It's sad he's not here to see it, but even though the magazine did not survive, the original premise ultimately came true. For John, that is a powerful legacy."

Despite the turmoil, John remained focused on getting issues onto the newsstands. Advice and criticism flowed from all sides: there was too much pop culture, and the colorful covers were a distraction; there was too much politics in the magazine and too few celebrities. John's leadership also came under scrutiny, with some deeming him too cautious and unable to take risks. In actuality, there was nothing cautious about John's handling of the magazine. He had determined to chart his own way and trust his own instincts, as revealed by his willingness to challenge both David Pecker and Michael Berman. On several occasions, he also overruled the advice of his senior editors. This new decisiveness did not mean that John always made the right choices—given the magazine's trajectory, he clearly did not—but it demonstrated a strong backbone and commitment.

One of Berman's complaints was that John never used his clout to persuade President Clinton to appear in the magazine. But Clinton's absence did not stem from a lack of effort on John's part. His first request to the White House came just weeks after *George*'s founding. He asked for permission to show readers photos depicting "the thrill of being inside the

President's own airplane." The request was denied because guidelines stated that photos of the interior of presidential/state aircraft represented a security risk. Two months later, John wrote the president a note thanking him for sharing his "wonderful remembrance" of George Wallace for their first issue. "I have been a bit reluctant to approach your office in the context of *George* magazine, since you have already done so much for our family. However, you are at the center of American politics, and we'd be honored to have you in the magazine in the future, if it suits you."

After the first issue launched, John pitched two ideas to the White House. On November 3, 1995, he wrote White House Press Secretary Michael McCurry to ask if Richard Ford, the author behind the popular book *Independence Day*, a powerful meditation on a man's midlife crisis, could pen a profile of the president. He asked that Ford be given access to Clinton for a week, following him when he traveled away from the White House as well as having three interview slots. "We realize that this is a substantial request, but if this piece is to have the insight, feeling, and depth that we envision, it is paramount that the President and Mr. Ford have sufficient time in which to become comfortable with each other." John planned to run the story in the magazine's fourth issue, which would hit newsstands in late March. Given the time frame, Ford would need access during the first few weeks of December. The second request was for the president to allow David Kennerly, President Gerald Ford's White House photographer, to conduct a one- or two-day photo shoot.

John did not shy away from using flattery to win Clinton's favor: "We would like to show our readers a side of the President that they rarely see in candids—his warmth, his humor, his personal style of governing, his intensity—all in the context of the work environment." John wanted the photos to lead off the fourth issue under the title "American Spectacle."

The deadlines themselves were enough to prevent either opportunity. In the margin of the request to shoot the photos by the third week in November, McCurry wrote, "Pretty well kills it." He then circulated John's memo around the White House communications office with the note, "Risky, of course, but what do people think? Too much?" Don Baer, the White House director of communications, nixed the idea, scribbling, "No way."

The Clintons liked and respected John, but they did not find *George* sufficiently serious to deserve a presidential appearance. Clinton, however, was eager to maintain his association with the Kennedys and to bring John into his administration, so he appointed him to serve two terms on the President's Committee on Mental Retardation. It was a natural fit for John, given his work with Reaching Up.

John also failed in his efforts to recruit Hillary Clinton for the July 1996 cover celebrating the twenty most fascinating women in politics. When she turned him down, John hatched a new idea. "I think we should dress up Madonna as my mother," he told Rose. "Wouldn't that be a riot? We'll have her in the pillbox hat, sitting on a stack of books." It was the kind of idea that no other editor would have proposed, especially because John's colleagues were still trying to understand how much of his family legacy was fair game and how much was off-limits. A few editors warned that the public might take offense at him parodying his mother. John had no such concerns. "If it doesn't bother me, why should it bother anyone else?"

Madonna denied John's request, saying she could never do his mom justice. "My eyebrows aren't thick enough," she joked. John then came up with another provocative idea: putting the young actress Drew Barrymore on the cover to re-create the image of Marilyn Monroe cooing "Happy Birthday, Mr. President" to his father at Madison Square Garden in 1962. "This was John's call," Blow recalled. "He had forcefully advocated for the idea but offered little more explanation than that it was a sexy image." Although he did not raise his concerns at the time, Blow considered the cover a "slap in the face" and a setback in their efforts to get other journalists to take *George* seriously.

Some wondered why John would choose an image that seemed to flaunt his father's sexual conquests and humiliate his mother. After first seeing the mock-up of the proposed Monroe cover, publicist Nancy Haberman looked at John and smiled. He missed a beat and then said, "I guess I'm working through my demons, one by one." The reality, however, was that John never believed that his father had an affair with Monroe. He therefore did not view the cover as an attempt to play with the truth but rather to toy with public perceptions of his family. It proved to be one of the most talked-about covers of the year, and it nearly doubled their newsstand sales.

In another bold move the following month, John sat down with Iain Calder, the retired British editor of the *National Enquirer*. After being harassed by writers from that publication his entire life, John would now be giving its figurehead space in his magazine. Some people believed he was committing a mistake by adding legitimacy to a third-rate gossip rag. John, however, was genuinely curious about the world of celebrity gossip. He viewed his interviews, whether of George Wallace or of Calder, as a way to understand the people and institutions that had shaped his life and his father's. Given his openness, John had no trouble engaging in a fair-minded conversation with Calder. His questions showed that he wanted a deeper knowledge of Calder's brand of "cowboy journalism," why it was so successful, and how the *Enquirer* had become the bestselling weekly newspaper in the country. Calder, nicknamed "Ice Pick" because he stabbed people in the front, characterized his style of journalism as mainstream, telling John that he was writing for "the mythical Mrs. Smith in Kansas City."

Near the end of the interview, John recounted a story about one of his many encounters with the *Enquirer*: "When I was at college, I once got a call, and it was a British voice on the other end. He said, 'We have information that you're gay, and we have photographs to prove it'—photographs taken in a bar or something." John assured the caller the story was false, but the writer then contacted his uncle Teddy's office and threatened to make the photos public if the senator did not pose for Christmas pictures. It's impossible to know whether doctored photos existed or if the caller was bluffing in the hopes that it could land him an interview. But John never forgot about it. "Could that have been the *National Enquirer*?" he asked. "I can't guarantee that it wasn't," Calder responded slyly, "but it certainly doesn't sound like us." "Why not?" John asked. Calder insisted that they would not have used the photos because "our readers consider you a beloved figure." John appreciated the flattery but was not buying it. "You're too kind," he retorted. "But wouldn't that be all the more reason?" John must have been shocked and horrified by Calder's response: "You're the little boy saluting his father," he confessed, claiming his readers "would have killed us for doing that."

Calder's response was revealing on many levels. Here was John, the cofounder and editor of a popular magazine, engaged in a serious interview, asking smart questions and engaging in thoughtful conversation, yet he could not escape his past. As much as he tried to reinvent himself and convince people to accept him as a serious adult, he was constantly forced back to the one moment that defined his life but that he could not remember.

John encountered a similar problem when, in September 1996, he agreed to sit down for an hourlong interview with Oprah Winfrey. Winfrey's daytime talk show, already the highest rated in America, could not have scored a better coup than snagging John for its eleventh season premiere. She had begged John in the past to appear on her show, but he always resisted. He did not want to rehash his childhood or be asked the same questions about his father. But now, John believed, circumstances had changed. He saw the interview as an opportunity to reintroduce himself to America as an adult and as the successful editor of a hot new magazine. To make sure the conversation stayed focused on the present, John extracted a promise from Winfrey that she would not show any photos of him as a child. Yet within the first few minutes, while John described the Calder interview, the audience at home saw a family photo revealing John as a child in his mother's arms. Later in the interview, Winfrey projected the famous image of John saluting his father's casket. When John returned to the office, he complained to Matt Berman, "I was three years old. I have no memory of doing that." He later called Winfrey to complain. "Well, it's television," she reportedly said. "Get over it."

Winfrey could be so dismissive partly because she got what she wanted from the appearance. John gave her show its highest season premiere rating ever. Her numbers surpassed the combined viewership total of talk-show runner-ups Rosie O'Donnell and Sally Jessy Raphael.

John continued to seek out other controversial figures that he found fascinating and mysterious. For the October 1996 issue, he sat down with Louis Farrakhan of the Nation of Islam one year after Farrakhan had organized a Million Man March on Washington to focus attention on the problems plaguing African American men. Farrakhan descended from a long line of African American leaders, from Marcus Garvey to Malcolm X, who exhorted their followers to distrust white people and to create separate institutions. John peppered him with questions about the potential conflict between being both a religious and political leader. "When you associate yourself with a political candidacy, should people still regard you as a religious leader?" he asked. John gave Farrakhan, who had spoken critically of Jews and been labeled an anti-Semite, a chance to explain his views. "Why do you single out Jews?" John asked when Farrakhan blasted those who he claimed repressed black people. Farrakhan managed to slip through that tough question and a few others, but John deserved credit for having the courage to ask them.

Continuing his string of daring choices, John ignored the advice of many of his top editors when he ran a story by the mother of Yigal Amir, who had assassinated Israeli prime minister Yitzhak Rabin in November 1995. She argued that her son belonged to a right-wing conspiracy within the Israeli government that opposed Rabin's peace overtures to the Palestinians. Her son, she charged, had been goaded into killing the prime minister by members of the Israeli secret service. John knew that running such an explosive story would be risky. He had his staff spend months fact-checking and hired investigators in Israel before he gave it the green light.

John had complicated reasons for deciding to publish the piece. He resented the many conspiracy theories swirling around his father's assassination, but now it appeared as if he were using his platform to promote a conspiracy theory about another head of state's murder. Nitsana Darshan-Leitner, an Israeli lawyer who negotiated the deal between *George* and Amir, raised the issue with John. He explained to her that too much time had passed since the deaths of his father and Uncle Robert for new evidence to emerge. But this case was fresh, and he encouraged the family to continue probing the details in hopes of finding some resolution.

The article, which appeared in the March 1997 issue, produced a harsh response from Rabin's widow: "I would expect John Kennedy, who lost his father to an assassin's bullet when he was a mere child and grew up in the shadow of that horrible tragedy, to adopt a higher moral stand in his paper." John stood by the story. While the claim that members of the Israeli secret service were involved remains controversial, a later investigation did reveal that a group of religious zealots had played a role in encouraging Amir.

It was also during *George*'s first full year that John asked me for help with writing his Editor's Letter, which had been spotty in the initial issues. Some of the letters had simply, sometimes blandly, provided the background for the magazine's featured interview. But John wanted to add more depth by situating contemporary issues in a richer historical context. That was where I came in. On a few occasions, I'd get home to find a message on my answering machine. "Stevie, this is John. I'm working on my letter and was hoping you could help offer some historical background. Oh, my letter is due tomorrow. Can you help?"

By the time John started *George*, I had left Yale and taken a position as a lecturer in modern history at Oxford University. I was sometimes not home to answer the phone when he called because I was participating in the Oxford ritual of high table, which resembles a scene from a Harry Potter movie. The weekly ritual is uniquely British and dates back hundreds of years. Dinner commences with the faculty marching into the ornate hall as students stand at attention until we are seated at a table atop a platform elevated over the students—hence the name high table. Everyone wears appropriate academic robes signifying his or her status in the academic pecking order.

I cannot remember how many letters I helped draft—maybe six, possibly a few more. Since we were five hours ahead, I would wake up early the following morning, write a few pages based on the skimpy outline that John had provided in his message, then fax them to New York so they arrived around nine. I never received a message back from John or even a note acknowledging that he received the fax. But later, I would pick up the magazine and realize that his letter looked awfully familiar. John always rewrote my material in his own words, extracting quotes to weave into his narrative, but the theme was identical to what I had suggested.

I must have helped with one of his letters in the first three issues because a few editors caught on to our arrangement. They could not understand how John could leave the office on Thursday night with only the vaguest idea for his letter and then, less than twelve hours later, turn in a crisp, thoughtful essay sprinkled with erudite quotes, ranging from Thomas Jefferson to Franklin D. Roosevelt. They eventually guilt-tripped John into publicly thanking me, something that I felt he did not have to do. At the bottom of his April/May 1996 letter, which dealt with virtue in politics and drew heavily on my memo, John wrote: "Special thanks to Dr. Steven Gillon, professor of American history at Oxford University and South Philly's only Anglophile."

In a little over a year, the magazine had lost its executive editor and its cofounder. These losses definitely took a toll. In the short term, however, John felt unburdened by Michael Berman's departure. He kept his office door open more often and could be seen casually strolling around the office. But in the long term, losing his friend and cofounder left John rattled and uncertain about the future of the magazine. Now it would be his instincts, and his alone, that would guide the magazine.

Furthermore, John faced many challenges that went far beyond Berman's departure. Critics, including some *George* editors, complained about the magazine's uneven quality, saying that what generated the most attention were the colorful and provocative covers, like that of Drew Barrymore dressed as Marilyn Monroe, not the articles. None of these critiques should have been of great concern, since most start-up magazines needed some time to find their legs. But Hachette was too impatient and frugal to allow its new magazine the typical chance to publish a few trial issues to work out the kinks. It was obvious to those who worked for *George* that theirs was not just another magazine and that the media would therefore judge it by a different standard.

In what was an ongoing theme, even *George* editors admitted candidly that the magazine often lacked discipline and focus. "John's vision was prescient," recalled associate editor Hugo Lindgren, "but it was one thing to have a vision; it was another to execute it." You also needed a certain measure of self-discipline and the capability to evolve and adapt to a changing marketplace. "There was a disconnect between Matt Berman's bizarre fashion statements and the second-rate, sometimes wonky content," Lindgren concluded. "The magazine was less than the sum of its parts."

Lindgren had a point, repeating a criticism that Michael Berman had expressed from the very beginning. *George* published some interesting articles, but it lacked a clear editorial voice and seemed to re-create itself every issue. Each editor clung to a different idea of the types of stories that should appear in *George,* so the magazine reflected eclectic interests that sometimes didn't mesh. John signed off on all the pieces, and he suggested a few of his own, but the magazine resembled more a chorus of competing singers than a solo performer with backup singers.

Hachette's budget-consciousness also damaged the magazine. Biz Mitchell estimated that they had roughly $50,000 to spend on the editorial in every issue, a fraction of what some of their competitors had and far less than what was needed to hire top talent. Hachette also never performed the necessary research to create the perfect reader profile for advertisers. They knew that *George* readership was 55 percent women and 45 percent male, an unusually balanced representation for a political magazine. Most political magazines leaned toward 75 percent to 80 percent men. But the *George* sales force did not possess granular demographic information on readers, making it hard to pitch and sell the magazine to advertisers. Hachette also worsened matters by deciding to go monthly so quickly. It made the announcement after the spectacular success of the first two issues, with the first monthly hitting the stands in July 1997. Elinore Carmody, who sold ads for *George*, claimed that decision "crippled" the magazine. Hachette assumed that it would get the same number of ads each month, but the math did not work that way. "I don't think they knew what the ramifications were," Carmody reflected.

After only a few issues, advertisers started expressing disappointment over the magazine's trajectory. When asked what he thought of *George*, Bob Guccione Jr., who had founded *Spin*, responded, "It has no bite." Again, the expectations for *George* ran much higher than for other magazines. Advertisers assumed that because of John's connections, his magazine would be close to the action, getting the scoop on the most newsworthy stories and uncovering something that readers did not already know. "I don't see where it is going," Ralph Lauren's team concluded. George Fertitta, head of a major advertising agency, put it more bluntly. "There's no 'Holy shit!' story in *George*," he said. "There's nothing that stops you in your tracks." GM's Michael Browner, who had been *George*'s largest advertiser for the first two issues, also questioned the magazine's direction. "The circulation was not developing the way we hoped," he reflected. "I came to the conclusion that maybe people were not as interested in politics as a subject matter as I thought they would be."

Other than the initial flurry of interest when the magazine first launched, the problem among advertisers had always been the same: they did not know how to categorize *George*, even two years in. *Sports Illustrated* was a sports magazine, and research revealed a specific profile of those who read it. But since *George* did not have similar detailed analytics, never mind a clear editorial profile and voice, imagining who would purchase it still involved a fair amount of guesswork. "It was kind of *Vanity Fair*, kind of *New Republic*, kind of *Esquire*. It was a little bit of different genres but never quite fit into any one," recalled Gary Ginsberg.

Keenly aware of these challenges, John decided to give his team a pep talk. In late January 1997 he gathered the entire staff in a large conference room and spoke in uncharacteristically personal terms about his motivations for creating the magazine and his continued optimism for its future. He confided about how his own experience shaped the magazine, how he grew up noticing a gap in the way he viewed politics and the way most journalists covered it. "There were only two ways I knew of to do something about this gap," John said. "One was to start a political career of my own. The other was to start a magazine." He insisted that he was proud of what they had accomplished, no matter what the critics said. "We have created a paradigm shift in journalism," John declared. "Someday we'll be able to look back on this and know that we created something truly new."

John went on to say that there would always be those who wanted *George* to fail. The media did not want him to succeed because they didn't want him to grow up. Declining numbers aside, John believed that other magazines worried because the publication they had once dismissed still threatened their advertising dollars. Although he did not mention names, John was clearly referring to Jann Wenner of *Rolling Stone* when he said, "I've lost friends because they're feeling the sting of ads that we're taking away from them, and they're pissed off about it." John had no intention of reverting to his former role as "Prince Charming." This magazine had been his momentous chance to reintroduce himself to the American people as a serious-minded adult, and he had no intention of quitting.

He recounted to the staff how people came up to him at Bill Clinton's 1997 inauguration to praise the magazine. Some said it was the only political magazine they had ever read. Those comments boosted his spirits, but John preferred to laugh at the naysayers. I think it was his way of letting us know that he did not take himself so seriously that he could not poke fun at himself. He enjoyed telling the story of a man who approached him one day as he walked to the office. The stranger came right up to John and poked his finger in John's face. "Kennedy, you know what's wrong with you?" he said. "You're mediocre."

CHAPTER 10

"SHE'S REALLY SPOOKED NOW"

I n June 1997 John found himself in a familiar place: standing by the bedside of Anthony Radziwill at the National Institutes of Health (NIH) in Washington, DC. With Anthony nearing the end of his life, John became a steady presence, reflecting a special bond that had existed ever since they'd been young. They resembled best friends as well as cousins: Anthony was the son of John's aunt, Lee Bouvier Radziwill, and Polish prince Stanislas Radziwill. Anthony grew up in London and moved to New York when he was sixteen years old. He finished high school at the exclusive Choate and then attended Boston University. After graduating in 1982, he relocated to New York and eventually became an award-winning television producer.

No matter the physical distance between them, John and Anthony had always managed to stay close. They were first cousins, but they grew up together because their mothers were close. As children, they frolicked on Scorpios, the private island owned by John's stepfather, Aristotle Onassis. Over the years, they took trips together, often to exotic locations, and rarely went more than a few weeks without speaking. Caroline Kennedy said they loved each other as "the brother they each did not have."

They were, however, a study in contrasts. While John was playful and outgoing, Anthony was serious and reserved. Anthony's wife, Carole, would later compare them to the characters in the popular 1970s television show *The Odd Couple*. "John is Oscar to Anthony's Felix," she wrote. Anthony embodied the "English schoolboy": neat and well mannered, his bed always made, his clothes tucked away. John was a different story. Some old habits were hard to break. He marked "his territory like a teenager, leaving trails of movement behind him: a dirty dish, an empty bottle, books and newspapers wrinkled from spilled drinks. If he has been in the kitchen, every cabinet is opened. In the bathroom there are towels on the floor and a toothpaste cap in the sink."

Their close relationship was defined by constant teasing and poking. Like mirrors of each other, John did a perfect imitation of Anthony, and Anthony did a perfect imitation of John. Often John would mock Anthony's royal heritage by calling him "petit prince." Once, when Anthony complained that an elderly woman was taking too much time at the grocery checkout counter, John told friends, "Do you know that Anthony hates children and old people?"

In the 1980s, Anthony suffered a bout of testicular cancer, but doctors assured him that the cancer was in remission. After that ordeal, John came up with a new nickname for Anthony: "Old One Ball." Then in January 1994 they discovered that the cancer had returned. The same night that Anthony was diagnosed, he received a call from John's mom. "I have something I need to tell you," Jackie said to her nephew. "So do I," he responded. Both had been diagnosed with cancer on the same day.

Despite the unfortunate news, Anthony carried on with his life. Later that year, he married Carole DiFalco, who grew up in the blue-collar suburb of Suffern, New York, in a family that loved "cheap wine, cigarettes, barbecues, and loud laughter." John served as best man at their wedding. Carole and Anthony had met while covering the murder trial of Erik and Lyle Menendez, two brothers who had gained notoriety for brutally murdering their wealthy parents in their Beverly Hills mansion in 1989. They appeared to be an odd couple: one from a working-class background, the other a descendant of Polish royalty and nephew of an American president. "It doesn't matter where you start from," Anthony told her. "What counts is where you end up." They dated for two years before he introduced her to his formidable mother, Lee.

On the last day of their honeymoon in Australia, Carole ran her hands over Anthony's scar from the previous surgery and discovered another bump. "I'm sure it's nothing," he reassured her. But it turned out to be something. Carole remembered the next few months as "a blur of hospital visits, men in white coats, more 'bumps,' talk of positive margins, radiation, and 'pulmonary nodules.'" The news could not have been grimmer: the cancer had colonized his body and traveled to his lungs. In November 1994 John called his uncle Teddy, who sat on the powerful Senate Health and Human Services Committee, and asked if he could get Anthony into the National Cancer Institute for some experimental, cutting-edge therapy.

John did his best to lift Anthony's spirits. After Anthony's first surgery at NIH, John walked into the recovery room with a grin that belied his heavy heart and said cheerily, "Hey, Tony Pro!" As usual, they proceeded to make jokes about the pleasure of getting sponge baths from nurses. "When they were kids, John was always the one who joked with Anthony and could make him laugh," Carole said in 2005. "He thought it would cheer him up, and it did. But he also told me that he was afraid that if he stopped joking, Anthony would know things were really bad and would just give up and die."

But Anthony's ordeal had barely begun, and John felt weighed down by a sense of helplessness. He'd helped Anthony get into the best hospitals, but there was nothing that his charm or connections could do to slow down the tumor's progression. John rarely talked about death or tragedy. It was not a part of his emotional makeup. He was never one to wallow in self-pity. He had lost so many people in his life, beginning with his father when he was just three, and, more recently, his mother. The same disease that had taken his mother at such a young age was now gradually bleeding life out of his best friend. It was as if John were now saying, "Enough. This can't happen to Anthony, too." He refused to acknowledge the seriousness of his illness or contemplate the possibility that his cousin was going to die. He blocked it out.

Worse still, Anthony's illness coincided with the creation of *George* and John's efforts to steer it through its first few years. John had grown up juggling many different roles, so he had developed the ability to compartmentalize his numerous responsibilities. But dealing with the demands of starting a new magazine while also caring for his best friend would challenge him both physically and mentally. He sorely wanted to spend more time with Anthony but found himself constantly called away to work long hours at the magazine.

Meanwhile, Carolyn had plenty of free time on her hands, so she soon became a devoted friend to both Carole and Anthony. In May 1996, when Anthony returned to DC for more surgery to remove malignant tumors from his lungs, Carolyn offered to accompany Carole. "I'm the only one without a life," she joked. "It's easy for me to go."

As they started to unpack in their shared hotel room, Carolyn noticed that Carole had brought along flannel-lined jeans.

"You're insane," she said. "And where did you get those jeans?"

"L. L. Bean."

"Oh my God, you can't wear those. I can't even believe we're friends."

"Laugh, but you'll see," Carole responded. "It's cold in the hospital; you'll wish you had flannel."

Carolyn grabbed lipstick from her small travel case. "Here," she said. "Ruby stain. It will look perfect on you. Keep it."

When they arrived at the hospital, Carolyn embraced Anthony and gave him a gift. "Look what I brought for you!" she said as she handed him an eight-by-ten photo of her dog Friday.

"Just what I've always wanted," he muttered.

"Everyone needs a dog!" Carolyn responded as she hung the photo on the wall. Still unsatisfied, she surveyed the room and noticed how dreary it looked. While Anthony had his preoperative lab tests, she told Carole, "We need to get flowers before he comes back." So they jumped into a car, turned up the radio, and drove to a flower shop to buy yellow tulips. As their last stop, they went to a 7-Eleven and grabbed SpaghettiOs, which they ate cold from the can.

Before departing, Carolyn asked the front desk to leave a note for Carole. "Lamb," it read, "please know that I am always thinking about you and worrying about you. It is so lonely and scary to go through that, and I can't bear the thought that you ever had to do it alone. I can't ever let you go again without me. It broke my heart."

The prognosis for Anthony looked bleak. With the cancer continuing to spread, he found himself back at NIH in April 1997. Once again Carolyn accompanied Carole. They checked into the same hotel and traveled back and forth to the hospital. During Anthony's surgery, they decided to take a shopping break at a local mall to buy Hush Puppies shoes. "It's all about a Hush Puppy," Carolyn said. "You aren't leaving this town without them." They first went to Bloomingdale's, where they gave each other makeovers at the counter, followed by sticky rolls at Cinnabon. But while they were at the shoe store, Carole noticed an older black woman staring at them from a few feet away. Carolyn walked over to her.

"Hi," she said as she reached for the woman's hand.

"Oh my goodness. Are you Mrs. Kennedy?" She put her hand to her mouth as if to keep a secret, then rummaged through her purse looking for something. "I don't have anything to write on—an envelope, here. Would you, please? Can I have your autograph?" Trying to deflect attention away from herself, Carolyn introduced Carole as her cousin, Princess Radziwill, adding, "She has three Emmys." But the woman remained focused on Carolyn. "I can't believe I'm talking to you!" she exclaimed. "I can't believe you're just out here. All by yourself! Don't you have security?" Carolyn held the woman's hand before quietly walking away.

While their wives were out shopping, John flew down from New York to spend a few hours with Anthony. He was shocked when he saw Anthony's condition. His friend had lost a great deal of weight and was clearly frail and weak. Anthony noticed his reaction and tried to lighten the mood. "Try not to embarrass yourself tonight," he said, ridiculing John's eating habits, which still typically involved shoving large quantities of food into his mouth. "Try to keep your tie clean." As much as John wished to stay longer, he again had other commitments pulling him away.

That evening, John needed to be at the White House for a screening of a new twelve-part HBO miniseries, coproduced by Ron Howard and Tom Hanks, that examined the Apollo missions to the moon in the 1960s. John had promoted the movie by putting Hanks on the cover of George. John had called me a few months earlier to tell me about the event and asked if I could develop some ideas for him. In February I sent a fax highlighting the controversy that surrounded the decision to put a man on the moon.

"It was surprising to see that almost everyone thought it was a crazy idea," I wrote. "Liberals worried that the program would drain resources from thirsty domestic programs. Conservatives, on the other hand, complained that the moon landing was distracting the nation's attention from the need to build up the defense program. Money could be better spent developing the military potential of space."

John, wearing a tailored double-breasted blue suit, gray tie, and white shirt, seemed nervous as he walked to the podium in the East Room of the White House. He launched into his speech before realizing that he had forgotten to thank the president and the first lady for inviting him. Reading from a white notepad, John began his talk using much of the material that I had provided before moving into a few touching personal stories about his connection to the

Apollo missions. He finished with a soaring tribute to man's successful mission to reach the moon. "But today there is an American flag on a windless plain on the moon," he declared, "because the challenge to explore space revealed something deep and indelible in the American character."

After the event, President Clinton took John and Carolyn on a tour of the White House. It was John's first time back since 1971, when Richard Nixon had invited him to the private residence. "We showed him the room where he slept, and we walked around the grounds where he and his sister played," reflected former first lady Hillary Clinton. "In the Oval Office, he saw the president's desk—the same desk under which he was caught by a photographer playing hide-and-seek as a toddler—and the garden named in honor of his mother." At one point, a photographer snapped a photo of the two couples gazing at the large portrait of John's father. While John enjoyed the evening, his mind likely still lingered on Anthony.

Like everyone else, John hoped for a miracle. Whenever he mentioned Anthony to me, he did not talk about the possibility of Anthony losing his battle with cancer, but, rather, about Anthony's courage in the face of death and his refusal to indulge negative thoughts. John admired toughness. "You should see this guy," he once told me. "He's been in and out of the hospital, his body is scarred from so many surgeries, and he is fighting an incurable disease. But the fucking guy refuses to give up. He just wants to get on with his life. He never whines or complains, even though he has every right to."

In November 1998 Anthony landed back in the intensive care unit with a massive septic infection. It had been two weeks since he finished the fifth cycle of chemotherapy, and he was not regaining his strength. With his temperature hovering around 103 degrees, Carole took him to the Columbia-Presbyterian Medical Center emergency room. Though it was not unusual for her husband to get rushed to the ER, this time was different. Even before he was checked in, a physician approached Carole and instructed her to call Anthony's mother. She could tell by the look on the doctor's face that Anthony could die at that very instant. The ER staff warned her that Anthony was fighting a massive infection. "It's not good," the doctor said. "His immune system is so compromised from the chemo, he's having difficulty fighting back. There is very little we can do except wait. The first twenty-four hours are the most important."

Carolyn arrived in the morning, and friends started showing up in the afternoon. John came later that night, still in the tuxedo he had worn to a *George* event. "He is the one who can save us somehow," Carole believed. "The one we count on. The one who brings magic dust and sparkle." When John entered the room, he kissed Carolyn and gave a quick hug to Carole before walking over to Anthony's bed. "Tony Pro," he said quietly as he grabbed Anthony's hand. He started humming and then quietly talking. Anthony responded by smiling and singing the words along with John. It was a musical rhyme, "Teddy Bears' Picnic," that John's mom used to sing to them when they were healthy, energetic kids, but now they were reciting it under very different circumstances:

> *If you go down to the woods today, you're sure of a big surprise.*
> *If you go down to the woods today, you'd better go in disguise.*
> *For every bear that ever there was*
> *Will gather there for certain because*
> *Today's the day the teddy bears have their picnic.*

They sang it over and over with John gripping Anthony's hand tightly. Tears streamed down the faces of Carolyn and Carole as they watched in amazement at these two old souls holding hands and singing a familiar childhood tune. "The boys who laughed and played and sang silly songs are all grown up now—John in a tuxedo, Anthony in a hospital gown," Carole reflected. "The doctors think Anthony will die tonight, and John takes him to the safest place he knows." Anthony made it through that night, and after seven days in the ICU, he recovered enough to be transferred to a private room. But it was becoming increasingly clear to John that his cousin's grit and courage would be no match for the disease ravaging his body, and that the battle would not last much longer.

I was seeing more of John during this time because of my involvement with *George*. Whenever I came to New York, I would call RoseMarie to let her know that I was around. I had stopped calling John at home because I could not keep track of his ever-changing phone number. Reporters would somehow get the number and fill up his answering machine with messages. I swear he changed his number every two weeks, and I always seemed to be a week behind. If he was in town and free, he would usually call right back, and we would arrange to play racquetball or just meet for lunch near the *George* office.

By this point, I had told John that I was gay, and I think that deepened our friendship. I wish I could say that I sat him down and told him directly, but that was not the case. One summer weekend I had been on Fire Island, a popular gay destination off the coast of Long Island, when I noticed a bunch of guys sprinting toward the beach. "What is going on?" I shouted to one guy as he ran past. "John Kennedy Jr. is playing Frisbee on the beach!" he said excitedly. While many gay men wished that John was gay, I knew otherwise. But I enjoyed the spectacle of about three dozen guys searching the beach for the Frisbee-throwing JFK Jr. Apparently, all they found was a John look-alike. A few weeks later, I was sitting in John's office at *George* and told him the story. He listened politely before asking, "So, Stevie, what were you doing on Fire Island?"

"Damn," I thought. I'd just outed myself, and not in the thoughtful way I had hoped. He deserved better.

The news was probably not a shock to John, and I never really worried about how he would react. That was not the reason I had hesitated to tell him in the past. I tend to be a private person, and we had established the habit of not talking about our personal lives, so there never seemed to be the right opportunity. Telling John you were gay was like admitting that you preferred chocolate ice cream over vanilla. It did, however, provide him with more fodder for teasing me.

In May 1997 I traveled to New York for a week and ended up having dinner three nights in a row with John. The first two were at Cafe Luxembourg on the Upper West Side, and the third time was at the Odeon, near his apartment on North Moore Street. At Cafe Luxembourg, we both ate the same meals two straight nights: a juicy hamburger with tons of French fries. He drank a beer, while I had a Coke. At these dinners, like many others, I was shocked by John's ability to inhale vast quantities of food without ever adding an ounce of fat to his lean, muscular frame. He also had a unique way of eating. He surrounded the plate with his arm as if to protect his meal from potential poachers, and then used his fork as a shovel to lift hefty portions into his mouth.

For the past few years, I had been appearing as a talking head on several History Channel shows but now felt ready for a bigger role. I decided that I wanted to switch chairs and act as a host. Earlier that day, I went to the head of programming at the network with my request. She sat me down and said, "Steve, there are two kinds of people on the History Channel: historians and talent. You are clearly not talent." Those words were still rattling around in my head when I met John that Monday night at Cafe Luxembourg. When I told him my story, John, who excelled at giving advice, suggested that I ask for smaller opportunities—maybe as guest host—to first make them more comfortable with me in that role. With his advice in mind, I raised the topic again on Tuesday and Wednesday.

The next day, my producer asked me to attend a meeting in his office. When I arrived, a sense of excitement filled the air and people whom I had never seen before were milling around. My producer rarely cracked a smile, but this afternoon he was beaming. "You won't believe what happened," he said. "This morning John F. Kennedy Jr. called the office and offered to sit down for a thirty-minute interview on the eightieth anniversary of his father's birth. But he would do it under one condition: that you host the show." John never hinted that he planned to make that offer, and I never would have asked. But he understood that he could dole out a little of himself and in the process give me a significant career boost. I would fly back from Oxford for the interview, and we agreed that John would use the interview to discuss the Profile in Courage Award that honored individuals who championed brave but unrecognized causes.

We filmed on a Friday in a studio around the corner from the History Channel offices. On most days, only the crew would be present. But on this day I noticed about a dozen well-dressed female executives standing in the dark behind the cameramen. John had not told RoseMarie that I would be conducting the interview, so she called a few minutes before John arrived to make sure the host stayed on topic. "Rose," I responded, "I'm the one doing the interview." She was almost as thrilled as me, not because she understood why it was such a big opportunity for me but because she knew that John was in safe hands. "Have fun," she said.

But *fun* is not a word that I would have used to describe the experience. I felt unbelievably nervous, almost as nervous as when I gave my first lecture about John's dad back at Brown. My worry was not over John, who made fun of me right up until the moment I introduced him. It was the teleprompter— the machine that sits a few feet away and scrolls your lines—that scared the hell out of me. Although I read books all the time, teleprompters always confounded me. My eyes read faster than my lips could speak, so I would try to catch up by pronouncing three words as one long syllable. My producer instructed me to slow down and lower my voice.

Most of the interview focused on how John and Caroline honored their father's legacy. John talked about the Institute of Politics at Harvard and, of course, the Profile in Courage Award. The recipient that year was Charles Price, an Alabama judge who wrote an opinion forcing another judge, Roy Moore, to remove the Ten Commandments from his courtroom, declaring it a clear violation of the First Amendment prohibition against state-sponsored religion. What struck me was how often John returned to the theme of inspiring people to get involved in public life and humanizing those who held office—in many ways, the animating theme of *George*. When asked why his father had recently been ranked as the best president in American history—ahead of Washington, Lincoln, and Franklin Roosevelt—John offered a dispassionate, analytical answer. He stated that his father had "inspired hope" and "created a sense of possibility"—a potential that had been tragically cut short. His death, he continued, "allowed people to project what they hoped for America and their own lives onto his memory." When asked about the specific impact of his father's legacy on him, John said that his father "would want both of his children to live their own lives and not try to mimic, for the sake of public expectation, his life."

At that moment, it occurred to me that John perceived *George* as an extension of his family's efforts to keep his father's legacy alive. Whether talking about the magazine or the Profile in Courage Award, John reiterated a core message that politics represented a noble endeavor. *George*, he stated, offered a "personal entry" into the public realm. "People in public life are never projected as the human, multidimensional, complex, self-sacrificing people they often are."

The interview proceeded without a hitch. Afterward, I decided to have fun with the young women who had gathered for the interview. John and I had large coffee mugs with the History Channel logo emblazoned on them. I knew that someone would steal John's cup, so as I got up to escort him from the studio, I switched mugs. When I returned, as expected, the mug in front of John's seat was missing. Someone out there still thinks she has John Kennedy's DNA on that coffee mug, but, unfortunately, it is only mine.

When the show aired about a month later, on Monday, June 2, 1997, I was on my summer break from Oxford and living in New York. I did not watch it because I disliked hearing my own voice. But the next morning, a few minutes after nine, my phone rang. On the other end was an agent from the William Morris Agency who had seen the show and wanted to sign me as a client. I was beyond thrilled. I called the head of programming at the History Channel, naïvely expecting her to share my excitement, but she remained silent. "Meet me for lunch today," she directed. "Do not sign with him until we have lunch." At our meeting, she offered to create a show for me. "I don't know what it will be, but you will soon have your own show." That show, *HistoryCenter*, aired for the next nine years, followed by other series. I spent two decades at the network, and it was all because of a generous act by my famous friend.

Carolyn demonstrated her best qualities when helping Carole cope with her dying husband, but she continued to be moody and unpredictable most of the time. According to John's close friend Rob Littell, she alternated between being lively and wisecracking and then being "like a caged animal backed against the wall." The more she insisted on privacy, the more aggressive the paparazzi became. "Billy, you don't understand," she told John's friend since childhood Billy Noonan. "When I walk up a street, they walk in front of me backward, knocking over old ladies and mothers with children. They don't care."

It soon became apparent that marriage to John was more of a double-edged sword than Carolyn had anticipated. She relished the glamor and fame that came with being the wife of an American prince, but she claimed not to have anticipated the intensive media scrutiny. While John tried to be supportive, he also grew frustrated with Carolyn's inability to make the transition. He felt responsible for her happiness, and he knew that his wife's coping mechanisms, and her attempts to balance the good and the bad, had been overwhelmed.

The August 1997 death of Princess Diana—often described as the most famous woman in the world—only exacerbated Carolyn's fear of the paparazzi. Diana's life ended in a grisly car crash when she was only thirty-six years old. Paparazzi on speedy motorcycles had been pursuing her Mercedes after she left dinner at the Hotel Ritz in Paris with her boyfriend, Dodi Fayed.

John, who had once met Diana at the Carlyle hotel, where he tried, unsuccessfully, to convince her to appear on the cover of *George*, described her as "sparkly." She had questioned him about details of his upbringing because she wanted to raise her sons, Princes William and Harry, in the same way that Mrs. Onassis had raised John and Caroline. She asked if John would meet with her boys. John was always amused by speculation that they were in constant communication, since he was considered American royalty and Diana was British royalty. "I always think that people imagine that we have a bat phone on my desk and Diana's desk and [Monaco's] Princess Stephanie's, and we can pick it up and the other will answer," he joked.

Diana's tragic death sent Carolyn into a tailspin. She obsessively watched every minute of television coverage, wondering if she would meet a similar fate. She identified with the young princess who was tormented by the media that literally chased her to her death. Whenever the subject of Diana came up, Carolyn would shake her head and mutter, "That poor woman." John noticed the change in her behavior. "I'm not sure what I'm going to do about Carolyn," he told Billy Noonan. "She's really spooked now."

Kathy McKeon, who had served as Jackie's assistant as well as John's and Caroline's governess when they were younger, had dinner with John and Carolyn in Hyannis Port on the day Diana died. When the topic of the princess's death came up, Carolyn, who had said little during the meal, suddenly opened up. Kathy observed that John was "clearly worried about his highstrung bride. 'Kat,' he said, 'tell Carolyn how Mom used to handle them.'" She told Carolyn that when Mrs. Onassis was at the Cape, "she'd leave the gate smiling, give them one good picture, and they let her go."

Carolyn shouted, "No! I hate those bastards! I'd rather just scream and curse at them." Kat responded, "That's exactly what they want you to do. They'll get great pictures." Carolyn described how she had been chased by a "wolf pack of photographers" who were "grunting and groaning and pushing each other" to get closer to her. "They were almost on top of me," she said in an agitated voice. "It was just awful. I can't take it!"

John intervened to calm her down. "You gotta just take it easy," he insisted. "Relax."

Diana's death resonated with John, too, because it exposed the tension between his professional responsibilities and his personal desires. Though it seemed like an obvious story for *George* to cover, John hesitated. "It was clear he was having an emotional reaction to the story," recalled Biz Mitchell. "He was annoyed that we were discussing it at all."

"I don't see any reason why we have to do it," he declared.

"We can't ignore it entirely," Biz pleaded. "We have to do something."

When they held their regular editorial meeting to discuss the topic, John kept the whole staff waiting. After he arrived and the subject came up, John announced that he could not talk about it. Instead of engaging the subject, John decided to clean his office. Ultimately, he agreed reluctantly to publish a photo essay.

John spoke often with his old friend Sasha Chermayeff about Carolyn and his frustrations with their marriage. For the most part, John liked to play sports and engage in physical activities with his male friends. But he'd confide in his female friends, and none more so than Sasha. By the late 1990s, she had married and was raising two children. John called her the morning after she gave birth to her first son.

"Sasha, did you have your baby?" he asked. John was ecstatic when Sasha said yes and told him her son's name: Phineas Alexander Howie.

"That's the greatest name I ever heard in my life!" he shouted over the phone. Sasha could hear his excitement in his voice. "Oh my God," he repeated, "Phineas Alexander Howie."

Sasha wanted John to be the godfather, but she did not want to impose on him. What she did not know was that John was eager. "I am going to be godfather," he told her one night over dinner. "I am going to be godfather of that baby. I am putting money away for him every year because when he grows up, I want him to buy a Ferrari."

A few years later, when Sasha was pregnant again, John insisted on also being *this* baby's godfather. Sasha joked, "No, no, for this one, I am going to get Michael Jordan." John, who thought she was serious, was clearly offended. John knew so many famous people that he assumed she knew the basketball star well enough to ask him to be the godfather. Sasha was thrilled to have John as a godfather again.

It was not surprising that John would turn to Sasha to help smooth over his relationship with Carolyn. After Diana's death, Carolyn became increasingly withdrawn and reclusive. "She just didn't want to leave the apartment," Sasha reflected. "She didn't want to go and be followed. She didn't want to go shopping. She stopped going to see her psychiatrist because one paparazzi walked backward in front of her, videoing her face after she came out of her therapy appointment." Sasha had watched the paparazzi interact with John since they'd been friends in high school. But their conduct toward Carolyn was different: seeing her vulnerability, they reacted like sharks sensing blood in the water, and fueled by their desire to earn a big paycheck, they swarmed around her, trying to incite a reaction.

"She wasn't delusional," Sasha emphasized. "They treated her horribly." One day Carolyn saw Sasha talking to one of the paparazzi outside their building. As soon as Sasha walked in the door, Carolyn pounced. "You can't talk to those people! They are not our friends!" she shouted. "They are not good people. You can't trust them." Sasha explained that she had known some of them since she and John were fifteen years old. "These guys are here all the time; you don't have to worry about them," she said soothingly. "They are not going to hurt you. It's sleazy, but they just want the money."

Carolyn shot back, "No! I don't want you talking to them. You can't talk to them. You can't be friends with them. These guys are the enemy. They are trying to ruin us. They are fucking with me."

Carolyn could not reconcile her inner desires with the pressures of public life. She did not want to interact with the photographers who hounded her, but she studied nearly every picture of herself she could find and became increasingly self-conscious about her appearance. Her hair kept getting lighter and her body thinner. Even after her nemesis Michael Berman had been banished from John's magazine, she went from being a free spirit who enthusiastically visited the *George* offices to a dark and fuming paranoiac.

Many close friends suspected that she had begun self-medicating, growing especially fond of cocaine. One friend described being on Martha's Vineyard when Carolyn and John started having a loud, angry fight. Carolyn stormed out and did not return until the following morning, "all coked out." While John used cocaine occasionally, his drug of choice had always been marijuana, which he began smoking as a teen. He rarely drank alcohol, and when he did, it was usually beer or an occasional glass of wine. Carolyn used drugs to lift her spirits, while John used pot to calm his racing mind. One of his favorite possessions was a bong made of white clay in the mold of Pegasus, the winged divine stallion of Greek mythology. Pegasus was quite popular among John's friends.

Rumors of problems in their marriage, both real and imagined, became a regular feature in the tabloids. Especially after their highly explosive fight in Washington Square Park, there was enough truth to make such accounts appear authentic. Typically, however, they veered off into voyeuristic fantasyland. When reporters saw John walking around with his arm in a sling, the rumor mill shifted into high gear. Had he been in a fight with his wife? Did Carolyn hit him with a wine bottle? The truth was that they had simply been having a quiet dinner at home before he left for a weeklong trip to India. John was washing dishes when he sliced a deep gash between his thumb and forefinger. He wrapped the wound himself and left for India the next day without seeking treatment. While in India, the injury began to hurt. When he returned home, he went to the hospital for minor surgery to repair nerve damage. But when the media asked why John had not explained himself earlier, a *George* spokeswoman said it was because "if he responded to every inquiry—about the state of his marriage, about his dog, about why he's wearing a hat—he would never have time for anything else."

Carolyn felt trapped and blamed John for her predicament. Not only was he the reason paparazzi were hunting her down, but also he was mostly absent, trying to keep his struggling magazine afloat. "She was doing anything she could to get his attention, most of it negative," reflected RoseMarie. John would call during the day to check on her, and she would refuse to answer. On those rare occasions when she did go out with friends, she would not tell him, and he would return to an empty apartment.

Caring for his wife and worrying about her emotional well-being occupied much of John's time. In September 1997 Rob Littell and his wife took John and Carolyn out for their one-year anniversary, arranging for a limousine to pick them up outside of John's apartment. When they exited the apartment together, John bounded into the car, but Carolyn walked away and sat on the stoop, saying she could not go. John sat down next to her, lovingly placed his arm around her shoulders, and whispered into her ear. After a few minutes, Carolyn rose to her feet and entered the car.

While John performed many acts of kindness toward his troubled wife, he could also be insensitive. He assumed that Carolyn would use her newfound celebrity to become involved in civic campaigns or join charity boards. For some reason, he chose to throw her into the deep end of the pool and see if she could learn to swim. "I didn't get the fucking employee handbook," she complained on many occasions. She had a point. John's expectations for Carolyn came from his own experiences and the way he'd been raised—the family never provided him with a public relations advisor or me-dia training. He learned how to succeed in public life the hard way, and he assumed that Carolyn would and could do the same. He could be thoughtless in other ways as well. He would occasionally tell Carolyn he would be home at a certain time for dinner. She would prepare something special for him, but, at the last minute, John would decide to go to the gym, then stroll home two hours late—without notifying her—and wonder why she was upset.

Carolyn complained that John let people take advantage of him, that he was too passive and refused to confront people—such as Michael Berman—who she felt were not acting in his best interest. His friends soon became the object of her suspicion and scorn. As Carolyn grew increasingly paranoid and reclusive, she started reducing her and John's exposure to outsiders. She cut down on the number of visitors, even barring some from visiting the Cape. According to Littell, Carolyn divided John's friends into three groups. There were "regular Joes," a small group who remained unfazed by John's celebrity; the "windblown," who were essentially good people but clearly trapped in John's cult of celebrity; and the "freaks," who were consumed by John's celebrity and would do anything to kiss up to him. "The freaks didn't last long," he said.

But her attempted purge went much deeper than just limiting con-tact. She came to resent some of the people who surrounded John, even those who had been his friends for a long time. According to Gustavo Pare-des, she had a special dislike for the privileged Andover and Brown friends who she complained were living off John. Some of her criticisms were not off the mark. "A lot of his friends had an agenda that was not necessarily in his best interest," recalled RoseMarie. "They got angry when Carolyn inter-vened and tried to put a stop to it. His friends were angry because she's call-ing bullshit on something that had always been done before. That pissed everyone off." In reality, however, it appears that jealousy, and not a rational concern for John's welfare, motivated Carolyn. As her relationship with John grew more troubled and distant, she begrudged the closeness that he shared with his old friends and deliberately tried to push them out of his life.

An element of paranoia definitely underlay Carolyn's efforts to segregate John from his friends. She wanted people around John who were loyal to her as well as to him. After helping to force out Berman, Carolyn later turned her attention to John's closest confidante at the magazine: RoseMarie. Carolyn knew that he entrusted RoseMarie with private information, and Rose made it clear from the beginning that her loyalty remained with John. One night Carolyn came by Rose's apartment to vent about John. "She was crying, and she sat on my couch, and we drank wine and we smoked cigarettes," Rose recalled. When Carolyn left, she warned Rose: "Don't tell John I was here." But Rose could not keep secrets from John. "I went right in the next morning and told him what happened. I pleaded with him not to tell her. 'You will ruin my relationship with her if you go back and tell her this, and it won't be pretty for either one of us,'" she said.

But as he had done in the past with Michael Berman, who shared his views of Carolyn on the condition of confidentiality, John told Carolyn everything that Rose had reported. Carolyn called Rose the next morning. "Did John pry it out of you?" she asked. "He pried it out of you that I was there last night, right?" Rose took the easy road out. "Yes, he pried it out of me."

This episode marked a turning point in Rose's relationship with Carolyn, who became increasingly distant. She even lobbied John to fire Rose and replace her with someone more "professional." Carolyn insisted that Rose's assistant bring packages to the house and perform other personal errands for her. At one point, John pulled RoseMarie into the office and said, "Carolyn said that you call the house too much and if you don't really have a reason that you shouldn't call the house." When RoseMarie told him that she called the house only for official business, John told her to confront Carolyn. "I want you to say to her, 'How dare you,'" John told Rose. But John refused to say anything that might antagonize his wife. "I am not getting involved in that," he stated, showing that he would hang RoseMarie out to dry the same way he had Michael Berman. The two most important parts of his life—his wife and his job—were at odds, but he refused to be proactive and resolve the problem, partly because he usually depended on others to handle conflict. He refused to recognize that in this case, he was the only one who could have nipped the tension in the bud.

Despite Carolyn's increasingly mercurial nature, she could also be warm, charming, and exceedingly generous. She stood by Anthony throughout his illness and served as a constant source of emotional support for Carole. She paid the therapy bills for one of John's closest but most troubled friends. At restaurants, she would leave extravagant tips. She would take *George* staff members out for expensive lunches and dinners, often spontaneously showing up with gifts. Once, Billy Noonan and his wife received in the mail a box from Tiffany's containing five or six smaller blue boxes with gifts for their young children. But her generosity did not always please John. "She's doing this all over town," he complained to Noonan. "She's sending presents to everyone. I can't imagine what my bill is going to be."

Several other flashpoints plagued their marriage. On the most basic level, John and Carolyn did not share the same interests. John loved to exercise and play sports, whether it be touch football in the park or kayaking on the Hudson. None of these activities interested Carolyn. Most nights, she was content to stay home with their dog, Friday, and cat, Ruby. She used to be a fixture on the New York party scene, but now she was afraid to leave the apartment. One time, John remarked, "I just can't come home and talk about the cat and the dog all evening." On other nights, she preferred to sit on the sofa, drink wine, smoke cigarettes, and gossip with her friends in the fashion industry. On a few occasions, John came home early to spend a quiet evening with his wife only to find her spread out on the sofa with a handful of pals, many of whom had keys to the apartment so they could come and go as they pleased.

Furthermore, they had different priorities when it came to raising a family: John was ready to have kids; Carolyn was not. "How can I bring JFK III into this world?" she asked Noonan. "They'll never leave me alone. They treat John like a national treasure, so what are they going to do to his *son*?" She echoed similar sentiments to Rob Littell. "Can you see me trying to push a carriage down the street? With all of them running behind me?"

One thing they did agree on was finding a second home closer than their place on Martha's Vineyard. If they were to have a family, Carolyn did not want to raise children in New York City. "If I'm going to have a kid at some point, I'm not walking around by myself in the streets in New York City with a stroller with every psycho in the world," she said. "They barely let me get across the street now." Ideally, they wanted a home base from which they could commute. They searched as far north as Columbia County, where Sasha lived, near Albany, because of its plentiful rivers and lakes. They also scouted out properties at historic Snedens Landing, a secluded town of about a hundred homes that sat along the Hudson River in the Palisades hamlet of Orangetown, New York. But they never found a place that they could agree on.

By 1998, John had grown increasingly desperate. Nothing he did seemed to make Carolyn happy. Rather than growing into her role, she was spiraling out of control, becoming more dependent on drugs and warring with many of his friends, including staff at *George*. Though he recognized how rudely the paparazzi acted, he felt she needed to ignore them and continue on with her life. Eventually, he believed, they would hound her less. But the more reclusive she became, the more precious and financially rewarding each photo of her became.

John begged Sasha to find a way to lure Carolyn from the apartment. "Can you convince her to go out? Can you convince her to go out to dinner with you? Can you convince her to go out and have a glass of wine with you?" he pleaded. "Please just get her out of the apartment." Sasha recalled that one night she managed to drag Carolyn out for a glass of wine. The first question that Carolyn asked was, "How do you keep passion in your relationship when you have been with somebody so long? How do you keep the passion?" The question shocked Sasha. "Well," she responded dismissively, "it's not something you are going to need to worry about for a long time. You have only known John for a few years." But it was a point that Carolyn would revisit often. "He's not my type," she would claim to friends. For some reason, she seemed to relish telling people that she was not sexually attracted to her husband, as if she alone did not share the common perception of him as one of the sexiest men alive.

Friends were puzzled: How could Carolyn be worried about losing passion when they had been married for only two years? They learned the answer in 2004 when former Calvin Klein underwear model Michael Bergin published his book *The Other Man: A Love Story—John F. Kennedy Jr., Carolyn Bessette, & Me.* Bergin had carried on a torrid romance with Carolyn while she was dating John. Once, John showed up downstairs at her apartment building while she was in bed with Michael. "Would you do me a favor?" she asked Bergin. "Would you go down and wait for me at our bagel place?" Once he left, she buzzed John up. Carolyn seemed to know that she could depend on Bergin's presence on the sidelines. The month after John and Carolyn's notorious fight in Washington Square Park, Carolyn visited his apartment.

Even after their marriage, the scandalous relationship continued. Bergin claimed that Carolyn called him often, professing her love for him. They met and had sex in a Los Angeles hotel in September 1997 and met again at a seedy Connecticut hotel around Thanksgiving. While John went kayaking in Iceland, Carolyn headed to Los Angeles and lived with Bergin for eleven days. Six months later, they met again. This time Carolyn, weeping hysterically, declared her love for Bergin. She justified the affair by saying that John was doing the same.

"We shouldn't be doing this, should we?" Bergin asked.

"I think John's having an affair," she said.

"Why would you think that?"

"I don't know. I just do."

In September she called Bergin again and insisted that she needed to see him. She told John that she was going to visit a girlfriend in Los Angeles. They spent a few nights together at a Days Inn on Sunset Boulevard. Apparently, John was not the only one in their marriage who welcomed danger. In the spring of 1998, they met again at a bed-and-breakfast in Seattle. Bergin noticed that she looked unhappy. "Save me," she pleaded. She wanted out of her marriage.

It's impossible to know the intimate details of John's and Carolyn's private lives, but from all the available evidence, it appears highly unlikely that John was having an affair. In fact, he confessed to friends, "I wish I could cheat on her." But he did not want to humiliate Carolyn the way his father had done to his mother. John often complained that Carolyn held a more casual view of marriage. "Carolyn looks at marriage like a man does, that it's not necessarily a lifetime thing, because of the way her mother got burned," John said. "It's made her cynical about marriage. Carolyn's father left her mother with three little kids."

When Bergin's book came out, two of John's friends matched enough logistical details to confirm the accuracy of many of its claims. "We figured it out," one recalled. "While John and Carolyn were married, she was in love with another man. And then everything changed in my mind. Maybe she had always been torn between John and her other lover."

Amid all the drama with Carolyn, *George* remained John's primary focus, a source of both great pride and considerable worry. Three years after its launch, the magazine was still struggling to turn a profit and earn the respect of established political journalists. On the surface, it seemed to be prospering. It had snared four hundred thousand readers and lured an array of blue-chip advertisers, from Tommy Hilfiger to General Motors. Such numbers seemed to indicate that *George* was considerably outpacing its political rivals, *The New Republic* (one hundred thousand) and its conservative counterpart, *The Weekly Standard* (sixty thousand). *George*, however, was still desperate to add subscribers and was heavily dependent on newsstand sales, which could swing wildly from month to month.

What struck Michael Voss when he joined *George* as marketing director in early 1999 was that no one was talking about the success of the magazine. "Everything was about John," he reflected. "*George*'s circulation was higher than the total combined paid circulation of all the other political magazines in the United States." The magazine, he pointed out, also had "great demos." It had a "thought-leader audience" that was "made up of readers in the thirties who were highly educated, affluent, or emerging affluent." *George*'s readership was "younger than readers of *The New Yorker* or *Vanity Fair* but had high disposable income and a wide variety of different interests."

However, signs of trouble brewed beneath the surface. Total ad pages had been declining since the first two issues in 1995, and this decline seemed only to be gaining momentum. By November 1998, *George*'s total ad pages had dropped 5 percent from the previous year. But the very next month, ad pages dipped by 20 percent in relation to December 1997. Compounding the problem of fewer ad pages, *George* was also discounting the ads it did sell—especially compared with its newsstand competitors. *George* received $24,000 for a four-color full-page ad. By contrast, *Men's Journal*, which boasted a similar circulation, earned $43,400, while *Vanity Fair* charged $67,800 for a onetime full-page advertisement.

Part of the problem stemmed from the fact that many advertisers remained skeptical of *George*'s focus on politics and popular culture. Even though it had entered its third year, the publication had yet to find its niche in the crowded magazine marketplace. And even at this juncture, *George* still struggled with the same issue that had existed since its launch: lacking a clear identity. "They are selling the political ads, but they are really much more an entertainment-oriented magazine," stated Michael Neiss from ad agency Lowe & Partners/SMS. "*Vanity Fair* is really their closest competitor, and when people find out *George* is just *Vanity Fair* light, they may say, 'Why read it?'" One magazine consultant judged that *George* was able to attract ads from Armani, DKNY, and Polo Ralph Lauren because its cover paraded stars such as Claudia Schiffer, Julia Roberts, and Cindy Crawford. Advertisers had limited budgets, and they put their money where they knew there would be celebrities. "It's simple," the consultant said. "The Hollywood publicity machine exists to turn down interview requests, except to the chosen few who will treat their clients with kid gloves. In return, those who get the access to celebrities know they can name their price with advertisers."

Even Joe Armstrong, who had educated John and Michael about the business and guided them toward launching the magazine, worried that *George* was "too light." "I wish they had done more investigative journalism," he reflected two decades later. "It could have been less *Vanity Fair* and *People* and a little bit more substantive. I felt *George* could have made a bigger name for itself with more investigative journalism and with more hard-hitting and provocative profiles. The editorial needed to have more substance, more teeth, more bite. And they could have made more news with their content." Armstrong had also hoped that John would make the magazine "a clearinghouse to connect readers with how to get involved in political activities and with volunteer and charity efforts." But that never happened.

As suggested by *George*'s association with celebrities, the magazine faced another more troubling identity problem. It remained unclear whether people were buying the magazine because they liked the stories or because they saw it as an avenue into John's private life. "The average consumer of *George* is not buying it to learn about politics," declared *The New Republic*'s Andrew Sullivan. "She is buying it to feel some intimate connection with John F. Kennedy Jr." Some critics dismissed it as nothing more than a "Kennedy fanzine" full of "editorial cotton candy." An editor at a competing publication claimed, "If Kennedy quit, that magazine would shut down in six weeks." Some publishers did not even call the magazine by its name, instead referring to it as "Kennedy." Such criticisms puzzled David Pecker. "I've never seen a community so negative about a person and wanting him to fail," he lamented. "People are very surprised that he was successful."

It is true that people still packed auditoriums to hear John speak, but they were more interested in getting a peek of him than they were in learning about the magazine. In February 1998 John gave a speech to an overflowing crowd at an advertising convention in the grand ballroom of the Disneyland Hotel in Anaheim, California. One attendee traveled all the way from New York to hear John. "I think it's neat to have a celebrity here," he said. "But from a business point of view, I could care less. He's been in the business for two-plus years. If he says something that will affect us, it will be amazing."

Yet in the face of such criticism, John remained unfazed and unapologetic. He complained that some critics judged the magazine solely by its colorful and provocative covers. "This is wrapping," he said. "And if there is anything that I feel somewhat frustrated about, it's that I think they suggest more frivolity than the magazine has inside." Though he acknowledged that *George* was more commercial than standard political magazines, he insisted that this quality was intentional: he wanted to reach a bigger audience. "I am an editor and I am an owner and a businessman," he asserted. "We owe an obligation to the magazine and to our advertisers and to our partners to make something that's going to sell and not sit back at night and be content that we delivered something highbrow."

On rare occasions John did get tired of the sniping. When veteran journalist Morton Kondracke, the editor of the congressional newspaper *Roll Call*, called *George* boring, John fired off a note. "I was crushed to hear we here at *George* have been guilty of boring you. But I don't feel too remorseful. *Roll Call* and a warm glass of milk [do] wonders for my insomnia." Another editor at *Roll Call* retorted, "He is supposed to be married to one of the most beautiful women in America—you'd think she'd be the one making sure he was tired enough to fall asleep at night."

Although *George*'s critics made some valid points, they failed to appreciate that John had launched a different type of magazine, and that it was far more robust than most assumed. It had hired gifted writers and, though the numbers had declined significantly, it still hosted some of the most exclusive advertisers in the world. The problem did not stem from the quality of the individual articles, some of which were first-rate, or the talent of its writers. Rather, *George* never solved the fundamental issue of its identity. "The magazine had this idea of what it wanted to be but never found a way to make it work," reflected Ned Martel. This indecisiveness regarding style and message was reflected in the constant aesthetic experimentation as well. Every month, *George*'s covers and designs would vary drastically. "It looked like a bunch of young people trying new stuff," said Martel.

But despite its apparent incoherence, the magazine still managed to attract a host of talented writers, including Lisa DePaulo, Naomi Wolf, Michael Lewis, Edmund Morris, Claire Shipman, Jake Tapper, and William Styron. John even hired the legendary Norman Mailer, who had covered the 1960 Democratic Convention that witnessed his father's nomination. Furthermore, in keeping with *George's* postpartisan appeal, John recruited commentators from both sides of the aisle, including Tony Blankley, who had been Newt Gingrich's press secretary and political consultant, as well as Democratic firebrand Paul Begala. He gave a stage to young conservative women, including Laura Ingraham and Ann Coulter. At one point, Coulter wrote a column announcing that she was leaving Washington and moving to New York because, she claimed, there were no suitable men to date in DC. John passed the piece along to a colleague with a note. "Should I," he asked, "put in an editor's note that Washington may not be the problem; it's that Ann is a ball-busting bitch?"

With this impressive roster of writers, the magazine tried to distinguish itself by publishing controversial and important stories—although not as many as critics wanted. For example, the June/July 1996 issue contained a devastating portrait of *Washington Post* reporter Bob Woodward, describing him as ruthless, manipulative, and dishonest. The January 1997 issue included articles by Mailer and Willie Morris, a former editor of *Harper's* magazine, who wrote about the ongoing struggle to bring the assassin of civil rights leader Medgar Evers to justice.

George also tackled tough, controversial topics. In April 1997 John decided to publish Russ Baker's article critiquing Scientology, which was founded in 1950 by L. Ron Hubbard and based on his controversial writings. The article examined the German government's decision to declare that Scientology was not a church but a "tyrannical cult." In response, the notoriously secretive, highly litigious, and well-connected church tapped into its Hollywood connections, raising the charge that Germany's crackdown on Scientology paralleled the "unspeakable horrors" of the Holocaust. Scientologists took out a series of ten full-page ads in *The New York Times* condemning the German government for "practicing religious intolerance."

Soon enough, the head of the Church of Scientology International, David Miscavige, came after Baker and John, who had signed off on the article. Miscavige accused Baker of being a Holocaust denier, even though his mother had escaped from Nazi-occupied Europe and several relatives had died in concentration camps. Scientologists bombarded *George* with letters and phone calls complaining about a story that none of them seemed to have read. Miscavige even flew to New York to personally confront John and editor Biz Mitchell about the piece. Frustrated by their reluctance to back down, Miscavige threw a book on the conference room table. The book bounced up and hit John squarely in the face. Then, over the next few weeks, John and Biz noticed strange men following them. Though John was used to being photographed, he found the stalking "creepy." But he did not hesitate to publish the article once it had been fact-checked. As expected, Scientologists threatened a lawsuit. *George* was ready to fight, but David Pecker intervened, promising to run two full-page ads for Scientology in *George* if they backed off on their threats.

Aside from its more serious articles, the magazine admittedly employed plenty of gimmicks to attract readers. If I Were President remained a regular feature, along with We the People, which consisted of a photo collage of famous individuals. John was especially partial to lists: "Top 10 Glamorous White House Weddings," "The 20 Most Fascinating Women in Politics," "The Power 50: Who's on Top of Politics and Who's Not," "Washington's Top 10 Media Hounds," "20 Most Fascinating Men in Politics." The two articles that I wrote for *George* fell into this category: "100 Most Important Laws in American History" and "Top 10 Big Laws That Bombed," a list of ten pieces of legislation that had unintended consequences.

John's Editor's Letter continued to be a mixed bag. Some of his essays simply offered quick summaries of the pieces appearing in that issue while trying, sometimes unsuccessfully, to find a common theme. Occasionally, John would include some insight about his life and family. "When I was younger," he wrote in the August 1998 issue, "I used to take a rafting trip with my family each summer about this time of year. One of my older cousins had a theory that we should include at least one person whom everyone else was sure to regard as a jerk. His logic was that it bonded the rest of the group together, uniting us in common antipathy against the chosen churl."

In another issue, John spoke about the year he spent in India after graduating from Brown. He focused on his visit to an organization in New Delhi that filed lawsuits on behalf of women who had been killed by their husbands. Most cases involved a dowry that the bride's family had not fully paid to the husband. In those cases, the deceased wife became a hostage in a contract dispute between families. If the wife died accidentally, the husband was allowed to keep the dowry and remarry. John reflected, "Throughout my year in India, I was always bumping up against this odd contradiction: How does a culture that subordinates its female population produce so many women of exceptional ability and character?"

Often the letters for which he sought my help tried to place contemporary events in historical context. For the July 1997 issue, featuring *Playboy* model turned TV personality Jenny McCarthy, he wrote about Thomas Jefferson, John Adams, and how Federalists and Republicans celebrated the Declaration of Independence differently. In the August 1996 issue, with a cover of Newt Gingrich posing behind a lion, he discussed the history of political conventions, charting dramatic moments from William Jennings Bryan's electrifying "Cross of Gold" speech at the 1896 Democratic National Convention, to Franklin Roosevelt's pledge to provide "a new deal" for Americans in 1932.

Some of his best essays were thoughtful meditations on the state of American society. In May 1997 he wrote about watching one of his father's appearances on *Meet the Press* in which "bland, deferential men in gray suits" asked easy questions. John contrasted the treatment his father received in 1960 with Tim Russert's recent grilling of Washington, DC's embattled mayor, Marion Barry. "How different it was from the mano a mano struggle between Russert and Barry I had just witnessed."

He went on to observe how a *New York Times* article had lamented the trend of politicians appearing in prime-time dramas and sitcoms, but John saw that phenomenon as part of an ongoing evolution in American politics. He pointed out that in the nineteenth century, it was considered unseemly for presidents to give stump speeches or even for candidates to campaign for votes. The essay touched on the central theme of *George* magazine: "The point is that politicians and journalists must now compete with an abundance of diversions for a share of the fickle public's attention. Exchanges between them must not only inform, they must also entertain; if not, plenty of other things will. Pass the remote, please."

Of all John's letters, the most notorious appeared in the September 1997 issue. He had just returned from a solo kayak excursion to Iceland. He found the trip refreshing because no one recognized him, giving him ample time to spend in solitary thought. When he returned home, his philosophical mood continued. For the cover, Matt Berman shot supermodel Kate Moss as Eve, so John thought it would be a good idea for him to play Adam. In the photograph accompanying his letter, John appeared to be naked and looking up at an apple. Seated, he showed only his limbs, chest, and face.

Naturally, his essay dealt with the topic of temptation. "I've learned a lot about temptation recently," he wrote. "But that doesn't make me desire any less. If anything, to be reminded of the possible perils of succumbing to what's forbidden only makes it more alluring." What John took special note of was how the public enjoyed "gawking at the travails of those who simply couldn't resist. We can all gather, like urchins at a hanging, to watch those poor souls who took a chance on fantasy and came up empty-handed—to remind ourselves to keep to the safety of the middle path." He went on to describe an article he had just read about temptation. "The author surmised that the more we live a life governed by conventional norms of proper behavior, and the nicer and more responsible we force ourselves to be, the further we drift from the essence of our true self—one that's ruled by passion and instinct. Give in to our deepest longings (like Mike Tyson and chop off your tormentor's ear) and become an outcast; conform utterly and endure a potentially dispiriting, suffocating life."

It was at this point that John connected these reflections on temptation to his cousins. "Two members of my family chased an idealized alternative to their life. One left behind an embittered wife, and another, in what looked to be a hedge against morality, fell in love with youth and surrendered his judgment in the process. Both became poster boys for bad behavior." John was referring to Representative Joseph P. Kennedy, son of Robert F. Kennedy, who was now a congressman preparing to run for governor of Massachusetts. His ex-wife had accused him of using his influence to have their marriage annulled. The other cousin, RFK's son Michael Kennedy, allegedly had an affair with an underage babysitter. The central point of John's meditation came in the next paragraph, when he blasted "the ferocious condemnation of their excursions beyond the bounds of acceptable behavior. Since when does someone need to apologize on television for getting divorced?" he asked. In John's estimation, people took "comfort in watching the necessary order assert itself. The discontents of civilized life look positively benign when compared with the holy terror visited upon the brave and stupid."

The following day, Joseph Kennedy, despite not having read the article, offered a stinging rebuke that paraphrased President Kennedy's inaugural address. "I guess my first reaction was, 'Ask not what you can do for your cousin, but what you can do for his magazine,'" he told reporters. Joe's response infuriated John. "That's a great quote, Joe," he told him in a phone conversation. "What idiot on your staff came up with that line? Or did you do it all on your own?" John knew that the media had hyped up his words, but he could not fathom why his family had turned on him so quickly. "But if they're too stupid to get the point," he told Billy Noonan, "who needs them?"

The media focused only on the sentence in which John described his cousins as "poster boys for bad behavior." The response was brutal, proving in John's eyes his exact point: venture outside the box society has placed you in, and you will get crucified. *The New York Times* denounced his essay "as a transparent marketing ploy" and "sophomoric." "Hunk's real agenda: polish his own image," declared the *New York Post* in a three-page spread devoted to "Camelot crumbling." *The Guardian* caricatured John's editorial as "a vicious attack on the conduct of two of his cousins." On *CBS This Morning*, author Daniel Horowitz claimed the letter amounted to "a family coup," asserting it showed that John was refusing to "cover up" his cousins' bad behavior. NBC's *Dateline* took a poll asking 503 Americans what they believed had motivated John's decision to criticize his family. Most agreed, at 33 percent, that it was all a ploy to sell magazines. Political ambition, at 22 percent, ranked second. Only 18 percent believed he wrote the piece for moral reasons.

The essay warranted criticism, but not for the reasons critics suggested. It was a convoluted letter, a collage of different ideas pasted together that made sense only in John's mind. As a result, the real meaning—that society rewarded conventional thinking and stifled the passion that makes us human—was lost in the jumble of competing thoughts. John was not condemning his cousins but rather doing just the opposite. He believed that they had admirably chosen to pursue their passions; the real villain was the media that punished and judged them for their indiscretions. John's mistake was that he let his cousins off the hook too easily. In truth, Michael's sexual relationship with an underage babysitter was not about pursuing a passion or creating a "hedge against morality." It was statutory rape.

Even worse, the story ended with a tragic twist. Several months after the magazine hit newsstands, Michael died in a skiing accident in Aspen,

Colorado. He and his siblings were playing their annual game of passing a football back and forth as they skied down a mountain at night. John was in Vero Beach, Florida, at the time of the accident. He flew to New York and asked his friend Billy Noonan to pick him up at Boston Logan International Airport. Noonan described him as "visibly shaken." They drove in silence for about forty-five minutes before John mustered up a sentence. "You know that stupid game they play. It's so dangerous." John pointed out that Michael's brother Max had broken his leg the previous year playing the same game. "They were warned about it, and now look what happened," he observed. "It's just the Kennedys acting like Kennedys."

The very public dustup with his cousins was yet another reminder that no matter what John accomplished, he was first and foremost a "Kennedy," with all the expectations and burdens that name involved. While battling with his cousins, John was also shadowboxing his past. In the spring of 1997, the investigative journalist Seymour Hersh published a scathing biography of John's father, *The Dark Side of Camelot*, depicting JFK as a reckless womanizer with ties to the Mob. Secret Service agents fed Hersh a string of gossipy details: JFK held daily skinny-dipping parties, had prostitutes brought to his hotel rooms while traveling, and suffered from a variety of venereal diseases. One of his mistresses was an East German spy. When a congressional committee started to investigate, the White House whisked her out of the country before she could be discovered.

The revelations troubled John deeply. "Will the book, and others like it that looked at my father's private life," he asked me, "change the way historians view Daddy's legacy?" John knew that public fascination with his father transcended reality. His father meant so much to the baby boom generation that efforts to undermine his legacy would gain attention for a few days and then disappear. But John worried more about historians who wrote the books that would shape the way future generations viewed his father. I assured him that the allegations, if true, would be weighed against his largely positive public record, and I found it unlikely that there would be a significant change in the perception that JFK would have been a great president had he lived.

Despite constant distractions, John remained actively involved in every facet of *George* magazine. He read articles, attended editorial meetings, and pitched ideas. He also surprised his staff with his eclectic interests. The magazine managed a house account at Coliseum Books, which was located just a few blocks from the office. John would often arrive at the office in the morning with pages ripped out of *The New York Times Book Review* or with scribbled notes containing titles of books he wished to read. Often John would read a novel, then ask the author to write a piece for the magazine. He would usually send Sasha Issenberg, a precocious intern who started working at *George* while finishing high school, to the store with his requests. "I was shocked by how catholic his curiosities were," Issenberg recalled. Once, John even asked Sasha to pick up a biography of Sun Ra, an Afrocentric jazz musician. "I was perpetually surprised, not just that he was deeply read, but by how wide his curiosities were."

That curiosity extended to music as well. John saw music, and the often politically engaged musicians who created and performed it, as another unconventional means for *George* to reach readers who would normally not be interested in politics. John loved classic rock, and the Rolling Stones remained his favorite band. But his interests ranged widely. "One time I was in my office and the door was open, and I had a Puff Daddy disc in," reflected Ned Martel. "I was playing it, and I could hear a weird reverberation. I turned around, and John was at the door singing along. He knew every word. That is a deep knowledge of pop culture that is not the usual for a thirty-eight-year-old white guy."

The highlight of the magazine, and perhaps the part that John enjoyed most, were his interviews with historical figures, many of them his father's contemporaries. These interviews complemented John's love of travel. He would always add a few extra days or weeks onto his trips so he could go kayaking or participate in some outdoor adventure. In one of his most anticipated trips, John traveled to Cuba in October 1997, the thirty-fifth anniversary of the Cuban Missile Crisis, to meet President Fidel Castro. It was hard for Americans to travel to Cuba, and Castro rarely gave interviews to US journalists. John spent months laying the groundwork for the trip. Typically, he signed letters simply as "John Kennedy," but he knew when to employ the full power of his name. He signed his letters to Castro, "John F. Kennedy Jr." The magazine sold extra ads knowing that a face-to-face encounter between the son of the American president and Castro would generate loads of buzz. It was JFK who had helped neutralize Cuba and the Soviet Union in the most dangerous confrontation of the nuclear age.

The trip, however, turned out to be a huge disappointment. Castro, then seventy-one, kept John waiting for days. A government representative would call in the morning, promising, "He will see you for dinner tonight, and we will contact you." Then John would hear nothing for hours. Around eight o'clock, the scheduled dinner time, he would receive another call. "El Presidente cannot meet you this evening. Perhaps tomorrow." *Click.* The next morning, John would call back to inquire about the interview. "You will be contacted later today," he was told once again.

This game continued for days, so John and his small entourage used the opportunity to sightsee. They spent four days traveling around Havana and western Cuba in a minivan. Ironically, John went swimming in the Bay of Pigs, the site of his father's biggest foreign policy blunder. In April 1961 President Kennedy signed off on an ill-conceived plan to orchestrate an invasion led by Cuban exiles to overthrow the Castro government. But the plan proved to be "a secret" only in Washington. Castro's forces were waiting for the exiles and slaughtered them on the beach.

Although he enjoyed exploring the island, John grew increasingly frustrated that Castro was toying with him. At one point, he called home and divulged all the details to Carolyn. She was predictably furious about the way the Cubans were treating her husband. "You get on that fucking phone to whomever you need to," she instructed him, "whether it's a US diplomat or Castro's guys, and you tell them that you are not going to sit around taking this shit. You came to see him, you are a Kennedy, you are a journalist with staff here, and if his office promised an interview, goddamn it, you're not leaving until you get one."

It's unclear whether John ever made that call, but the day before they were scheduled to leave, someone from the foreign ministry assured him that he would be meeting Castro for dinner that evening. There was a twist, however: though John came to conduct a formal interview, he was now told there would be no interview and no photographer.

That night at eight thirty, the official from the foreign ministry appeared at the hotel. They went down to the hotel basement, walked through the kitchen to an underground parking garage, and climbed into the same minivan they had been using the whole trip. But this time, the curtains were closed. "Whether this was to stop people [from] looking in or to prevent us from looking out, who knows," reflected Inigo Thomas, a *George* editor who accompanied John on the trip. Thomas vividly remembered the eerie blackness that night. "It was the darkest city at night I'd been to," he recalled. "There were few streetlights, and cars only had one headlamp. We couldn't have seen anything if we'd wanted to."

The dinner finally proceeded, as bizarrely as the rest of the trip. A handful of other government officials attended, including José Ramón Fernández, who had helped crush American-backed forces in the Bay of Pigs. "Are you the same height as your father?" Fidel asked John bluntly through a translator a few minutes into their meeting. "He was a little taller," John replied, and "a little thinner." After they had all been seated at a large table covered with an embroidered cloth, Castro launched into a five-hour monologue. John, who had a notoriously short attention span, tuned out the Cuban leader after a few minutes, but he stayed mesmerized by the uneaten shrimp perched on the tip of Castro's fork. "That fucking shrimp," he named it, recalling how Castro would use it to make points and then, just as he appeared ready to eat it, would jab it again into the air. John, who was a great storyteller and mimic, recounted that story with great gusto, often reenacting the scene using Castro's accent.

At the end of the evening, Castro brought up the subject of JFK's assassination. Many of the conspiracy theories swirling around the assassination pinpointed Castro, claiming that he sought retribution for American efforts to kill him. Castro was acutely aware of these accusations and likely saw his meeting with John as a chance to reassure him that he had not been involved. "You know Lee Harvey Oswald was trying to get to Cuba," he said. John nodded. Weeks before he killed President Kennedy, Oswald had been in Mexico City, shuttling between the Soviet embassy and the Cuban consulate in a failed effort to get a visa to enter Cuba and, likely, to return to the Soviet Union. "It was hard to allow Americans into Cuba at that time," Castro explained. Again, John nodded but said nothing. John understood what Fidel was trying to accomplish, but he maintained his policy of not speaking about his father's death. John never believed in Castro's involvement, so he felt no need to engage him on the topic.

John ended up disliking Castro almost as much as he did Oliver Stone, so when he returned to New York, he announced that Castro would not appear in the magazine. Pecker pleaded with John to write about his meeting, but he refused. "I don't want him in my magazine," John insisted. That last-minute decision, made as the magazine neared production, forced the staff to rush to fill the space.

In August 1998 John traveled to Southeast Asia to meet with Vietnamese military hero Võ Nguyên Giáp. The eighty-seven-year-old general had been the mastermind behind the repulsion of the French in 1954; two decades later, he led North Vietnamese forces again to defeat the United States. Renowned photographer Robert Curran, who accompanied John on the trip, recalled that the plan was to interview Giáp and then spend two weeks touring the country. But the trip turned out to be more complicated than expected. The Vietnamese government, which had close ties to China, feared that Giáp, an outspoken critic of the Chinese government, would say something that would complicate relations between the two nations. "The Vietnamese government told John that Giáp was senile and infirm and incapable of conducting a meaningful interview," Curran recalled.

While they tried smoothing things over with the government, John, Curran, and a handful of other friends traveled around, visiting sites that had played a central role in the Vietnam War. They trekked to Dien Bien Phu, where in 1954 Vietnamese and Communist Chinese soldiers forced the surrender of twelve thousand French troops. Their victory led to France's withdrawal and opened the door to American involvement. The highlight of the trip was a four-day kayaking outing on Ha Long Bay in the Gulf of Tonkin. Even here John could not escape history. On August 4, 1964, while operating in heavy seas about sixty miles off the North Vietnamese coast in the Tonkin Gulf, the US destroyers *Turner Joy* and *Maddox* reported they were under attack by North Vietnamese torpedo boats. President Lyndon Johnson used the skirmish to justify expanding US involvement in the conflict.

John turned what could have been a peaceful getaway into a life-or-death adventure. Ha Long, which means "where the dragon descends into the sea," was a popular destination for kayakers because of its peaceful waters and thousands of soaring limestone karst islets. John and his team arrived in the afternoon and spent a few hours assembling their portable kayaks. "We got the kayaks built around five or six, and it's going to be sunset soon, but he wanted to set off," Curran recalled. "We told him that it would be dark in a couple hours, but he still wanted to go. We voted him down and went the next morning." After about three hours without a break from the boiling sun, some of them started to show signs of sunstroke. They found a little rocky outcrop to rest upon while John sent a few guys to hire a Vietnamese trawler to serve as a support boat for the rest of the adventure.

While they were traveling, their local contact reached an agreement for the Giáp interview, but there was one condition: John had to have his picture taken with a newborn baby. The couple had close ties to the general, and they believed having the picture would bring their child good luck. Once that was out of the way, John finally got to meet with the general on a Sunday afternoon that also happened to be the general's eighty-seventh birthday. "Contrary to what we'd been told," Curran recalled, "the general was remarkably spry and quick witted."

After sitting down, John started asking him questions about the Vietnam War, using a translator, as he'd done with Castro. Over the next two and a half hours, Giáp told John that the war could have been averted if the United States had continued its policy during World War II of supporting the nationalist revolution. Rather than boasting about his own greatness, Giáp contended that "the Vietnamese people" had been the best general. "It was a war fought by the whole people," he added. "This is a point that American generals and politicians didn't understand." Giáp revealed that he had told his Soviet allies that a guerrilla war was the only way Vietnam could defeat France and the United States. Moscow had wanted to know the ratio of American tanks and jets compared with his army. The general replied to the Soviets, "If we were to fight your way, we would not last for more than two hours."

Giáp asked John why the United States decided to enter the war. John handed him declassified documents that shed some light on the American rationale for intervention. Giáp told him that he believed President Kennedy would not have sent ground troops to Vietnam, as his successor did in 1965. But Giáp wanted to focus on the future, not the past. "I think the cooperation and friendly ties between Vietnam and the US will be an important factor for peace, development, and stability in Southeast Asia," the general assured John.

On Saturday, January 17, 1998, internet columnist and provocateur Matt Drudge published a sordid story about an affair President Clinton was having with an intern. The scandal presented both an opportunity and a challenge for

George. The opportunity was obvious. The very man who had seamlessly woven together politics and popular culture, who helped inspire the magazine, was now trapped in an all-consuming sex scandal. But focusing on the sexual peccadilloes of public figures violated John's philosophy of highlighting the positive attributes of politicians. "Why do people care so much about Clinton's private life?" he asked me. The question was rhetorical.

On Monday, John convened an editorial meeting. The editors thrilled over the possibilities. Clinton had inspired John's desire to create a magazine merging politics and popular culture, and now he was providing them with even more fodder. The story pulled together the key ingredients defining the intersection between politics and entertainment: power, partisanship, and passion. Yet John seemed uncomfortable and stayed silent, fidgeting in his chair and staring out the window as his editors buzzed with excitement about potential angles. Richard Blow noticed the irony of the press hunting down an unfaithful president while "the magazine owned by the son of a famously libidinous president was racing to join the pack."

There is no doubt that John was also struck by this irony, especially in light of the Hersh book that spelled out his father's sexual indiscretions in intimate detail. But John's reluctance to pursue the story went even deeper. John enjoyed a close relationship with the Clintons. Just a few months earlier, following John's presentation about the space program in the East Room, they had taken him on a private tour of the White House. The Clintons had helped raise money for the JFK Presidential Library and spent time with his mom, who also appreciated their company.

Most of all, John genuinely believed that presidents should be judged by their policies and by how much they improved the nation. He thus felt buoyed by public polls showing the public was far more forgiving of Clinton's mistake than the Washington establishment was. "The scandal," John wrote in an AOL chat, "has revealed an important facet of the American people, which is that they are not swayed by endless naysaying regarding politics. They recognize real achievement. They want their leaders to produce and do well. They respect our government institutions, if not always the people who run them. And they have realistic expectations about what people in public life can and should accomplish." In John's opinion, an affair between two consenting adults was not illegal. It was a private matter between the president and his wife.

John always shared an affinity for anyone being attacked by the media. "John felt that when people with pitchforks and torches came after Clinton, he needed to defend him from the mob," reflected Ned Martel. Over the years, John had witnessed his uncle Teddy subjected to similarly unfair attacks. And although the media had usually treated him well personally, John remembered how it felt to be under siege after failing the bar exam. "John fought against the reflex to condemn somebody who was in the stockade of publicity," said Martel.

Despite his sympathy for Clinton, John did not want to insert himself into such a high-profile and deeply partisan debate. But there was another person who John felt was being treated unfairly by the press and whom he rushed to defend: former heavyweight boxing champion Mike Tyson. John had loved boxing ever since he was a kid watching and idolizing Muhammad Ali. In June 1997 John was in the crowd at the MGM Grand Garden Arena for Tyson's bout with Evander Holyfield, who had defeated Tyson the previous year to claim the heavyweight title. Holyfield vs. Tyson II, billed as "The Sound and the Fury," did not last long: the referee disqualified Tyson in the third round after he bit off a piece of Holyfield's ear. On July 9 the Nevada State Athletic Commission suspended Tyson's boxing license, effectively banning him from the sport.

Upon hearing the news, John took out a legal pad and started scribbling a letter to Tyson. Few people could have given the advice that John offered in this seven-paragraph letter, which he asked boxing promoter Don King to hand deliver to Tyson. (I viewed the letter while doing research for this book.) Speaking from his own experience, he reassured the disgraced boxer that he had special insight into the unique pressures of his life, saying, "I'm familiar with the demands of being a public figure." He also told Tyson that he understood how it felt to be scrutinized by the press, which was clearly treating him unjustly. Yet John advised him never to allow the media to "dictate the decisions you make in your life." Everything would be fine, he promised, if the boxer retained "the respect of those" around him. The people who fascinated the public, John continued, were "not the relentlessly good, but rather those who in their best efforts and worst failure, show themselves to be human." That humanity was the reason, John claimed, the public remained so fascinated by his own family. The Kennedys were flawed, but human. He ended his letter by reminding Tyson to ignore what was being said in the press. "It's here today, gone tomorrow," he wrote. "They crucify saints and anoint fools as kings."

Two years later, Tyson faced more trouble, this time for assaulting two motorists following a traffic accident. On February 5, 1999, he was sentenced to a year in prison. Perhaps feeling helpless that he could do little to help Clinton, John made a dramatic gesture in support of Tyson. In March he visited the boxer at the Montgomery County Jail in Rockville, Maryland. Afterward, John held an impromptu press conference on the jailhouse steps. He announced to reporters that Tyson was a good man "trying to put his life together," and he suggested that his one-year sentence was too severe. "By coming here and talking about it," he said, "maybe people will start to believe" that Tyson deserved a second chance.

Media pundits and Washington politicians were still debating whether President Clinton deserved a second chance. According to early press reports, which turned out to be true, Monica Lewinsky, a twenty-two-year-old White House intern, crawled under the desk in the Oval Office to perform oral sex on Clinton. That desk, the *Resolute*, was the same one that John's father had used. In February, just one month after the scandal broke, John faxed a handwritten note to the president. "I was under that very desk 35 years ago," he wrote. "I could tell you there's barely room for a three-year-old."

At times, John felt that his editors pursued the story too aggressively and that their Clinton treatment ended up too judgmental. When preparing an issue ranking "best and worst" of politics in 1998, the editors chose Bill Clinton as the "least valuable politician." John erupted, finally making the private thoughts he'd been having very public. "So what if Clinton fooled around with an intern?" he challenged them. "The media is doing to Clinton what it has been doing to my family for the past thirty years." The president, John declared, worked hard and led admirably, so he should be judged by his policies, not his personal life. In fact, John pointed out, FDR had had a mistress as well. Applying the same logic to past presidents, he argued, FDR would have been listed as "least valuable" and "so would my father." When asked by *USA Today* about the scandal, John responded similarly, "It's making people really reflect on what matters in their leaders."

John knew that the magazine had to cover the story, but he wanted to make sure that such coverage would not be salacious. "He thought it was destructive to our political message if we wasted time pursuing scandals," Biz Mitchell recalled. "The real mission was to help readers understand how people thought and operated in DC. He wanted to offer a different reality: that most of the people in politics try to do something noble. You may not agree with them, but they do have a mission, and it's worth understanding."

The scandal, with all its twists and turns, dominated headlines for the rest of the year. As readers and viewers learned throughout 1998, on the evening of November 15, 1995, Clinton allegedly invited Lewinsky into his private study for the first in a series of sexual rendezvous. The story and investigations that followed revealed the intrigue unfolding behind the scenes to torpedo the Clinton presidency. After their initial encounter, the president and Lewinsky continued their clandestine meetings for the next twenty months. After the lovesick Lewinsky was transferred to work in the Pentagon, a conniving Linda Tripp befriended her and cajoled her into sharing tales of her sexual trysts with Clinton. Eventually it emerged that Tripp had secretly amassed seventeen tapes covering twenty hours of conversation. Through an interlocking network of conservative lawyers and activists, Tripp managed to tip off the attorneys for Paula Jones, who had a sexual harassment suit pending against the president that claimed he had exposed himself to her at a Little Rock hotel when he was governor of Arkansas. She then turned the tapes over to Independent Counsel Kenneth Starr.

On January 17, 1998, when he gave his deposition in the Jones case and denied having had a sexual relationship with Lewinsky, Clinton unknowingly stepped into a legal trap. What made this incident different from all the other allegations was that it raised the possibility that the president had committed an impeachable offense. The list of possible crimes included suborned perjury (bribing someone to commit perjury), perjury, and obstruction of justice.

John and I had several conversations about the scandal as the story unfolded. What I remember most was his escalating anger. He resented how money was being poured into efforts to bring down Clinton and the hypocrisy of many politicians, such as House Speaker Newt Gingrich, who had his own history of infidelity. He lashed out at the "sanctimonious prude" Ken Starr for setting up a perjury trap. He also could not understand why the media, including respectable publications such as *The New York Times* and

The Washington Post, obsessed over the story, often at the expense of covering more meaningful issues. John had a point. From January until the Senate trial the following winter, the Associated Press assigned twenty-five full-time reporters to the story, resulting in 4,109 total pieces, or an average of eleven stories per day on just this topic. The evening news broadcasts for the three major networks, along with Fox News, devoted 1,931 minutes to the scandal—more than the next seven topics combined.

The scandal broke at a key moment in the evolution of the media industry. When *George* launched in 1995, it stood largely alone in its quest to merge politics and pop culture. But by 1998, everyone had started joining the act. Political talk shows were cheap to produce, and the Clinton scandal turned talking heads into media stars. Cable television, which expanded its reach in the 1990s, filled the airwaves with chat shows: *Hardball, Rivera Live, Crossfire, Washington Unwrapped*, and *The Beltway Boys*. At the same time, comedian Bill Maher started hosting *Politically Incorrect*, which included actors, rock stars, and politicians along with his unique brand of biting commentary.

Just as John was trying to humanize political leaders, a cultural shift was occurring in the opposite direction. Berman and Kennedy viewed the merge of politics and popular culture as a positive development and one that could be harnessed to reach apathetic voters and make them feel better about their elected leaders. There was, however, already emerging a darker side to this merger. A key starting point occurred in 1988, when the *Miami Herald* staked out the home of Gary Hart, front-runner for the 1988 Democratic nomination for president, to catch him having an affair with a young model named Donna Rice. (The two were later photographed together on a boat aptly named *Monkey Business*.) In 1992 the *Star*, a supermarket tabloid, published a story about Gennifer Flowers, who claimed she had had a twelve-year affair with then presidential candidate Bill Clinton. The story forced Clinton and his wife to sit down on the popular television news program *60 Minutes* to discuss their marriage.

These two events, and others that followed, symbolized the blurring of lines between mainstream media and sensational tabloid exposés. Television networks increasingly hustled to feed the twenty-four-hour news cycle with scandal and innuendo. Mock reporters stood alongside serious journalists to interrogate Flowers. "Did Governor Clinton use a condom? Will you be sleeping with any more presidential candidates?" asked "Stuttering John"

Melendez, who worked for radio shock jock Howard Stern. Soon enough, Matt Drudge, who had broken the Clinton-Lewinsky story and who thrived on gossip, was competing with mainstream news organizations. *Time* magazine once dubbed Drudge "the king of the new junk media." But whatever his critics called him, Drudge still could be seen on NBC's venerable *Meet the Press*, mingling with the paragons of the Washington press corps.

Technological changes helped create and sustain the new politics of scandal. In his 2005 bestselling book, *The World Is Flat: A Brief History of the Twenty-First Century*, journalist Thomas Friedman of *The New York Times* described how technology and globalization were flattening hierarchies and removing the middleman between manufacturers and consumers. The same phenomenon impacted journalism in the 1990s, as technology broke down traditional ways of providing information. In the past, editors and producers decided which information was newsworthy. But the proliferation of information outlets—the internet, all-news cable TV channels, talk radio— removed mediating institutions and allowed people to choose for themselves which news sources to trust. While roughly 60 percent of adults watched television network news regularly in 1993, fewer than half did so in 1998. Major newspapers suffered a corresponding decline. Digitization quickened the pace of news and privileged gossip over fact. "The digital age does not respect contemplation," observed James M. Naughton, former executive editor of *The Philadelphia Inquirer*.

The Lewinsky scandal uncomfortably highlighted the flawed assumptions upon which *George* rested. John had misread history. In 1995 he and Michael Berman had launched the magazine with tremendous enthusiasm, convinced that Bill Clinton's election signaled a new age of optimism and a powerful affirmation of the benefits of government activism. Technological transformation would galvanize a new generation of voters by turning political leaders into pop icons. But John proved wrong on both counts. Instead of establishing a positive view of government, the decade witnessed a reactionary conservative backlash, and the same technology that enabled Clinton to forge an emotional bond with Democratic voters would later be responsible for fueling the scandal that almost destroyed his presidency. While Clinton was impeached in the House, the Senate did not remove him from office, and ironically, he left the White House in 2001 with sky-high approval ratings in polls.

By 1998, numerous burdens weighed on John's shoulders, but you would never have known it. He remained as fun loving and lighthearted as always. He spent long weekends at the Vineyard and took advantage of summer holidays—Memorial Day, July 4, Labor Day—to invite close friends over to relax and play games while he served as cruise captain. Breakfast was open season, with everyone making his or her own. John enjoyed a multicourse meal consisting of cereal, eggs, and lots of bacon. His guests would then hop into a jeep and drive across the property to the beach, where John would organize touch football games. When not running around with the adults, John would traverse the dunes, playing with his friends' children. For lunch, they would head back to the house, where Mrs. Onassis's chef, who stayed on after her death, would have a hearty meal already prepared. In the afternoon, John would sometimes arrange trips into town or go waterskiing on the bay. After dinner, John loved to play a word game in which guests would either recite a real quote from *Bartlett's Familiar Quotations* or make up their own. People had to guess what was real and what was not. The game produced some hysterical reactions, but few were as animated as John, who always clapped his hands while roaring with laughter.

Tragically, the summer of 1998 would be his last full season on the Vineyard, and there would be few opportunities for laughter in 1999, as John's world closed in on him.

CHAPTER 11

"THE ONLY PLACE THAT I
WANT TO BE IS WITH
ANTHONY"

T he last six months of John's life were the most difficult since his father's assassination. *George* continued its struggle to gain readers
and attract advertising revenue. Amid this struggle, Hachette made
clear to John that it planned to walk away from their partnership once their
contract expired at the end of 1999. In his private affairs as well, John confronted the prospect of loss. While he adored his sister, their relationship
had quietly soured over the past few years. Even more troubling, the two
most meaningful people in John's life were slipping away. Cancer intensified
its relentless conquest of Anthony Radziwill's body, while Carolyn grew still
more distant and erratic. Despite all these problems, John remained resilient, exploring new opportunities that might keep his business afloat and
salvage his marriage. On Friday evening, July 16, as John departed from Essex County Airport in New Jersey for a stopover on Martha's Vineyard before continuing on to Hyannis Port, hopeful signs suggested that his life
might be getting back on track.

On January 6, 1999, the *New York Post* published a headline: "John Jr. Searching for New No 2." The article announced that John was "searching for a
hands-on editor for his *George* magazine to try to bring it to the next level."
The article appeared shortly after John attended a Hachette-organized meeting in Los Angeles with the syndication arm of Barry Diller's USA Networks
to discuss his possible participation in a *George* television show. John had

always understood the value of extending the *George* brand to TV, but he insisted that whatever they created needed to focus on the magazine and not on him. It was clear to John, however, that Hachette was pushing for him to play a larger role. "Fuck this!" he shouted as he stormed out of the room. He then called David Pecker, and the two men engaged in what one *George* editor called "a fiery phone call."

Prior to this media ploy in January, the once promising relationship between John and Pecker had already begun disintegrating. Pecker blamed John for the magazine's ongoing troubles. In the first quarter of 1999, ad pages dropped by 32.7 percent, and ad revenue tumbled 20.4 percent. When combined with the declines over the previous two years, the figures gave the clear impression that *George* was in trouble. Despite the fall, *George* still had a healthy one hundred pages of ads. But all the financials were moving in the wrong direction, which did not bode well for the future.

While it's true that *George* could sell more copies if John posed with his shirt off in every issue, the magazine confronted much bigger problems. Editorially, *George* remained of uneven quality and never found a clear way to distinguish itself from competitors or to create its own category. The highly partisan trial and impeachment of President Bill Clinton further complicated *George*'s mission. How could a magazine designed to celebrate the nobility of politics cover a story about the unseemly relationship between a White House intern and a dishonest president? The intersection between politics and culture turned out to be a far less savory place than John had imagined. His desire to project a neutral, nonpartisan message was rapidly overwhelmed by an angry partisanship dividing Americans into rival camps of liberals and conservatives. And the internal problems never went away, either: John never, even after four years, found a true editorial focus, and David Pecker and Hachette never committed to a subscription drive and the magazine's long-term growth.

John's and David Pecker's relationship devolved so badly that John worried Pecker was using him primarily to support other Hachette properties. John found himself on the road every few weeks meeting with enthusiastic advertisers, but for some reason, the ad pages in *George* continued to shrink. "John suspected Pecker was playing a shell game," observed Richard Blow, "cashing in on John's celebrity and using the money for his other titles." John became convinced that Hachette was stealing from *George*, overbilling for back office work while keeping a larger share of the revenue than it was entitled to. At first glance, it did appear that Hachette was taking a $3 million bite out of *George* profits. That amount not only translated to smaller budgets for editors but also drained money from John's own pocket, since his contract guaranteed him a percentage of the revenue that he generated. In the fall, John asked Biz Mitchell to help him find a forensic accountant. John arranged several secret meetings with the accountant at a hotel near the office. It's unknown what, if anything, came of these meetings.

That information, however, would have likely come to the attention of the top of the company. "There was just no way David Pecker didn't know that John's people [were] asking questions about the budget," Biz recalled. "There's not a chance."

The timing of this battle with Hachette could not have been worse. John was trying to fulfill a lifelong dream to earn his pilot's license, and in order to qualify, he needed to log hours in the sky. Earlier, John had asked for Biz's permission to do so, knowing that he would be away from the office for long stretches of time. Biz did not like the idea of John sitting behind the wheel of an aircraft suspended twenty-thousand feet in the air. "I have driven with you," Biz responded. "I don't think it's a good idea." She always declined his invitations to accompany him. "That's all right," he responded, "because Mommy and Daddy can't fly at the same time because of what will happen to the magazine if we crashed."

Mitchell had good reason to be concerned. I, too, had driven with John and, given his aggressiveness, would not have wanted to be in an airplane with him at the controls. When driving, he would weave in and out of lanes, often at high speed. Once, when we were stuck in traffic, he steered the car onto the sidewalk. His flight instructors swore that John was a careful pilot, yet he was naturally absentminded and prone to take unnecessary risks. But he had been fascinated with airplanes and helicopters since childhood. "I have loved flying since I was a little kid," he told Biz, repeating a story he had once shared with me. "You know that picture of me running into my daddy's arms? Well, I am running to the aircraft behind him." Whenever John spotted an interesting aircraft, he would call people to the window to witness it with him.

John had started taking flying lessons in the 1980s but stopped at his mother's request. She was well aware of the Kennedy family's track record of flying mishaps. John's uncle Joseph P. Kennedy Jr. died while piloting a dangerous mission over the English Channel during World War II, and his aunt Kathleen "Kick" Kennedy died in 1948 when a small aircraft in which she was a passenger smashed into the Cévennes Mountains in France. When John was three years old, his uncle Ted Kennedy was on his way to the Massachusetts Democratic Convention to accept his nomination for a second term as senator when his plane crashed due to bad weather. The pilot and the senator's legislative aide both died, and Teddy was left with a broken back that bothered him for the rest of his life. More distant relatives, from Aunt Ethel's parents to Aristotle Onassis's son, Alexander, also perished in plane crashes. Yet this history had little impact on John, who eagerly resumed flying after his mother passed away.

Biz agreed to let John pursue his flying fantasies, but after his fight with Hachette, John's hours away from the office left her to contend with the fallout. After the contentious meeting in Los Angeles, John decided to fly his plane back to New York in order to gain the flying time needed to earn his pilot's license. It was during John's multiday flight in his small plane, a single-engine Cessna 182 Skylane, that Hachette decided to ratchet up the aggression. First, the publisher canceled Biz's subscriptions to other magazines. "They were sending back writer contracts unprocessed," Mitchell recalled. Hachette fired Negi Vafa, whom John had hired to organize *George* events, cut up her credit card, and escorted her out of the building. "They were clearly on the attack," said Mitchell.

While all of this was going on, John was calling Biz from pay phones in small towns as he made his way across the country. "I'm coming back, just sit tight," he repeatedly told her. "Just don't put up with anything, just ignore it, and I'll be there shortly." A few days after the publication of a second critical *New York Post* article, John returned to *George* and called Biz into his office. He looked tired and uncharacteristically frazzled, apparently overwhelmed by events unfolding around him. "He and I understood the situation was untenable," Mitchell recalled. "He had urged me to stay and fight, but they had escalated the assault in the intervening days."

It was all too much for John to handle. Sitting with his head resting on his desk, John started sobbing inconsolably. "I don't have very many good friends in the world, and you are one of my best friends," he confessed. Now Hachette was trying to take her away. "I was surprised he was telling me how important I was to him and with this much emotion," Mitchell reflected in

2018. "I felt very clear that he and I understood each other well, were close, and really enjoyed each other. But I tended to grant him his privacy, and as his employee, I guarded some of mine, and that did not allow for the level of communication best friends usually had. I was surprised he was putting me in that small group of his closest people."

They both knew that she, as the "No. 2" who was allegedly being replaced, could no longer remain as the editor. The *Post* article, by conveying the impression that there was no one in charge at *George*, eroded her authority to lead the magazine. Biz did not pull any punches with John. "What really bothers me," she told him bluntly, "is that you left me to handle this situation for all these days when you were calling me, telling me to just hang tough." At the time, Biz was in a relationship with a man who had recently been diagnosed with acute myelogenous leukemia, but she never used that misfortune as an excuse and always did everything John asked of her. "I always came through on my end," she said, looking back. John and Biz "agreed that it would have been hell to fight our way through this, with Hachette on the attack, and that with my boyfriend in the hospital, I could use the time to be with him." He never asked her to resign and instead offered to pay her the near equivalent of her salary for six months if she did not accept another job.

Of all people, John knew the value of getting as much time as possible with a sick loved one. He had counseled Biz when she first learned of her boyfriend's diagnosis. He had told her about his experience trying to be the best friend he could be to Anthony during his treatments. And within months, John would be facing the challenge, and the anguish, of supporting Anthony full on.

By the spring, it became evident to everyone that Anthony was rapidly deteriorating and living on borrowed time. Doctors informed Carole that his heart had expanded to three times its normal size. "Carole, he's not going to recover from this," a physician told her matter-of-factly. "I'm very sorry. I assumed you knew. Your husband is dying. He has a few weeks left at best." It was the first time in five years that any doctor had stated with such finality that Anthony was going to die.

John had been slow to realize that Anthony was dying, but now it was impossible to ignore. "John, for the most part of the five years, was really stoic," Carole reflected in 2019. "He thought he could call the person who had the cure. Get us to the right doctor. He thought he could fix it. And when he realized that was not going to happen, it weighed heavily on him. It did not matter if we had the top doctor at the NIH. It did not matter that he got us into a clinical trial with some experimental medicine. He was not going to save Anthony. He was having difficulty dealing with it."

It was still hard for all of them—Carole, Carolyn, and John—to comprehend a future without Anthony. Carole noticed that John was coming to their house as if he were "frantically trying to create memories," even though he "still wanted to believe that everything was going to be fine." They all did. With Anthony withering away, they talked about future plans, including a trip to Cuba. John suggested that they all go back to Scorpios—the magical place where John and Anthony had once played in the sand and blue waters. "I suppose this was nothing more than nostalgic, since Anthony was not well enough to make these big trips," Carole recalled.

The reality of Anthony's impending death hit John hard, but once he accepted it, he pushed Carole to prepare her husband for the end. "Right after Anthony had the heart operation and it was clear that he would only live for a few more weeks, John called me early one morning," Carole recalled. "Hey, sorry to wake you," he said. "I need to talk." He thought the time had come to have an honest conversation with Anthony about his prognosis. "He's in denial," John said, "and he needs to come to terms with this." John had been reading a book, Elisabeth Kübler-Ross's *On Death and Dying*, which described the five stages of death: anger, denial, fear, acceptance, peace. Carole found John "oddly formal," almost rehearsed. John believed that Anthony was holding on because he thought Carole was afraid to let go. "You have to tell him," John insisted. "Carole, he can't go on like he is. He needs to accept that he is going to die." For a moment, John's voice cracked. But Anthony's wife was not buying the stages-of-grief argument. "Don't you think that's a conversation I wanted to have with him for months? Years?" John was silent and then whispered quietly, "No, I don't."

"I'm not telling him," she responded, "because he did not want to know. Anthony does not want to think about dying. He does not want to talk about it." In his case, she reflected, "denial outlasted death, which is rare. But Anthony was determined to live until the very end."

Very few people were aware of the enormous pressure John was under in the summer of 1999. "To say that John was complicated is an understatement," recalled a close friend. "There was a lot of stuff going on in his head." Anthony's illness and the declining revenue at *George*, along with the problems plaguing his marriage, added to the many burdens he carried already. In the past, John had always channeled stress and anxiety into activity. "He was like a shark that needed to be constantly in motion," Carole recalled. That restiveness explains why a Memorial Day weekend accident at his home in Martha's Vineyard involving his latest flying contraption, the Buckeye, would prove so devastating.

John had purchased the three-wheeled go-kart with a parachute (dubbed "the flying lawnmower" by friends) from a manufacturer in Ohio. The contraption rolled across the grass until it had enough lift to take off, but John struggled to gain altitude and crashed to the ground. Friends watched in horror before rushing to rescue him. "We were the first people there," recalled Sasha Chermayeff. Although he had crushed his ankle and was in horrible pain, John reassured Sasha's six-year-old son, Phineas (Finn), that he was not seriously hurt. Struggling to remove his helmet, which bore the insignia of his uncle Joe's old flying squadron, John joked that he needed a smaller head. As they carried John back to the house, he kept repeating, "Finney, I hurt my leg. I hurt my leg, Finney. I'm fine. I just hurt my leg."

They rushed him to the local emergency room, where doctors told him he needed surgery, which John scheduled later at Lenox Hill Hospital in New York. John always looked forward to summertime, because that was when he could play a wide range of activities. Now he faced surgery and six weeks locked in a cast, unable to exercise. Initially, John was angry with himself, but he never dwelled on negative thoughts, and he refused to feel sorry for himself. Instead, he viewed the accident as an opportunity. "That night, he was very emotional," recalled Sasha. He talked about how he needed to spend the summer with Anthony. "I am literally going to be sitting in a rocking chair next to Anthony for the next six weeks," he concluded. "And that is exactly where I belong." The plan was for Anthony to come to Martha's Vineyard for the Fourth of July weekend and spend the rest of his life there. They would be staying at Jackie's massive 366-acre Red Gate Farm, which she had purchased in 1978 and left to John and Caroline following her death. "They were going to be sitting there in their two rocking chairs," Sasha reflected.

Meanwhile, John's accident seemed to overwhelm an already fragile Carolyn. While at the hospital, Carolyn noticed people staring at John as he lay helplessly on a stretcher. Normally she would have ignored the gawkers, but not this time. "Haven't you seen a guy in a cast before?" she snapped. "Stop staring! Please!" She then called Carole to vent her frustration. "I don't know if we can survive a broken ankle," she said. "It's such a goddamn bad time for this." Carole described her at this moment as "angry, exhausted." She sensed that Carolyn had neared the end of her rope and could not deal with any more stress.

"Six weeks in a cast!" Carolyn shouted. "No kayaking, no waterskiing, no swimming. No physical activity of any kind." Carolyn knew how emotionally difficult it would be for John to stay still and how such inactivity would only add more tension to their already troubled marriage. "I heard in her voice, she didn't have a lot of fight left in her," Carole recalled. "'We're not going to make it through the summer with him like this.' Looking back, it was an ominous foreshadowing."

The following weekend, they were all gathered on Martha's Vineyard. Carole and Anthony were staying at a friend's house because John needed to rearrange the beds in his house so that Anthony could sleep on the first floor. To cheer them up, Carole and Carolyn suggested they walk the fifty yards to the beach. Both John and Anthony loved the ocean. John hobbled out on one leg with crutches. Anthony had a cane to steady him. When Anthony got to the water's edge, he took off his sweatshirt. "He probably weighed ninety pounds," Carole recalled. "His chest and back were crisscrossed with five years' worth of scars." John, who had never seen the scars, put his head into his hands and sobbed. Anthony could not hear John crying because of the deafening sound of the crashing waves. "Come on, Johnny!" he yelled. "John's shoulders were heaving," Carole recalled. "The denial and stoicism just fell away."

Eventually the accident sent Carolyn into an emotional tailspin. Carole believed that at that point Carolyn gave up on any ambitions she had of improving her life. She stopped seeing her therapist, refused to go to the gym, and abandoned plans to enroll in college and take classes toward earning a degree. She became a bundle of anger and resentment. Friends noticed the change in her personality. Some *George* staff members used to welcome her visits because she was so energetic, irreverent, and full of life. Not anymore.

One confidant described her as "dark and paranoid." She had already turned against Michael Berman and RoseMarie. Surprisingly, creative director Matt Berman, perhaps her closest ally at the magazine, became her next target.

As she had sensed, her relationship with John hit a new low. "The constant scrutiny of their marriage had taken a toll," RoseMarie observed. "Where they once laughed off problems or misunderstandings, they now blew them out of proportion and were both too stubborn to work things out on their own." Since John could often be thoughtless, Carolyn decided to retaliate by not showing up for lunch dates or by going out with her girlfriends all evening and not telling him anything. John would frequently call Rose to see if she knew Carolyn's whereabouts. Rose would then try to defuse the situation by joking, "Oh, she's probably just blowing you off like you've done to her a million times." But John could not be humored.

The relentless travel to meet with advertisers and potential investors was also a burden. In the spring, John and Carolyn had traveled to London. She did not want to be there, and the trip ended up being a disaster. At one point, Carolyn called Carole to ask about Runnymede, the memorial garden dedicated to President Kennedy that John had visited as a child. "He wants to go to Runnymede, and I want to come home. I think he was mad because I didn't know what Runnymede was," she told Carole. Even when they returned home, John seemed to be constantly traveling or attending events: the White House Correspondents' Dinner, the Profile in Courage Award announcement, and the Newman's Own–*George* Awards dinner where John and actor Paul Newman teamed up to recognize the most philanthropic companies in America. Carolyn reluctantly attended the most important public events, but more often she hid at home, stewing in private and relying on cocaine to deal with the loneliness.

Yet they continued to carry on, inviting friends to Martha's Vineyard as they did every Fourth of July weekend. It was always an enjoyable holiday full of long days on the beach, fun games, and plenty of physical activity. But this year was different. On July 3 Anthony and Carole moved into the main house. It was here that Anthony planned to spend his final days. John placed a bed in a downstairs room off the patio so that Anthony would not have to climb stairs. He also arranged to have his mother's former assistant Effie stay to cook and manage the house. John was spending a great deal of time traveling for *George*, but he planned to spend every weekend at the Vineyard with his cousin.

It soon grew clear to many guests that something was not right in John and Carolyn's relationship. At one point during the weekend, John stood in front of the fireplace, venting candidly to Billy Noonan about the state of his marriage. He wondered out loud whether having a baby would save it. "I really need to start thinking about having a family," Billy recalled him saying. "This is going to suck—a baby makes everything better, right?" He quizzed Billy about how long he and his wife had been married before having kids, and then announced that he had already settled on a name for his son: "Flynn. Flynn Kennedy—now, that's a name. What do you think?"

But Carolyn, for good reason, had grown more adamant that it was not time to have a baby. As Rose reflected, "Anthony is dying. The magazine is struggling. Carolyn is a basket case, and John says to her, 'Let's start a family and buy a house.'" Carolyn was not opposed to having children but found John's timing mind-boggling. "We are in the middle of complete chaos here," she told him. "You are flying around trying to find funding for a magazine, we are dealing with Anthony literally 24/7, wondering who's at the hospital with him, and you want to start a family." Still, John could not understand her reluctance. "What does she want?" John asked Rose. "Like her life is so hard."

According to Noonan, John disappeared for hours the day after this latest quarrel with Carolyn over the weekend. Without telling anyone, he flew his plane to the Cape to check on the family house. Furious, Billy confronted John, explaining how difficult it had been for him to get to the Vineyard and how rude it was of John to leave him alone. "Well," John responded, "I wanted to be alone, and I didn't think you'd want to fly with me." Billy believed that John had changed into someone "selfish and insensitive and scattered." But that judgment was harsh, for although John had always possessed a rather callous and thoughtless streak, his mind was currently preoccupied by too many thoughts. It made sense that John needed to clear his head, and what better place to retreat to than his father's Hyannis Port home, which John had been using as an occasional weekend refuge?

It's possible that John found the inspiration he was seeking, because the next day, he had a candid conversation with Sasha about his marriage. John was lying on the lawn of Red Gate Farm, gazing up at the sky. Sasha, who was also part of the weekend group, was standing next to him. "He told me how fucked up it had gotten with Carolyn, and that they were emotionally very distant," she recalled. Carolyn refused to have sex with him, and they seemed to be leading entirely separate lives. He never used the word *divorce*, but it was clear to Sasha that that was what he was alluding to. "Oh my God, this is it," Sasha thought. Carolyn, she realized, "has no idea how badly this is going to take her out, because her whole life revolves around the fact that she is this important person who is JFK Jr.'s wife, and when he tells her that this marriage is falling apart and he's done, it's going to be so hard for her." Sasha predicted that while divorce would be difficult for both, John would recover more quickly. "It's going to be shitty for him for a while—like, two or three years—and then he is going to be fine."

Although John and I had an unspoken arrangement that we would not talk about our private lives, he confessed to me once in the spring, while we were sitting in the steam room at the New York Athletic Club, that he had "blue balls." I honestly did not know what the expression meant and was afraid to ask a follow-up question that would sound stupid. I thought for a second about looking over to see if his balls really were blue but realized that he would probably not appreciate the gesture. Only later did someone explain to me that it meant that he had been denied sex for so long that his balls were (figuratively) turning blue.

Carole Radziwill, however, saw no evidence that weekend that John and Carolyn's marriage was careening toward divorce. "There was nothing, not one conversation, not anything to indicate that there was an impending divorce," she recalled. "It's certainly easy to sit around and talk about arguments and fights and divorces, but very few people knew really what was going on." The last six months of their lives were stressful: they were fighting over many different issues, and the shadow of Anthony's death hung over them. Carole used the metaphor of a husband and wife having an argument in a fast-moving car when they crash into a wall and are killed. No one knows how that conversation would have ended. The same was true of John and Carolyn, she maintained. "He loved her, and she loved him," she reflected. But they also "drove each other crazy."

The weekend before the plane crash, Carolyn invited close friends Christiane Amanpour and her husband, Jamie Rubin, to the Vineyard to help cheer everyone up. Anthony's impending death, which they all knew could happen any day, put a lot of pressure on all of them. The tension between John and Carolyn was palpable. Christiane and Jamie provided them with a break and lightened the moment. "We spent the days on the beach and had fun dinners," Carole recalled. "Except for the dying, it was a weekend like any other, with great friends and laughs and good food."

At the end of the weekend, John hit the road again in search of a new publishing partner to replace Hachette. During his travels, John made sure to call Carole late every night to check in on Anthony. He discussed what he planned to say in his eulogy. "Big life stuff," Carole reflected. "We talked about how hard a lot of this has been on Carolyn and how he felt a large responsibility for that." He did not mention his own life and dreams. Instead, he talked about "how he had lived his life with Anthony by his side, an ally in a sometimes confusing world. He couldn't believe that he was going to be gone." Carole described his mood as melancholy. "There was a softness in his voice that I hadn't heard before," she said. "I suppose it was resignation."

On Monday, July 12, John flew from Martha's Vineyard to Toronto with a flight instructor to meet with potential investors Keith Stein, Leslie Marshall, and Belinda Stronach. John may have finally accepted that he could not save Anthony, but he was not resigned to allowing *George* to die. He had already found several leads, including Rupert Murdoch and the auto parts consortium Magna International in Canada. Stein met John's Piper Saratoga at the hangar and escorted him to the meeting. Stein began the conversation by asking John why Magna and why Toronto. "I like to do things off the radar," John responded. Stein remembered the meeting as very casual and informal. "It was a forty-thousand-foot conversation," he recalled. It was clear to him and his colleagues, however, that John was committed to *George* and looking for the right partner. "We were interested," Stein reflected, "because *George* was ahead of its times," and also because of the opportunity to be associated with John. "That publication was about John," he said. Stein and his colleagues came away impressed by John and convinced that he could be a good partner. The next step would have been for John to meet with the company's founder, billionaire Frank Stronach. "The window was open," Stein said.

As the meeting ended, John offered Marshall, who had flown commercial from New York, a ride if she wanted to fly back with him. She was tempted, but Keith intervened. He was not impressed by the plane or the young copilot who accompanied John on the trip. "Leslie," he said, "I flew you in, and I'm flying you out."

But John continued to fear that most potential investors and partners were more interested in him than his magazine, a problem that, he believed, had doomed his relationship with Hachette. "It was a tough time for John, who hated flying around the globe with his hat in his hand," Rob Littell reflected. John confided to Rob that he worried the magazine would likely come to an end. His efforts to keep *George* afloat had clearly taken a toll on him. According to Rob, "he gained weight, he looked tired, his hair was noticeably grayer."

John, however, never revealed his inner doubts to his staff. It was not only his pride but also his future on the line. "This magazine has to be a success; otherwise I can't move on to the next venture, whatever that may be," he declared. He remained outwardly upbeat about *George*'s prospects, reassuring the staff, "We *will* find a new home." Near the end of June, John gathered everyone into the conference room. He apologized for being withdrawn, confessing that he had been distracted by a personal issue, "a family problem." It had consumed much of his time, he said, but that problem "will be resolved soon." He also promised them that no matter what they read, *George*'s situation was not as bleak as naysayers claimed. Talk of the magazine closing was nonsense. *George* would persist, he guaranteed them. "Don't worry," John said. "We will all have our jobs at Christmas." Still later in the afternoon, he met with the business staff. "As long as I'm alive," John pledged, "this magazine will continue to publish."

RoseMarie had no doubt that John planned to stay at *George* until it was successful. "John was absolutely going to stick with *George* until it was a success on its own," she reflected in 2019. He made her a promise: "I will not go do the next thing, whether it's politics or something else, until this magazine is a success."

But the magazine, which was now almost four years old, was still trying to establish its identity. In addition to the internal challenges of articulating a consistent message, John worried that the media still focused too much on him and not enough on the product. Once again, John wanted to find a way to "sell *George* as *George*," and not as John Kennedy's magazine. In response, marketing director Michael Voss revamped the media kit, which hadn't been reworked since the launch, and he met with companies that could help them to streamline their pitch to potential advertisers. One such company was Leifer-Stieffel, run by the husband-and-wife team of Cheryl Stieffel and Peter Leifer, who had developed an interactive computer program that would have allowed the magazine sales staff "to take people through a very dynamic presentation that showed the essence of the publication," reflected Leifer. By hitting a few keys, the *George* reps could summon statistics, demographics, and other content that would be directly relevant to an advertiser. Their proposal highlighted *George* as a brand and made no mention of John. Unfortunately, Cheryl and Peter never had the chance to meet with John personally, and their proposal was still sitting on his desk when he left for Martha's Vineyard on July 16.

Along with finding another business partner and developing more sophisticated ways to describe *George* to advertisers, John began exploring whether to transform *George* into a web-based magazine—which in 1999 was considered cutting edge. He raised the idea with a number of people, including Rich Blow, who took over as editor after Biz Mitchell left. "Maybe we should just turn *George* into a website," John suggested to him. "If we abolish the printed magazine, we would save on paper, printing, trucking, and mail costs." Blow said he did not imagine *George* as a website, but John responded, "It would solve a lot of our problems."

Blow was not the only person with whom John was having this conversation. "I think he was interested in other alternatives and perhaps producing an online magazine," recalled Jeffrey Sachs, who had helped John create Reaching Up. "He talked about turning it into an online magazine—an idea that was very much ahead of its time." John was fascinated by how technology could potentially change the media landscape. The late nineties were an exciting time in the evolution of the internet. "This is the Kitty Hawk era of electronic commerce," one internet entrepreneur boasted, referring to the site of the Wright brothers' 1903 flight that marked the dawn of air travel. Although still primitive, the World Wide Web, as it was initially called, was the central character in a larger unfolding drama: the explosion in digital communications technology that made it possible to convert text, sound, graphics, and moving images into coded digital messages that would transform the way people worked and played.

John recognized the potential of the internet, although he never anticipated how quickly or dramatically the media landscape would change. Voss recalled joining John on a trip to San Francisco and Seattle, where he met with people at Microsoft to discuss the future of technology. "John was very interested in what was happening online," Voss recalled. "How should we be using the web to get more of our content out there and engaging better with our audience?" John asked.

Moving the magazine to the internet was not just a hypothetical question. John had also been having conversations with an old friend, Dan Samson, who had just sold a highly successful premium ice-cream company that he had created in Seattle in 1983. John respected Samson, admiring that he had built such a profitable business from scratch. Now he wanted to approach Dan about a new business venture. He began leaving voice messages for Samson, talking vaguely about "wrapping up conventional print, audio, and visual media concepts" and placing them on the internet. John revealed that he wanted a partner who could "mind the store" but not "some expert or big named person." Rather, Samson recalled, "he just wanted someone that he knew he could trust to oversee the operations of the company."

In these conversations with Samson, it was unclear whether John had gone a step further with his dreams about *George*, imagining it could be interactive as well as online, or whether he had a completely different business in mind. John told Sasha Chermayeff that he was also considering going back to his original idea of mass-producing kayaks, which he and Michael Berman had investigated and dismissed before starting *George*. But the cryptic messages he left for Samson suggested that John was definitely focused on a venture that would involve tapping into the power of the still-nascent internet. On July 17 Samson was waiting at the airport to greet John in Hyannis. Afterward, they planned to go to the Vineyard "to spend two or three days hashing out his vision and developing the game plan."

I met Carolyn for the first time on May 19, 1999, at the Newman's Own–*George* Awards ceremony. I had arrived in New York earlier that afternoon and called Rose to let her know I was in town. John got on the phone and told me that he was hosting a big event at the US Customs House Building downtown and wanted me to come. I tried to get out of it, insisting I had to prepare for my show, *HistoryCenter*, which I was filming two days later. But he refused to accept no for an answer. "Stevie, I better see you there," he said.

I tried to arrange a car service, but it was a rainy day, so I went outside and hailed a yellow taxi. As we made our way closer to the event, traffic started slowing down. When we were about three blocks away, I could see a line of black cars ahead of me, and after a few minutes, more limos appeared behind me. I decided to get out and walk the last few blocks, but security guards were patrolling the street. "Get back into the car," one advised me. "You need to disembark at a special location." Because it was a rainy day and John did not want paparazzi running around the area, *George* had created a tent by the building entrance. Each car needed to pull up directly in front of the tent so that photographers could take pictures of the guests. I sat helplessly in my taxi with my eyes transfixed on the meter as the cost of the trip seemed to increase by the second. Finally, I made it to the photographers' tent. I was hoping that at least a few flashbulbs would go off, but as I exited the taxi, I heard one photographer ask, "Who is he?" to which another responded, "He's nobody."

Dejected, I walked into the hall and stood alone in the reception area. Everybody seemed to know one another, but I knew no one. Finally, John and Carolyn arrived, holding hands and looking like the king and queen of the event. All eyes turned when they entered to a round of applause. I was taking in the moment, always marveling at the way people responded to John when he entered a room. He and Carolyn were making their way deeper into the reception area when John suddenly saw me standing alone and separate from the crowd. "Stevie!" he shouted. "You made it!" He rushed over, put his arm around my shoulders, and escorted me into the dining area. It occurred to me that John was just as happy to see a friendly face as I was.

I headed to my assigned table, but after a few minutes, John came over and asked me to join him at the head table with designer Kenneth Cole, actor Paul Newman, and his wife, actress Joanne Woodward. Several of his guests were arriving late, and he did not want the table to look empty. I became a seat warmer for Alfonse D'Amato, the recently retired New York senator, and Puff Daddy. I leaned into John's ear and whispered, "Do I call him 'Puff' or 'Mr. Daddy'?" John pushed me away. "Don't embarrass me, Stevie."

John seated me next to Carolyn, who was stunningly beautiful, refined, and delicate. She was also aloof and guarded, qualities that were understandable, since she knew nothing about my relationship with John. At this point, I knew of their mercurial marriage from conversations with mutual friends and comments that John had made, but I did not really know what to expect. We made small talk, discussing the awful weather and a few other innocuous topics. Eventually the other guests arrived, so I went back to my regular table.

A few weeks later, John had just returned from a long trip and asked me to have dinner with him at his favorite local restaurant, Odeon. The dinner was uneventful, but John seemed tired, which I assumed was the result of jet lag. I realized something was wrong when halfway through the meal he still had not made fun of me. "John, are you feeling okay?" I asked. "You are unusually subdued and uncharacteristically respectful." I hoped to elicit a laugh, but instead he spoke in subdued tones about contentious negotiations with Hachette. He had come home to a nasty letter that day and wanted a fresh pair of eyes to read it and give him an opinion. While I was a contributing editor at *George*, I did not work there and wasn't embroiled in office politics, so I agreed.

It was now obvious that he had invited me to dinner to discuss the letter and to suggest that I come to his apartment to read it. It would be my first time at his Tribeca apartment. We walked down a busy street, populated with countless bars and restaurants, onto a dark side street with only one dimly lit streetlamp. "Why would John live here?" I thought, as I scanned a neighborhood full of old, abandoned warehouses. His building looked like an outdated industrial factory. We approached the front door, which John opened with a key. We entered a small, nondescript lobby with linoleum floors. No doorman. No security. He used another key to call the elevator. John's apartment was on the top floor of a nine-story building. The apartment was dark, so I did not get to see much other than some mismatched furniture. Somehow I'd imagined John living in a fancy high-rise with a doorman and dramatic floor-to-ceiling windows. But John was always the rustic type. He would have been perfectly comfortable living in a tent in Central Park.

As we walked in, John told Carolyn that he had brought a friend over to read "the letter." Carolyn, whom I had met just a few weeks earlier at the awards ceremony, was wearing an oversized Columbia University sweatshirt. It was probably ten o'clock, and she looked exhausted. We went into a tiny kitchen with a small counter. John handed me the letter, and as I pulled it out of the envelope, John nervously lit a cigarette, and the two passed it back and forth. I was somewhat surprised—I knew that John smoked cigarettes occasionally and that he enjoyed pot, but he had never smoked either in front of me.

I cannot recall who wrote the letter, or the specific language, but I do remember it being an unrelenting assault on John's stewardship of the magazine, essentially attacking him for being both lazy and stupid. I told him that this letter would almost definitely serve as Hachette's defense for refusing to renew the contract with Random Ventures. It represented a clear warning shot, putting John on notice that if he protested, they would go after him personally.

At this point, Carolyn jumped into the discussion, enraged. I knew that she was fiercely protective of him, but I never expected what followed: a string of expletives like I had never heard before. "John, they are trying to fuck you!" she shouted. "Everybody fucks you, John, and you just take it! You let everybody fuck you, John. When are you going to grow some balls and start fighting back? You need to start fucking people back, John."

"Was this the same person I had met at the dinner?" I asked myself. She was seething with anger that seemed directed more at John than at the business partner who was about to abandon him. That night, I got a glimpse of John's troubled marriage, along with his struggling magazine, and had the clear sense that both were coming to an end. Until then, I knew the magazine was limping along and that John and Carolyn, like most married couples, had problems. But not until I witnessed both firsthand—Hachette's blistering letter and Carolyn's rage and anger toward John—did I understand that both had become untenable.

John solemnly guided me out of their apartment. He said he needed to clear his head. When we got to the curb, I shook his hand and turned right toward civilization. John turned left down the dark street. After taking a few steps, I turned around and saw his silhouette, head down and hands in his pockets. It was the last time I would ever see him.

As if things were not bad enough in John's life, he was also feuding with his sister, Caroline. They had been so close growing up and shared countless memories, but tragically, they were barely on speaking terms in the final months of John's life. The two had great affection for each other, but they were very different people, and their lives had taken divergent paths. She was disciplined, focused, and book smart, while John was laid-back and mellow, relying more on his charm than his brains. Caroline had always been dismissive of *George*, believing that John was wasting his time when he should have been forging a real career path. On several occasions, she even visited the *George* offices and shared her concerns with John's coworkers. "He's irresponsible," one staff member recalled her saying. "Can't he keep his shirt on?"

Her constant needling bothered John, because he felt judged, even for his passion. "She loved him, and they loved each other, but she was always making fun of him," recalled Sasha. What John could tolerate even less, however, were her friends, who he thought did not respect him at all. While Caroline dismissed John and his friends as "potheads," John described Caroline's friends as "entitled snobs" and "know-it-alls." John would often scoff at their pretentious conversations. "No, no, no," he said in a mocking voice, "that was not who translated Freud." He interpreted their attitude as, "Look, Caroline, there's your cute, dumb brother." After their mom died, John and Caroline would often find themselves on Martha's Vineyard together, but they rarely interacted when they were with their spouses or friends. "John's and Caroline's friends never crossed over," recalled Sasha, who spent considerable time with John at the Vineyard. "We stayed separate. She didn't think much of his friends, and he didn't think much of her friends, but I always felt there was an old closeness between the two of them. They really loved each other."

Their respective marriages further strained their relationship. Edwin Schlossberg, who was fifteen years John's senior, made a genuine effort to reach out to John after marrying Caroline in 1986. But John found him to be just as pretentious and arrogant as the other people in Caroline's life. "John just never liked Ed," recalled Sasha. When asked what Ed did for a living, John responded, "You tell me!" According to a close friend, John regularly referred to his brother-in-law as "Ed the dickhead" and dismissed his art as drivel. "He hated the guy," said one of John's close friends. Carolyn also added a new element to the combustible mix. She repeatedly told John that his sister and brother-in-law treated him "like shit" and that they viewed him as the "family fuckup." John, Noonan said, initially ignored her comments, but he eventually started to take them seriously. "When it's just Caroline and me, we're fine," John reflected, but "add a spouse and look out."

Tensions between John and Ed escalated further during the auction of Mrs. Onassis's estate, which unfolded over the course of four days beginning on April 23, 1996. The auction consisted of six thousand items from Jackie's homes. She wished for John and Caroline to sell most of her belongings, saying, "Sell them! Tell them it was from Jackie's love nest." Jackie left all her tangible property to John and Caroline, asking them to donate items of historical significance to the Kennedy Library. The library received thirty-eight thousand pages of documents, thousands of photographs, and around two hundred artifacts. John and Caroline could then keep what they wanted and sell everything else. Even Caroline's rocking horse and John's high chair were auctioned off. Sotheby's calculated a conservative presale estimate of around $5 million for the entire auction.

An estate sale is always stressful for a family, but John seemed to blame Ed—often unfairly—for making the whole affair more difficult than it should have been. "What I understood from John was that Ed was such a prick [about selling memorabilia]," a close Kennedy confidant recalled. "Ed insisted that they divide up the estate and sell items that had great sentimental value to John, including his father's rocking chair." Caroline and Ed rarely went to Hyannis Port, while John and Carolyn made regular trips during the summer. John resented how Ed and his sister "plundered" the house for auction items, dividing everything in half, including plates, glass, and silverware. Ed also insisted on a public auction that would garner maximum attention and profits. John pleaded for a private auction, where the estate could be sold discreetly and largely out of the public eye.

In reality, Ed and Caroline were probably right. Everyone agreed that it was important to keep the Martha's Vineyard home, but they needed to raise lots of money from the estate sale to pay for the taxes. They were more likely to raise the sum of money needed from a public auction. Also, John and Caroline were required to tag and declare all the items in the Hyannis Port house. Whatever items they decided to keep would be charged to them and deducted from the money they received at the end of the sale.

What John resented most was the way that Ed took control and seemed to be bossing him and his sister around. John believed in bloodlines, and while Carolyn and Ed had married into the family, they were not direct descendants of their mother or father. He felt that only he and Caroline should have been making decisions about how to divide up their mother's estate. Instead, Ed inserted himself into what should be considered a "family affair." John characterized the tone of Ed's involvement as, "All of this material needs to be settled up. This is just valuable stuff, and you and your stoner friends can't be rocking in this rocking chair and dancing on this rug. We are doing stuff with it."

The frenzied sale of his mom's estate brought in $34.5 million, well above the original estimate. An oak rocking chair used in the second-floor Oval Room fetched $453,500. A plastic replica of Air Force One, valued at $300 to $500, sold for $48,875. The highest price—$2.6 million—was paid for the 40.42-carat diamond gifted to Jackie by Aristotle Onassis. Arnold Schwarzenegger purchased President Kennedy's wooden golf clubs for $772,500.

John was so disgusted by the whole spectacle that he left the country during the auction. And while the final sale far exceeded expectations, John received less than $100,000. The bulk of the money went to paying off taxes due from the transfer of Mrs. Onassis's estate. John was not impressed by the check. "After all that, this is what we get: less than a hundred grand," he told Rob Littell. Had the sale not been successful, however, he would have been writing a check, not cashing one.

Later in the summer, John felt that Ed overstepped his bounds again when he tried to spearhead a Kennedy Center project to produce a film honoring President Kennedy's contribution to the arts. Ed should not even be included in such a project, John believed. He was not a Kennedy; he was only married to one. This film was an issue, John said, that should have been brought directly to him or Caroline, not Ed. John voiced his discontent, and the project was canceled.

These conflicts soured John's relationship with Ed, making it even more difficult to remain close with Caroline. The most serious blowup occurred in the fall of 1998. RoseMarie received a call one day from HBO, revealing that Ed was going to be an executive producer of a documentary about President Kennedy's assassination and he had suggested that John serve as narrator. Everyone who knew John was aware that he never commemorated the day his father died. Never. He rarely discussed it even in private. RoseMarie went into John's office and relayed the message to him. "Are you really going to participate in a documentary about your father's assassination?" she asked incredulously.

John exploded. He could not believe that Ed would be so dumb, or Caroline so clueless, as to get involved in such a project. What infuriated him most was that Ed was once again crossing the line by thinking that because he had married a Kennedy, he was one. "Who the fuck is he to tell me how to honor my dad's death?" he shouted. "I've never seen him so mad," recalled a close friend. I happened to be in the *George* office one day when the conflict was unfolding. I walked in while John was having a heated phone conversation with Caroline. "You would never be doing this if Mummy were alive!" he bellowed before slamming down the receiver. He then turned to me as if nothing had happened, and we went out to lunch.

John stewed for days before he decided to tackle the problem head-on by summoning Caroline and Ed into his office. He sat at the head of a conference room table, Caroline settled a few seats away on his right, and Ed parked himself across the table from his wife. John, refusing to even look at Ed or acknowledge his presence, began lecturing his sister. "If you want *him* to be involved in defining your relationship with our father, then go ahead. But he will not interfere with my relationship with my father and his legacy. Is that understood?"

They were still at odds over the sale of Mrs. Onassis's estate. While they had sold off many of her possessions, they still needed to decide what to do with the Hyannis house, which was one of three Kennedy homes on the compound. There was a lot of history in that house. JFK used it for his successful presidential bid in 1960 and later turned it into the summer White House. It was the place where John and Caroline would gather with their cousins during holidays and summer breaks even after JFK was assassinated. Caroline wanted to sell it, but the family worried about the possibility of having a stranger living on the compound, so they rented it to a member of the Shriver family for two years. When that lease ended, Caroline pressured John to sell. "Doesn't she realize that it was the house where our father lived?" he asked a friend. He could not understand her eagerness to get rid of a house that played such an important role in their lives, and which he now considered a second home.

"If anything contributed to the tension between John and Caroline that summer, it was the sale of the Hyannis Port house," recalled a close friend. In June, rather than sell the house, John chose to buy out his sister's share. "I remember Carolyn saying that he [John] hated that he had to write a check to his sister for eight hundred thousand dollars, [which was] then half the value of the home." And all of this took place after Caroline had taken half of all the possessions in the house and put them up for auction.

John's relationship with his sister hit rock bottom in the summer of 1999.

The visits to see her and her children—Rose, Tatiana, and Jack—whom he adored, had become less frequent. It was not the relationship that either wanted, but John could not stomach being in the same room with Ed. Occasional phone calls happened, but usually to discuss family matters. Their emotional bond, however, remained strong, and John likely assumed that they would soon make things right. And that they still had plenty of time to do so.

Despite being under enormous pressure, John was still capable of gestures of empathy and generosity. I learned that firsthand. In the spring of 1999, I had developed a tremor in my left arm, along with unexplained twitches throughout my body. By this point, I had left Oxford and accepted a position as the dean of the Honors College at the University of Oklahoma. Theoretically, the move made it easier for me to commute to New York to tape my History Channel show, but since there were no direct flights, it actually took longer.

John noticed something was wrong one day while we played racquetball. During our last game, roughly a week before his Buckeye accident, I held out my left hand and showed him the tremor. I put on a brave face, telling him that I did not plan to see a doctor and would not let it interfere with my life. In fact, I was too afraid to visit the doctor, so I had no choice but to continue with my life. Without prompting, John started talking about Anthony and how courageous he was in dealing with this horrible disease. John never told me that Anthony was dying. All he talked about was how Anthony refused to complain. He used the word *tough* a handful of times in just a few minutes, as if prodding me to follow Anthony's example.

On Friday, July 9, I finally decided to make an appointment to see the chief of neurology at the University of Oklahoma Medical Center. These were the early days of the internet, so I did what any reasonable person would do: I went online and found the worst possible disease with symptoms matching my own. After a few hours, I had convinced myself that I suffered from Parkinson's disease, but I decided to see a doctor who could confirm my self-diagnosis.

I realized how primitive neurology was when I went for my two-hour exam. Much of it consisted of standing on one leg, touching various parts of my body, and using a small hammer to test my reflexes. At the end of the exam I sat on the table and asked the neurologist, "So do I have Parkinson's?" He shook his head and said, "Well, I have good news and bad news." The good news was that

I did not have Parkinson's; the bad news was that I could be in the early stages of ALS, popularly known as Lou Gehrig's disease. He scheduled a series of additional tests the following Tuesday that would be more revealing.

Shaken, I called a mutual friend when I returned home and broke the news, instructing him to tell no one. He ignored my request and immediately phoned John. That evening I wandered around Norman, Oklahoma, for hours. Even though there was no official diagnosis I played out different scenarios in my head. Finally, around nine thirty, I headed back home and found two messages on my answering machine. "Stevie, it's John. I hear we have something we need to talk about. Call me." The second message came about an hour later. "Stevie, I know you're home. It's ten thirty P.M. on a Friday night. You never go out on a Friday night. Call me back." I was not prepared to have that conversation with him, so I went to bed without returning his calls.

At seven o'clock central time on Saturday morning, the phone started ringing again. Fearing that something bad had happened, I picked it up and heard that familiar voice. "Stevie, I hear we have something we need to talk about." He then gave a reassuring chuckle, letting me know he knew everything but wanted to hear it directly from me. After listening to my detailed description of the exam, which involved stripping down to my underwear and standing on one leg, John started speaking. I can still hear his voice. "For better or worse," he said, "my family is very well connected in New York medical circles. If there's anything you need, you let me know." There was then a pause. "Stevie," he said, "I'll take care of you." To make sure that I heard it right the first time, he repeated. "I'll take care of you, Stevie." He then followed with a comment that only someone worth about $100 million could utter: "And don't worry about all that insurance stuff." For John, medical insurance, which serves as a lifeline and often a source of constant frustration for most Americans, including me, was just "stuff."

On Tuesday, I returned to the University of Oklahoma Medical Center for a series of excruciatingly painful tests, which consisted of shooting electricity through my arms. I felt like I was in the electric chair. But afterward, the doctor explained that I actually suffered from "benign essential tremor," the operative word being "benign." After the appointment, I walked out to the parking lot and used my new cell phone to call John. He was thrilled by the good news and even more excited that he was getting his cast off that week. "Not being able to exercise has been playing with my head," he said. We made plans to play racquetball the following Monday at the New York Athletic Club. I joked that we would look like two invalids. "Stevie," he said, "I can kick your butt with a lame leg."

Many Americans were still awaiting the moment when John would enter public life to fulfill his father's unfinished agenda. The best opportunity came in November 1998, when New York senator Daniel Patrick Moynihan announced that he would not seek reelection in 2000. Several challengers emerged, including Housing Secretary Andrew Cuomo, but First Lady Hillary Clinton soon overshadowed him when she expressed interest in the seat.

Even many of her staff members counseled the first lady against seeking the seat, suggesting that she wait for a position to open up in her home state of Illinois. "Hillary had disadvantages running for the Senate in New York," recalled campaign manager Patti Solis Doyle. "She wasn't from the state. People viewed her as a carpetbagger. New York was a tough media market, and she did not have a good relationship with the media." They assumed that her two toughest potential challengers for the Democratic nomination would be Congresswoman Nita Lowey and John. After lots of discussion, Lowey agreed to step aside for Clinton.

But no one on the campaign knew what John planned to do, and it caused the Clinton people many sleepless nights. "We were scared shitless that John F. Kennedy Jr. would run," Solis Doyle recalled in 2019. The thinking on the campaign was that John "would be serious competition and the one person that she would not be able to beat in the primary." He had too many built-in advantages. "John was American royalty," she recalled. "He built his life in New York. He was a New Yorker. He was beloved nationally." He had a close relationship with the local media, and he was one of the few potential candidates who could raise more money than the first lady. "I don't think she would have run if John was going to run. It was going to be tough enough," said Solis Doyle.

In February 1999, John confided in Dennis Rivera, the powerful head of Local 1199, the Service Employees International Union, that he was interested in running for the open Senate seat. But was he ready to finally make that move? On the evening of St. Patrick's Day, Jeffrey Sachs, who was well connected in New York political circles, and Rivera met with John over dinner to discuss that question. Dennis, who had already spoken to major figures in New York Democratic politics, told John that if he wanted to run for Moynihan's seat, "there are a number of us who will go to Hillary and tell her to stand back." Although John had never run for public office and possessed no real track record, Rivera knew that he boasted near-universal name recognition and was beloved by people of all political persuasions. That did not mean his election would be a cakewalk. The central question that John needed to answer was, "Are you really ready to run?" It was not clear to either man that he was ready to make that decision or that he possessed the passion for campaigning.

Although John had asked for the meeting, Sachs noted that he appeared "edgy in his chair" and "was very uncomfortable" as the dinner progressed. "Is this the right thing for me to do?" John asked. "Will people take me seriously as a candidate?" John promised Dennis that he would get back to him, but he never did. Sachs called him two days later to hear his thoughts, and John confessed he was not interested. "I'm committed to *George*," he said. "I have investors. And I'm very flattered, but I don't think it's time for me." After this conversation, the possibility of John joining the political fray seemed to fade. At least for now, John placed his political ambitions on hold.

From the time I met him in the early 1980s, the question of whether John would enter politics swirled around him. I always sensed that other people thought more about it than he did. We all teased him about which jobs he had planned for us or which rooms in the White House we would occupy. But though he was civic-minded and well read in political history, I never detected in him a burning desire to enter the family business blindly. People speculated that his mom was holding him back, but the dynamic between them was complicated. Jackie was not opposed to John entering public life but she wanted him to make an informed decision and not feel that he was required to enter the family business. And as I watched him mature over the last sixteen years, it became clear that the prospect of running for office grew progressively more appealing to him.

John would occasionally make off-the-cuff comments that suggested he had a calling to be president. In 1989, while watching television coverage of George H. W. Bush's inauguration, he told Rob Littell that he wanted to go home someday—home being the White House. In the mid-1990s, I had lunch with John and some annoying friend who kept badgering him about running for Congress. "How many members of Congress ever become president?" John snapped. In a moment of pique, John revealed his desire to be president, but at the time, I was more interested in pointing out the fallacy of his argument. "Well, John," I interjected, "you could start with your father," and then I rattled off a list of other names of presidents from recent history who had once been members of Congress: Lyndon Johnson, Richard Nixon, and George H. W. Bush.

I tracked John's growing affinity for public life by how he referred to his father. When at Brown, and for a few years after, I never heard him designate his father as anything other than President Kennedy. By the early 1990s, he started identifying him as "my father." Then, in the final years of his life, John often called his father "Daddy." In my eyes, John did not want to join politics, as did some of his cousins, only because he felt a sense of family obligation. He first needed evidence that he had something to contribute, a concrete accomplishment that would serve as his foundation to run. Simply being JFK Jr. was not enough.

Had *George* been successful, it would have offered an ideal launching pad, but by the end of 1999, his magazine was limping along, its future uncertain. When he sat down with Sachs and Rivera, the timing still did not feel right, but he was leaning closer.

On the Sunday before he died, John called me to complain that Clinton planned to seek the Democratic nomination to fill the Moynihan Senate seat. He likely had seen the press coverage of her July 6 announcement that she had set up an exploratory committee and would begin a "listening tour" of the state. Although John had decided not to run for the seat, he believed that it should go to a native New Yorker, and not someone moving to the state solely for the purpose of seeking the office. "Stevie," he said, "somebody [meaning me] should write an article about this carpetbagger Clinton moving to New York solely to run for a Senate seat." I gently reminded him that his uncle Robert moved his residence to New York to run for (and win) a Senate seat in 1964. "Someone with the last name of Kennedy should not be complaining about carpetbaggers moving to New York to run for a Senate seat," I told him. He quickly changed topics.

On Wednesday, July 14, John met Carolyn and her sister Lauren, a rising star at the Morgan Stanley Dean Witter investment bank, for lunch at the Stanhope Hotel's Café M. The three had made weekend plans to fly together.

John and Carolyn would be attending the wedding of his cousin Rory, the youngest daughter of John's aunt and uncle Ethel and Robert F. Kennedy, at the family compound in Hyannis Port. They planned to drop off Lauren at Martha's Vineyard on the way. But now Carolyn was reluctant to go to the wedding, and it appeared that John had enlisted Lauren to help persuade her to change her mind. "Oh, come on now," a diner seated nearby heard Lauren say, "we'll have fun."

The previous few weeks had been especially difficult for the couple. Carolyn had become more withdrawn and more dependent on drugs. "I went over to their house two weeks before he died to watch a basketball game, and it was weird," recalled a friend. "She was definitely doing a lot of coke, and I think she was involved with her coke dealer who lived across the street. She was out of control." Friends had been telling John that they thought Carolyn was having an affair. At this point, he did not know what to believe. Now she seemed to be taunting him by not attending the wedding. "I'm not going to go to the wedding, how's that?" she said to him. "I am going to make a big scene, and I am not going to go to the wedding, and then you are going to have to explain it, and you are going to come home and feel really bad that I wasn't there."

John probably saw Carolyn's threat as the last straw. He knew that her absence, and not the wedding of his cousin, would dominate the headlines as a result. If Carolyn was so insensitive that she would embarrass him in front of his entire family, there seemed little left to salvage in their relationship. "If she's done, I'm done," he told a friend, who wished to remain anonymous. They agreed that John should move into the Stanhope Hotel on Fifth Avenue. It would not be his first stay there, though. He had spent many nights at the hotel in the past and often retreated there following similar fights with Carolyn.

This time was different. John told friends that he was not going back to Carolyn and would instead continue to live at the Stanhope for the foreseeable future. It was a painful decision, but a necessary one, he thought. He knew that the tabloids would eventually discover that he and Carolyn were living apart, which would only intensify public scrutiny of their private lives. He still wanted to make the marriage work, but he needed to send Carolyn a clear signal that the status quo was not acceptable. For now, he planned to make it through the weekend without becoming an unwanted distraction before Rory's wedding.

After lunch, John returned to his office and called Caroline, who was leaving for Idaho the next day on a rafting trip to celebrate her and Ed's thirteenth wedding anniversary and Ed's fifty-fourth birthday. He told his sister that Carolyn was not going to be attending the wedding that weekend and that his marriage was imploding. He wanted her to know before the story flooded the tabloids. He apologized for being distant and suggested that they both make more of an effort to spend time together. Caroline responded graciously and compassionately. She invited John over, but he said that they could talk more after the wedding. For that brief moment, they recaptured the genuine affection that had animated most of their lives. It was the last time they would speak.

John stayed in the office reading copy, chatting with editors, and making phone calls until eight at night. He left the office and headed to the Stanhope, where he checked into room 1511. He told the receptionist that he was staying at the hotel because "my wife kicked me out." John always got special service wherever he traveled, and the Stanhope was no different. Less than an hour after he arrived, a waiter showed up with his favorite turkey club sandwich and a bottle of mineral water. He also received a visit that evening from Julie Baker, a former model whom he had dated before marrying Carolyn.

Unlike with his other girlfriends who faded out of his life, John remained close to Baker long after their romantic relationship ended. Their relationship now rested on mutual trust and respect. "John and I had an easy, uncomplicated friendship," Baker reflected in 2019. "We had a very special bond that throughout the years became stronger and stronger. I believe we knew we would always be there for each other." Their close friendship was no secret to Carolyn, who was completely comfortable with the arrangement. "John and Julie remained friends and were in touch about once a month," recalled Rose-Marie. "Their friendship was completely transparent, and Carolyn even invited Julie to one of John's birthday celebrations at their apartment."

During these difficult final months of his life, John reached out to Baker for comfort and conversation. They talked about many of the topics that close friends discuss. John would mention a book that he was reading or say something about the *George* issue they were working on at the time. They were close enough that they could also sit in silence for long periods of time. But Julie was one of the few people whom John would open up to and discuss his personal issues with. A few weeks earlier, John had come over to her apartment, where the two "hung out." Now, on his first night alone at the hotel, he asked her to join him.

Baker remembers John as being "conflicted" in those final days. Conflicted about *George* and what should be his next steps. He did not want to abandon the magazine, but he was not sure if he could attract other investors. Most of all, he was conflicted about his marriage. He had heard from many of his friends that Carolyn was abusing cocaine. But she denied it. The biggest issue was whether he should stay with her or leave. John felt that Carolyn had stopped working on the marriage a long time ago. Why, then, should he work so hard to keep the marriage going? "I cannot begin to know what would have happened on all fronts of his inner turmoil," Julie told me. "But I know he wouldn't just lie down and sulk about things. He would have taken thoughtful steps" and made the best choices possible.

Julie remembers John speaking openly of his fear of being alone. It was understandable, given the circumstances. He had come to terms with the prospect of losing his lifelong best friend at any moment. Anthony was the brother that John never had. He also had to contend with his marriage ending. The loss of those two people—one was certain, the other likely—would have left a huge hole in John's life. But he would have recovered. "John was the most resilient person I ever met in my life," RoseMarie reflected. John had lots of close friends who would have been happy to help to fill the void, but it is extremely hard to replace your best friend and your spouse all at once.

On Thursday morning, July 15, John returned to Lenox Hill Hospital, where his surgeon removed the cast that had been molded to his ankle for the previous six weeks and gave him the go-ahead to fly. According to a reliable source, Carolyn accompanied him, and the two were very affectionate, kissing passionately while seated in a small reception area. The scene revealed the volatility of their relationship. They could be fighting one minute and then unable to keep their hands off each other the next. Carolyn was no doubt relieved that they had survived the past six weeks with her husband immobile. John emerged from the hospital on crutches and went straight to the *George* offices on Broadway in midtown Manhattan. He had an important meeting later that afternoon with his new boss at Hachette, Jack Kliger.

In May, David Pecker had left Hachette and purchased American Media Company, which owned the *National Enquirer* and other tabloids—the very ones that bought pictures from the same paparazzi who tortured Carolyn.

Hachette replaced him with Kliger, a low-key numbers guy who lacked Pecker's dramatic flair and had no emotional attachment to *George*. When he took over as CEO, the French told Kliger that one of the early questions he would face was what to do with *George*. He was informed that the magazine was losing money and that Hachette did not see a viable way forward for the partnership. Hachette's priority was protecting *Elle* and figuring out how to make the company operate more efficiently. They asked him to look further into the issue and make a recommendation on how to proceed. "It was the first big issue that I faced," he recalled.

Kliger met often with John over the next few weeks and told him that the current business plan was not working. "My point to John in the beginning was we have to either figure out if the business model can be redone, or, if not, what's a graceful way for us to part," he shared in 2017. He made clear to John, however, that parting ways did not mean shuttering the magazine. If they chose to end their association, Hachette would stick with him for a reasonable amount of time until John could find another partner.

John took Kliger's recommendations to heart and submitted a revised business proposal in June. "I thought it was a viable plan," Kliger admitted. It called for cutting the number of pages in the magazine, producing fewer copies, and raising the newsstand price. However, Kliger never presented John's modified business plan to the French executives because he still concluded that the partnership could not be rescued. There was not, he recalled, "much faith at Hachette in *George*." Hachette, he pointed out, was a "bottom-line-driven company that didn't really have as big a franchise in either news or lifestyle." While John was picking up hints that Hachette was going to pull out of their partnership, he retained a glimmer of hope.

Kliger extinguished that glimmer on Thursday, July 15. The two men had a meeting scheduled for two in the afternoon, but John kept pushing it back. He finally showed up at four o'clock. "Jack, I am very sorry," John apologized. "I wish we could come to a final decision on the plan." Kliger broke it to him that Hachette did not want to continue as partners but that it would stay with *George* until he was able to find another buyer. John made it clear that he did not want Hachette to help in the search and that he would do it himself.

Afterward, John went downstairs to his office with a big grin on his face. "So, Jack told me they're not going forward with *George*," he told Rose. She was stunned, not so much by the news as by the image of John's gleaming smile while he shared it with her. John said he figured it out even before Kliger opened his mouth. "You know how I knew?" he asked. "When I went into his office, I put my water bottle on his desk. And he was so nervous, he picked up *my* bottle of water and started drinking from it." Later that evening, John recounted a similar story to his close friend and former *George* editor and legal counsel Gary Ginsberg. "I knew I was fucked," he said, "because I met with Kliger today, and I brought a bottle of water, and I put it on the table between us. Kliger was so nervous that he took my bottle of water and started drinking it. That was when I realized, this guy's so nervous because he knows he's going to cut the cord on me."

That evening, John attended a Yankees game with Ginsberg, who introduced John to James and Lachlan Murdoch, the children of News Corporation CEO Rupert Murdoch. Gary, a senior executive at News Corp, organized the meeting in the hopes that the Murdoch family would want to partner with John. As they watched the Atlanta Braves rock Yankees starter Roger Clemens, a television crew spotted John and flashed his face to New Yorkers following the game at home. The evening went well, but they left the game without securing a commitment.

George was not the only topic of conversation that evening. In the long car ride to and from the stadium, Gary talked with John about his political ambitions. John mentioned that he was eyeing the New York governor's race in 2002. "That's the race," John told Gary. He had stopped brooding over the Senate seat that Hillary Clinton had moved to claim. "I'm intellectually and temperamentally better suited to be an executive than a legislator," he said. "My dad didn't like it, either," he revealed, referring to his father's time in the House and the Senate. John felt he could beat incumbent George Pataki, a bland moderate Republican who was seeking a third term. John realized that he had to get his house in order before he could make the move. He worried whether Carolyn would ever be emotionally capable of dealing with him running for office. And then there was *George*, which was hanging like a dark shadow over his future ambitions. "He was looking for a graceful way out of *George*," Ginsberg recalled.

Even on the last night of his life, John felt trapped between two worlds. He had finally come to acknowledge his political ambitions and embrace his role as the heir to his father's legacy, but before he could seek office, he needed to come to terms with a troubled marriage and a failing magazine.

When John arrived at his office on Friday morning, he told RoseMarie that Carolyn would not be accompanying him to the wedding. Rose decided to stage an intervention. "John," she said, "I need to have a little chat with your wife in private." She asked him to leave his office so she could make the important call.

Despite her frustration with both, Rose understood the necessity of Carolyn showing up at the wedding. "I don't know what the hell you are trying to prove," RoseMarie declared, "and I don't know what the hell you are doing, but it's not working. You are smarter than this; you are better than this. Why are you staying out, and not calling?" Rose told Carolyn that she was acting "like a teenager." By this point, Carolyn was crying hysterically. "I'm so sick of everything," she sobbed. Rose told her that whatever her legitimate grievances, she was dealing with them the wrong way. "I don't know what you are looking for, what kind of attention you are looking for, but you are not getting it, and you are fucking up your life." In fact, she was only aggravating the situation. "If you are trying to get him to pay attention, he's not," Rose said. "He is getting angrier and pulling further away." By this point, Carolyn was distraught. "I am just so sick of my life. I am exhausted from this, there's always an event, there's always something, it's always about him, it's always about the magazine. It's never about me."

Rose empathized but insisted that this was not the time to take a stand. "His whole family is going to be at this wedding, and you need to go with him." Carolyn finally backed down. "I just want some normal married time," she confessed. Rose realized that despite all their fame, John and Carolyn needed what every couple desired: privacy and sufficient time to spend together without distraction. "Listen, Carolyn," she told her. "You don't want to put John in a position where he has to explain where you are, and you don't want to put yourself in a position of being judged. You get enough of that." Reluctantly, Carolyn agreed to go to the wedding.

Could Carolyn's decision to attend the wedding have been a possible turning point in their relationship? It certainly marked the first positive development in months and revealed that Carolyn still wanted to improve their marriage. There would have been ample work ahead. Carolyn needed to come to grips with her newfound celebrity and find some cause to occupy her time, while John had to talk less about having children and instead listen to Carolyn's legitimate concerns. But despite all the obstacles that loomed,

Carolyn's gesture was a meaningful one, and according to RoseMarie, John clearly appreciated it.

The rest of the day proceeded routinely for John. He went to lunch with a group of *George* editors and attended an afternoon staff meeting. At 4:05 P.M. he sent a message to his old friend John Perry Barlow, who had just buried his mother. John praised him for staying by his mother's side while she died. "I will never forget when it happened to me," John wrote, "and it was not something that was all that macabre." Meanwhile, now that she was going to the wedding, Carolyn needed a new dress and spent most of the afternoon shopping in midtown Manhattan. Late in the afternoon, she went to Saks Fifth Avenue, where she found a short, black dress by Yves Saint Laurent that cost $1,640.

John left the office immediately after sending the email to Barlow and went to visit his old friend from Brown, Pat Manocchia, who now owned the exclusive fitness center La Palestra. As he headed toward the door, Rose reminded him that he had to meet Lauren Bessette in the lobby at six thirty. She then asked him if he was okay with her leaving at five thirty that evening. "Sure, Rosie, no problem. I'll call you later." He took a few steps before turning and looking at Rose. "Rosie, you're the best. Thanks for smoothing things over." Before she left for the day, Rose put a pink sticky note on the table in his office: "Meet Lauren in the lobby at six thirty." Rose knew it never hurt to remind John twice. She was planning to spend the weekend at John and Carolyn's apartment. The forecast was for hot, muggy nights, and Rose's air-conditioning was broken, so John and Carolyn had offered her their place for the weekend.

John took a car to Pat's Upper West Side gym. "We trained a lot that last couple weeks because of his injury," Pat recalled. "On that last day, we did some soft tissue work to try to get some range of motion back." Pat described John as "despondent." He was happy to have the cast off, but he was not sure what he was going to do about *George*. "He was demoralized by his meeting with Hachette," he recalled. "He wasn't sure whether the magazine could survive or if he wanted to continue with the magazine even if it did." Pat declined to say what, if anything, John said about his marriage.

John returned to the office just in time to meet Lauren. He first went to his office and checked the weather conditions for Martha's Vineyard and the surrounding area. The official report gave little evidence of the trouble that lay ahead, indicating clear skies and visibility at between four and ten miles along his route. The forecast was crucial since he was flying under visual flight rules, or VFR, which meant that he was navigating on his own rather than relying on instruments. At the time of his flight, John was enrolled in an instrument training course and had completed half of the twenty-five lessons.

Reassured by the forecast, John grabbed his bag and descended to the lobby. At a quarter to seven he and Lauren hopped into his white Hyundai convertible for the short trip to Essex County Airport in Fairfield, New Jersey. As they crawled through Times Square, people spotted John and waved. Normally it would have taken about forty minutes, but on a July weekend, it took seventy-five minutes.

They arrived at the airport shortly after eight and pulled into a Sunoco gas station across the street. The owner of the station thought it was too late for John to be flying. "He usually showed up between five and seven," he told *Time* magazine. But John showed no signs of being in a hurry. Wearing a light gray T-shirt, he made small talk with the cashier and bought a banana, a bottle of Evian, and six AA batteries. The attendant asked John how his leg felt. "I just got the cast off yesterday," John responded, "but it's feeling better." On his way out, he scanned the magazine rack near the front door, perhaps looking for a copy of *George*. He then climbed into his car and drove across the street to the airport.

What John did not know was that weather conditions had deteriorated rapidly since he had checked the forecast a few hours earlier, and a thick fog had descended over the ocean. Munir Hussain, who had sold John his plane, had just landed at Essex after a short trip from Long Island. He went over to warn John, but John was still in the convenience store across the street. If he had not lingered for those extra minutes in the store, John might have received a warning that could have saved his life. "If only I'd seen him," Hussain lamented. "I would have told him, 'Don't go up.'"

After John and Lauren loaded their luggage into the cargo hold, John hobbled around the plane checking its wing flaps and fuel tanks. Just as he finished, Carolyn pulled up in a black car. John climbed into the pilot's seat, while Lauren and Carolyn sat in the rear of the six-seat cabin directly behind him. Before they took off, Carolyn called Carole, notifying her they would be at the Vineyard in time for dinner on Saturday.

According to recently released FBI files, there was a hiccup right before departure that foreshadowed worse to come. A woman told the FBI that she, her husband, and their three children ate at a Mexican restaurant near the airport that evening. After dinner, their kids wanted to watch the planes take off and land at Essex County Airport. It was quiet at the airport but after a brief period her husband heard an engine. They drove to the edge of the airport grounds where a red-and-white single-engine airplane was revving its engine. A white convertible car was parked near the plane, and the roar of the engine set off the car alarm. "A blonde woman then exited the plane and reset the car alarm," she told the FBI. According to the witness, the woman "proceeded to walk around the left side of the aircraft and reentered the airplane from behind the pilot seat. The airplane then departed for the runway." She noted that "the right-side door of the airplane was left ajar as they departed for the runway." There is no evidence to suggest, however, that an open door played a role in the tragedy that was about to occur.

According to the control tower, John's plane departed at 8:38 P.M. on run-way 22, climbed to 5,600 feet, which was a typical altitude for small planes, then headed east across the Hudson toward Long Island Sound. Eleven min-utes into his flight, John ascended directly into the flight path of American Airlines Flight 1484, which was coming in for a landing at New York's La-Guardia Airport. Air traffic control scrambled to warn both John and the pilot of the American flight in order to avoid a collision. Apparently, John received the message and maneuvered out of danger.

The flight was uneventful as they passed the southern Connecticut coast. The lights of homes and businesses that lined the coast served as beacons, helping John to navigate northward. At 9:26 P.M., just forty-eight minutes into the flight, John passed Westerly, Rhode Island, banked right over the ocean, and headed directly into a thick fog. He was now flying blind. He could have altered his plan and gone straight to Hyannis, but John continued to Martha's Vineyard. An instrument-trained pilot could have guided the plane to its destination, but John had to use his own senses, which were now betraying him.

It is impossible to know what was happening in the plane during the final minutes or what was going through John's mind. Most experts believe that he suffered from spatial disorientation, often referred to as Spatial-D. Unable to see stars, lights, land, or even the ocean, John lost his bearings. The plane had an automatic pilot function, but John never deployed it. "It's an excellent autopilot," Al Pregler, a retired airline captain told the *Los Angeles Times*. "It probably could have gotten him down to the last one hundred feet."

Instead, John needed to reconcile what his body was telling him with what his instrument panel indicated. "If you are not able to fly by instruments, you are dependent on your body," Pregler explained. "Your sense of balance is determined by your inner ear—and your inner ear can lie to you. You can lose awareness. You don't know if you are turning or climbing or diving. What you may perceive is happening can be entirely different from what is really happening."

About thirty-four miles west of Martha's Vineyard Airport, the plane began a descent that varied between four hundred and eight hundred feet per minute. At twenty seconds past 9:40 P.M., John made a left turn, but his wings were not even. John pulled frantically on the plane's yoke, trying to lift the plane's nose, but instead he was losing altitude. Clearly disoriented, John banked to the right, sending the plane into a downward spiral. While I hate to even think about it, John and his passengers experienced a horrifying final few seconds of life as the plane entered a violent, plunging spin that sent them smashing into the ocean at two hundred miles per hour. In the clinical language of National Transportation Safety Board (NTSB) investigators, John failed "to maintain control of the airplane during a descent over water at night, which was a result of spatial disorientation."

Fatal air crashes result from a series of mistakes. John's first error was to choose to fly that evening without a flight instructor. In April, John had traded in his Cessna 182 Skylane for the faster and more complex Piper Saratoga. Although he had logged approximately 310 flying hours, including 55 at night, John had only flown 36 hours in the Saratoga, and only 10 of those were at night. Furthermore, he had not flown in two months because of his ankle injury. If he ever needed an instructor seated next to him, it was this night.

Second, he was not experienced enough to fully understand how unpredictable the weather could be around Martha's Vineyard, where fog could roll in and smother the island within minutes. The National Transportation Safety Board interviewed pilots who flew a similar route that evening. One pilot said that the visibility was well above VFR minimums. Before taking off, he asked if there were any adverse conditions along the route. He was told emphatically: "No adverse conditions. Have a great weekend." Another pilot, also flying to Martha's Vineyard, stated that his entire flight was conducted under VFR, with visibility of three to five miles in haze. He said that over land he could see lights, but over water there was no horizon to reference. But these were both seasoned pilots. John was not. Many experienced pilots chose not to fly that evening. Some who did take off traveling the same route radioed the FAA for permission to land at alternative airports farther inland, where the visibility was better.

Even if he did not have an instructor, and he chose not to land at an alternative airport, John still could have used his radio to ask for help. But John never made radio contact. I think I know why. John enjoyed danger and risk, and he always found a way out. He no doubt realized that he was in trouble, but no more trouble than when he camped alone in the wilderness for a week, strapped himself into his Buckeye, or skied down steep cliffs. Whatever it was that attracted him to danger—a genetic predisposition or a psychological response to the trauma of childhood, or both—John had supreme confidence in his ability to get himself out of tight jams. If his own skill and determination were not enough, he could count on some other force to protect him, like the unpredictable wave that once lifted his kayak over a large boulder and past the jagged coral on a Jamaican beach. He assumed that this flight would be another challenge that he would conquer. He likely worried more about the embarrassment of a leaked recording of him asking for help than he did about crashing his plane.

At midnight on Friday, July 16, the phone starting ringing at John and Carolyn's Martha's Vineyard home where Carole and Anthony were staying. Both were sleeping, but Anthony picked it up and handed Carole the receiver. She went into the bathroom and shut the door before putting the phone to her ear.

"Hi," she whispered, assuming it was John. "Is everything okay?"

"Oh, hi, Carole. I'm sorry to wake you," the caller said. It was Dan Samson, nicknamed "Pinky," who was supposed to pick him up at the airport in Hyannis.

"I know it's late. I'm really sorry. Maybe I'm confused, but I think I was supposed to pick John up at the airport at ten o'clock, and he is not here yet."

"Pinky, what are you talking about?" Carole asked.

He did not want to sound too alarmist, so he tried to lighten the mood. "I'm sure it's nothing. You know John, he probably just changed his plans [and] didn't call anyone."

"They're in Hyannis, Pinky," she told him. "Carolyn called me before they left. You must be mistaken."

"I know," he said. "You're right. I thought maybe he changed his mind and stayed in the Vineyard after dropping Lauren off."

Carole hung up the phone and walked quietly out of the bathroom hoping not to alarm Anthony. But he was awake.

"What's wrong?" he asked.

"Oh. Well, you know John," she said. "I'm just going to make a few calls to make sure everything is okay. Go back to sleep. Everything's fine."

Carole, a talented producer for ABC News, used her investigative skills to immediately start tracking down sources of information. One of the first calls she made was to John and Carolyn's apartment in New York, hoping that maybe they had decided at the last minute to postpone flying until morning.

That Friday night, Rose was sitting on John and Carolyn's sofa, sipping a huge glass of white wine and talking on the phone to Matt Berman, the magazine's creative director, about an upcoming shoot with actor Rob Lowe, who was promoting a new TV show called *The West Wing*. Carole had been trying to get through for hours, but Carolyn had refused to buy call waiting because she thought it rude to interrupt one phone conversation for another. Finally, shortly after midnight, the fax machine started ringing. Rose knew that only a handful of people knew that fax number, so she hung up on Matt and picked up the fax line.

"Hello?" Rose said.

"Oh, Carolyn, thank God you're home."

"Carole, it's Rose. What's going on?"

"Where are they?" Carole asked.

"What do you mean, where are they?"

"Oh God!" Carole gasped.

EPILOGUE

"YEP, YOU REALLY
WERE SPECIAL"

I woke up at 7:15 A.M. CST on Saturday morning, July 17, 1999. Three days earlier I had moved into a new house in Norman, Oklahoma. I hadn't found any time to go shopping for furniture, so I had only a bed, an old sofa, and a television. That morning I got out of bed, made coffee, grabbed a bowl of cereal, and strolled into my two-story study, which was the centerpiece of the house. I immediately began multitasking: sipping coffee; shoveling nondescript sugar-coated flakes into my mouth; turning on the computer to access my AOL account; checking for phone messages.

I must have bypassed AOL's news page and gone directly to my inbox, where I had a message from my research assistant that read, "I'm sorry to hear about your friend. I'm sure everything will turn out okay." Having no idea what she was referring to, I wrote back saying that all my friends were doing fine. I hit the send key and then turned to access the voicemail on my landline. Since I had checked for messages late the previous evening, it was unlikely, I thought, that I had any new ones. Even if someone did call, I would not have heard the ring because the only working phone was in my study, which was far from the bedroom. But right when I realized I had eighteen new voice messages, I glanced at the computer screen and saw the headline: "JFK Jr.'s Plane Missing."

For a moment I froze. I looked at the clock above my desk and noticed that it was 7:24 A.M., almost the exact time that John had called me the previous Saturday to offer his help during my health crisis. I felt overwhelmed by a sense of powerlessness. John had offered to take care of me in a moment of need, and now I was trapped in the middle of nowhere, unable to do anything to help him.

During the night and into the early morning, both Carole Radziwill and RoseMarie Terenzio had frantically alerted the authorities and reached out to John's friends in hopes that they might know his whereabouts. Carole contacted numerous airports along the Northeast corridor to see if John had decided to take a last-minute detour. RoseMarie called the New Jersey airport where John's plane had taken off and insisted on speaking to the air traffic controller who had been on duty Friday evening so he could confirm that the plane had left. At 2:00 A.M., the controller reported that the flight had indeed taken off at 8:49 P.M. on Friday evening. "At that point, I panic," RoseMarie reflected, "and I know that something is wrong." She decided that it was time to inform Ted Kennedy, who was in Hyannis Port for the wedding.

When RoseMarie called the senator's home around 2:15 A.M., a housekeeper answered the phone and said that the senator was sleeping. "You need to wake him up," Rose insisted. The housekeeper remained unconvinced. "Oh, John is just being John," she said. "He probably went to a friend's house, or he decided not to go and didn't tell anybody. He's going to come walking in the door, and it's going to be no big deal." Rose grew increasingly frustrated as the housekeeper brushed off the urgency of her request. Only when Rose specified that the flight departed at 8:49 P.M. and never arrived at the Vineyard did the housekeeper agree to wake up Ted Kennedy.

The senator called about ten minutes later. RoseMarie told him everything she knew: the plane had left New Jersey and never landed at Martha's Vineyard and no one had been able to reach either John or Carolyn. "Okay," he responded, "just sit tight." It's unclear who he called next, but by the time I woke up, the search for John's plane had already begun.

To be honest, my memory of the next few days is a blur. I recall snapshots of what I felt and experienced, but I do not remember the connective tissue between these events. At one point, I flew to New York but have no recollection of being on a plane that week. I must have met people for lunch and dinner but cannot say for sure.

Snapshot 1: I spent Saturday afternoon pacing back and forth across my living room while talking to friends and colleagues at *George*. Overnight, almost everyone hoped that John had simply landed at an alternative airport and somewhat characteristically decided not to tell anyone. By noon, however, that possibility was looking less likely. While John might have made a last-minute change without notifying anyone, Carolyn would have checked in with someone. But I remained upbeat and confident that John would be found alive.

Snapshot 2: Later Saturday evening, reports emerged that a luggage tag from a garment bag that belonged to Lauren Bessette had washed up on the shores of Martha's Vineyard. Even then, I remained in denial. John was such a vital force it felt inconceivable that he could be gone. As much as I'm embarrassed to admit it, I kept telling everyone that this occurrence would be John's "yuppie" version of PT-109, when his father rescued his crew after their ship had been sliced in half by a Japanese destroyer during World War II. Rescuers, I assured, would find him with a rope clenched in his teeth, pulling the plane behind him with Carolyn and Lauren sitting on the wing doing their nails.

Snapshot 3: I woke up Sunday morning and quickly realized that I needed a break from the constant news coverage. I turned off the television, disconnected my landline, and went shopping. Shortly after 10:00 A.M., I left my cell phone at home and went to Mathis Brothers, a giant furniture warehouse in Oklahoma City. I was clearly in shock and not able to think straight because I purchased enough furniture to fill three houses. When I returned home later that afternoon I walked in the house, picked up the remote, turned on the television, and there it was: a photo of John with the dates "1960–1999." While I was out, the US Coast Guard had announced that it had given up hope of finding anyone alive. All the calls with *George* colleagues and other friends ceased. Everyone was now in mourning. Either that evening or early the next morning I must have flown to New York, but I don't remember.

Snapshot 4: Throughout the week, people kept calling and leaving messages to confirm a gathering point for that evening. I received a call on Tuesday afternoon that a group of close friends would meet at seven o'clock at the home of Randy Poster, who'd met John at Brown. I was reluctant to go because I feared there would be security, no one would be able to vouch for me, and I would be turned away. I stood outside the building for a few minutes before mustering enough courage to approach the doorman. When I mentioned Randy's name, the doorman simply waved me onto the elevator. I had passed the first test. Now the bigger test: would John's other friends know me? Most of my time with John had been one-on-one, and while I occasionally ran into Randy and others who belonged to his inner circle, the interactions had been brief. When I knocked on the door, Randy answered. "Hi," I said nervously, "I'm Steve Gillon." His face lit up. "The professor!" he exclaimed, as he started flexing his right wrist as if going through the motions of playing racquetball. Now I knew how John had described me to his other friends. As I mingled with the other guests it became clear that many were aware of the role that I had played in John's life.

Snapshot 5: For most of the week I refused to watch television news, listen to radio, or read a newspaper. There was something liberating about living in a news vacuum. On Wednesday afternoon, as I walked near Forty-Second Street on my way to the gym, I passed a newsstand with a television. The novelty of the scene caught my attention, so I glanced over and saw a CNN headline declaring that the coast guard had found the bodies submerged in about 116 feet of water. Although I knew that John was dead, there was something jarring about learning that his body, along with those of Lauren and Carolyn, had been at the bottom of the ocean for days. I could have continued on to the gym, but the revelation drained all my energy. I returned to my hotel, pulled the curtains closed, and sat in the silent dark for the rest of the day and evening. I needed that time to pull myself together and come to terms with what had taken place. "Life is for the living," John used to say. No one understood death better than John, and he would have been horrified that I was wallowing in grief. I could hear his voice in my ear. "Get the fuck up, Stevie, and get on with your life." I was in a somewhat better place by the time I left the hotel on Thursday morning.

Snapshot 6: I turned on the television in my hotel room for the first time on Thursday morning, July 22, to briefly watch the ceremony burying John's and Carolyn's cremated remains at sea. I felt enormous empathy for Caroline. Her relationship with John had hit a rough patch, but their deep affection and respect for each other had been both genuine and heartfelt. If only they had had more time, they would have worked out their difficulties.

I was honored to be one of the 350 guests invited to the eleven o'clock memorial service at St. Thomas More Church on East Eighty-Ninth Street, located just a few blocks from Jackie's old Fifth Avenue apartment and the place where John and Caroline had attended Mass as children. John's dear friend Gary Ginsberg, who had helped launch *George*, his wife, Susanna, and I took a car together to the Upper East Side. As we traveled up the FDR Drive, we witnessed President Clinton's helicopter landing along the river.

We met with about two dozen people from *George* at Sarabeth's restaurant on Ninety-Second Street and Madison Avenue and walked through a gauntlet of barricades, showing our white invitations at each one. It was a sunny, hot, and humid morning. The oppressive heat outside was soon replaced by the feeling of overwhelming sadness inside the Gothic-style church. I was immediately struck by its small size, with only fifteen rows of pews, all covered in crimson velvet cushions. An extended center pew ran across almost the entire width of the church, with smaller pews on either side that could easily fit three adults. I sat in one of the side pews near the middle of the church with a colleague from *George*. Just as the service began, a tall man knelt down, crossed himself, and gently pushed his way into the pew. It was Senator John Kerry, who ended up weeping throughout the entire service. I understood how he felt but had no tears left.

Famous people from the world of politics and entertainment poured into the church and maneuvered for seats. I noticed that many guests had square jaws and big teeth, so were probably part of the extended Kennedy family. Sitting across from me in the center aisle was John's childhood idol Muhammad Ali.

After everyone had been seated, President Clinton, Hillary, and their daughter, Chelsea, entered the church and took seats directly behind the Kennedy family in the center aisle, near the front.

Readings and prayers soon filled the space. Anthony Radziwill read Psalm 23: "The Lord is my shepherd; I shall not want." RoseMarie, Sasha Chermayeff, and Caroline also did readings. A gospel choir sang "Swing Low, Sweet Chariot." Wyclef Jean performed the reggae song "Many Rivers to Cross," which was one of John's favorites.

The eulogies were reserved until after Communion. The family had hoped that Anthony would deliver John's eulogy, but because he was too weak, Caroline enlisted Ted Kennedy, who had become the family mourner-in-chief. The senator turned to his favorite speechwriter, Robert Shrum, who recalled getting a call from Ted early in the week before the coast guard had abandoned the search for survivors. "There's no hope," Teddy said before asking Shrum to start working on the speech. "The words almost wrote themselves," Shrum recalled.

Not surprisingly, Ted rose to the occasion and offered an eloquent farewell to his nephew. He delivered so many lines that reverberate in my head to this day. He eulogized John for "seem[ing] to belong not only to our family, but to the American family. The whole world knew his name before he did." Everyone had hoped, Ted continued, "that this John Kennedy would live to comb gray hair, with his beloved Carolyn by his side. But like his father, he had every gift but the length of years." I was also stunned by the eloquence of Hamilton South, who spoke about Carolyn. "When she was your friend, it was like having a lion in your life," he reflected. "She was protective of her cubs, and woe to anyone or thing that would do them harm."

The whole service ended after ninety minutes.

I walked out of the building next to Theodore Sorensen, JFK's wordsmith, who had written many of his most famous speeches, including his inaugural address. Now nearly blind, he gripped the railing with his right hand as he descended the steps. I greeted Arthur Schlesinger Jr., whom I had come to know over the years. It occurred to me that these men had buried John's father and now his son. A few of us lingered outside the church for a few minutes. I walked over and hugged RoseMarie, who remained in a state of shock. Rob Littell, who had been John's Brown roommate and dear friend for two decades, stood alone, staring in disbelief at the church. He had lost his closest friend.

I walked the two blocks up Madison Avenue to the Convent of the Sacred Heart, a girls' school that Caroline Kennedy had once attended and where the reception was being held. I had shut myself off from the news for the past week and thus had been oblivious to the scale of public mourning. Now I experienced it firsthand as I passed hundreds of people lining the sidewalks, standing in the hot sun, wishing to say good-bye to a man they had never met. Though the crowds were large, they remained remarkably solemn. The city itself seemed uncharacteristically quiet and still. Because of the police blockades, no vehicles filled the streets. Without the sound of car horns or sirens, just an empty silence hung in the air. All week I had been mourning the loss of my friend, not realizing that the entire nation was grieving the loss of its reluctant prince. As I looked around I thought, "Yep, you really were special."

We entered the school through a side door and mounted a flight of marble steps to the auditorium. Caroline, looking pale and drawn, stood at the top of the steps greeting everyone as they filed in. I don't think I had ever seen so much sadness on anyone's face as I saw on Caroline's that afternoon.

There was nothing fancy about the reception. The room had round, cloth-covered tables and metal chairs. Along the wall, long tables offered assorted piles of food—slices of salmon, bowls of pasta, and salad. I rarely walked past a dessert table without eating something, but on this day I had no appetite. Off to the side of the larger room, a small sitting area had been arranged with a comfortable sofa and fireplace. While many people mingled, I parked myself on the sofa for the next hour. People would come and go, sharing stories about John. We talked about our plans for the future—a future without John.

Up to this point, I had never met Anthony, and I was determined to say hello and tell him what he already knew—that John loved and admired him. I dislodged myself from the sofa and walked into the main room. I was shocked when I saw him: frail, alone, sitting in a metal chair, leaning forward on a cane to support his weight. I decided to leave him alone. I was struck by the tragic irony. John had spent the last few weeks of his life writing Anthony's eulogy and here Anthony sat, clinging tenuously to life while mourning his best friend. A few weeks later, Anthony would succumb to the disease he had fought so gallantly for nearly a decade.

I learned later that the reception turned into a traditional Irish wake, with Teddy leading the group in song. But by then, I had left. It was the saddest week of my life, but I finally made the decision to stop mourning and try to move on.

"Will a magazine die without its editor?" asked *The New York Times*. That question was certainly on the minds of heartbroken editors and staff at *George*. The future of *George* was now in the hands of Jack Kliger, who had been on the job for only a few weeks. On Thursday he had told John that Hachette would not be renewing its partnership with *George* but would stick with him until John found another partner, at least for a reasonable amount of time. Now, however, Kliger was telling the media a different story, claiming that John had still been working on a business plan and that their last meeting had ended on a positive note.

On Monday morning, July 19, Kliger organized a meeting for *George* editors in the forty-first-floor conference room, where they often held editorial meetings. Kliger arrived with a retinue of about a dozen people who filled most of the chairs around the table. "You had crying and pregnant people forced to stand around the outside of this room because his people came in and took the seats," recalled Sasha Issenberg. "It was just the first indication that this outreach was not infused with compassion."

George editors present in the room described Kliger's presentation as "cold" and "businesslike." RoseMarie claimed that Kliger "addressed John's death with all the sensitivity of a serial killer." Such assessments, however, were too harsh. *George* editors wished to commiserate and share their grief; Kliger convened the meeting to provide a clear assessment of where the magazine stood. He bluntly told them that he could not give specific answers about the magazine's future. "I wish I could tell you, but we just don't know. This is a business, and for now, we have to keep going." One big unknown was what Caroline planned to do with the 50 percent share of the magazine that she had inherited from John.

John's death complicated Hachette's plan to pull out of *George*. According to Kliger, on the same day that he met with *George* editors he received a call from Jean-Luc Lagardère, the CEO of the French conglomerates that owned Hachette. "Look, Jack," he stated, "I am not just the head of Lagardère. I am a citizen of the world, and I am not going to be the man who shut down John Kennedy's magazine. You will continue to publish it for at least a year."

Oddly enough, John's death inspired new interest in *George*, producing a brief glimmer of hope that the magazine might have a life post-John. The July issue sold 493,000 copies; August, 582,000; September, 625,000; and an October memorial issue sold an estimated 707,000. Hachette decided that with some marketing changes, it could salvage the magazine. In September, it purchased Caroline's 50 percent interest. She had no desire to be involved in the magazine business and never really approved of John's being in it, either. The purchase marked an unusual turn of events. On the day before John died, Hachette had been prepared to pull the plug on *George*. Now, less than two months later, it bought out his share and owned the magazine outright.

Hachette started interviewing potential candidates to assume John's role as editor in chief. Rich Blow, who filled the role until someone new took over, recommended Al Franken, a comedian who made a name for himself on *Saturday Night Live* and had also written a bestselling, highly critical book about right-wing radio host Rush Limbaugh. Franken expressed interest in the position and sat down with Kliger and Jean-Louis Ginibre, the head of editorial for Hachette's publications. Franken talked about giving the magazine more of a comic flair. Then Jean-Louis, who spoke with a thick French accent, talked for a few minutes. When Jean-Louis finished, Franken responded, "Monsieur Ginibre, I don't understand." Surprised, Ginibre asked, "What don't you understand?" Franken, with perfect comedic timing, said, "I don't understand one word you just said." Ginibre did not appreciate Franken's humor and ended the meeting abruptly.

In late November, Kliger named Frank Lalli, who had previously served as managing editor of *Money* magazine, as the new editor in chief of *George*. He proved an uninspiring leader, but it was unclear if anyone could have saved the magazine. *George* struggled through eighteen more months before being shuttered in March 2001. There had been "a softening of the advertising market," Kliger said in announcing the decision. "The likelihood that *George*'s prospects will improve in this environment has become remote."

However, the demise of the magazine should not detract from its significance. When they developed the idea for *George* in 1994, Michael Berman and John understood the importance of the convergence between culture and politics. John, in particular, saw the trend as a positive development that could motivate apathetic citizens, humanize politicians, and engender a postpartisan future. But John failed to appreciate the seismic political shift pushing American politics in a much different direction and underestimated how culture could also be used as a political weapon to demean public figures and accentuate partisanship. While *George* never truly succeeded, it was indeed prescient.

News of John's death sparked an eruption of grief and nostalgia. In New York, where John sightings had been common, strangers shared stories of their encounters with John—picking up bagels at the market, walking on the street, playing in Central Park. Newspapers published numerous on-the-street interviews with people who praised John for being unfailingly polite and respectful. Mourners turned John's North Moore Street apartment into a makeshift memorial, bedecked with flower bouquets, candles, and handwritten notes. John would have been appalled at these expressions of sorrow, but he would have chuckled at one note left on his steps. "Thanks for the inspiration, from someone who also passed the bar on the third try."

Television provided saturation coverage from Saturday morning, when it was first learned that John's plane had gone missing, until Friday afternoon following the memorial service. Between Saturday morning and the funeral on Friday, television news magazines—*20/20, 48 Hours, Dateline, Primetime*—devoted forty-seven prime-time segments to the story, representing 66 percent of all stories. The three morning shows—*This Morning* (CBS), *Today* (NBC), and *Good Morning America* (ABC)—aired 224 stories, beginning with the search and ending with the funeral, making it the most intensely covered topic that year. Newspapers and magazines followed suit. Polls showed that four out of five Americans followed the coverage of John's death and funeral. Women were more interested than men. Not surprisingly, those over the age of sixty—the ones who remembered John's famous salute—showed the greatest interest.

Looking back at the coverage two decades later, it is clear that editors and producers desperately searched for a new angle on John's life but ended up returning to the same themes. An older generation recalled John's salute and reflected on the enormous grief the Kennedy family had repeatedly endured. "Not this family. Not again," declared NBC's Tom Brokaw. "He was the prince for all of us," proclaimed ABC News anchor Sam Donaldson. The *New York Post* headline read "More Tears." Most commentators and writers highlighted the connection between John's death and his father's assassination. "Even now, no words prompt so much anguish, so much grief, so much disbelief as these: John F. Kennedy is dead," observed *The Boston Globe.* "Those words flew around the country yesterday in frantic electronic pulses, though this time it was not news of the death of a president but of his son." Inevitably, commentators noted the many tragedies that had befallen the family and speculated about a "Kennedy curse."

The rest of the world also mourned John's passing. In Brazil, television networks preempted soccer to provide coverage of the search for his body. The British mass-circulation tabloid *The Sun* described John's death as "an utter tragedy." The French *Le Figaro* described him as "the symbol of a lost Romanticism." *The Sydney Morning Herald* wrote that John "had yet to make his definitive mark," but "when he did, it would be a mark etched into the core of the nation's destiny." The editors of *The Philippine Star* observed, "This is not the way fairy tales are supposed to end."

Commentators and editorial writers both at home and abroad struggled to explain why John meant so much to the nation and why he deserved such nonstop coverage. In trying to answer that question many overreached, assigning John a significance that he did not deserve. "The news that John F. Kennedy Jr., Carolyn Bessette Kennedy and Lauren Bessette are missing at sea and presumed dead has struck such a crippling blow to my generation," the historian Douglas Brinkley wrote in *The New York Times*. A CNN commentator described John as "the moral leader for the next generation of young Americans." None of these estimations were true. John was not—nor did he ever strive to be—a "moral leader," and it was simply silly to characterize his death as a "crippling blow" to any generation.

The Clinton administration, which took the unprecedented step of ordering the coast guard to spend days searching for the bodies and then enlisted a navy destroyer for the burial at sea, struggled with a similar question. Why should coast guard and navy resources, along with taxpayer money, be spent looking for someone who never served in the armed forces? The government estimated that the recovery operations cost the coast guard and the navy an astonishing $1.2 million.

A handful of people criticized these decisions. They pointed out how uncommon it was for the coast guard to conduct such an extensive, five-day search to find a downed plane, remove the bodies, and then send a navy ship for the sea burial. "Who was Mr. Kennedy that he should rate a U.S. Coast Guard Cutter and a U.S. Navy destroyer to be buried at sea?" a Louisiana resident wrote Senator John Breaux. "He never served in the armed forces, nor did his wife or sister-in-law. A veteran of the armed forces would not have the same offer to his or her family if they wish to be buried at sea. It must be nice to be a Kennedy and have the whole nation bow at your feet." In a similar vein, a Texas resident told his congressman, "It is beyond my comprehension how our government could spend literally millions of tax dollars to find the bodies of private citizens."

These observers had a point. Every year the navy buried five hundred service members at sea, but at Portsmouth, one of five navy sites that handled the remains of individuals who qualified for such rites, the waiting time stretched to six months. Furthermore, no special provision existed to have these service members buried individually. Instead they were buried en masse, with their ashes scattered during normal military operations. Family members were not permitted on board and instead were sent a videotape, along with the flag and a letter from the ship's captain. "I can't square how Kennedy, who never served, got special privileges," thundered the highly decorated colonel David H. Hackworth. "It's a national disgrace."

Compounding this political problem, John's burial happened while the military had cut back its participation in veterans' funerals. The military claimed that it could no longer afford to provide a military detail, such as two soldiers present to fold the American flag and a third to play "Taps" on the bugle.

But for Clinton, who maintained a close relationship with the Kennedy family and had entertained John recently at the White House, the decision was easy. Clinton recalled in a 2019 interview that the coast guard would usually search for people missing at sea for twenty-four hours. They would then call off the search if no one was found. But Clinton remembered that when the coast guard asked him if they should call off the search, he said no. "I think that he's a good man," he recalled saying to the guard, "and he and his wife and sister-in-law deserve to be found and his family is important to this country. We have to keep going. Just stay out there, you'll find them." When the guard raised objections about continuing the search, Clinton responded, "You have to. We have to! We owe this to his family and to the country."

At the time, however, Clinton struggled to justify his decision. Initially, the administration claimed there was nothing unusual about either the search or the burial. The US Coast Guard, the White House said, "places a high value on each and every human life," describing the effort as "a fairly typical response." In response to questions about using a navy ship for the burial, the White House issued a broad and unconvincing press release saying the navy could perform a burial of US citizens "who are determined eligible by the Chief of Naval Operations due to notable service or outstanding contributions to the United States." The White House highlighted John's work with Reaching Up and the Profile in Courage Award as his "notable service." However, it remained hard to believe that someone who wasn't a

Kennedy would have received a burial at sea had their only claim to success been involvement in these programs. The White House did acknowledge that John was also the son of a president and World War II navy hero.

But not even the White House officials charged with explaining such decisions to the public found them credible. In a private White House conversation, Press Secretary Joe Lockhart confessed his reluctance to hold press conferences because he worried that "people might say, 'Why do you have so many resources out there? Would you do this for the average Joe Smith?'" Lockhart admitted that he did not "know how to respond to that. This phase of the search is something the coast guard does not do normally." Later Thurgood Marshall Jr., who served as the liaison between the White House and the coast guard and navy, added, "This is not the type of investigation that the NTSB has normally done. Everything, as far as we're concerned, is extraordinary."

Why did the nation have such an emotional investment in John? What does his death tell us about our own hopes and longings? Most of all, we felt an emotional connection with him because we watched him grow up. Photographers documented the key milestones in his life, from his birth, to his graduation from Brown, to his struggles with the bar exam, and to his marriage to Carolyn Bessette. Even people who never met him knew who he was. Based on my own observations, I believe that attitudes toward John varied by generation. Older Americans, both men and women, who remembered his father and John's tragic salute, viewed him with a degree of reverence. It was as if they were observing a living historical artifact and, if they approached him, they would immediately tell him how much they loved his father and mother. Meanwhile, a younger generation, especially women, treated John like a rock star. They likely knew him more as "the sexiest man alive" than as the son of a slain president. In the end, however, something about John appealed to everyone. He was rich, handsome, and charismatic. He displayed many of the personal qualities that parents hoped their children would come to possess. Even his struggles with the bar exam helped humanize him.

The older generation felt his loss the greatest. From the moment on his third birthday when he raised his right hand to salute JFK, John became a living memorial to his slain father's legacy. Deep down, many older Americans dreamed of a resurrection, hoping that John would return to the White House and that Camelot would live again. When his plane crashed, both a literal and metaphorical death occurred: the tragic loss of a promising young man and two innocent bystanders, as well as the end of a fantasy that would remain forever unfulfilled.

John's death occurred at a critical moment in his life, when he for the first time began openly discussing his plans to enter politics. Thus, many people were left with the same sense of unfulfilled expectations that followed his father's assassination. What if John had lived? Could he have rekindled the sense of idealism that defined the sixties? It's impossible to know what the future held for John. I prefer to remember him for the life that he lived and not for what might have been. He certainly would have been shocked by the state of contemporary politics. John treasured civility, and he admired leaders, whether Republican Ronald Reagan or Democrat Bill Clinton, who offered the nation a hopeful vision of the future. He disdained demagogues who tapped into the dark aspects of the American character.

What constituted John's greatest achievement? *George* was certainly ahead of its time, but its fate remained uncertain when John took flight on July 16, 1999. Reaching Up trailblazed an innovative approach to improving health care by providing the opportunity for caregivers to earn a college degree and qualify for better jobs in the field. While John focused on helping workers who cared for the mentally disadvantaged, his approach has spread to many other fields. That influence alone represents a notable accomplishment.

But John's greatest success was personal. His parents' generation made its mark in the public arena: running for office, passing important legislation, fighting for civil rights, and standing firm against the spread of Communism. John's greatest achievements unfolded in private, in his ability to carve out a healthy identity in the face of enormous public expectations. John lived his life burdened by a myth, but he never allowed that myth to define him or dictate the choices he made.

I am honored to have called him my friend. My heart ached the day he died. It aches still.

ACKNOWLEDGMENTS

This book would not be possible were it not for the help and guidance of many colleagues, archivists, and research assistants. My thanks to archivists at the John F. Kennedy and Lyndon B. Johnson Presidential Libraries for identifying relevant materials in their collections, and to the staff of the William J. Clinton Presidential Library who processed my Freedom of Information Act (FOIA) request in record time and opened nearly thirteen thousand pages of documents. Attorney Scott Hodes skillfully handled my lawsuit against the Department of Homeland Security, negotiating a settlement that produced thousands of documents. My agent, Steve Troha, skillfully guided the project from start to finish. Research assistant Eric England tracked down sources, while Scott Russell helped with research at the Ronald Reagan and Richard Nixon Presidential Libraries. The Ryan brothers, Will and Sam, reviewed dozens of hours of audio and visual materials. My sister Karen Laverack adeptly transcribed the many hours of interviews. I owe a special debt to Andrina Tran (PhD, Yale University), who read every word of the draft manuscript, made extensive comments, and offered numerous suggestions for revisions. She made this a better book.

I have been fortunate to have mentors who have entered my life at key moments, offering their guidance, encouragement, and support. As an undergraduate at Widener College, Dr. Lawrence Buck saw potential in me that I did not know existed. In graduate school at Brown University, I was fortunate to study under James T. Patterson, who taught me—with limited success—how to think like a historian. No one has done more to enrich my life than Abbe Raven, who took me under her wing at History and offered opportunities that I never imagined would be available to me.

A number of people encouraged me to write this book. RoseMarie Terenzio has been a source of unfailing support. I still remember the evening over dinner when she implored me to take on this project. "If John knew he would be dead at the age of thirty-eight he would want someone to write a book about him," she said. "And he would want you to write it." Nick Davatzes, the CEO emeritus of A&E television networks, has supported my career for the past two decades, offering sound advice along the way. I value his friendship and his counsel. Rob Sharenow, president of programming at A&E Networks, commissioned a documentary based on the book. I am grateful to the production team at Left/Right, especially John Marks and Molly Raskin, for turning the words on these pages into a compelling documentary. They were also able to secure an interview with former president Bill Clinton. I am grateful to many of John's friends, including those who have never spoken before, who trusted me to tell their stories.

At Dutton, my thanks to my talented editor, Jill Schwartzman, for providing me with the opportunity to write this book, and to all the members of Team Dutton: Christine Ball, John Parsley, Amanda Walker, Maria Whelan, Carrie Swetonic, Kayleigh George, Susan Schwartz, Linda Rosenberg, Alice Dalrymple, and Marya Pasciuto.

I could not have written this book without the love of my family and the support of my many friends. My siblings: Fran, Mike, and "little" sister, Karen, have always been supportive and caring. My dear friends, especially Jim and Kate Ryan, Robert and Debbie Raines, Ken Orkin and Sondra Baker, Gary Ginsberg and Susanna Aaron, Ross Baker, Sam Stoia, Maged Shenouda, David Courier and Charlie Mustachia, Bill Miller, and Bill Rindfuss—and so many others—have provided moral support and, on rare occasions, even laughed at my jokes. My spouse, Vantuir L. Borges, stood by my side for the entire process offering gentle encouragement and much-needed affection.

Nearly three decades ago, I dedicated my first book to my parents, Frank and June Gillon, and now I have the privilege to do the same today. My love for them has only grown over the years.

SOURCE NOTES

MANUSCRIPTS

John F. Kennedy Presidential Library
Rose F. Kennedy Personal Papers
David Powers
Jacqueline Kennedy
Walter Heller

Lyndon Baines Johnson Presidential Library
John F. Kennedy Jr.
Lyndon B. Johnson Papers

Richard M. Nixon Presidential Library and Museum
Richard Nixon Presidential Materials
Daily Diary

Ronald Reagan Presidential Library
Speechwriting Office

William J. Clinton Presidential Library
John F. Kennedy Jr. (FOIA 2017-0713-f)

Brown University Archives
Howard Swearer
The Brown Daily Herald

Wesleyan University Special Collections and Archives
William Manchester

National Archives (JFK Assassination Records)
J. Lee Rankin

Bodleian Library, Oxford University
Harold Macmillan

Department of Homeland Security (*Gillon v. Department of Homeland Security*)
United States Secret Service
Federal Bureau of Investigation

PRIVATE COLLECTIONS

Michael Berman
Sasha Chermayeff
Steve Gillon

Charlie King
Elizabeth "Biz" Mitchell
RoseMarie Terenzio

INTERVIEWS

Joe Armstrong
Julie Baker
Jim Barnhill
Paul Begala
Matt Berman
Michael Berman
Bruce Breimer
Linda Thomas Brooks
Michael Browner
Elinore Carmody
Phineas Chermayeff
Sasha Chermayeff
President William J. Clinton
Robert Curran
Patti Solis Doyle
Bill Ebenstein
John Emigh
Gary Ginsberg
Mary Gluck
Richard Gray Jr.
Nancy Haberman
Clint Hill
Stephen Hill
Sasha Issenberg
Kenneth Robert Jones II
Charlie King
Jack Kliger
Peter Leifer
Hugo Lindgren

Nina Link
Victor Malafronte
Pat Manocchia
Ned Martel
Elizabeth "Biz" Mitchell
Charles Neu
Gustavo Paredes
David Pecker
Carole Radziwill
Tina Radziwill
Dennis Rivera
James Rogers
Ben Ryan
Jeffrey Sachs
Dan Samson
Lawrence Schwartzwald
Michael Sheehan
Robert Shrum
Brian Steel
Keith Stein
Cheryl Stieffel
Sam Stoia
RoseMarie Terenzio
Barbara Vaughn
Michael Voss
Thomas Wells
Richard Wiese
Don Wilmeth

ORAL HISTORIES

John F. Kennedy Presidential Library
Lawrence Arata
Laura Bergquist
Preston Bruce
Christine Camp
William F. Connors
Joseph J. Karitas
Katherine "Kay" Murphy Halle
Maud Shaw
Stanley Tretick

Lyndon Baines Johnson Presidential Library
Cecil Stoughton

NOTES

CHAPTER 1: "I WAS PROUD OF THE LITTLE GUY"

9 **"as a precautionary measure"**: Clint Hill, *Mrs. Kennedy and Me* (New York: Gallery, 2012), 20–21.

9 **had Seiler not intervened**: Dean R. Owen, *November 22, 1963: Reflections on the Life, Assassination, and Legacy of John F. Kennedy* (New York: Skyhorse, 2013), 339–41.

10 **gives up and stops breathing**: The description of the ailment comes from "Infant Respiratory Distress Syndrome (Hyaline Membrane Disease)," Boston Children's Hospital online, accessed September 10, 2018, www.childrenshospital.org.

10 **"was in doubt"**: "Nancy Tuckerman Called with the Following Information from Mrs. Onassis," Rose Fitzgerald Kennedy Personal Papers, series 3, box 55, John F. Kennedy Presidential Library (cited hereafter as JFKPL), Boston.

11 **"a new administration and a new baby"**: Sally Bedell Smith, *Grace and Power: The Private World of the Kennedy White House* (New York: Random House, 2004), 5.

12 **crippling back condition**: Robert Dallek, *An Unfinished Life: John F. Kennedy, 1917–1963* (New York: Little, Brown, 2003), 193.

13 **Caroline in November 1957**: Ibid., 193–94.

15 **"natural language of politics"**: Mary Ann Watson, *The Expanding Vista: American Television in the Kennedy Years* (New York: Oxford University Press, 1990), 8.

15 **separate press plane**: Hill, *Mrs. Kennedy and Me*, 19–20; "Nancy Tuckerman Called," Rose Fitzgerald Kennedy Personal Papers, series 3, box 55, JFKPL. Rose was writing her memoir and asked Jackie about John's birth. Tuckerman relayed her response to Rose.

15 **Walsh arrived five minutes later**: W. H. Lawrence, "Kennedy Alters Schedule to Stay Close to New Son," *The New York Times*, November 26, 1960.

16 **Salinger's reply is not recorded**: "Powers interview," David F. Powers Personal Papers, series 3, box 9, JFKPL; "Delighted Father," Powers Papers, n.d., series 5, box 17, JFKPL; W. L. Beale Jr. to Pierre Salinger, November 29, 1960, JFKCAMP1960-1047-015, JFKPL.

16 **"Why, it's John F. Kennedy Jr."**: Merriman Smith, "President-Elect Proud of Son to Be Named John F. Kennedy Jr.," UPI, November 25, 1960.

17 **"because she was so jealous of John"**: Maud Shaw, Oral History Interview, JFK #1, April 27, 1965, JFKPL.

17 **gave him an autograph**: Lawrence, "Kennedy Alters Schedule to Stay Close to New Son."

17 **removed John from the incubator**: "John Kennedy Jr. Pays First Visit to Mother," *The New York Times*, December 4, 1960.

17 **"People were fascinated by her"**: Hill, *Mrs. Kennedy and Me*, 29–30.

18 **"I think John suffered a great handicap":** Maud Shaw, *White House Nannie: My Years with Caroline and John Kennedy, Jr.* (New York: New American Library, 1965), 97–98.

18 **"I didn't come to meals":** Laurence Leamer, *The Kennedy Women: The Saga of an American Family* (Villard: New York, 1994), 515.

18 **Jackie desperately needed rest:** Richard Reeves, *President Kennedy: Profile of Power* (New York: Touchstone, 1994), 146–47; Susan Sheehan, "The Happy Jackie, the Sad Jackie, the Bad Jackie, the Good Jackie," *The New York Times*, May 31, 1970; Hill, *Mrs. Kennedy and Me*, 16; Leamer, *The Kennedy Women*, 515.

18 **from the Georgetown home:** Hill, *Mrs. Kennedy and Me*, 82–83; "Description of Children's Rooms," February 3, 1961, Jacqueline Kennedy Papers, series 1.1.2, Pamela Turnure Files, box 25, JFKPL; Shaw, *White House Nannie*, 82–83.

19 **smearing some peanut butter:** J. B. West, with Mary Lynn Kotz, *Upstairs at the White House: My Life with the First Ladies* (New York: Open Road, 2016), 201–2; Traphes L. Bryant, Oral History Interview, JFK #1, May 13, 1964, 2–3, 9–10, JFKPL.

19 **growing up at 1600 Pennsylvania Avenue:** Shaw, *White House Nannie*, 40–46.

20 **"moat with crocodiles":** Leamer, *The Kennedy Women*, 512–13; Letitia Baldrige, *A Lady, First: My Life in the Kennedy White House and the American Embassies of Paris and Rome* (New York: Viking, 2001), 177; Barbara Leaming, *Mrs. Kennedy: The Missing History of the Kennedy Years* (New York: Free Press, 2001), 20–21; Dallek, *An Unfinished Life*, 473–74; West with Kotz, *Upstairs at the White House*, 205.

20 **"rented Glen Ora or built Wexford":** West with Kotz, *Upstairs at the White House*, 212–13, 265–66.

20 **a stinging memo:** Pierre Salinger, *With Kennedy* (New York: Doubleday, 1966), 84.

20 **avid reader of gossip magazines:** Hill, *Mrs. Kennedy and Me*, 206.

21 **"rapidly expanding":** Memo, February 3, 1961; "Pam's Briefings, JFK, Jr.," May 1, 1961; "John F. Kennedy, Jr.," August 25, 1961, October 17, 1961, November 21, 1961, November 15, 1962, Jacqueline Kennedy Papers, series 1.1.2, Pamela Turnure Files, box 25, JFKPL.

21 **"the White House's most popular attraction":** "The Latest on J.F.K.," *New York Herald Tribune*, October 20, 1961; Don Shannon, "Caroline Captures 'Top Billing,'" *Los Angeles Times*, April 15, 1961.

21 **protect Caroline's privacy:** Thomas J. Walsh to Mrs. John F. Kennedy, October 23, 1962; "Dear Tom," October 26, 1962, Jacqueline Kennedy Papers, series 1.1.2, Pamela Turnure Files, box 25, JFKPL.

22 **better-educated reader:** Kate Anderson Brower, *First Women: The Grace and Power of America's Modern First Ladies* (New York: HarperCollins, 2016), 108.

22 **"in no uncertain terms":** Baldrige, *A Lady, First*, 179–80.

22 **"charm and charisma of President Kennedy":** Amanda Hopkinson, "Cecil Stoughton" obituary, *The Guardian*, November 19, 2008.

23 **"to be called Camelot":** Margalit Fox, "Cecil Stoughton Dies at 88; Documented White House," *The New York Times*, November 6, 2008; Cecil Stoughton, Oral History Interview, Lyndon Baines Johnson Presidential Library (cited hereafter as LBJPL), Austin, TX; Cecil Stoughton and Chester V. Clifton, *The Memories: JFK 1961–63* (New York: W. W. Norton, 1973), 135–37, 153.

24 **"an absolute rule of divine right":** Christine Camp, Oral History Interview, JFK #2, January 14, 1966, 78, JFKPL.

24 **The bushes stayed:** Shannon, "Caroline Captures 'Top Billing.'" The president was not the only one who complained. The Secret Service was also upset. "How the hell do you expect us to guard this place if we can't see who's climbing over the fence?" an agent complained. In response, the police stationed another man at the gate and electrified the fence. But that did not work because the alarm went off every time a bird flew over. Eventually they installed ground lights among the bushes. West with Kotz, *Upstairs at the White House*, 205.

24 "an order from the president": Shaw, *White House Nannie*, 131–32.

24 Kennedy's hotel room: Dirck Halstead, "A Tribute to Stanley Tretick," *The Digital Journalist*, 1999.

25 plum Washington assignment: Ibid.

25 "The president loves those pictures": Stanley Tretick, Oral History Interview, JFK #1, September 15, 1964, 21–28, 32–34, JFKPL.

26 "near my children again": Jackie Kennedy, "Memo for Pierre Salinger," August 6, 1963, Jacqueline Kennedy Papers, series 1.1.4, Nancy Tuckerman File SF93, JFKPL.

26 "I didn't say that, but it might be a good idea": Tretick, Oral History, 37–42, 44–45.

26 "kind of sticky": Ibid., 45.

26 "'can you, Stan?'": Ibid., 47.

27 "wets his pants": Evelyn Lincoln, *My Twelve Years with John F. Kennedy* (New York: David McKay, 1965), 357; Benjamin C. Bradlee, *Conversations with Kennedy* (New York: W. W. Norton, 1975), 159–61, 168–69.

27 under the furniture: Kay (Katherine Murphy) Halle, Oral History Interview, JFK #1, February 7, 1967, 19, JFKPL; Stoughton and Clifton, *Memories*, 137.

28 traveled to Dallas: Laura Bergquist Knebel, Oral History Interview, JFK #2, August 1, and 11, 1977, JFKPL.

29 "a trio of uncles": Shaw, *White House Nannie*, 109–10; Hill, *Mrs. Kennedy and Me*, 113.

30 enjoy such a luxury: Hill, *Mrs. Kennedy and Me*, 33–34.

30 see the Secret Service as more intrusive: Clint Hill, interview by author, December 9, 2017.

31 "follow on foot": James Jeffries to Chief U. E. Baughman, "Protective Procedures Being Used and Recommended for Mrs. Jacqueline Kennedy and Children," February 16, 1961, *Gillon v. Department of Homeland Security*, Civil Action No. 17-cv-02529-APM. All references to Secret Service material, unless indicated otherwise, came from files Homeland Security provided in response to my lawsuit.

32 "have a special agent, of the service, in a bathing suit": Lynn Meredith to Chief U. E. Baughman, "Swimming Pool Incident Concerning Caroline Kennedy," July 6, 1962.

32 "protect her children from kidnapping": James Jeffries to Chief U. E. Baughman, "Protection of Mrs. Kennedy's Children, While at the Beach or in a Swimming Pool," July 11, 1961.

33 agents did not clear a path: Lynn Meredith to Gerald A. Behn, n.d.

33 rational heads prevailed: Hill, *Mrs. Kennedy and Me*, 193.

34 "an often confusing world": Jim Mathis to Pamela Turnure, May 7, 1963, Jacqueline Kennedy Papers, series 1.1.2, Pamela Turnure Files, box 25, JFKPL.

34 "children's hour": West with Kotz, *Upstairs at the White House*, 204.

34 lifelong habit of bowing: Baldrige, *A Lady, First*, 179–81.

35 "children tumbling around him": Jacqueline Kennedy, *Historic Conversations on Life with John F. Kennedy* (New York: Hyperion, 2011), 157, 333–34.

35 rabbits and guinea pigs: Shaw, *White House Nannie*, 89–91; Shaw, Oral History, 8, JFKPL; West with Kotz, *Upstairs at the White House*, 202.

35 "Canon! Canon!": Preston Bruce, Oral History Interview, JFK #1, June 16, 1964, JFKPL; Joseph J. Karitas, Oral History Interview, JFK #1, June 23, 1964, 7–10, 98–99, JFKPL; Lawrence J. Arata, Oral History Interview, JFK #1, 1964, 1–3, JFKPL.

36 "He will grow another one": Thomas Wells, interview by author, December 9, 2017.

36 "all with gusto": Memo on Children's Activities, Jacqueline Kennedy Papers, series 1.1.2, Pamela Turnure Files, box 25, JFKPL.

36 children tucked into bed: Shaw, *White House Nannie*, 103–4; Bruce, Oral History, JFKPL; Karitas, Oral History, JFKPL; Arata, Oral History, JFKPL; Wells, interview.

37 unlimited Coke: Shaw, *White House Nannie*, 135–37, 140.

37 "I'm John F. Kennedy Jr.": Ibid., 112.

37 bought the ducks: Brower, *First Women*, 101, 105–6.

38 a cookie and ginger ale: Shaw, *White House Nannie*, 149–50.

38 **the meaning of death:** Ibid., 158.

39 **"an even greater preoccupation":** Hill, *Mrs. Kennedy and Me*, 248–49; Hill, interview; Edward M. Kennedy, *True Compass: A Memoir* (New York: Twelve, 2009), 199–200.

39 **"the nurse's technique":** Walter Heller, "Confidential Notes on Breakfast Briefing Session with the President," Wednesday, October 9, 1963, Walter W. Heller Personal Papers, series 3, box 6, JFKPL.

39 **John's concoction:** Heller, "Notes on a Quick Meeting with the President and Other Leading Members of the Kennedy Family," November 19, 1963, Heller Papers, series 3, box 6, JFKPL.

40 **"always very proud of him":** Shaw, Oral History, 7–8, JFKPL.

40 **It just so happened that his father was in the way:** Wells, interview.

40 **"a torrent of tears":** Shaw, Oral History, 7, JFKPL.

40 **"could barely sit still":** Hill, *Mrs. Kennedy and Me*, 155.

41 **"Daddy's hebrecop":** Ibid.; Stoughton and Clifton, *Memories*.

41 **mimicking the sound of the helicopter:** Shaw, *White House Nannie*, 145–46.

41 **"he is going to be a pilot":** Hill, *Mrs. Kennedy and Me*, 251–52; Hill, interview.

41 **"What are all those flags?":** Baldrige, *A Lady, First*, 181–82; Hill, *Mrs. Kennedy and Me*, 190–91.

42 **"use his left hand":** Hill, interview.

42 **"right-hand salute":** William F. Connors, Oral History Interview, JFK #1, April 15, 1964, JFKPL.

42 **"proud of the little guy":** Hill, *Mrs. Kennedy and Me*, 267–68.

CHAPTER 2: "PLEASE, MAY I HAVE ONE FOR DADDY?"

43 **occupied with toy planes:** William Manchester, *The Death of a President* (New York: Harper & Row, 1967), 56–58.

44 **bill banning segregation:** The account of the assassination draws on my book *The Kennedy Assassination* (New York: Basic Books, 2009).

44 **Air Force One lifted into the clouds:** Manchester, *Death of a President*, 63–64; Gerald Blaine, *The Kennedy Detail* (New York: Gallery, 2010), 158.

44 **"Just in time for your birthday":** Blaine, *Kennedy Detail*, 210–11.

45 **usually Jackie's mother:** Manchester, *Death of a President*, 90.

45 **six, on Wednesday:** Shaw, *White House Nannie*, 8–9.

45 **"she looks better than we do when she does it":** Tom Wicker, "Kennedy Is Killed by Sniper as He Rides in Car in Dallas; Johnson Sworn in on Plane," *The New York Times*, November 23, 1963.

46 **matching pillbox hat:** David Powers notes, William Manchester Papers, Wesleyan University Special Collections and Archives (WM-WU), Middletown, CT.

46 **"cool in the tunnel":** Theodore White notes, December 19, 1963, WM-WU.

46 **"They've killed my husband!":** Mimi Swartz, "The Witness," *Texas Monthly*, November 2003, 114. The detail about Mrs. Kennedy saying, "I have his brains in my hand," was omitted from the official Warren Commission report but can be found in earlier drafts. See J. Lee Rankin Papers, box 19, JFK Assassination Records, National Archives, College Park, MD.

47 **signaled thumbs-down:** Paul Landis, November 30, 1963, Warren Commission, vol. 18, exhibit 1024, 755.

47 **"wanted you and John to be home":** Blaine, *Kennedy Detail*, 234–36.

48 **"I'll call you back as soon as I hear how it is":** Ibid., 210–11.

48 **"shock that now lay in store for them":** Shaw, *White House Nannie*, 10–11.

48 **More than 90 percent:** Thomas J. Banta, "The Kennedy Assassination: Early Thoughts and Emotions," *Public Opinion Quarterly* 28, no. 2 (Summer 1964): 216–24; Bradley S. Greenberg, "Diffusion of News of the Kennedy Assassination," *Public Opinion Quarterly* 28, no. 2 (Summer 1964): 225–32.

49 **"a ghost town"**: Wicker, "Kennedy Is Killed by Sniper."

50 **"Here they come!"**: Bradlee, *Conversations with Kennedy*, 75–76.

51 **stayed with their grandparents**: Hill, *Mrs. Kennedy and Me*, 298.

51 **"I was shattered by the thought"**: Shaw, *White House Nannie*, 11–12.

51 **It had absolutely no impact**: Manchester, *Death of a President*, 415–16.

52 **"put them to bed"**: Janet Lee Bouvier Auchincloss, Oral History Interview, JFK #2, September 6, 1964, 32, JFKPL.

52 **"Put your coat on"**: Shaw, *White House Nannie*, 15–17; Manchester, *Death of a President*, 407.

52 **second-floor bedrooms**: Wicker, "Kennedy Is Killed by Sniper"; Wendy Leigh, *Prince Charming: The John F. Kennedy Jr. Story* (New York: Dutton, 1993), 71.

53 **buried her face in the pillow**: Manchester, *Death of a President*, 208–9; Shaw, *White House Nannie*, 18–20.

54 **"The rest of us followed"**: Arthur M. Schlesinger Jr., *Journals: 1952–2000* (New York: Penguin, 2007), 203–6.

54 **closed-coffin ceremony**: Ibid.

56 **"A man shot him, didn't he?"**: Bouvier Auchincloss, Oral History Interview.

56 **too big for his coffin**: Arthur M. Schlesinger Jr., *Robert Kennedy and His Times* (New York: Houghton Mifflin, 1978), 611.

56 **knelt in front of the casket and prayed**: Leigh, *Prince Charming*, 74–75.

56 **"on the verge of fainting"**: Smith, *Grace and Power*, 444–45; Shaw, *White House Nannie*, 20–21; Mary Barelli Gallagher, *My Life with Jacqueline Kennedy* (New York: David McKay, 1969), 332.

57 **"When is he coming back?" Manchester**, *Death of a President*, **464–65.**

57 **"His jaw flew open"**: Leigh, *Prince Charming*, 74–75.

57 **"it will be a great help"**: Shaw, *White House Nannie*, 20–21.

57 **"I don't have anyone to play with"**: John H. Averill, "Grieving Mrs. Kennedy, Children in Seclusion," *Los Angeles Times*, November 24, 1963.

58 **the flag-draped coffin**: Schlesinger Jr., *Robert Kennedy*, 611.

59 **"Please, may I have one for Daddy?"**: Shaw, *White House Nannie*, 22–23; Manchester, *Death of a President*, 540–41; Marjorie Hunter, "Mrs. Kennedy Leads Public Mourning," *The New York Times*, November 25, 1963.

60 **grasping his church booklet**: Shaw, Oral History, 13, JFKPL; Blaine, *Kennedy Detail*, 295.

60 **"the toughest men I knew"**: Manchester, *Death of a President*, 590; Tom Wicker, "A Hero's Burial," *The New York Times*, November 26, 1963.

61 **"I'm glad they are happy"**: Shaw, *White House Nannie*, 26; Smith, *Grace and Power*, 455–56; John H. Davis, *The Kennedys: Dynasty and Disaster, 1848–1983* (New York: McGraw-Hill, 1984), 450; Manchester, *Death of a President*, 617–18.

63 **"It's uncomfortable for me"**: Michael Berman, interview by author, July 2, 2018.

63 **"I have a new airplane!"**: Steven M. Gillon, *The Kennedy Assassination—24 Hours After: Lyndon B. Johnson's First Pivotal Day as President* (New York: Basic Books, 2009), 217; Gallagher, *Life with Jacqueline Kennedy*, 336–37.

64 **three flights of stairs**: Shaw, *White House Nannie*, 164.

64 **"don't have time to think"**: Thomas Maier, *The Kennedys: America's Emerald Kings* (New York: Basic Books, 2003), 468–73; Gallagher, *Life with Jacqueline Kennedy*, 340; Jackie to Prime Minister, January 31, 1964, Harold Macmillan Papers, General Correspondence, Bodleian Library, Oxford (cited hereafter as HMP-BL); Caryle Murphy, "Jackie Kennedy's Spiritual Crisis," *The Washington Post*, November 13, 2003.

65 **"That's where we used to live, Caroline"**: Shaw, *White House Nannie*, 165, 178–79.

66 **Lincoln was too overcome**: Leigh, *Prince Charming*, 84.

66 **the president's favorite dish**: Ibid., 66.

66 **security room in the main garage**: Gerald A. Behn, "Survey Report," February 3, 1964; *Gillon v. Homeland Security*, No. 17-cv-02529-APM.

66 **"the grown-ups temporarily forgot the grief"**: Shaw, *White House Nannie*, 166.

67 **"drown my sorrows in vodka"**: Gallagher, *Life with Jacqueline Kennedy*, 344, 349–50.

67 **"scrambles with his uncle"**: Ibid., 350; Ellen Key Blunt, "School Bells Will Ring for John-John," *The Washington Post*, May 22, 1964.

67 **"Caroline doesn't let people get close to her"**: Leigh, *Prince Charming*, 88–89.

67 **his cousins Kerry and Michael**: Ibid., 88–89.

68 **"fully aware of his father's death"**: Wells, interview.

68 **their future in the city**: Hill, *Mrs. Kennedy and Me*, 333; Shaw, *White House Nannie*, 175; Winzola McLendon, "Nurse Shaw Recalls: John-John Brought His Own Tribute," *The Washington Post*, January 21, 1966.

CHAPTER 3: "JOHN, WHAT DO YOU WANT TO BE WHEN YOU GROW UP?"

71 **Francis, not Fitzgerald**: "JFKs Abound at 1040 Fifth," *The Washington Post*, July 31, 1964.

71 **"so ridiculous as asking for their autographs"**: Shaw, *White House Nannie*, 189.

72 **"people connected with November 22"**: Bishop to Salinger, November 29, 1963, "Name File: Bishop," LBJPL; "Beleaguered Author: William Raymond Manchester," *The New York Times*, December 17, 1966, 19; "Battle of the Book," *Time*, December 23, 1966.

72 **it was published in early 1967**: Gillon, *Kennedy Assassination*, xii –xvi.

73 **tried to play checkers**: Shaw, *White House Nannie*, 187.

74 **whether John had won the fight**: "John-John Is the New Boy with Punch," *Herald Tribune News Service*, May 26, 1965; Christopher Andersen, *The Good Son: JFK Jr. and the Mother He Loved* (New York: Gale, 2014), 176–78.

74 **refer to Mrs. Kennedy as "Madam"**: Kathy McKeon, *Jackie's Girl: My Life with the Kennedy Family* (New York: Gallery, 2017), 11–13, 15.

75 **Mrs. Kennedy was not pleased**: Ibid., 66–68.

75 **"favorite wooden truck"**: Ibid., 64.

75 **retrieved the snake**: Ibid., 172–73; Shaw, *White House Nannie*, 187.

76 **"yeah, yeah, yeah!"**: Christina Haag, *Come to the Edge: A Memoir* (New York: Spiegel & Grau, 2012), 116–17.

76 **lengthen the side**: Marylin Bender, "Side-Burns Key to John-John Haircut," *The New York Times*, January 10, 1967.

76 **"set the bar for American families"**: Sam Stoia, interview by author, January 10, 2019.

77 **the correct right-handed salute**: McKeon, *Jackie's Girl*, 298.

77 **"pitiful lack of imagination"**: Ibid., 124–26.

78 **"America the Beautiful"**: Maier, *The Kennedys*, 478–79.

78 **"I feel inadequate about saying anything"**: Ibid., 278–80.

78 **he asked innocently**: Ibid., 479.

78 **"London to see the Queen"**: "John-John Is the New Boy with Punch."

79 **at the actual event**: Shaw, *White House Nannie*, 194–95.

79 **"one person missing"**: Ibid., 195–96.

79 **flub his lines**: Tina Radziwill, interview by author, July 5, 2017.

80 **"He's absolutely safe as he is'"**: Ibid.

80 **mesmerized by the changing of the guards**: Shaw, *White House Nannie*, 200–1.

81 **still had their heads**: Ibid., 182–83.

81 **American royalty meets real British royalty**: Leigh, *Prince Charming*, 102.

81 **"Where's the cook and butler?"**: Shaw, *White House Nannie*, 202–3.

82 **JFK's legacy would remain a burden**: Jackie to Mr. Macmillan, May 17, 1965, HMP-BL.

82 **"vengeance on the world"**: Jacqueline to Mr. Macmillan, September 14, 1965 HMP-BL.

82 **Jackie gently intervened**: Leigh, *Prince Charming*, 104.

82 **"things were all right"**: Ibid., 105–6.

83 **"John always belonged to the sky"**: Andersen, *Good Son*, 192; McKeon, *Jackie's Girl*, 124.

83 **"You can't die!":** Andersen, *Good Son*, 187.

83 **hobbling around on crutches:** "John Kennedy Jr. to Have Surgery," *The New York Times*, July 3, 1966.

84 **burned skin had to be cut away:** SAIC Lardner to Rufus W. Youngblood, "Accident to John F. Kennedy Jr.," July 6, 1966; "John F. Kennedy Jr. Burned by Hot Coals," *The New York Times*, July 2, 1966.

84 **the exclusive Bailey's Beach:** Leigh, *Prince Charming*, 114–16.

84 **slapped his hand on the table:** McKeon, *Jackie's Girl*, 164–65.

84 **"I can too!":** "John Jr. Goes Swimming After Candy Gambit Fails," *The New York Times*, June 18, 1967.

85 **hung it proudly in John's room:** Sheehan, "The Happy Jackie, the Sad Jackie."

86 **"Santa Claus was going to find out":** McKeon, *Jackie's Girl*, 78.

86 **By October 1967:** Nancy Zaroulis and Gerald Sullivan, *Who Spoke Up?: American Protest Against the War in Vietnam, 1963–1975* (New York: Doubleday, 1984), 71–74; Thomas Powers, *The War at Home: Vietnam and the American People, 1964–68* (New York: G. K. Hall, 1984), 116–18.

87 **"snot-nosed little son of a bitch":** Jeff Shesol, *Mutual Contempt: Lyndon Johnson, Robert Kennedy, and the Feud That Defined a Decade* (New York: W. W. Norton, 1998), 100; Robert Dallek, *Flawed Giant: Lyndon Johnson and His Times, 1961–1973* (New York: Oxford University Press, 1998), 9–12; Gillon, *Kennedy Assassination*, 30–33.

88 **"quote his letter by heart":** All the correspondence can be found in the Lyndon Johnson Papers, President, 1963–1969, Messages EX ME 2/B-R, box 87, LBJPL.

88 **RFK announced his candidacy:** Schlesinger Jr., *Robert Kennedy*, 845.

89 **"fatalistic, like me":** Schlesinger Jr., *Journals*, 285–86.

89 **funeral services in Atlanta:** Jacqueline Kennedy, *Historic Conversations*, 260.

91 **kitchen of the Ambassador Hotel:** Cecil Beaton, *Beaton in the Sixties: The Cecil Beaton Diaries* (London: Weidenfeld & Nicolson, 2003), 245.

91 **John and Caroline burst into tears:** Andersen, *Good Son*, 221–23.

91 **"He'll always take care of you":** McKeon, *Jackie's Girl*, 184–85.

93 **walked solemnly away:** Judith Martin, "Kennedy Clan Keeps Quiet Vigil," *The Washington Post*, June 8, 1968.

93 **"brought quick, involuntary tears":** Leroy F. Aarons, "'Good and Decent Man': Last Brother Eulogizes Robert Kennedy," *The Washington Post*, June 9, 1968.

93 **"mourners lined the tracks":** McKeon, *Jackie's Girl*, 189–90.

94 **"throwing bouquets of flowers":** Ibid., 195.

94 **candles and flashlights:** Robert J. Donovan, "Nation Pays Final Honor to Kennedy," *Los Angeles Times*, June 9, 1968; Donna Gill, "Bobby Buried Near Brother in Arlington," *Chicago Tribune*, June 9, 1968.

94 **"I want to get out of this country":** Michael Gross, "Favorite Son," *New York*, March 20, 1989.

CHAPTER 4: "IF ANYTHING HAPPENS TO JOHN . . ."

95 **One parent predicted:** Enid Nemy, "Here, John Kennedy Jr. Will Be 'Just Another Boy,'" *The New York Times*, August 22, 1968.

95 **"exuberant and restless":** "John F. Kennedy Jr. to Become a Pupil at Collegiate School," *The New York Times*, August 16, 1968; Gross, "Favorite Son."

96 **"They were not happy":** Bruce Breimer, interview by author, February 7, 2019.

97 **She personally invited Onassis:** Sam Kasher, "The Complicated Sisterhood of Jackie Kennedy and Lee Radziwill," *Vanity Fair*, May 2016.

97 **"she's finally free of the Kennedys":** Frank Brady, *Onassis: An Extravagant Life* (Englewood Cliffs, NJ: Prentice Hall, 1977), 160–70, 172; Sheehan, "The Happy Jackie, the Sad Jackie."

98   **"my life was engulfed in shadows"**: Sheehan, "The Happy Jackie, the Sad Jackie"; Brady, *Onassis*, 176.

98   **$5,000 a month**: Brady, *Onassis*, 176–77.

98   **"the prospect of getting a stepfather"**: McKeon, *Jackie's Girl*, 206–7.

99   **The way into John's heart**: Leigh, *Prince Charming*, 126.

99   **old enough to be John's grandfather**: Sheehan, "The Happy Jackie, the Sad Jackie."

99   **"a magnificent coastline"**: Lee Radziwill, *Happy Times* (New York: Assouline, 2000), 118.

100   **"He was really sweet with John"**: McKeon, *Jackie's Girl*, 260; Brady, *Onassis*, 191; Tina Radziwill, interview.

100   **"a special chemistry"**: J. Randy Taraborrelli, *Jackie, Janet & Lee: The Secret Lives of Janet Auchincloss and Her Daughters Jacqueline Kennedy Onassis and Lee Radziwill* (New York: St. Martin's Press, 2018), 314.

102   **"the curse is part of our family"**: McKeon, *Jackie's Girl*, 269–70.

103   **Jackie renounce further claims**: Helen Lawrenson, "Jackie at 50," *The Washington Post Magazine*, July 28, 1979.

103   **"slip in unobtrusively"**: Jackie to Mrs. Nixon, January 27, 1971, Kennedy Letters, box 21, PPS 320, Richard Nixon Pre-Presidential Materials (Laguna Niguel), Richard Nixon Presidential Library, Yorba Linda, CA (cited hereafter as RNPL).

104   **"Congress together in 1947"**: Alan Peppard, "As Friend, Foe of Kennedy, Nixon Was Near—Even at End," *The Dallas Morning News*, November 19, 2018.

104   **a rewarding afternoon**: President Richard Nixon, "Daily Diary," February 3, 1971, RNPL.

104   **"nice seeing it all again"**: John to President Nixon, February 4, 1971, Kennedy Letters, box 21, PPS 320, RNPL.

104   **refused to attend**: Jackie to Rose Kennedy, Rose F. Kennedy Personal Papers, series 3, box 57, JFKPL; Rose to Jackie, July 8, 1971, JFKPL.

105   **"She didn't trust the Secret Service"**: Hill, interview.

106   **"He just didn't like the attention"**: Gross, "Favorite Son"; Leigh, *Prince Charming*, 136–37.

107   **whatever the case may be**: "Conversation with Mrs. Jacqueline Onassis," December 2, 1968. All references to Secret Service correspondence come from *Gillon*, No. 17-cv -02529-APM.

107   **protect John from threats**: Hill, interview.

108   **"rather than vice-versa"**: Jacqueline to Rowley, December 11, 1968, *Gillon*, No. 17-cv -02529-APM.

108   **"will most certainly consider your suggestions in my decision"**: Rowley to Jacqueline, December 13, 1968, *Gillon*, No. 17-cv-02529-APM.

109   **"unauthorized entry to the house"**: "Dear Jacqueline," draft, n.d., *Gillon*, No. 17-cv -02529-APM.

109   **her apartment on April 18, 1969**: Rowley to Jacqueline, March 3, 1969, *Gillon*, No. 17-cv -02529-APM.

110   **They ranged in age from twenty-three to forty-five**: "Athens: Plot Aimed at JFK's Son," *The Washington Post*, July 16, 1972; Leigh, *Prince Charming*, 157–58.

110   **"periodically throughout the lifetime"**: Hill, interview.

110   **let Billings decide**: SA John J. List to Clinton J. Hill, December 7, 1972, *Gillon*, No. 17-cv -02529-APM.

111   **The incident, which made headlines**: "John F. Kennedy Jr., 13, Robbed of Bike in Park," *The New York Times*, May 15, 1974. In September a Manhattan jury indicted a young man accused of selling the bicycle to John. Robert Lopez, twenty, was charged with first-degree robbery, third-degree grand larceny, and possession of a dangerous weapon. It said that the man threatened John with "a dangerous instrument, to wit, a stick." On September 9 criminal court charges against Lopez were thrown out because John failed to appear for the fourth time.

111 "If anything happens to John": USSS New York (SAIC J. F. Walsh) to USSS Washington (DSD Paul S. Rundle—Protective Forces), May 16, 1974, *Gillon*, No. 17-cv-02529-APM.

112 "traditionally employed in detective work": Jacqueline Kennedy Onassis to Mr. Secretary, July 3, 1974, *Gillon*, No. 17-cv-02529-APM.

113 "the restrictive circumstances": David R. Macdonald to H. Stuart Knight, June 5, 1974, *Gillon*, No. 17-cv-02529-APM.

113 "developing the self-reliance": Jacqueline Kennedy Onassis to Mr. Secretary, July 3, 1974, *Gillon*, No. 17-cv-02529-APM.

114 "very difficult": Hill, interview.

115 sent Mrs. Onassis a pleasant note: Knight to Macdonald, July 22, 1974; Macdonald to Knight, July 24, 1974; Macdonald to Mrs. Aristotle Onassis, July 24, 1974, *Gillon*, No. 17-cv-02529-APM.

116 Schlesinger once joked: Thomas Brown, *JFK: History of an Image* (Bloomington: Indiana University Press, 1988), 50–79.

117 "titillated and amused": Landon Y. Jones, "Too Many Celebrities, Not Enough Heroes," *The Washington Post*, February 28, 2014.

118 the first of hundreds of items: Frank DiGiacomo, "The Gossip Behind the Gossip," *Vanity Fair*, December 2004.

119 Hong Kong, Japan, and Australia: Ron Galella, *Jacqueline* (New York: Sheed and Ward, 1974), 9–10, 58.

119 "I feel threatened when he is present": McKeon, *Jackie's Girl*, 264–65; Leigh, *Prince Charming*, 168; *Jacqueline Onassis v. Ronald E. Galella*, March 1971, *Gillon*, No. 17-cv-02529-APM.

119 twenty-five feet and thirty feet: Galella, *Jacqueline*, 167, 179–80.

120 "He looked like an unmade bed": William Sylvester Noonan with Robert Huber, *Forever Young: My Friendship with John F. Kennedy, Jr.* (New York: Viking, 2006), 20.

121 "Ethel's children were raised wildly": Leigh, *Prince Charming*, 186.

121 "reminded me of Jack with all his curiosity": Jackie to Rose Kennedy, August 1972, Rose Kennedy Personal Papers, series 3, box 57, JFKPL.

121 "prison camp": Tully to Director, "Survey Report re: Visit of John F. Kennedy, Jr. to London and Plymouth, England, July 29 through August 14, 1971," *Gillon*, No. 17-cv-02529-APM.

122 "JFK . . . isn't that an airport": Noonan with Huber, *Forever Young*, 40–41.

122 "I'll never allow myself to be that hungry again": "Teens Outward Bound in Maine Wilderness," *Boston Sunday Globe*, July 31, 1977.

123 A few days later, John showed up: John Perry Barlow, *Mother American Night: My Life in Crazy Times* (New York: Crown Archetype, 2018), 109–10. He recalls that John arrived in the summer of 1977, but given the clear record that John was in Maine that summer, Barlow must be mistaken.

123 partially flooded bunkhouse: Ibid., 111.

124 Such escapades: Ibid., 111–12.

124 readied their cameras: Noonan with Huber, *Forever Young*, 52–54.

124 "I told Billy to take the lead": Gustavo Paredes, interview by author, January 24, 2019.

125 pushed to the ground in the confusion: Noonan with Huber, *Forever Young*, 65–68.

125 Jenny jumped in with John: Paredes, interview.

125 "you should write a note": Noonan with Huber, *Forever Young*, 65–68.

125 overlooking Rabbit Pond: Advance to Walsh, "Preliminary Survey Report," September 14, 1976, *Gillon*, No. 17-cv-02529-APM.

126 "platonic love of my life": John to Alexandra (Sasha) Chermayeff, July 28, 1979, Chermayeff Papers, private.

128 "a facility for acting": Leigh, *Prince Charming*, 199.

128 received a warning: Ibid., 200–1.

129   **"He certainly wasn't at the top of his class"**: Gross, "Favorite Son."

129   **"Let him go"**: Breimer, interview.

CHAPTER 5: "THE QUESTION IS, WHERE IS THIS ALL TAKING ME?"

132   **"I do not enjoy being a university president"**: Ben Leubsdorf, "The New Curriculum Then," *The Brown Daily Herald*, March 2, 2005.

132   **independent studies, and interdisciplinary efforts**: Luther Spoehr, "Making Brown University's 'New Curriculum' in 1969: The Importance of Context and Contingency," *Rhode Island History* 74, no. 2 (Summer/Fall 2016): 52–71. For the best overall history of Brown, see Ted Widmer, *Brown: The History of an Idea* (New York: Thames & Hudson, 2015). Also useful is Janet M. Phillips, *Brown University: A Short History* (Providence: Office of Public Affairs, 2000).

133   **twenty-eight courses to graduate**: Fox Butterfield, "Brown Outpacing Rivals in Ivy League Popularity," *The New York Times*, March 20, 1983; Neil Miller, "How Now, Brown U?," *The Boston Globe Magazine*, October 23, 1987.

133   **"doormat of the Ivy League"**: Ellie McGrath, "Keeping Brown in the Black," *Time*, May 24, 1982.

134   **Approximately 46 percent**: "Special University Enrollment Needs," February 12, 1979, Howard Swearer Papers, box 23, Brown University Archives.

134   **John's application materials**: In 2017 the nation got a glimpse of John's application to Brown when an autograph dealer called Moments in Time posted it on its website after acquiring it from the estate of a deceased former Brown administrator. It's unclear, however, why a former Brown official would have had John's essay among his personal possessions.

136   **The Panamanian government desired a settlement**: Gaddis Smith, *Morality, Reason and Power: American Diplomacy in the Carter Years* (New York: Hill & Wang, 1987), 109–132; Marlise Simons, "U.S. to Retain Defense Rights in New Treaty," *The Washington Post*, August 11, 1977; Edward Walsh, "Panama Treaty-Signing Here Weighed," *The Washington Post*, August 23, 1977.

137   **its flexible curriculum**: Phillips, *Brown University*, 95; "Freshman Kennedy Gets Arrival 'Quiz' at Brown," *The Providence Journal*, September 11, 1979. For the best account of Brown's celebrity culture, see Daniel Golden, *The Price of Admission: How America's Ruling Class Buys Its Way into Elite Colleges—and Who Gets Left Outside the Gates* (New York: Three Rivers, 2007). Reichley's quote can be found on page 95.

137   **"would be followed by other students"**: James Rogers, interview by author, September 18, 2017; Golden, *Price of Admission*, 99.

137   **two Beatles**: Golden, *Price of Admission*, 94.

138   **ambitious goal of $158 million**: "Swearer to List," press release, March 1, 1979, April 11, 1980, Howard Swearer Papers, box 23, Brown University Archives; "Admission Office Swamped; 11,600 Applications Expected," *The Brown Daily Herald*, January 11, 1980; Miller, "How Now, Brown U?"

138   **"John Kennedy goes there"**: "Applications to Brown Reach All-Time High, Up Seven Percent," press release, January 28, 1980, Howard Swearer Papers, box 23, Brown University Archives; Richard Gray Jr., interview by author, September 25, 2017.

139   **"people began to talk about Brown"**: Rogers, interview.

139   **National Outdoor Leadership School course in Kenya**: Jeanne O'Brien, correspondence with author, November 11, 2018.

139   **"this grueling course"**: Leigh, *Prince Charming*, 200.

139   **"GREAT REEFER"**: John to Sasha Chermayeff, August 12, 1979, Chermayeff Papers, private.

140   **"pleasant and accommodating"**: "Freshman Kennedy Gets Arrival 'Quiz' at Brown."

140   **"I'll kick his ass"**: Theodore White, *America in Search of Itself* (New York: Harper & Row, 1982), 270–75; Elizabeth Drew, *Portrait of an Election: The 1980 Presidential Campaign* (New York: Simon & Schuster, 1981), 49–87.

140 **"But he was gorgeous":** Leigh, *Prince Charming*, 214.

141 **apologize profusely to John's mom:** Noonan with Huber, *Forever Young*, 48–49.

142 **"I'm glad to do anything for my uncle":** "Brown Freshman Kennedy Says He'll Campaign a Bit for Uncle," *The Providence Journal*, January 16, 1980.

143 **the most embarrassing of his life:** Debra Scott, "The Shy Kennedy," *The Boston Sunday Herald Magazine*, August 9, 1987; Charlie King, interview by author, March 7, 2019.

144 **Carter became the first Democrat:** John to Sasha Chermayeff, November 4, 1980, Chermayeff Papers, private.

145 **"no credit for the class":** Charles Neu, interview by author, September 20, 2018.

145 **"he had little interest in writing a paper":** Ibid.

146 **"he is off probation":** Jacqueline Kennedy Onassis to Dean Romer, July 2, 1980; Jacqueline Kennedy Onassis to Dean MacIntosh, August 30, 1980.

146 **field trip to Newport:** Pat Manocchia, interview by author, August 17, 2017.

147 **"we had lines outside the door":** Richard Wiese, interview by author, January 22, 2018.

147 **"self-deprecating sense of humor":** Ibid.

148 **drove the pig back to the farm:** Robert T. Littell, *The Men We Became: My Friendship with John F. Kennedy Jr.* (New York: St. Martin's Press, 2004), 29–32.

148 **dampen their friendship:** John to Sasha Chermayeff, November 4, 1980, Chermayeff Papers, private.

149 **the phone in his room:** Wiese, interview.

150 **genuine warmth and kindheartedness:** Ibid.

150 **took a stack of his albums:** Manocchia, interview.

150 **"Get your own money":** Ibid.

152 **She never showed up again:** Littell, *Men We Became*, 41–42.

152 **"I don't really go out a lot":** Andersen, *Good Son*, 226.

153 **constantly losing his key:** Littell, *Men We Became*, 62–63, 70–72.

154 **"John was wonderful":** John Emigh, interview by author, May 12, 2018.

154 **"That's going to follow you for the rest of your life":** Emigh, interview.

154 **"made his voice smaller":** "Western World Uninviting," *The Brown Daily Herald*, May 12, 1982.

154 **"Pacino-type movements":** "Boom-Boom Hits Hard," *The Brown Daily Herald*, December 14, 1981.

155 **"He wanted to be right for the role":** Gray, interview.

155 **how fiercely protective John was of Jackie:** Stephen Hill, interview by author, September 22, 2017.

155 **"I'll slap the hell out of you":** Gray, interview; Kenneth Robert Jones, interview by author, September 27, 2017.

155 **"a line between us":** Jones, interview.

156 **He pushed himself physically:** Ibid.

156 **"it definitely will not be politics":** Ibid.

156 **"just another proud mother":** Gray, interview.

156 **no escaping his past:** Christopher Andersen, *The Day John Died* (New York: Morrow, 2000), 164; Alexandra (Sasha) Chermayeff, interview by author, January 12, 2018.

168 **"glued himself unnaturally":** Littell, *Men We Became*, 74.

169 **"business as usual":** Maer Roshan, "Prince of the City," *New York*, August 2, 1999.

170 **His efforts eventually earned Stretch's respect:** Barry Clifford, *The Pirate Prince: Discovering the Priceless Treasures of the Sunken Ship* Whydah (New York: Simon & Schuster, 1993), 111–12; Roshan, "Prince of the City."

170 **the sharp metal had ripped:** Clifford, *Pirate Prince*, 116; Roshan, "Prince of the City"; "Cape Cod Diver Retrieves Cannons Once ID'd by JFK Jr.," Associated Press, August 19, 2009; "Pirates, the Reality: Loot from the *Whydah*," *The Washington Post*, July 3, 2007; "Barry Clifford—Diver, Explorer, Adventurer," Whydah Pirate Museum online, accessed July 10, 2018, www.discoverpirates.com/barry-clifford-diver-explorer-adventurer.

171 **"the meaning of life"**: Haag, *Come to the Edge*, 76.

171 **Indian Institute of Technology**: Kabir Taneja, "When John F. Kennedy Jr. Came to India," *The New York Times*, March 29, 2013.

172 **"in a Dixie cup"**: John to Sasha Chermayeff, Fall 1983, Chermayeff Papers, private.

172 **"this crazy Westerner"**: Ibid., January 27, 1984.

172 **devoutly Catholic paternal grandmother**: Taneja, "When John F. Kennedy Jr. Came to India."

174 **"a good man"**: Barlow, *Mother American Night*, 239–40.

174 **"The question is, where is this all taking me?"**: John to Sasha Chermayeff, April 1984, Chermayeff Papers, private.

CHAPTER 6: "I'M NOT MY FATHER"

175 **switch rooms every six months**: Littell, *Men We Became*, 78–80.

175 **"If I stop to think about it all"**: Noonan with Huber, *Forever Young*, 72.

178 **scurrilous gossip**: Sally MacMillan, "The Man Born to Be President," *The Mail on Sunday* (UK), April 16, 1989; Joe Armstrong, interview by author, December 10, 2018.

179 **both women forgave him**: Littell, *Men We Became*, 153–54.

179 **professed his love**: Haag, *Come to the Edge*, 87, 171, 218; Littell, *Men We Became*, 150.

180 **He always managed to survive**: Haag, *Come to the Edge*, 207–8.

180 **"reasonably well behaved"**: Manocchia, interview. All the material in this section comes from these interviews.

184 **"unity, patriotism, the office of the presidency"**: Timmons to Noonan, June 17, 1985, Ronald Reagan Library, Speechwriting Office, box 225, FOIA S07-0069/01.

184 **"speech of the workingman"**: "Presidential Remarks: Fundraiser for J. F. K. Memorial Library, McLean, Virginia," Monday, June 24, 1985, RRPL, Office of the President: Presidential Briefing Papers, March 11, 1985, Ronald Reagan Library, Speechwriting Office, box 225, FOIA S07-0069/01; Donnie Radcliffe, "In Tribute to JFK: A Moving Reagan Speech as Ted, Jackie, and Kennedy Clan Join for a Fundraiser," *The Washington Post*, June 25, 1985; John Robinson, "A Party for JFK," *The Boston Globe*, June 25, 1985.

185 **"be a fuckup"**: Lester David, "Caroline Kennedy at 30," *McCall's*, September 1987, 15, 19–20.

185 **"the depth of John's emotions"**: Littell, *Men We Became*, 120–21.

187 **That coldness proved too much**: Haag, *Come to the Edge*, 182–83.

187 **"William is my cousin"**: "John F. Kennedy Jr. Visits Smith Trial," *Los Angeles Times*, November 19, 1991.

188 **Pfizer, Hallmark, and Johnson & Johnson**: Michael Berman, interview. Much of the material in this section comes from interviews with Berman.

189 **John trusted Michael**: Nancy Haberman, interview by author, November 13, 2017.

190 **Sheehan joked to the senator**: Michael Sheehan, interview by author, June 20, 2018.

191 **introduction of Uncle Ted**: Charles Goldsmith, "John Kennedy Jr. Charms Convention," UPI, July 19, 1988.

191 **"I'm not sure anyone remembers one word of what he said"**: Maureen Dowd, "A Tame Day, by the Party's Standards, and Kennedy Memories," *The New York Times*, July 20, 1988; Karen S. Schneider, "And Now, the Rest of His Life," *People*, January 16, 1995.

191 **"Whenever any of the cousins need help"**: "JFK's Son Makes His Party Debut," *Chicago Tribune*, July 20, 1988; Joyce Wadler, "The Sexiest Kennedy," *People*, September 12, 1988.

192 **Christmas on *Good Morning America***: Michael Berman, interview.

193 **"Most of the time, he would just let them talk"**: Haag, *Come to the Edge*, 175–76.

194 **"the morally right thing to do"**: Leigh, *Prince Charming*, 267.

194 **"was willing to learn"**: Sheehan, interview.

194 **"'The Hunk Flunks'"**: Ibid.

196 **"the family business"**: Gary Ginsberg, interview by author, May 3, 2017.

197 **"terribly fractured environment"**: Michael Berman, interview.

197 **He retreated into his room**: Littell, *Men We Became*, 84.

198 **"the kind of offense that rated national coverage"**: Leigh, *Prince Charming*, 248–49; Littell, *Men We Became*, 89.

198 **"a bad grade"**: Haag, *Come to the Edge*, 176; Gross, "Favorite Son"; MacMillan, "Man Born to Be President."

199 **appearing in the *New York Post***: King, interview.

199 **"the way he acted in public"**: Ibid.

199 **Such criticisms were unfair**: Leigh, *Prince Charming*, 252–53.

200 **For John, that meant paying all his tickets**: MacMillan, "Man Born to Be President."

200 **"cleanest office in the building"**: Jim Dwyer, "He Had the Time of His Life in the DA's Office," *New York Daily News*, July 20, 1999.

201 **read their Miranda rights**: Brian Steel, interview by author, November 15, 2017.

201 **Steel watched in horror**: Ibid.

201 **"a good lawyer"**: Scott, "The Shy Kennedy."

201 **"He wasn't above embarrassment"**: Manocchia, interview.

202 **the seven who failed**: "John Kennedy Jr. Fails Bar Exam 2nd Time; Says He'll Take It Again," *Deseret News*, May 1, 1990.

202 **"I'm not my father"**: Littell, *Men We Became*, 90.

202 **off-site location**: Michael Berman, interview by author, March 22, 2019.

203 **"The verdict: guilty"**: Charles Strum, "For the People, Kennedy; for Jurors, Kennedy!," *The New York Times*, July 10, 1992.

204 **"developmentally disabled and poor people"**: Jeffrey Sachs, interview by author, October 12, 2018.

204 **flip hamburgers at McDonald's**: Ibid.

205 **"was ahead of his time"**: Bill Ebenstein, interview by author, November 7, 2018.

205 **Initially, CUNY**: Ibid.

205 **using his celebrity status**: Ibid.

205 **"brought the spotlight"**: Dennis Rivera, interview by author, January 12, 2019.

206 **"the hands-on people"**: Albor Ruiz, "JFK Jr.'s Legacy Lives On: Scholars Recall His Humanity," *New York Daily News*, July 26, 1999. Juan Gonzales, "He Quietly Laid Gifts on Needy Fellowships Helped Hundreds Travel Road to Success," *New York Daily News*, July 23, 1999.

206 **"secret ingredient"**: Ebenstein, interview.

207 **"I do not worry about things that I can't do anything about"**: Armstrong, interview.

207 **a firm career choice**: Manocchia, interview.

208 **Jackie look-alike**: Leigh, *Prince Charming*, 263.

208 **Manhattan's Upper West Side**: Nadine Brozan, "Chronicle: A Kennedy-Hannah Idyll in Palau," *The New York Times*, August 4, 1993.

208 **"a little hamster track"**: Littell, *Men We Became*, 152.

209 **"thrown for a loop"**: King, interview.

209 **"afraid of his name"**: Littell, *Men We Became*, 163.

210 **A health care worker told *The New York Times***: Lawrence K. Altman, "Death of a First Lady: No More Could Be Done, Mrs. Onassis Was Told," *The New York Times*, May 20, 1994.

210 **"Mummy loves you two so much"**: Armstrong, interview.

211 **"series of steps in death"**: Noonan with Huber, *Forever Young*, 126.

211 **run around in the park**: *I Am JFK Jr.*, documentary, directed by Steve Burgess and Derik Murray (Newtown, PA: Virgil Films, 2016), Video Prime streaming online video, 92 mins.

211 **"All for Mummy"**: Noonan with Huber, *Forever Young*, 127.

212 **A clueless Daryl**: Ibid., 128.

212 **"too young to be a widow in 1963"**: John J. Goldman and Robert L. Jackson, "Kennedy's Widow Recalled as a 'Blessing' to Family, Nation," *Los Angeles Times*, May 24, 1994.

212 **touch the simple bronze grave marker**: Marylou Tousignant and Malcolm Gladwell, "A Day of Farewells to a First Lady," *The Washington Post*, May, 24, 1994.

212 **"You hold it inside"**: Sasha Chermayeff, interview; Ginsberg, interview.

213 **"And I hope it comes soon to you"**: John to Charlie King, October 1994, King Papers, private.

213 **"bearer of his parents' legacies"**: Littell, *Men We Became*, 166.

CHAPTER 7: "WHAT ABOUT A MAGAZINE ABOUT POLITICS?"

215 **a mass-produced version**: Michael Gross, "Citizen Kennedy," *Esquire*, September 1995; Michael Berman, interview.

215 **Berman nixed this idea**: Michael Berman, interview.

215 **"It just got a little better in my mind"**: Michael Berman, interview; Haberman, interview.

216 **all aspects of the race**: Michael Berman, interview.

217 **"a greater risk with *George*"**: Nina Link, interview by author, March 22, 2018.

217 **"launch a successful political magazine"**: Ginsberg, interview; Michael Berman, interview.

221 **spotlight shined on him**: Ibid.; Rivera, interview.

221 **"how much he loved flying"**: Armstrong, interview.

221 **a successful businessman**: Michael Berman, interview.

222 **"wholly vested in the political process"**: "*George*: A Proposal," n.d., Berman Papers, private.

224 **"extravagantly starstruck"**: David Samuels, "Hollywood or Bust," *The Weekly Standard*, August 18, 1997; Maureen Dowd, "Washington Is Star-Struck As Hollywood Gets Serious," *The New York Times*, May 9, 1993.

224 **"We the people . . . define our times"**: Samuels, "Hollywood or Bust."

226 **bowling alone**: Robert Putnam, "Bowling Alone: America's Declining Social Capital," *Journal of Democracy* 6, no. 1 (January 1995): 65–78.

227 **"policy wonk"**: "*George*: A Proposal."

227 **potential readers also responded warmly**: RoseMarie Terenzio, interview by author, March 13, 2017; Michael Berman, interview.

227 **reserved for sports**: Matt Berman, *JFK Jr., George, & Me: A Memoir* (New York: Gallery, 2014), 131; Edward Klein, "Secrets and Lies," *Vanity Fair*, August 2003.

228 **substance of policy**: Francis Fukuyama, "The End of History?," *The National Interest* 16 (Summer 1989): 3–18.

230 **take-no-prisoners**: Gross, "Citizen Kennedy."

230 **outnumbered Democrats by 2 to 1**: Gary C. Jacobson, "The 1994 House Elections in Perspective," *Political Science Quarterly* 111, no. 2 (Summer 1996): 203–23; Peter Applebome, "The Rising G.O.P. Tide Overwhelms the Democratic Levees in the South," *The New York Times*, November 11, 1994.

231 **the bestseller list**: Louis Bolce, Gerald DeMaio, and Douglas Muzzio, "Dial-In Democracy: Talk Radio and the 1994 Election," *Political Science Quarterly* 111, no. 3 (Autumn 1996): 457–81.

231 **"the sympathy in the Kennedy office"**: Michael Berman, interview.

231 **take whatever papers**: RoseMarie Terenzio, *Fairy Tale Interrupted: A Memoir of Life, Love, and Loss* (New York: Gallery Books, 2012), 13–14; Terenzio, interview.

232 **dislodged from her office**: Terenzio, *Fairy Tale Interrupted*, 17–19.

232 **dear, lifelong friend**: Terenzio, interview.

232 **"*Premiere* is to films"**: Armstrong, interview; Michael Berman, interview, October 25, 2017; Gross, "Citizen Kennedy."

233 **an impressive 5.1 response**: Michael Berman, interview, January 22, 2019.

233 **In the summer of 1990:** Michael Bergin, *The Other Man: A Love Story—John F. Kennedy Jr., Carolyn Bessette & Me*, (New York: HarperCollins, 2004), 19–21.

233 **"stood him up":** Richard Wiese, interview, March 10, 2018; Carole Radziwill, interview, January 18, 2019.

235 **"the campus man-eater":** Andersen, *The Day John Died*, 219.

235 **"hanging out in nightclubs":** Nathan Cobb, "Carolyn Bessette Kennedy: From Shy Student to Accomplished Celebrity Wife," *The Boston Globe*, September 24, 1996.

235 **"aside from looking great":** Andersen, *The Day John Died*, 219.

235 **"He always had one eye on her":** Carole Radziwill, interview.

236 **not going to wait for John:** Andersen, *The Day John Died*, 220.

236 **$1 million to meet with John:** Gross, "Citizen Kennedy"; Michael Berman, interview.

236 **"kick them out":** Michael Berman, interview.

237 **"he was so worked up":** Gross, "Citizen Kennedy"; Evan Thomas and Martha Brant, "Coming of Age," *Newsweek*, August 14, 1995.

237 **"betrayed by Jann":** Gross, "Citizen Kennedy"; Michael Berman, interview.

237 **"$9.5 million":** Michael Berman, interview.

237 **"a racehorse":** Ibid.

238 **Metropolitan Home and Car and Driver:** Robin Pogrebin, "Once a Renegade, Hachette Magazine Chief Gains Respect," *The New York Times*, April 6, 1998; Jeffrey Toobin, "The National Enquirer's Fervor for Trump," *The New Yorker*, July 3, 2017.

239 **"lunch with John Kennedy":** David Pecker, interview by author, June 27, 2017.

239 **"ad sales machine":** Ibid.; Pogrebin, "Once a Renegade, Hachette Magazine Chief Gains Respect."

239 **This tension was never resolved:** Pecker, interview.

239 **"a little SWAT team":** Ibid.

240 **publish twice in 1995:** Mary Huhn, "The Politics of 'George,'" *Mediaweek*, March 6, 1995.

240 **venerable Vanity Fair:** Ibid.

240 **"screaming as if he was Mick Jagger":** Pecker, interview; Pogrebin, "Once a Renegade, Hachette Magazine Chief Gains Respect."

240 **Despite the uncomfortable start:** Pecker, interview.

241 **"This is the life":** Terenzio, *Fairy Tale Interrupted*, 51–52.

241 **more appropriate space:** Michael Berman, interview.

242 **"unpleasant first day":** Ibid.

243 **"That's why I thought it was interesting":** Linda Thomas Brooks, interview by author, March 16, 2018.

243 **their distinctive message:** Ibid.

243 **"I was extremely impressed by him":** Michael Browner, interview by author, March 20, 2018.

244 **"John wanted to edit":** Ibid.

244 **smuggling John out:** Brooks, interview.

244 **the premier advertiser:** Ibid.

244 **"Everyone wanted to see the guy. Everyone":** Nina J. Easton, "Is John Kennedy Jr.'s 'George' Making American Politics Sexy?," *Los Angeles Times*, August 11, 1996; Oscar Suris, "This Audience Was in the Market for the Salesman, Not the Pitch," *The Wall Street Journal*, April 24, 1995.

245 **the magazine's largest advertiser:** Browner, interview.

245 **"successful publishing venture":** Easton, "Is John Kennedy Jr.'s 'George' Making American Politics Sexy?"; Gross, "Citizen Kennedy."

245 **childhood idols:** Thomas and Brant, "Coming of Age"; Suris, "This Audience Was in the Market for the Salesman, Not the Pitch"; Gross, "Citizen Kennedy."

245 **"Go get married":** Elinore Carmody, interview by author, December 11, 2018.

246 **"closely with consultants"**: Ibid.

246 **female-driven fashion:** Ibid.

246 **"It legitimized the adventure"**: Ibid.

247 **"I know this sounds crazy"**: Ibid.

247 **"Down the road"**: Lisa Lockwood, *"George:* Fashion's New Camelot?," *Women's Wear Daily,* September 8, 1995.

248 **"twirling around"**: Michael Berman, interview.

248 **Without missing a beat:** Browner, interview.

CHAPTER 8: "LADIES AND GENTLEMEN, MEET *GEORGE!*"

249 **the work environment:** Elizabeth "Biz" Mitchell, private notes.

250 **the *New York Observer* in 1994:** Elizabeth "Biz" Mitchell, interview by author, August 12, 2018.

250 **"less than powerful"**: Richard Blow, *American Son: A Portrait of John F. Kennedy, Jr.* (New York: Henry Holt, 2002), 9–10.

250 **relatively vague concept:** Matt Berman, interview by author, September 27, 2018.

251 **sign the agreement:** Michael Berman, interview; Ginsberg, interview.

251 **meticulous note taking:** Ginsberg, interview.

251 **"people who don't know much about politics"**: Hugo Lindgren, interview by author, September 25, 2017.

251 **forty uninterrupted days:** Mitchell, interview.

252 **Rice 'n' Beans:** Matt Berman, interview.

252 **"his other commitments"**: Mitchell, interview.

253 **popped up unannounced:** Terenzio, *Fairy Tale Interrupted,* 67; Matt Berman, interview; Mitchell, interview.

253 **the cost-conscious Hachette:** Terenzio, interview.

254 **"intoxicated white male"**: Declassified FBI Files, John F. Kennedy Jr., 7-HQ-19719, May 14, 1985, *Gillon,* No. 17-cv-02529-APM.

254 **informed John of the threat:** San Francisco to Director FBI, New York, Miami, Jacksonville (priority), 7A-SF-114974, July 12, 1995; Jacksonville to FBI Director, July 13 and July 20, 1995; Jacksonville to New York, 7A-NY-254901, September 7, 1995; Jacksonville to New York, 7A-NY-254901, May 14, 1996, *Gillon,* No. 17-cv-02529-APM.

255 **"tore up the magazine"**: Lindgren, interview.

256 **left on the cutting-room floor:** Ned Martel, interview by author, May 8, 2018.

256 **how gerrymandering shaped elections:** Ibid.

256 **"going to open doors"**: Lindgren, interview.

258 **come out of the closet:** John to "M" (Madonna), n.d., private collection.

259 **"nodding in agreement"**: Matt Berman, interview; Blow, *American Son,* 37; "Poster Boy for Poster-Boy Behavior," *Spy,* March 1998, 30–38. Although the article appeared in *Spy,* Biz Mitchell described it as "remarkably accurate" and sat down with me to go through the story line by line, identifying the parts that were true and those that were not.

259 **"sassy street attitude"**: Terenzio, *Fairy Tale Interrupted,* 61.

260 **"they got the message"**: Ibid., 58–59.

260 **debilitating symptoms:** Blow, *American Son,* 41.

261 **"darken my door"**: Martel, interview.

261 **"back-hall closet"**: Blow, *American Son,* 44–45, 76–77.

262 **trendy SoHo neighborhood:** Martel, interview.

262 **broad and eclectic interests:** Mitchell, interview.

263 **"That settled the issue"**: Matt Berman, *JFK, Jr., George, & Me,* 71–72; Matt Berman, interview.

263 **superimposing a political icon:** Matt Berman, interview.

263 **John killed the piece:** Blow, *American Son,* 33–34.

264 **confront Wallace back in 1963:** Ginsberg, interview.

264 **powerful painkillers:** Ibid.

264 **signing pictures of his father:** Gary Ginsberg, "Remembering the Essence of John F. Kennedy Jr.," CNN online, last modified July 16, 2014; Ginsberg, interview.

265 **John nixed it:** Blow, *American Son*, 36–37.

265 **"love hard":** Liz McNeil, "John F. Kennedy Jr. and Carolyn Bessette: The Way They Were," *People*, August 6, 2014.

265 **a rocky relationship:** Carole Radziwill, *What Remains: A Memoir of Fate, Friendship and Love* (New York: Scribner, 2005), 128–30.

266 **"Home Depot, the warehouse":** Ibid., 140; Carole Radziwill, interview.

266 **"I will be judged":** Terenzio, interview.

266 **a more normal life:** Radziwill, *What Remains*, 141; Terenzio, interview.

267 **the engagement news:** Michael Berman interview, January 31, 2018; Terenzio, *Fairy Tale Interrupted*, 97–98.

267 **"You're the only one I fucking trust":** Michael Berman, interview; Terenzio, *Fairy Tale Interrupted*, 99–100.

267 **"comment on John's personal life":** Terenzio, *Fairy Tale Interrupted*, 101.

267 **"But everything I know tells me not to":** Michael Berman, interview; Blow, *American Son*, 60.

268 **"Please leave the dog at home":** Haberman, interview; Michael Berman, interview, September 27, 2018.

269 **"central operative fact":** Ginsberg, interview.

269 **"electricity of the magazine itself":** Ibid.

270 **"they tend to get overshadowed":** Haberman, interview; Michael Berman, interview.

270 **"single most important piece of advice":** Rita Ciolli, "By George, He's Got It: JFK Jr. Unveils New Political Magazine," *Newsday*, September 8, 1995; Haberman, interview.

270 **"a strobe light":** Ciolli, "By George, He's Got It."

271 **write about his modesty:** Blow, *American Son*, 61.

271 **"She would be very proud":** Ciolli, "By George, He's Got It"; Blow, *American Son*, 61–62.

271 **"Today was a three":** Michael Berman, interview.

271 **"a persuasive case":** Ciolli, "By George, He's Got It"; George Rush and Joanna Molloy, "It's the New George," *New York Daily News*, September 8, 1995; Deirdre Carmody, "George Didn't Look Like This in 1789," *The New York Times*, September 8, 1995.

271 **"you're not going to get one of those back":** Michael Berman, interview.

272 **"instrument of public relations":** Easton, "Is John Kennedy Jr.'s 'George' Making American Politics Sexy?"; Carmody, "George Didn't Look Like This in 1789"; "John-John's Journal," *U.S. News & World Report*, September 15, 1995; Maureen Dowd, "Liberties: Giant Puppet Show," *The New York Times*, September 10, 1995.

272 **"pay full newsstand price":** Michael Berman, interview.

273 **"but I'm not sure I really do":** John F. Kennedy Jr., interview by Larry King, *Larry King Live*, November 24, 1995, CNN, transcript.

273 **the O. J. Simpson murder trial:** Haberman, interview.

273 **appear on *Larry King*:** Pecker, interview.

274 **"passionate about pursuing for the rest of my life":** John F. Kennedy Jr., interview by Dan Rather, November 25, 1995, CBS, transcript. On July 18, 1999, the network re-aired an interview originally conducted in 1995 following the *George* launch.

274 **in response to the threat:** Boston to Director, FBI (priority), "John F. Kennedy, Jr—Victim; Extortion Matter," September 21, 1995, *Gillon*, No. 17-cv-02529-APM.

275 **the Buffalo Club:** Michael Berman, interview.

275 **"dinner is over":** Ibid.

276 **"a ho-hum one":** Blow, *American Son*, 67.

276 **Berman faked a photo:** Matt Berman, interview.

278 **handed over the reins to Biz:** Mitchell, interview.

278 **at the end of January 1996:** Frederick M. Winship, "Success Propels John Kennedy's Magazine," UPI, January 30, 1996.

278 **stimulated or provoked them?:** Keith Kelly, "The Best Magazines," *Advertising Age*, March 11, 1996; Ann Marie Kerwin, "Numbers Don't Tell Whole Tale of 'George,'" *Advertising Age*, February 9, 1998.

CHAPTER 9: "SHE'S ACTING CRAZY"

280 **"I had never seen in business before":** Blow, *American Son*, 72; Carmody, interview.

281 **being sidelined:** Michael Berman, interview.

281 **an alternative direction:** Ibid.

282 **"I don't need more":** Blow, *American Son*, 73.

282 **"I blame him for that":** Ibid.

283 **John knew that Rosie:** Terenzio, interview.

283 **"put into a box":** Ibid.

284 **mimeographed photo:** Michael Berman, interview.

284 **"'He doesn't know what he's talking about'":** Ibid.

284 **But his grievances again went unaddressed:** Ibid.

286 **"other voices weighing in":** Ibid.

286 **scandalous eight-photo spread:** "Sunday in the Park with the *George* Editor," *New York Daily News*, March 3, 1996; Helen Kennedy, "Big Newsstand Play for JFK Jr.'s Brawl Pix," *New York Daily News*, March 4, 1996.

287 **leaked into public view:** Sasha Chermayeff, interview.

287 **John remained unconcerned:** Terenzio, interview; Michael Berman, interview, October 4, 2018.

287 **very-much-in-love couple:** Terenzio, interview; Michael Berman, interview; Haberman, interview.

288 **fewer than three hundred thousand:** Blow, *American Son*, 79.

288 **"*George* was going to be judged differently":** Michael Berman, interview; Carmody, interview.

289 **"perspective on fashion and culture":** Michael Berman, interview.

289 **Pecker decided to raise the issue again:** Pecker, interview.

290 **"a tremendous amount of influence":** Matt Berman, *JFK Jr., George, & Me*, 69; Pecker, interview.

291 **"starts listening to her":** Terenzio, interview.

291 **an uncomfortable laugh:** Michael Berman, interview.

292 **"the perfect solution":** Mitchell, interview; Berman, *JFK Jr., George, & Me*, 69–70; Matt Berman, interview.

293 **"freaks and sycophants":** Matt Berman, interview.

293 **"you're John F. Kennedy Jr.":** Klein, "Secrets and Lies."

294 **"It made absolutely no sense":** Michael Berman, interview. The account that follows is from Berman's recollection of events.

296 **"not getting married here":** Terenzio, interview.

296 **National Park Service:** Kevin Sack, "The Island That Kept a Wedding a Secret," *The New York Times*, September 26, 1996.

296 **accommodated at Greyfield:** Judith Gaines, "'Most Eligible' No Longer," *The Boston Globe*, September 23, 1996.

297 **Indian Head nickel:** Terenzio, interview; Carole Radziwill, interview.

297 **an old fishing boat:** Littell, *Men We Became*, 182.

298 **"Think of me when you wear them":** Littell, *Men We Became*, 184–85.

298 **cross made of sticks and twine:** Sack, "The Island That Kept a Wedding a Secret"; Carole Radziwill, interview.

298 **"big heart of gold":** Littell, *Men We Became*, 156.

299 **"Just stand there":** Terenzio, *Fairy Tale Interrupted*, 159.

299 **"It was very demoralizing"**: Lawrence Schwartzwald, interview, May 10, 2018; Terenzio, interview; Carole Radziwill, interview.

299 **"that seemed ill-advised"**: Michael Berman, interview, January 31, 2018.

300 **the public yearned**: Terenzio, *Fairy Tale Interrupted*, 157–58.

300 **matter-of-factly**: Victor Malafronte, interview, May 12, 2018.

300 **if a daughter, Jacqueline**: "Yes, Carolyn Is Pregnant," *New York Post*, October 20, 1996; "Jet Set Hails King John II," *New York Post*, November 6, 1996.

300 **$600-a-month**: "Carolyn Accused in Sublet Scam," *New York Post*, October 22, 1964.

301 **"I was furious"**: Berman, *JFK Jr., George, & Me*, 90–91; Terenzio, interview; Michael Berman, interview.

301 **negotiating book deals**: The author has copies of handwritten notes of John's presentation to advertisers. There are no dates; Michael Berman, interview.

302 **"He would not be asked to promote it"**: Michael Berman, interview.

302 **"It's not what I want to do"**: Terenzio, interview , January 31, 2018.

302 **"Get her the hell out"**: There have been numerous accounts of this fight, but it's the first time that Berman has spoken about it.

303 **"ripped my shirt"**: Michael Berman, interview; Matt Berman, interview; Terenzio, interview.

303 **small and petty**: Blow, *American Son*, 125–26.

303 **Michael's 25 percent share**: Carmody, interview.

304 **dazzle people with his presence**: Ibid.; Klein, "Secrets and Lies"; Blow, *American Son*, 134.

304 **Michael never spoke with John again**: Haberman, interview; Michael Berman, interview, October 4, 2018.

305 **"a powerful legacy"**: Michael Berman, email to author, December 8, 2018.

306 **"center of American politics"**: Dmcdew/WHMOOEOB to James A. Hawkins, "JFK, Jr's Request to Photograph AF-1," May 4, 1995, box 2, William J. Clinton Presidential Library (cited hereafter as WJCPL), Little Rock, AR; John to President Bill Clinton, July 14, 1995, box 1, WJCPL.

306 **"American Spectacle"**: John to Michael McCurry, November 3, 1995, box 1, WJCPL.

306 **"No way"**: John to George Stephanopoulos, May 15, 1996, box 1, WJCPL.

307 **"why should it bother anyone else?"**: Terenzio, *Fairy Tale Interrupted*, 135–36.

307 **doubled their newsstand sales**: Blow, *American Son*, 105–6; Nancy Haberman, email to author, December 20, 2018; Mitchell, interview.

309 **"Get over it"**: Berman, *JFK Jr., George, & Me*, 35; Mitchell, interview.

309 **talk-show runner-ups**: Richard Huff, "JFK Appearance Gives 'Oprah' a Hunk of Hot Nielsen Ratings," *New York Daily News*, September 5, 1996.

310 **finding some resolution**: Nitsana Darshan-Leitner, "JFK Jr.'s Advice to Israel," *The New York Jewish Week*, July 30, 1999.

310 **group of religious zealots**: Richard Sisk, "Rabin's Wife Blasts JFK Jr.," *New York Daily News*, April 2, 1997.

311 **"South Philly's only Anglophile"**: *George*, April/May 1997.

311 **guide the magazine**: Blow, *American Son*, 134.

312 **"less than the sum of its parts"**: Lindgren, interview.

313 **"knew what the ramifications were"**: Mitchell, interview; Carmody, interview.

313 **"politics as a subject matter"**: Carmody, interview; Browner, interview.

313 **"never quite fit into any one"**: Ginsberg, interview.

314 **"we created something truly new"**: Blow describes the meeting in *American Son*, 122–23.

314 **"You're mediocre"**: Lindgren, interview.

CHAPTER 10: "SHE'S REALLY SPOOKED NOW"

315 **"the brother they each did not have"**: Kieran Crowely, "Kennedy Cousin Mourned: Caroline Gives Eulogy for JFK Jr.'s 'Brother,'" *New York Post*, August 14, 1999.

316 **"toothpaste cap"**: Radziwill, *What Remains*, 90–91.

316   "**children and old people?**": Ibid., 91.

316   **In November 1994**: Ibid., 117–18.

317   "**give up and die**": Michael Shelden, "'Their Deaths Brought Me to My Knees,'" *The Daily Telegraph* (UK), October 25, 2005.

318   "**It broke my heart**": This account is from Radziwill, *What Remains*, 148–51.

319   "**keep your tie clean**": Ibid., 165–66.

319   "**military potential of space**": Gillon to John, February 16, 1998.

320   **While John enjoyed**: "Hillary Honors JFK Jr.," Associated Press, July 19, 1999.

321   **grit and courage**: Radziwill, *What Remains*, 196–209; Carole Radziwill, interview.

325   "**They don't care**": Littell, *Men We Became*, 200.

325   **coping mechanisms**: Ibid., 212–13.

326   "**a bat phone**": Martel, interview.

326   "**She's really spooked now**": Noonan with Huber, *Forever Young*, 200.

326   "**Relax**": McKeon, *Jackie's Girl*, 294–95.

327   **photo essay**: Mitchell, interview.

328   "**They treated her horribly**": Sasha Chermayeff, interview.

328   "**They are fucking with me**": Ibid.

329   "**why he's wearing a hat**": Terenzio, interview.

329   **empty apartment**: Ibid.

329   **Carolyn rose to her feet and entered the car**: Littell, *Men We Became*, 211.

330   "**That pissed everyone off**": Littell, *Men We Became*, 200; Terenzio, interview.

331   "'**You will ruin my relationship**'": Terenzio, interview.

331   "**he pried it out of me**": Ibid.

331   **nipped the tension**: Matt Berman, interview; Terenzio, interview.

332   "**what my bill is going to be**": Noonan with Huber, *Forever Young*, 193.

332   "**running behind me**": Littell, *Men We Became*, 214.

333   **sexiest men alive**: Sasha Chermayeff, interview.

334   "**I just do**": Bergin, *The Other Man*, 208–9.

334   **She wanted out of her marriage**: Ibid., 212–13, 218.

334   "**three little kids**": Noonan with Huber, *Forever Young*, 157.

335   **swing wildly from month to month**: Keith J. Kelly, "George of the Ad Jungle," *New York Daily News*, August 25, 1997.

335   "**readers of *The New Yorker***": Michael Voss, interview by author, December 21, 2018.

335   **onetime full-page advertisement**: Daniel Jeffreys, "JFK's Trouble with George," *The Independent* (UK), March 24, 1997; Carl Swanson, "*George* Magazine Loses a 'Yes' Woman as Hachette Steps In," Observer.com, January 18, 1999, accessed June 10, 2018.

336   "**name their price**": Jeffreys, "JFK's Trouble with George."

336   **But that never happened**: Armstrong, interview.

336   "**People are very surprised that he was successful**": Ibid.

337   "**it will be amazing**": "JFK Jr. Delivers Pitch as Advertised," *The Orange County* (CA) *Register*, February 13, 1998.

337   "**something highbrow**": Robin Pogrebin, "George Wins Readers, but Little Respect," *The New York Times*, February 10, 1997.

337   "**one of the most beautiful women**": Ibid., Jeffreys, "JFK's Trouble with George."

337   "**bunch of young people**": Martel, interview.

339   **two full-page ads for Scientology**: Mitchell, interview.

342   "**who needs them?**": Noonan with Huber, *Forever Young*, 141.

342   **Only 18 percent**: *CBS This Morning*, CBS, transcript, August 12, 1997; *Dateline*, NBC Transcripts, August 15, 1997; "Joe Kennedy Shrugs Off JFK Jr.'s Moral Musings," *The Patriot Ledger* (Quincy, MA), August 12, 1997.

343   "**Kennedys acting like Kennedys**": Noonan with Huber, *Forever Young*, 19.

343   **a great president**: I learned later that John asked a similar question of a family friend, the esteemed historian Arthur Schlesinger Jr., who noted in his journal on December 27, 1997,

that John had called, perplexed by the popularity of Hersh's book. "Is there a real backlash against Daddy?" he asked. "Or is it just a perennial interest in anything about the Kennedys?" Schlesinger did not record his response. Schlesinger Jr., *Journals*, 826.

344 **"how wide his curiosities were"**: Sasha Issenberg, interview by author, October 26, 2018.

344 **"thirty-eight-year-old white guy"**: Martel, interview.

345 **"You will be contacted later today"**: For a full account of the trip, see Inigo Thomas, "JFK Jr, Castro and Me" (LRB blog), *London Review of Books*, November 22, 2013, www.lrb .co.uk/blog/2013/november/jfk-jr-castro-and-me.

345 **"you are a Kennedy"**: Noonan with Huber, *Forever Young*, 189.

347 **"Giáp was senile and infirm"**: Robert Curran, interview by author, December 14, 2018.

348 **"stability in Southeast Asia"**: "Vietnam's Legendary Giap Wants to be 'General of Peace,'" Agence France-Presse, October 21, 1998; Curran, interview.

349 **"famously libidinous president"**: Blow, *American Son*, 178–79.

349 **a private matter**: Ibid., 190.

351 **"fools as kings"**: John to "Mr. T" (Mike Tyson), July 9, 1997, private.

351 **Tyson deserved a second chance:** Manuel Perez-Rivas and Martin Well, "JFK Jr. Sees Tyson in Jailhouse Visit," *The Washington Post*, March 12, 1999.

351 **"a three-year-old"**: Martel, interview; Peter Madaus to Roger Berg et al., February 13, 1998, John F. Kennedy Jr. Files, box 13, WJCPL.

351 **"It's making people really reflect"**: Blow, *American Son*, 178–80, 188–91.

352 **"it's worth understanding"**: Mitchell, interview.

353 **1,931 minutes:** Michael Gartner, "How the Monica Story Played in Mid-America," *Columbia Journalism Review*, May/June 1999, 34.

354 **Washington press corps:** David Friend, "Before Trump Was President, Online Sex Videos, Bill Clinton and the Naughty '90s Changed America," *Newsweek*, September 15, 2017.

354 **"The digital age does not respect contemplation"**: John Merline and Claude Marx, "So What Is 'Journalism' Today?," *Investor's Business Daily*, January 29, 1998.

CHAPTER 11: "THE ONLY PLACE THAT I WANT TO BE IS WITH ANTHONY"

357 **"a fiery phone call"**: Keith J. Kelly, "John Jr. Searching for New No. 2," *New York Post*, January 6, 1999; Swanson, "*George* Magazine Loses a 'Yes' Woman as Hachette Steps In."

357 **did not bode well for the future:** Keith J. Kelly, "JFK Jr. Talking About Taking Title to TV," *New York Post*, April 28, 1999.

358 **"There's not a chance"**: Mitchell, interview. The discussion that follows is from the same interview.

360 **Anthony was going to die:** Radziwill, *What Remains*, 225.

361 **"He was having difficulty dealing with it"**: Carole Radziwill, interview.

361 **"these big trips"**: Ibid.

361 **"No, I don't"**: Carole Radziwill, interview; Radziwill, *What Remains*, 226.

361 **"determined to live"**: Carole Radziwill, interview.

362 **"I just hurt my leg"**: Sasha Chermayeff, interview; Phineas Chermayeff, interview by author, September 20, 2018.

362 **"two rocking chairs"**: Sasha Chermayeff, interview.

363 **"ominous foreshadowing"**: Carole Radziwill, interview; Radziwill, *What Remains*, 221–22.

363 **"denial and stoicism"**: Carole Radziwill, interview.

364 **became her next target:** Ibid.

364 **John could not be humored:** Terenzio, *Fairy Tale Interrupted*, 192.

364 **relying on cocaine:** Radziwill, *What Remains*, 218.

365 **"What do you think?"**: Noonan with Huber, *Forever Young*, 204–6.

365 **"Like her life is so hard"**: Terenzio, interview.

365 **occasional weekend refuge:** Noonan with Huber, *Forever Young*, 206–8.

366 **"he is going to be fine"**: Sasha Chermayeff, interview.

366 **"drove each other crazy"**: Carole Radziwill, interview.

367 **"laughs and good food"**: Ibid.

367 **"I suppose it was resignation"**: Ibid.

367 **"The window was open"**: Keith Stein, interview by author, November 16, 2018.

368 **"noticeably grayer"**: Littell, *Men We Became*, 8–9.

368 **"I will not go . . . a success"**: Blow, *American Son*, 254–55; Terenzio, interview.

369 **Martha's Vineyard on July 16**: Voss, interview; Cheryl Stieffel and Peter Leifer, interview by author, November 15, 2018.

369 **"a lot of our problems"**: Blow, *American Son*, 230.

370 **"operations of the company"**: Dan Samson, email to author, September 13, 2018.

370 **"game plan"**: Ibid.

374 **"They really loved each other"**: Ibid.

374 **"add a spouse"**: Sasha Chermayeff, interview; Noonan with Huber, *Forever Young*, 203.

376 **wooden golf clubs**: John J. Goldman, "Final Take for Jackie O. Auction Tops $34 Million," *Los Angeles Times*, April 27, 1996.

376 **writing a check, not cashing one**: Littell, *Men We Became*, 167.

376 **the project was canceled**: Ibid.

380 **"It was going to be tough enough"**: Patti Solis Doyle, interview by author, February 12, 2019.

381 **passion for campaigning**: Sachs, interview; Rivera, interview.

381 **ambitions on hold**: Sachs, interview.

383 **"we'll have fun"**: Andersen, *The Day John Died*, 10–11.

383 **similar fights with Carolyn**: Terenzio, interview.

384 **"John's birthday celebrations"**: Julie Baker, interview by author, March 3, 2019.

385 **"best choices possible"**: Ibid.

386 **"first big issue"**: Jack Kliger, interview by author, April 24, 2017. The discussion that follows is from this interview.

387 **"cut the cord"**: Terenzio, interview; Ginsberg, interview.

387 **"a graceful way out"**: Ginsberg, interview.

388 **the important call**: Terenzio, interview.

388 **"It's never about me"**: Ibid.

388 **Reluctantly, Carolyn agreed**: Terenzio, *Fairy Tale Interrupted*, 197–98; Terenzio, interview.

389 **hot, muggy nights**: Manocchia, interview; Terenzio, *Fairy Tale Interrupted*, 199–200.

389 **"magazine could survive"**: Manocchia, interview.

390 **"'Don't go up'"**: Much of the account of John's final hours is from the following sources: Dale Russakoff and Lynne Duke, "JFK Jr.'s Joyful, Fateful Final Hours," *The Washington Post*, July 21, 1999; Jeffrey Kluger and Mark Thompson, "The Last Day," *Time*, August 1, 1999; Douglas A. Lonnstrom, "10 Mistakes JFK Jr. Made," Aircraft Owners and Pilots Association online, last modified July 5, 2010, www.aopa.org/news-and-media/all-news/2010/july/pilot/10-mistakes-jfk-jr-made; Ricardo Alonso-Zaldivar, "Instructor Offered to Fly with JFK Jr.," Report Says," *Los Angeles Times*, July 7, 2000. For the final NTSB report, see: *NTSB Identification: NYC99MA178*, National Transportation Safety Board online, accessed August 10, 2018.

390 **dinner on Saturday**: Radziwill, *What Remains*, 9.

391 **no evidence to suggest**: Federal Bureau of Investigation, Records Management Division, *Gillon*, No. 17-cv-02529-APM.

394 **"Everything's fine"**: Carole Radziwill, *What Remains*, 234–35.

394 **"Oh God!"**: Terenzio, *Fairy Tale Interrupted*, 200–201.

EPILOGUE: "YEP, YOU REALLY WERE SPECIAL"

400 **"The words almost wrote themselves"**: Robert Shrum, interview by author, July 10, 2018.

402 **"infused with compassion"**: Issenberg, interview.

402 **50 percent share:** Terenzio, *Fairy Tale Interrupted*, 223.

402 **owned the magazine outright:** Ann Marie Kerwin, "Lalli Steps up to Helm of Troubled 'George,'" *AdAge*, December 6, 1999.

403 **Franken's humor:** Kliger, interview.

404 **"on the third try":** Alona Wartofsky and Hannah Allam, "In New York, the Improvisations of Grief," *The Washington Post*, July 19, 1999.

404 **over the age of sixty:** Donna Petrozzello, "Ratings: Newsmags Do Well in Week of Kennedy Coverage," *New York Daily News*, July 28, 1999; Richard Huff, "JFK Jr. Coverage Nearly Par to Di's," *New York Daily News*, August 4, 1999.

404 **"Kennedy curse":** Frank Manciewicz, "'There Are No Curses,'" *The Guardian*, July 19, 1999.

405 **"fairy tales":** "Summary of International Media Coverage," July 18–22, 1999, FOIA 2017-0713-f, box 5, WJCPL.

405 **an astonishing $1.2 million:** White House aide Sean Maloney pointed out that the White House flag was not lowered when John's mom died. Nor was it lowered for Senator William Fulbright, Dean Rusk, or Mother Teresa. "It's a difficult decision, but it would be out of proportion to previous episodes of this kind for the president to order the lowering of all US flags." He suggested that the president could "consider lowering the flag over the White House residence (as opposed to all U.S. Flags) for a period of 24 hours once the fate of Mr. Kennedy and his party is known with more certainty." Maloney to John Podesta, July 19, 1999, FOIA 2017-0713-f, box 1, WJCPL; "Kennedy Salvage Costs," July 21, 2017-0713 -FCL, box 1, WJCPL.

405 **"bodies of private citizens":** Don and Marlene Dunbar to Senator John Breaux, July 22, 1999. Breaux forwarded the letter to the president. Breaux to Clinton, June 15, 2000, 2017-0713-FCL, box 1, WJCPL; Bernard M. Brady to Congressman Kenneth E. Bentsen Jr., August 1, 1999, 2017-0713-FCL, box 1, WJCPL.

406 **"a national disgrace":** David H. Hackworth, "U.S. Warships Are Not Royal Yachts at Beck and Call," *South Florida Sun Sentinel*, August 5, 1999. The article was circulated among White House aides. White House email, August 5, 1999, 2017-0713-FCL, box 6, WJCPL.

406 **"Taps" on the bugle:** Anne E. Kornblut, "Expansive Naval Aid Tied to Family's Service to US," *The Boston Globe*, July 23, 1999.

406 **"We owe this to his family and to the country":** President Bill Clinton, interview by John Marks as part of the A&E documentary *JFK Jr.: The Final Year*, which is based on this book, March 6, 2019.

407 **World War II navy hero:** "Kennedy Aircraft Missing Press Guidance," July 19, 1999, 2017-0713-FCL, box 1, WJCPL; "Kennedy Burial at Sea," July 26, 1999, 2017-0713-FCL, box 2, WJCPL.

407 **"as far as we're concerned":** "Transcript of conversation," n.d., 2017-0713-FCL, box 1, WJCPL.

INDEX